Hi

Unveiling

Prophecy

Also Available from LutheranLibrary.org

- *First Elements of Sacred Prophecy* by Thomas Birks.
- *Romanism and the Reformation* by H. Grattan Guinness.
- *The Great Exodus* by James Wylie.
- *The Origin of Dispensational Futurism and its Entry Into Protestant Christianity* by H.C. Martin.

About The Lutheran Library

The Lutheran Library is a non-profit publisher of good Christian books. All are available in a variety of formats for use by anyone for free or at very little cost. There are never any licensing fees.

We are Bible believing Christians who subscribe wholeheartedly to the Augsburg Confession as an accurate summary of Scripture, the chief article of which is Justification by Faith. Our purpose is to make available solid and encouraging material to strengthen believers in Christ.

Prayers are requested for the next generation, that the Lord will plant in them a love of the truth, such that the hard-learned lessons of the past will not be forgotten.

Please let others know of these books and this completely volunteer endeavor. May God bless you and keep you, help you, defend you, and lead you to know the depths of His kindness and love.

Works by the Author On Prophecy

- The Approaching End of the Age. 1878.
- Light for the Last Days. 1887.
- Romanism and the Reformation from the Standpoint of Prophecy. (*Exeter Hall Lectures.*) 1887.
- The Divine Program of the World's History. 1888.
- The City of the Seven Hills. 1891.
- Creation Centered in Christ. (*Two volumes.*) 1896.
- Key to the Apocalypse, 1899.

History Unveiling Prophecy

Or Time As An Interpreter

By H. Grattan Guinness, D.D.

FELLOW OF THE ROYAL ASTRONOMICAL SOCIETY. AUTHOR OF
"THE APPROACHING END OF THE AGE"

New York

FLEMING H. REVELL COMPANY

LutheranLibrary.org

Copyright Notice

This book was published 2020 by The Lutheran Library Publishing Ministry LutheranLibrary.org. Some (hopefully unobtrusive) updates to spelling, punctuation, and paragraph divisions have been made. Unabridged. A few pages were missing from the source book in Chapter 12 of the last section. These have been noted in the text.

Originally published 1905 by the Fleming H. Revell Company, New York.

Cover image "Contrasting Protestant and Catholic Christianity" by Lucas Cranach the Elder, 1545.

Image on imprint page is *Still Life With Bible* by Vincent Van Gogh.

640 – v5
ISBN: 9798643544609 (paperback)

Table of Contents

Preface by Lutheran Librarian

In republishing this book, we seek to introduce this author to a new generation of those seeking authentic spirituality.

The Lutheran Library Publishing Ministry finds, restores and republishes good, readable books from Lutheran authors and those of other sound Christian traditions. All titles are available at little to no cost in proofread and freshly typeset editions. Many free e-books are available at our website LutheranLibrary.org. Please enjoy this book and let others know about this completely volunteer service to God's people. May the Lord bless you and bring you peace.

A Note about Typos [Typographical Errors]

Please have patience with us when you come across typos. Over time we are revising the books to make them better and better. If you would like to send the errors you come across to us, we'll make sure they are corrected.

Preface

THE LOFTY DECREE of Papal Infallibility issued by the Vatican Council of 1870, immediately followed by the sudden and final fall of the Papal Temporal Power, after a duration of more than a thousand years, was the primary occasion of my writing that series of works on the fulfillment of Scripture prophecy which has appeared during the last quarter of a century.

I left Paris, where I had been laboring in the Gospel, at the outbreak of the Franco-German war in July, 1870. It was in the light of the German bombardment of that city, of the ring of fire which surrounded it, and of the burning of the Tuileries, that I began to read with interest and understanding the prophecies of Daniel and the Apocalypse. Subsequent visits to Italy and Rome enlarged my view of the subject. A library of books bearing on it was accumulated, historical, astronomical, and prophetic, including 150 commentaries on the Apocalypse, ancient and modern, from the commentary of Victorinus in the third century, down to those of Elliott and others in the nineteenth. These studies laid the foundation of my works on prophecy.

The present work, which differs in important respects from my previous works, as being chiefly historical in character, may be fitly introduced by a brief explanation of the method of interpretation which it follows.

A great and incontrovertible principle underlies the method it pursues in the interpretation of the Apocalypse. Simply stated that principle is that

God Is His Own Interpreter

In two ways does the great Revealer of the prophecy explain its meaning — by words, and deeds; by written words, and acted deeds. He has given us a verbal explanation of its most central and important vision, one which stands in close and commanding connection with all its other visions; and in the long course of Christian history he has fulfilled its predictions.

Thus Scripture is the key to Scripture; and Providence to Prophecy.

The historic interpretation of the Apocalypse which rests on this twofold foundation has been slowly developed under the influence of the divine action in Providence; it has changed in details with the changing currents of Providence; it has grown with the growth of the knowledge of the plans of Providence; it has been confirmed and sealed by the whole course of Providence. It is no vain, or puerile, or presumptuous speculation. It is a reverent submission to the very words of God, and a reverent recognition of His acts. God has spoken; He has given an explanation of the central and commanding vision of the prophecy; and God has acted; He has fulfilled its predictions. In pointing to the words and deeds of God we act as His witnesses. What hath God said? What hath He done? These are the questions. We are wearied with vain speculations as to the meaning of prophecy which have no other foundation than the assertions of men. We are wearied with speculations as to imaginary future fulfillments of prophecies which have been plainly accomplished before our eyes in the past; prophecies on whose accomplishment in the events of Christian history the structure of the great Reformation of the sixteenth century was built; on the fact of whose accomplishment in their days the confessors stood, and the martyrs suffered. Alas! the speculations of men have clouded these facts and brought into disrepute the Holy Word of God. Even good men have been led to neglect the voice of divine prophecy, and to refuse its lamp to light their steps, through the follies of its exponents. Is it not time that the last prophetic book in the Word of God, a book bearing the seal of the signature of the name of "JESUS" should be lifted up from the dust of neglect, and set upon a candlestick in the midst of the house, to shed its clear light and cheering beams on all around? Let the reverent believer who "trembles" at God's word, the patient student who has searched the records of the past, the uncompromising witness who fears not the faces of men, lift up that fallen lamp from the soil on which men have cast it, and place it where Copernicus placed the sun, as a kingly light enthroned in the center of its system.

In agreement with the foregoing principle I have written, among others, two works on the interpretation of the symbolical prophecies in Daniel and the Apocalypse by means (1) of divinely given explanations of their meaning contained in the books themselves, and (2) by the events of history. The first of these works, published in 1899, is entitled "*A Key to the Apocalypse, or the seven divinely given Interpretations of symbolic prophecy.*" The second is the present work. In the first of these I have shown that as God has graciously given us His own all-wise and infallible explanations of the meaning of certain leading and determinative portions of the symbolical prophecies in the book of Daniel and the Apocalypse, no interpretation of these prophecies can be secure and trustworthy which does not rest on these divine explanations, and employ them as keys to unlock the meaning of the prophecies as a whole.

The seven divinely given interpretations of Daniel and the Apocalypse are the following:

1. The interpretation of the vision of the great image in Daniel 2.

2. The interpretation of the vision of the great tree in Daniel 4.

3. The interpretation of the handwriting on the wall of Belshazzar's Palace in Daniel 5.

4. The interpretation of the ram and he-goat in Daniel 8.

5. The interpretation of the four wild beast kingdoms, and of the kingdom of the Son of Man, in Daniel 7.

6. The interpretation of the seven stars, and seven candlesticks in Revelation 1.

7. The interpretation of the woman "Babylon the great," and of the seven-headed, ten-horned beast that carries her, in Revelation 17.

Concerning the last of these interpretations I have shown that "of all the visions in the prophetic part of the Apocalypse (chaps, 6-22), that of Babylon and the beast in chap, 17, is the only one divinely interpreted and that through the interpretation of this vision a door is opened to the understanding of the rest of the prophecy.

(1) The woman is interpreted as signifying the city of Rome.

(2) The city is represented as sitting on "seven hills," the well known seven hills of Rome.

(3) The "many waters" over which she rules are interpreted as "peoples, and multitudes, and nations and tongues."

(4) The wild beast which sustains and carries her — the ten horned wild beast of Daniel's prophecies, the fourth of his four Gentile kingdoms, the kingdom of Rome — is interpreted in detail. (a) Its seven heads are interpreted to represent ruling powers. Of these it is expressly stated "five are fallen, and one is, and the other is not yet come." Thus the sixth head of the wild beast power which carried the harlot is stated to have been in existence when the Apocalypse was written; and must necessarily therefore refer to the government of the Caesars, as then represented by the Emperor Domitian. This locates the visions of the Apocalypse as relating to Roman and Christian history. (b)

The ten horns are interpreted as ten kingdoms, then future, into which the empire should be divided. These horns, or kingdoms first submit to the harlot city, and then rise against her and "make her desolate and naked, and eat her flesh, and burn her with fire."

Three Visions of the Ten Horned Wild Beast Power

As to the use of this central interpreted vision to explain the other visions of the Apocalypse I have pointed out that there are three visions in the Apocalypse of the ten horned wild beast power:

- The first in chapter 12.
- The second in chapter 13.
- The third in chapter 17.

(1) That the interpretation of one of these in chapter 17, determines the meaning of all three.

(2) That these three visions of the wild beast power represent successive stages in the history of the Roman Empire, as first under the government of its seven heads; secondly under the government of its ten horns, for in the prophecy the crowns are transferred from the heads to the horns; and thirdly as carrying, and then casting off and destroying, the harlot Babylon.

(3) That the story of Babylon and the Beast occupies the largest and most central part of the Apocalyptic prophecy, being referred to in no less than ten successive chapters: Chapters 11, 12, 13, 14, 15, 16, 17, 18, 19, 20.

(4) That to the visions relating to the Roman Empire under its revived eighth head prophetic times are attached representing —

1. The period of the sun-clothed woman in the wilderness (chap. 12).
2. The period of the rule of the eighth head of the wild beast (chap. 13).
3. The period during which the outer temple court is trodden under foot by the Gentiles (chap. 11).
4. The period during which the witnesses prophesy in sackcloth (chap. 11).

These four periods are manifestly the same period stated in three forms, as days, months, and "times," or years — 1,260 days; forty-two months, and three and one-half "times," or years: and are to be interpreted on the year-day scale; a scale recognized in both the law and the prophets; the scale on which the "seventy weeks" to Messiah are universally interpreted; a scale justified by the course and chronology of Christian history, and confirmed by the discoveries of astronomy as to the cyclical character of the prophetic times.

The interpretation of the Apocalypse thus reached is in harmony with that of the book of Daniel, and links both prophecies with one and the same series of events — the course of five kingdoms, the temporal kingdoms of Babylon, Persia, Greece, and Rome, and the eternal kingdom of God. The Apocalypse is simply the story told in advance of the two last kingdoms of Daniel's prophecy; the story of the decline and fall of the Roman Empire, and of the rise and establishment of the kingdom of God.

From the interpretation of the Apocalypse by means of the divinely given explanation of its most central and commanding vision, we now advance to the subject of the present volume, the interpretation of the prophecy by the events of history.

History has ever been the interpreter of prophecy. It was so notably in New Testament times, for the sufferings and glories of our Lord, foretold in the Old Testament, remained uncomprehended until their meaning was revealed by the events of history. Similarly the predictions concerning the great apostasy, or "falling away" from the faith and practice of Apostolic times which has taken place in the Christian Church, were not comprehended till explained by historical events. And thus has it been all along. From the beginning of the world to the present day Time has ever been the chief interpreter of prophecy. For prophecy is history written in advance. As the ages roll by history practically takes the place of prophecy, the foretold becoming the fulfilled.

A clear and comprehensive view of the leading events of Christian history up to the date of the Reformation is afforded by Gibbon's noble work on "The Decline and Fall of the Roman Empire." This standard work embraces in a single view the history of the Roman Empire and Christian Church for fourteen centuries, from the time of the Antonines to the fall of the Eastern Roman Empire at the capture of Constantinople by the Turks in 1453. It is enhanced by its extensive learning, its philosophic spirit, the lucidity of its arrangement, and the majesty of its style. The value of Gibbon's work as an unintended key to the Apocalypse is exhibited by the well-known commentator Albert Barnes in the following interesting account of his own experience:

"Up to the time of commencing the exposition of this book (the Apocalypse) I had no theory in my mind as to its meaning. I may add, that I had a prevailing belief that it could not be explained, and that all attempts to explain it must be visionary and futile. With the exception of the work of the Rev. George Croly, which I read more than twenty years ago, and which I had never desired to read again, I had perused no commentary on this book until that of Professor Stuart was published, in 1845. In my regular reading of the Bible in family and in private, I had perused the book often. I read it, as I suppose most others do, from a sense of duty, yet admiring the beauty of its imagery, the sublimity of its descriptions, and its high poetic character; and though to me wholly unintelligible in the main, finding so many striking detached passages that were intelligible and practical in their nature, as to make it on the whole attractive and profitable, but with no definitely formed idea as to its meaning as a whole, and with a vague general feeling that all the interpretations which had been proposed were wild, fanciful and visionary.

"In this state of things, the utmost that I contemplated when I began to write on it was, to explain, as well as I could, the meaning of the language and the symbols, without attempting to apply the explanation to the events of past history, or to inquire what is to occur hereafter. I supposed that I might venture to do this without encountering the danger of adding another vain attempt to explain a book so full of mysteries, or of propounding a theory of interpretation to be set aside, perhaps, by the next person that should prepare a commentary on the book.

"Beginning with this aim, I found myself soon insensibly inquiring whether, in the events which succeeded the time when the book was written, there were not historical facts of which the emblems employed would be natural and proper symbols, on the supposition that it was the divine intention in disclosing these visions to refer to them, and whether, therefore, there might not be a natural and proper application of the symbols to these events. In this way I examined the language used in reference to the first, second, third, fourth, fifth and sixth seals, with no anticipation or plan in examining one as to what would be disclosed under the next seal; and in this way also I examined ultimately the whole book: proceeding step by step in ascertaining the meaning of each word and symbol as it occurred, but with no theoretic anticipation as to what was to follow. To my own surprise, I found, chiefly in Gibbon's 'Decline and Fall of the Roman Empire,' a series of events recorded such as seemed to me to correspond to a great extent with the series of symbols found in the Apocalypse. The symbols were such as it might be supposed would be used, on the supposition that they were intended to refer to these events; and the language of Mr. Gibbon was often such as he would have used, on the supposition that he had designed to prepare a commentary on the symbols employed by John. It was such, in fact, that if it had been found in a Christian writer, professedly writing a commentary on the book of Revelation, it would have been regarded by infidels as a designed attempt to force history to utter a language that should conform to a predetermined theory in expounding a book full of symbols. So remarkable have these coincidences appeared to me in the course of this exposition, that it has almost seemed as if he had designed to write a commentary on some portion of this book; and I found it difficult to doubt that that distinguished historian was raised up by an overruling Providence to make a record of those events which would ever afterwards be regarded as an impartial and unprejudiced statement of the evidences of the fulfillment of prophecy. The historian of the 'Decline and Fall of the Roman Empire' had no belief in the divine origin of Christianity, but he brought to the performance of his work learning and talent such as few Christian scholars have possessed. He is always patient in his investigations; learned and scholar-like in his references; comprehensive in his groupings, and sufficiently minute in his details; unbiased in his statement of facts, and usually cool and candid in his estimates of the causes of the events which he records; and, excepting his philosophical speculations, and his sneers at everything, he has probably written the most candid and impartial history of the times that succeeded the introduction of Christianity that the world possesses; and even after all that has been written since his time, his work contains the best ecclesiastical history that is to be found. Whatever use of it can be made in explaining and confirming the prophecies will be regarded by the world as impartial and fair; for it was a result which he least of all contemplated, that he would ever be regarded as an expounder of the prophecies in the Bible, or be referred to as vindicating their truth.

"It was in this manner that these Notes on the Book of Revelation assumed the form in which they are now given to the world; and it surprises me — and, under this view of the matter, may occasion some surprise to my readers — to find bow nearly the views coincide with those taken by the great body of Protestant interpreters. And perhaps this fact may be regarded as furnishing some evidence that after all the obscurity attending it, there is a natural and obvious interpretation of which the book is susceptible" (Barnes on the Revelation, preface, pp. xi-xiii).

The present volume traces the history of that interpretation, describes its progressive development under the modifying influence of the events of the last nineteen centuries from stage to stage, from its germinant form in the pre-Constantine centuries, through Mediaeval and Reformation times, down to the present day.

As written later than Elliott's great work on the Apocalypse, the *Horae Apocalypticae,* whose five editions appeared in the years 1844-1862, the present work takes into account the long expected fall of the papal temporal power in 1870, immediately following the decree of papal infallibility; and the present deeply interesting Zionist movement dating from 1897, for the national restoration of the Jews to the land of their fathers.

An important confirmation of the historical interpretation of the Apocalypse afforded by the discovery of the astronomical features of the prophetic times, is briefly set forth at the close of the volume. The extensive astronomical tables published by the author in 1896 are based on the remarkable fact that the prophetic times of Daniel and the Apocalypse are extremely perfect astronomical cycles harmonizing solar and lunar revolutions. The year-day theory resting on Scripture analogy and historic fulfillment is strongly confirmed by the discovery, and the 1,260, 1,290, 1,335, and 2300 "days" of Daniel and the Apocalypse proved to represent the same number of years in Jewish and Christian history.

It is a deep satisfaction to the author to remember that whatever may be the views of a modern section of skeptical or speculative interpreters of the Apocalypse, who either see no reference to definite historical events in the prophecy, or relegate its fulfillment to future times, in accepting and advocating its historical interpretation, in regarding it as the story told in advance in symbolic language of the events of the Christian centuries, he is treading in the steps of the greater part of Apocalyptic interpreters from the earliest times, of Justin Martyr, Irenaeus, Tertullian, Hippolytus, Victorinus, Methodius, Lactantius, Eusebius, Athanasius, Jerome, and Augustine among the Fathers; of Bede and Anspert, Andreas and Anselm, Joachim Abbas and Almeric of the middle ages, of the Albigenses and Waldenses, of Wickliffe and the Lollards, of John Huss and Jerome of Prague of pre-Reformation times; of the Reformers, English, Scottish, and Continental; of the noble army of Confessors and Martyrs who suffered under Pagan and Papal Rome; of the Puritan theologians, of the Pilgrim Fathers of New England, of Mede and More, and Sir Isaac Newton, and Jonathan Edwards that greatest of American theologians, of Bengel the learned German exegete, of Alford and Wordsworth, of Birks and Bickersteth, of Faber and Elliott in England, and a host of others, men distinguished for their ability, their assiduity, their spirituality, their deep study of the prophetic word, in short by what appear to be the greatest and best of the expositors of the book. Modern historical interpreters of the Apocalypse are in good company; they stand with the Fathers, the Confessors, the Martyrs, the Reformers, with men who suffered for the truth they believed, and were practically guided and inspired by the interpretations they have handed down to posterity. The fanciful interpretations of the Preterists who falsely conceive the Apocalypse to bear a Neronic date, and to be Neronic in its references, have never been a practical power in the history of the Church; the vague interpretations of a modern school, German and English, which ignoring the clearly defined order of the Apocalyptic Visions, their synchronisms and successions, their system of prophetic times, fixed and absolute, and sure as the times of the celestial luminaries, reduce the prophecy to a nebulous mass of anticipations of things in general in human history, have wrought no victories, have accomplished no reformations, have sustained no martyrs, and are self-refuted by their impotence, and unworthiness as expositions of the last great revelation of Jesus Christ concerning "the things" which were to "come to pass." The same may be said as regards the reveries of the Futurists; barren of practical and worthy effects, they have denied accomplishments recognized by the great mass of prophetic interpreters in the past; they have invented future fulfillments, as unsubstantial and impossible as the dreams of those who mistake bizarre imaginations for sober realities; they have forsaken the great trend, the main path, the well trodden highway of Apocalyptic interpretation, based upon divine explanations of prophetic symbols, and unquestionable historic facts, for empty speculations about the future; unprofitable speculations as to the coming universal dominion of a short-lived infidel antichrist, to be seated in a literal temple to be erected by the Jews in Palestine, who in the brief space of three and a half years is to fulfill all the wonders of the Apocalyptic drama, and exhaust the meaning of the majestic prophecy which the Church of God has been blindly misinterpreting and misapplying throughout all these ages. Surely it is time for such interpreters to consider the unscripturalness and unreasonableness of the method of interpretation which they employ, the absence of authority, of warrant, for their views, the entire lack of demonstration human or divine; and the fruitlessness of their speculations, as affording no present guidance to the Church, and their injuriousness as extinguishing the lamp which God has given His people to guide their steps along the perilous way of their pilgrimage. I am well convinced from wide observation that many excellent persons adopt these modern prophetic speculations because good men have advocated them, here and there, and for no better reason; they have heard them advanced in prophetic conferences, they have read them in books, and tracts, full of confident assertions, superficial and dogmatic compositions on the sublimest questions which can exercise the human mind, and they have been satisfied to believe without proof, and to repeat without independent investigation the marvelous inventions of busy brains as to the antichrist of the future, without ever having soberly inquired whether the Reformers and Martyrs were right or not in their recognition of the antichrist as already come, and as long reigning in the professing

Church, the Standard Bearer of an abominable apostasy, the very Masterpiece of Satan for the delusion of mankind. Let us appeal to such to open their eyes to the facts of history, to turn their thoughts for awhile to the sublime story of the decline and fall of the Roman empire, of the rise of the great apostasies in the Eastern and Western Church, of the testimony and sufferings of the Christian witnesses of the middle ages, and Reformation days, and of the retributive acts of Providence in our own time, the manifest and awful judgments which have been poured forth on Papal Rome in and since the French Revolution, judgments whose afterwaves are rolling and reverberating still, uttering with no uncertain sound the solemn conclusion that so far from living in days preceding the fulfillment of Apocalyptic prophecy, we are living in the closing days of the accomplishment of the things which it has foretold.

In writing thus, and in making this appeal, I write as one who has long and deeply studied both Prophecy and History, and as one who knows that his days are numbered, and that he must give account before long of his stewardship as a teacher in the Christian church, for in the present year of the publication of this volume I have entered on the fiftieth year of my ministry, a ministry in which I have striven to teach in harmony with "the oracles of God," and to declare, as far as in me lies, "the whole counsel of God." I have no private ends to accomplish by the publication of this book; it is written in the interest of truth, as a heritage for my children, a guide to those whom I would not and dare not mislead, a help to young men and women prosecuting their studies in their homes or colleges with a view to future usefulness; and for ministers of the gospel, most of them my younger brethren, to whom I would be of service; and for the sake of any into whose hands it may come, of open heart and unprejudiced mind, desirous of understanding more clearly the meaning of the last predictions in the Word of God. Brethren, beloved in the Lord, in writing thus, it is not I who testify, but the voice of a multitude of Witnesses, mostly gathered now before the throne of God. We shall spend eternity with them;

are we prepared to join their songs of triumph, to echo the hallelujahs which break from their lips? Is the testimony of the Word of God to us what it was to them? Is our testimony in the world in harmony with theirs? Can we join the Reformers in their witness, and the Martyrs in their song? They stand on the sea of glass mingled with fire, having the harps of God, proclaiming the accomplishment of God's judgments in the fall of Papal Babylon; shall we stand apart from them, electing to sing some little song of our own out of harmony with the great volume of the voice of God's redeemed? Let it not be! It would be unworthy of us. Compassed about with "so great a Cloud of Witnesses," let us lay aside indifference and ignorance, prejudice, and misconception, and take our place with these in the great arena of conflict, dyed with martyr blood, to maintain "the Testimony of Jesus Christ," looking away from all beside to Him as the Author and Finisher of our faith, whose hand has given us this final prophecy to be our armor in the day of battle, our guide in the perils and perplexities of our pilgrimage, our morning star amid the darkness which precedes the dawn of eternal day. Behold the volume whose seals his hand, his providence, have loosed. Seal it not again. Neglect it not. Doubt no more its meaning. For lo Time, that great Interpreter, has rolled back the veil which once hung upon its mysteries, and is irradiating its pages as with the sunlight of heaven.

Introduction

IT WAS TOWARDS the close of the first century of Christian history, in the year 95 or 96, that the aged Apostle John, banished by the Roman Emperor Domitian, to the lonely island of Patmos, in the Aegean Sea, beheld the visions described in the Apocalypse. More than sixty eventful years had elapsed since the ascension of his blessed Lord. During that long period he had looked back to that sublime and glorious event, as the closing incident in his Master's earthly history, and often had retraced in thought every step of his last walk with the risen Saviour over the Mount of Olives, to the sloping fields above the little village of Bethany with the deep Jordan valley and the blue far-off hills of Moab full in view. On countless occasions he had recalled his Lord's last charge, and parting blessing, and gazed in thought on His ascending form, and on the white robed angels whose words directed the minds of the bereaved disciples from the sorrowing contemplation of their Lord's departure, to the glad anticipation of His return, saying, "This same Jesus which is taken up from you into heaven, shall so come in like manner as ye have seen Him go into heaven." But when was it to be, that promised return? Was it to take place in the lifetime of the disciple whom Jesus loved? Had not the Master said concerning that disciple when speaking to Peter, "If I will that he tarry till I come, what is that to thee? Follow thou Me." Peter had died, following his Lord to the cross. Was he, John, to escape death? Was he to enjoy translation with the saints who were to be "alive and remain" to the Second Advent? Yet he remembered that Jesus had not promised he should not die, but had only said, "If I will that he tarry till I come." What could that mean? The strange mysterious sentence lived and lingered in his thoughts; he ends his gospel narrative with it. Was he to behold before his departure some glorious prefiguration of his Lord's return, like the scene on the Mount of Transfiguration; some vision, unveiling the secrets of the future more fully than they had been foreshadowed by that memorable event? No such revelation had been given, and he was now grown old; a venerable, patriarchal man, gentle and gracious in mien; the last survivor of the apostles. He had shared the promised baptism of Pentecost; had witnessed the marvelous growth of the Christian Church; had seen the fall of Jerusalem; the destruction of its glorious temple, of which now not one stone was left standing upon another; had witnessed the accomplishment of those dreadful judgments on the Jewish nation in anticipation of which his Master's tears had fallen on the Mount of Olives, bedewing the palm branches spread by the multitudes beneath His feet. He had seen too the preliminary fulfillment of the signs of the approach of the Second Advent which his Master had predicted; the earthquakes, famines, pestilences, wars, and persecutions, the appearance of false prophets, and false Christs, of fearful signs and wonders in heaven. The idolatrous ensigns of the desolating Roman power had been planted within the precincts of the Holy City. The triumphal arch of Titus had been reared in Rome, the mighty metropolis of the world, to commemorate Jerusalem's fall; that arch on which were represented in striking sculpture the sacred vessels of the sanctuary carried in triumph by heathen hands; the seven branched golden candlestick, the table of the shew bread, and the book of the law. Jerusalem was no more. The Jewish Dispensation founded ages before by those supernatural revelations granted to Moses and Israel on Mount Sinai had come to an end. The kingdom of heaven had taken its place, growing up silently as a grain of mustard seed, from small and despised beginnings to far reaching development. From the upper chamber of Jerusalem it had spread through Judea, Samaria, Galilee, and across the Roman Empire, in which there was scarce a city of importance which had not a Christian Church. It had reached

Antioch and Alexandria, Crete and Corinth, Philippi and Thessalonica, Ephesus and Smyrna, Pergamos and Thyatira, Athens and Rome; it had spread throughout Asia Minor, Greece, Italy, Egypt, and even as far as the western confines of Spain, and the distant isles of Britain; and this in spite of the most violent opposition and persecution from Jews and Gentiles. The gospel had penetrated even to Caesar's household, and won the hearts of some of his nearest kindred. The aged Clement presided over the Christian Church in the city of Rome, undeterred by threats of imprisonment and martyrdom; while another Clement of high born position had just witnessed for Christ even unto blood, whose wife Domitilla had been banished to the desolate island of Pandateria, where she was suffering the same punishment for the Christian faith as John himself was enduring in Patmos.

And with the lapse of time changes for the worse had taken place in many Christian Churches, gross corruptions of the pure doctrines of the gospel had appeared. Self-righteous legalism and Judaic ritualism on the one hand, and false philosophy, the boasted wisdom of the Gnostics on the other, had perverted the minds of many, corrupting them from the simplicity which is in Christ. Sects had arisen in the Church which denied the divinity of Christ, and the atoning character of His death. Tares had been sown by the enemy among the wheat, and were already flourishing on every side. It appeared as though the Antichrist so long before foretold by Daniel, and so emphatically predicted by Paul, might speedily come; springing up as a horn or ruler among the kings of the divided Roman Empire, and exalting himself as an overseer in the Christian Church, in whose symbolical temple it was foretold he would sit supreme, clothed with divine honors and prerogatives, and deceiving many to their eternal destruction. These things were to be, and the times seemed dark enough to indicate that they might even then be at hand. Daniel had revealed in mystical language the time of the manifestation of this antichristian power, and the period of its continuance. But what was the exact meaning of those times of Daniel? What meant the "time, times, and a half time," of which he spoke; the 1,260, 1,290, and 1,335 days; the 2,300 "evenings and mornings"; the periods which were to reach to the resurrection and promised "rest" of the righteous at the end of the days? Were they literal days which were meant, or were the days he spoke of symbolical of larger periods? Were these revelations in Daniel the last to be granted on the subject, or was more light to shine forth through communications of the truth yet to be given to the Church of "the last days"? Questions such as these may well have occupied the mind of the aged apostle in the lonely hours of his banishment.

We can conceive him standing on the rocky height of some Patmos headland watching the western sun descending over the blue waters of the Aegean Sea, making a broad pathway of golden light on the waves, till they shone like "a sea of glass mingled with fire," or beholding the sun rise in the glowing east over the Asiatic shores, transporting his thoughts to the advent of the "morning without clouds," yet to shine upon the world. Or when he watched the host of heaven come forth by night, and fill the glittering canopy above the lonely isle, while the "many mansions" of which his Master had spoken came to his mind, and the angel hosts who do His bidding, can we not conceive him longing that one of these glorious beings might be sent to him as of old one had been sent to Daniel, the man "greatly beloved," to impart some of that knowledge of the future enjoyed in higher and holier realms? We know not what he thought or desired, but we know what God granted to the aged and privileged apostle.

It was on one Lord's day of his sojourn in Patmos, the day commemorating Christ's triumphant resurrection, that being alone, and "in the spirit," or wrapped in ecstasy from the outward world, and oblivious of its presence, he suddenly heard behind him a great voice as of a trumpet, speaking to him such words as mortal ear had never heard before.

"I am Alpha and Omega, the first and the last, and what thou seest write in a book and send it unto the seven Churches which are in Asia; unto Ephesus, and unto Smyrna, and unto Pergamos, and unto Thyatira, and unto Sardis, and unto Philadelphia, and unto Laodicea ."

And turning in the direction of the Voice he saw seven golden candlesticks, and standing in their midst, One whom he recognized as "like unto the Son of Man," but O how changed from the Christ on whom he had so often looked in Galilee, and on whose bosom he had leaned in the upper chamber at Jerusalem! For every trace of humiliation was gone. No tears upon the cheek, no thorns upon the brow, He stood there transfigured and glorified; His face as the noonday sun shining in its strength; His garment white and glittering, and girt at the waist with a golden girdle; the hair of His head white with the snows of dateless years, as the "Ancient of days" beheld by Daniel; His eyes like a flame of fire; needing no exterior light to aid their vision, but penetrating the secrets of the soul with holy searching gaze; His feet as burning brass, strong as the pillars of heaven, and glowing as though they burned in a furnace; His voice as the mighty and majestic sound of many waters; seven stars glittered in His right hand, and a sharp two-edged sword, the evident symbol of the Word of God, living and powerful, and piercing to the dividing asunder of # soul and spirit, proceeded from His lips.

At this sudden and marvelous apparition of the glorified Redeemer all strength forsook the aged apostle. Falling at the feet of the Son of God he lay there as one dead. Then touching his prostrate form with His right hand, the Lord strengthened him, saying in His own well-remembered voice, "Fear not; I am the First and the Last; I am He that liveth, and was dead, and behold I am alive forevermore, Amen; and have the keys of death and of hades."

And now aroused to wondering attention, the aged apostle received from the lips of Christ the divine commission to communicate to the seven Churches of Asia, representing symbolically the entire Christian Church throughout the world, a faithful record of all that he had seen, and was yet to behold.

"Write the things which thou hast seen, and the things which are, and the things which shall be hereafter."

And first to the seven Churches of Asia Minor John is directed to write brief letters, charged with lofty meaning; letters appreciating, judging, encouraging, rebuking, and counseling these representative Churches; and conveying through them messages from the glorified Redeemer to the whole Christian Church throughout the world. In these letters, bearing on their forefront descriptive titles of Christ referring to attributes suited to the character and condition of the Churches addressed, our Lord speaks in the tone of sovereign authority, perfect knowledge, burning holiness, and tender love. His eyes as a flame of fire search the secrets of hearts, yet beam with infinite compassion. His lips are full of promises, his hands of gifts and graces. Every sentence in these celestial communications bears the impress of His personality. In listening to their words we hear the very voice of the Son of God speaking to our individual souls, out of the world of glory. "I know thy works." "I have somewhat against thee." "I am He that searcheth the reins and hearts." "I will give unto every one of you according to your works." "I have set before thee an open door." "I have loved thee." "I will keep thee." "I would thou wert cold or hot." "I will spew thee out of My mouth." "I counsel thee." "As many as I love I rebuke and chasten." "I stand at the door and knock; if any man hear My voice and open to Me, I will come in to him and sup with him, and he with Me." Each letter closes with a special promise of glorious and eternal reward "to him that overcometh"; and with the solemn appeal to the individual Christian conscience, "he that hath an ear let him hear what the Spirit saith to the Churches."

Having received these communications from the Lord Jesus Himself, standing amid the golden candlesticks which symbolized the Churches He addressed, John now beholds heaven opened, and sees the throne of God, and the worshiping hosts before the throne, and hears them crying, "Holy, holy, holy, Lord God Almighty, which was, and is, and is to come;" "Thou art worthy, O

Lord, to receive glory, and honor, and power, for Thou hast created all things, and for Thy pleasure they are and were created." In the right hand of Him who sits on the throne, John now beholds a seven sealed book, and hears an angel cry with a loud voice, "Who is worthy to open the book, and to loose the seals thereof?" None in heaven or earth is found worthy to open the book or look thereon. Then appears the sublime and solitary Exception. In the midst of the throne, standing among the four living creatures and adoring elders, is seen "a Lamb as it had been slain." He who had redeemed man by His blood shed on Calvary's tree, is there enthroned. Lo! the Lamb advances and takes the seven sealed book from the hands of Him who sits upon the throne, while the songs of the redeemed proclaim Him worthy to open its seals, and countless myriads of holy angels cry, "Worthy is the Lamb that was slain to receive power, and riches, and wisdom, and strength, and honor, and glory, and blessing." The whole creation takes up the anthem and sounds forth His praise. Then the Lamb opens the seals of the sacred and mysterious book, and unveils the contents of this final revelation of providence and prophecy.

As He opens the seven seals, successive visions appear to the gaze of the inspired seer of Patmos. First four horses, white, red, black, and livid, are beheld issuing forth, with their various riders. The souls of the martyrs are seen under the altar of sacrifice, and their cry for righteous retribution is heard. Heaven and earth are then shaken with the judgments attending the day of "the wrath of the Lamb." A pause follows in which the destructive winds of judgment are stayed, while a definite number of saints are sealed out of the twelve symbolical tribes of Israel. Then an innumerable multitude of the redeemed from all nations, kindreds, peoples, and tongues, is seen gathered before the throne of glory, with palm branches of victory, and songs of grateful joy. "They have come out of great tribulation, and have washed their robes, and made them white in the blood of the Lamb." The Lamb who has redeemed them leads them to fountains of living water, and God wipes away all tears from their eyes.

At the opening of the seventh seal there is silence in the symbolical heaven of the vision, during which seven angels prepare to sound trumpets of woe. At the successive sounding of these trumpets various judgments fall on the earth, seas, rivers, and sun of the symbolical world scene. After the sixth of these woe-trumpets occur parenthetical visions, followed by the sounding of the seventh trumpet, proclaiming the advent of "the Kingdom of our Lord and of His Christ." The parenthetical visions are then continued. There is seen the persecution of a sun-clothed woman by a wild beast power. Three stages of the conflict are marked. First the Draconic world power is cast down by "Michael and his angels," who overcome by "the blood of the Lamb," and the witness of martyrs who "loved not their lives unto the death." Then the woman flees to the wilderness, from the persecutions of the revived wild beast power, who makes war against the saints and overcomes them. Lastly, under the judgments of the seven vials, the persecuting wild beast power, and that of Babylon the great, are utterly destroyed. Great Babylon is burned, the beast is cast into the lake of fire, and Satan bound for a thousand years, while the saints and martyrs reign with Christ. The final judgment of the great white Throne succeeds, and the New Jerusalem, arrayed in the glory of God, as the Bride of the Lamb, descends from heaven into the new earth, and becomes the everlasting abode of righteousness and bliss.

Such in brief is the general outline of the Apocalyptic drama. How great the progress it depicts! At the beginning the crowns of glory and dominion are worn by the potentates of the world; the saints are oppressed and persecuted, forced to flee to the wilderness, and trodden under foot; at the close, dominion, crown, and glory are transferred to the suffering saints and their great Leader. The Lamb is crowned with "many crowns," and the victorious martyrs are exalted to reign with Him in His eternal kingdom.

Prefacing his description of these visions by the title "The Revelation of Jesus Christ which God gave unto Him to show unto His servants things which must shortly come to pass," John wrote as he was directed to the seven Churches of Asia; opening his message with greetings of "grace and peace" from the Eternal Father, the Spirit, and the Son. A doxology of praise bursts from his lips to Him "Who loved us and washed us from our sins in His own blood, and made us kings and priests unto God and His Father." The keynote of the Apocalyptic prophecy is sounded, "Behold He cometh with clouds" indicating its character as the book of the Advent of Christ, and of the Kingdom of God. At the close is added the seal of Christ's own name and authorship. "I Jesus have sent mine angel to testify unto you these things in the Churches. I am the root and the offspring of David, and the bright and morning star." "Surely I come quickly," is the final word of the prophecy.

The Reception of the Apocalypse by the Early Church

From the seven Churches of Asia Minor copies of the Apocalypse, multiplied by Christian hands, rapidly spread in all the Churches throughout the Roman Empire. Its apostolical authorship was recognized from the first, and its sacred character admitted. Early added to the Canon of the New Testament, it became the closing book of the entire Word of God.

No book of the New Testament was accorded a more general reception. The chain of evidence on the subject is complete. Justin Martyr, a Christian philosopher, born about A.D. 103, six or seven years after John's banishment to Patmos, in his dialogue with Trypho thus refers to the Apocalypse: "A man from among us by name John, one of the apostles of Christ, in the revelation made to him, has prophesied that the believers in our Christ shall live a thousand years in Jerusalem." Justin Martyr suffered martyrdom for the Christian faith about A.D. 165. Irenaeus, Bishop of the Lyonnese Church, in his book on Heresies written between A.D. 180 and 190, speaks of the Apocalypse as the work of John the disciple of the Lord, that same John that leaned on His breast at the last supper. Melito, Bishop of Sardis, about A.D. 170, wrote a treatise on the Revelation of John. Theophilus, Bishop of Antioch, about 181, according to Eusebius, made use of quotations from John's Apocalypse. So also did the martyr Apollonius, at the close of the second century, in an eloquent apology before the Roman Senate, in the reign of Commodus. Clement of Alexandria, who flourished about 194, frequently quoted the Apocalypse. Tertullian, the contemporary of Clement, one of the most learned of the Latin fathers, quotes or refers to the Apocalypse in more than seventy passages in his writings, and declared that "the succession of bishops traced to John 'rested' on John as its author."[1] Hippolytus, a greatly esteemed Christian Bishop, and martyr, who flourished about A.D. 220, in early life a disciple of Irenaeus, wrote an express commentary on the Apocalypse. Origen, the most critical and learned of the early fathers, received the Apocalypse into the Canon of Scripture. "What shall we say of John," he asks, "who leaned on the breast of Jesus? He has left us a gospel:... he wrote likewise the Revelation, though ordered to seal up those things which the seven thunders uttered: he left, too, one Epistle of very moderate length, and perhaps a second and a third, for of these last the genuineness is not by all admitted."[2] Cyprian, Bishop and martyr, the contemporary of Origen, held similar views. Victorinus wrote a commentary on the Apocalypse in the third century, which is still extant; Methodius, Arnobius, Lactantius, Athanasius, Cyril of Alexandria, Ambrose, Jerome and Augustine all received the Apocalypse, and regarded it as the inspired production of the last of the Apostles. In the centuries which followed the times of these Fathers, the acceptation of the Apocalypse by the Christian Church, both in the east and in the west, was universal. In all the early and later translations of the Scriptures, the Apocalypse found a place; and the literature to which its exposition has given rise has proved by its exceptional

---

1 Adv. Marcion Book IV, Ch. 5.
2 Quoted by Eusebius, H. E. VI, 2 5.

magnitude the interest which the prophecy has awakened in almost every age of the Church's history.

Interpretation of the Apocalypse

I. Pre-Constantine, Or Martyr Church Stage

AS THE DIRECT GIFT of the ascended and glorified Redeemer, His message from heaven, His last message through the last of His apostles, the Apocalypse possessed from the very first for the Christian Church a special and incomparable interest. Granted in the days of Domitian towards the close of the first century while the Church was suffering from the cruel persecutions of heathen Rome, this prophecy of the sufferings and triumphs of her saints and martyrs, struck a cord which strongly vibrated in every Christian heart. To the Martyr Church of the first three centuries, this book of martyrs was at once the mirror of her experiences, and the treasury of her hopes. It illuminated the darkness and dreariness of her lot with rays of celestial brightness. It was recognized as the golden crown of Revelation; the highest stone of its structure; the most triumphant note of its lofty music. What wonder that every sentence of the mysterious prophecy should have been studied with earnest attention by the Church of primitive times? What wonder that its visions should have arrested the gaze of men eager to read the meaning of the present, and to pierce the secrets of futurity? What wonder that the hands of humble sufferers, of lonely exiles, of holy martyrs, should have transcribed its pages with loving care, and transmitted them to their beloved companions in "the Kingdom and patience of Jesus Christ?"

And that they did so study this closing prophecy of Scripture is evident from the fact that the entire Apocalypse can be reproduced from its quotations in the writings of the early Fathers which remain in our hands.[3] One complete commentary on the book has come down to us from the third century, that of the martyr Victorinus; a brief and simple exposition, exhibiting the views of the Church of that period on its mysterious meaning.

And now, going back in thought to those early days of purer faith, and nobler heroism, let us endeavor to realize what were the first faint dawnings of the comprehension of this mysterious prophecy which penetrated the mind of the primitive Church; and mark the dawn light slowly increasing, as the course of history unfolded the meaning of the prophecy, and the secrets of Providence became revealed to every eye.

I. Title and subject of the prophecy.

On opening the Apocalypse the early saints and martyrs saw plainly written upon its forefront its descriptive title, — "The Revelation of Jesus Christ which God gave unto Him to show unto His servants things which must shortly come to pass... for the time is at hand." Here then they beheld an authoritative definition of the subject of the prophecy. Not to some distant period in the future of the Church's history, did this prophecy relate, but to events whose occurrence was even then, nineteen centuries ago, "at hand." This inspired declaration determined the primitive interpretation. Not a single trace is to be found in that interpretation of the "gap theory" of modern futurism, the theory that the prophecy, overleaping the last nineteen centuries of Christian history, plunges at once into the remote future, and occupies itself with the events of a brief closing period, a mere stormy sunset hour, in the story of the world. To the Church of the first three centuries the fulfillment of the Apocalypse bad already

---

3   See index to quotations from the Apocalypse in the writings of the early Fathers at the close of this chapter.

begun, and was to continue without a break to the final consummation of all things.

II. Her study of the prophecy revealed to the primitive Church its Christian character.

It was evident that the Apocalypse was sent to Christian Churches; that it was prefaced by letters addressed to these Churches; that its leading prophetic features had their parallels in these prefatory letters; that the warnings and promises in the letters related to things set forth more fully in the visions of the prophecy; that the saints of the prophetic portion of the book were those who kept "the commandments of God and the faith of Jesus,"[4] and that its martyrs were "the martyrs of Jesus."[5] Hence a Christian meaning was attached by the early Church to the entire book. It was regarded as the prophetic story of the trials and triumphs of the Church of Christ.

III. The early Church regarded the Apocalypse as the New Testament continuation of the prophecies of Daniel.

The history of the Gentile world from the period of the Jewish captivities presented then, as now, the succession of four great Gentile Kingdoms; those of Babylon, Persia, Greece, and Rome. The last of these, the greatest of the four, was at that time in the fullness of its strength, and at the acme of its glory. Ptolemy of Alexandria, the great astronomer and chronologer of the second century, had traced and tabulated in his invaluable Canon, the order and succession of these four kingdoms; associating with a series of dates in the reigns of their kings the whole of his astronomical observations. To the early Church these four

---

4   Rev. 12:12.
5   Rev. 17:6.

kingdoms of history were mirrored in the visions of prophecy. Daniel had doubly foretold their course in his vision of the quadripartite image, of gold, silver, brass and iron; and in his vision of the four beasts; the lion, bear, leopard, and ten-horned wild beast which trod down and crushed, with iron strength, the nations of the earth. The visions of the Apocalypse were recognized as the continuation of those of Daniel, as relating to the fourth of these Gentile kingdoms, and to that divine eternal kingdom which Daniel foretold, destined to destroy and replace the kingdoms of the world.

The following is Ptolemy's canon of the four kingdoms of Babylon, Persia, Greece, and Rome, composed in the second century, just after the Hadrian destruction of Jerusalem.

THE CANON OF PTOLEMY
Kings of the Babylonians

	Each.	Sum.
Nabonassar	14	14
Nadius	2	16
Khozirus and Porus	5	21
Jougaius	5	26
Mardocempadus	12	38
Archianus	5	43
First Interregnum	2	45
Belibus	3	48
Apronadius	6	54
Regibelus	1	55
Mesesimordachus	4	59
Second Interregnum	8	67
Asaridinus	13	80
Saosduchinus	20	100
Khuniladanus	22	122
Nabopolassar	21	143
Nabokolassar	43	186
Ilvarodamus	2	188
Nerikassolasar	4	192
Nabonadius	17	209

Kings of the Persians

Cyrus	9	218
Cambyses	8	226
Darius I	36	262
Xerxes	21	283
Artaxerxes I	41	324
Darius II	19	343
Artaxerxes II	46	389
Ochus	21	410
Arogus	2	412
Darius III	4	416

Kings of the Greeks

Alexander of Macedon	8	424
Philip, after Alexander the Founder	7	7
Alexand. Ægus	12	19

Kings of the Greeks in Egypt

Ptolemy Lagus	20	39
" Philadelphus	38	77
" Euergetes I	25	102
" Philopator	17	119
" Epiphanes	24	143
" Philometor	35	178
" Euergetes II	29	207
" Soter	36	243
" Dionysius	29	272
Cleopatra	22	294

Kings of the Romans

Augustus	43	337
Tiberius	22	359
Caius	4	363
Claudius	14	377
Nero	14	391
Vespasian	10	401
Titus	3	404
Domitian	15	419
Nerva	1	420
Trajan	19	439
Hadrian	21	460
Antoninus	23	483

That the early Fathers interpreted the fourfold image, and four wild beasts of Daniel, as prophetic symbols of the four kingdoms of Babylon, Persia, Greece, and Rome, is clearly seen in the following striking passage from the writings of Hippolytus.[6]

"The golden head of the image, and the lioness, denote the Babylonians; the shoulder and arm of silver, and bear, represented the Persians and Medes; the belly thighs of brass, and the leopard,

---

6 Hippolytus, "Treatise on Christ and Antichrist." Secs. 28, 3a, 33.

meant the Greeks, who held the sovereignty from Alexander's time; the legs of iron, and the beast, dreadful and terrible, expressed the Romans, who hold the sovereignty at present; the toes of feet, which were part of clay and part of iron, and the horns, were emblems of the kingdoms that are yet to rise; the other little horn that grows up among them meant Antichrist in their midst; the stone that smites the earth and brings judgment upon the world was Christ. Speak with me, O blessed Daniel. Give me full assurance I beseech thee. Thou dost prophesy concerning the lion in Babylon, for thou wast a captive there. Thou hast unfolded the future regarding the bear, for thou wast still in the world, and didst see the things come to pass. Then thou speakest to me of the leopard; and whence canst thou know this, for thou art already gone to thy rest? Who instructed thee to announce these things, but He who form thee in thy mother's womb? That is God, thou sayest. Thou hast spoken indeed, and that not falsely. The leopard has arisen; the he-goat is come; he hath smitten the Ram; he hath broken his horns in pieces; he hath stamped upon him with his feet. He has been exalted by his fall; (the) four horns have come up from under that one. Rejoice, blessed Daniel! thou hast not been in error! all the things have come to pass. After this again thou hast told us of the beast, dreadful and terrible. 'It has iron feet and claws of brass: it devoured and brake in pieces, and stamped the residue with the feet of it.' Already the iron rules; already it subdues and breaks all in pieces; already it brings all the unwilling into subjection; already we see these things ourselves. Now we glorify God, being instructed by thee."

IV. The early Church interpreted the first vision, that of the crowned Rider seated upon a white horse, armed with a bow, going forth "conquering and to conquer," as a representation of Christ going forth on His victorious mission.

Thus Victorinus in his commentary on the Apocalypse written in the third century says, "The first seal being opened he saw a white horse and a crowned horseman bearing a bow. For this was at first drawn by Himself. For after the Lord ascended into heaven and opened all things. He sent the Holy Spirit, whose words the preachers sent forth as arrows, reaching to the human heart that they might overcome unbelief."

A comparison of this opening vision with that in the nineteenth chapter, of the rider on the white horse, whose name was "King of Kings and Lord of Lords," justified in the view of the early Church the application of the first seal to Christ's victorious mission.

The fact that Christ had founded a Kingdom whose power was greater even than that of Rome, became early apparent. The words of Origen in his answer to Celsus strikingly exhibit the conviction of the primitive Church, that its marvelous progress could only be explained by attributing it to the action of supernatural power. "Any one who examines the subject," says Origen, "will see that Jesus attempted and successfully accomplished works beyond the reach of human power. For although from the very beginnings all things opposed the spread of His doctrine in the worlds — both the princes of the time, and their chief captains and generals, and all, to speak generally, who were possessed of the smallest influence, and in addition to these the rulers of the different cities, and the soldiers, and the people, — yet it proved victorious as being the Word of God, the nature of which is such that it cannot be hindered; and becoming more powerful than all such adversaries, it made itself master of the whole of Greece, and a considerable portion of barbarian lands, and converted a countless number of souls to his religion."[7]

"The outcry," says Tertullian, "is that the State is filled with Christians; that they are in the fields, in the citadels, in the islands; they make lamentation as for some calamity, that both sexes, every age and condition, even high rank, are passing over to the profession of the Christian faith."[8]

The triumph of Christianity over Paganism described by the historian Gibbon is in striking harmony with the view of the early Church as to the destinies of Christ's kingdom. "While the Roman world," says Gibbon, "was invaded by open violence, or undermined by slow decay, a pure and humble religion quietly insinuated itself into the minds of men; grew up in silence and obscurity; derived new vigor from opposition; and finally erected the triumphal banner of the Cross on the ruins of the Capitol. Nor was the influence of Christianity confined to the period, or to the limits of the Roman Empire. After a revolution of thirteen or fourteen centuries that religion is still professed by the nations of Europe, the most distinguished portion of humankind in arts and learning, as well as in arms. By the industry and zeal of the Europeans, it has been widely diffused to the most distant shores of Asia and Africa; and by the means of their colonies has been firmly established from Canada to Chili, in a world unknown to the ancients."

With the vision of Christ going forth on His world conquering mission, the Apocalypse most naturally begins. At the outset of the drama, the glorious Conqueror goes forth to whose head at the close are transferred the "many crowns" of universal dominion.

And in the vision thus interpreted is found a key to the entire prophecy; for this is the starting point of the whole. Seals, trumpets, and vials set forth a continuous course of history stretching to the consummation, having as its commencement the

---

7 "Origen against Celsus," Ch. XXVIII.
8 "Tertullian's Apology," Sec. I.

going forth of the Gospel of Christ to accomplish its world-subduing work. The inference is unavoidable that the Apocalypse presents a prophetic foreview of the entire course of Christian history, from the foundation of the Church to the end of the world. Nor was any other interpretation ever known in the Christian Church till the rise of modern futurism.

V. The red, black, and livid horses, and their riders, of the second, third, and fourth seals, were explained by primitive interpreters as signifying the wars, famines, and pestilences which our Lord had predicted in the twenty-fourth of Matthew, as salient events which would occur in the interval between His departure and His return.

Thus in the commentary of Victorinus, who died as a martyr under the persecution of Diocletian, after the application of the going forth of the rider on the white horse of the first seal to the victorious Kingdom of Christ, he adds, "The other three horses very plainly signify the wars, famines, and pestilences announced by our Lord in the gospel."

VI. The vision under the fifth seal of the souls of the martyrs beneath the altar, was interpreted by the Church of the first three centuries as representing the continuous persecutions and martyrdoms of Christ's saints;

while the sixth seal was regarded as a vision of the judgments attending the consummation, or close of the age. No other view of the meaning of the seals was possible to the early Church. Their scope seemed to reach to the consummation, and it was most natural that their mysterious symbols should be interpreted in the light of our Lord's plain unmetaphorical predictions concerning the events whose occurrence should extend to His Second Advent. Both prophecies were by the same divine Revealer; and both seemed to predict the same course of events; wars, famines, pestilences, earthquakes, persecutions; a universal proclamation of the gospel, a great tribulation; and then the darkening of the sun and moon; the falling of the stars; the shaking of the powers of heaven; and the advent of the Son of Man in the power and glory of His kingdom.

Holding this view as regards the six first seals, the early Church, unable to anticipate the long course of history which lay concealed in the future, considered that in the remaining visions of the book the revealing Spirit retraced the steps leading up to the consummation, in order to fill in the features omitted in the introductory sketch. Thus Victorinus says with reference to the trumpets and vials, which succeeded the seals, "we must not regard the order of what is said, because frequently the Holy Spirit, when He has traversed even to the end of the last times, returns again to the same times, and fills up what He had (before) failed to say." To this interpreter the brief "silence" under the seventh seal was "the beginning of everlasting rest"; while the judgments of the trumpets represented generally events connected with the coming of Antichrist.

VII. According to Victorinus the mighty cloud-clothed angel of the covenant of Revelation 10, "is our Lord."

His position as standing on sea and land signifies that "all things are placed under His feet." The command to "measure the temple" he regarded as relating, not to the rebuilding of the Jewish Temple, but to the right ordering of the Christian Church. By the assembly of its bishops its faith was to be brought into agreement with the teachings of the Word of God. The slaughter of the witnesses he explains as representing the slaying of holy prophets by Antichrist in the last times. The 1,260 days of their prophesying he interprets literally, as the period of three years and six months, during which the witnesses should prophesy in their sackcloth clothed character, as despised and persecuted by the world. To have interpreted the 1,260 days as symbolically representing 1,260 years of a suffering and subjected condition of witnesses to gospel truth, was of course impossible at that early period of the Church's history. The latter view only dawned upon the minds of Apocalyptic interpreters during the actual fulfillment of the prophecy in the middle ages.

VIII. The woman clothed with the sun, with the moon under her feet, and a crown of twelve stars, of Ch. 12, is, according to Victorinus, and all the early interpreters, "the ancient Church of fathers, and prophets, and saints, and apostles."

In his treatise on Christ and Antichrist, Hippolytus says, "By the 'woman clothed with the sun' he meant most manifestly the Church, endued with the Father's word, whose brightness is above the sun... the words 'upon her head a crown of twelve stars,' refer to the twelve apostles by whom the Church was founded." The "three and a half times" of her seclusion in the wilderness is the period of 1,260 days, or three and a half years, during which the Church "seeks concealment in the wilderness," from the persecutions of Antichrist; finding no safety but in flight.

IX. The 144,000 sealed out of the twelve tribes of Israel, of Chs. 7 and 14, are interpreted by Tertullian as not Jews but Christians.

"With the same anti-Judaic view he markedly speaks of the Apocalyptic New Jerusalem (though with the names of the twelve tribes of Israel written on its gates) as Christian, not Jewish; the Jerusalem spoken of by St. Paul to the Galatians, as the Mother of all Christians."[9]

The same view was clearly and powerfully advocated by the celebrated Origen; and was held by Methodius, and Lactantius; in fact was a leading feature of primitive exposition.

X. On the important subject of Antichrist

"While there was a universal concurrence in the general idea of the prophecy, there was in respect of the details of application, a considerable measure of difference; these differences, arising mainly out of certain current notions of the coming of Antichrist as in some way Jewish as well as Roman, and the difficulty of combining and adjusting the two characteristics."[10] The Roman view was derived from the Antichrist being represented in the prophecy as the eighth head of the Roman beast, arising after the healing of his deadly wound.[11] His Jewish character, where held, seems to have arisen from his being regarded as in some sense a false Christ, such as our Lord predicted in Matt. 24. Hence Irenaeus and Hippolytus imagined that the place of his manifestation would be the Jewish sanctuary, and that its time would synchronize with the last half week of the "seventy weeks" of Daniel 9. The whole subject was necessarily involved in great perplexity to these early expositors. No correct anticipation of the fulfillment of the predictions relating to

---

9 Elliott, *Horae*, IV, p. 281.
10 Ibid p. 303.
11 Ch. 13.

Antichrist, viewed as a whole, was possible in the opening centuries of the Church's history. Certain points, however, were clearly and correctly seen. Justin Martyr, one of the earliest of the Fathers, considered the Apocalyptic ten-horned beast, or rather its ruling head, to be identical with St. Paul's Man of Sin, and St. John's Antichrist: and Irenaeus directed his readers to look out for the division of the Roman Empire into ten kingdoms, as that which was immediately to be followed by Antichrist's manifestation. He also remarkably explained the number of Antichrist's name, 666, as symbolizing *Lateinos*, the Latin man, "seeing that they who thus held the world's empire were Latins."[12]

XI. To the early Fathers the Babylon of the Apocalypse represented Rome.

This is an important point owing to the magnitude of the position occupied by "Babylon the Great" in Apocalyptic prophecy; and also to the fact that the angelic interpretation of the vision relating to Babylon makes it the key to the whole prophecy.

"Tell me, blessed John," says Hippolytus, "thou apostle and disciple of the Lord, what thou hast heard and seen respecting Babylon: wake up, and speak; for it was she that exiled thee to Patmos." "Babylon, in our own John," says Tertullian, "is a figure of the city of Rome, as being equally great and proud of her sway, and triumphant over the saints." On Revelations 17:9, Victorinus says, "The seven heads are the seven hills on which the woman sitteth — that is the city of Rome." "On the Apocalyptic Babylon's meaning Rome, all agreed."[13]

---

12 The numerical value of the Greek letters in the name *Lateinos* is equivalent to 666.
13 Elliott, *Horae*, IV, p. 308.

XII. The continued existence of the Roman Empire was commonly regarded by the early Fathers as the "let" or hindrance to the manifestation of "the Man of Sin," or Antichrist.

In his magnificent apology addressed to the rulers of the Roman Empire, Tertullian says that the Christian Church prayed for the stability of the empire, because they knew "that a mighty shock impending over the whole earth — in fact the very end of all things, threatening dreadful woes — was only retarded by the continued existence of the Roman Empire. We have no desire to be overtaken by these dire events; and in praying that their coming may be delayed we are lending our aid to Rome's duration." As to the "let" or hindrance to die manifestation of the "Man of Sin," "we have the consenting testimony of the early Fathers," says Elliott, "from Irenaeus, the disciple of the disciple of St. John, down to Chrysostom and Jerome, to the effect that it was understood to be the imperial power ruling and residing at Rome."[14]

XIII. The Martyr Church of the first three centuries interpreted the first resurrection foretold in the twentieth chapter of the Apocalypse as a resurrection of the literal dead.

Hence they believed in the premillennial Advent of Christ. On no point of interpretation was their agreement more remarkable. "On the millenary question, all primitive expositors except Origen, and the few who rejected the Apocalypse as unapostolical, were premillenarians; and construed the first resurrection of the saints literally."[15] They looked for the appearance of Christ to destroy

---

14 *Horae*, III, p. 101.
15 Ibid., IV, p. 310.

Antichrist. They believed that the Roman Empire would fall into ten kingdoms, then Antichrist would appear, and then Christ would come in the glory of His kingdom. Thus Lactantius held that after the destruction of Antichrist "the saints raised from the grave would reign with Christ through the world's seventh Chiliad, a period to commence, Lactantius judged, in about two hundred years at furthest: the Lord alone being thenceforth worshipped in a renovated world; its still living inhabitants multiplying incalculably in a state of terrestrial felicity; and the resurrection saints, during this commencement of an eternal kingdom in a nature like the angelic, reigning over them."[16]

At the conclusion of his treatise on Christ and Antichrist, Hippolytus expresses himself as follows — "Moreover, concerning the resurrection, and the kingdom of the saints, Daniel says, 'And many of them that sleep in the dust of the earth shall arise, some to everlasting life.' Esaias says, 'The dead men shall arise, and they that are in their tombs shall awake; for the dew from thee is healing to them.' The Lord says, 'Many in that day shall hear the voice of the Son of God, and they that hear shall live.' And the prophet says, 'Awake thou that sleepest, and arise from the dead, and Christ shall give thee light.' And John says, 'Blessed and holy is he that hath part in the first resurrection; on such the second death hath no power.'

Concerning the resurrection of the righteous, Paul also speaks thus in writing to the Thessalonians... 'The Lord Himself shall descend from heaven with a shout, with the voice and trump of God, and the dead in Christ shall rise first. Then we which are alive and remain shall be caught up together with them in the clouds to meet the Lord in the air; and so shall we ever be with the Lord. These things then, I have set shortly before thee, O Theophilus, drawing them (from Scripture itself) in order that maintaining in faith what is written, and anticipating the things that are to be, thou mayest keep thyself void of offense both towards God and towards men, "looking for that blessed hope and appearing of our

---

16 Elliott, *Horae*, IV, p. 301.

God and Saviour," when having raised the saints among us, He will rejoice with them, glorifying the Father. To Him be the glory unto the endless ages of the ages. Amen'"

Such were the leading features of the interpretation of the Apocalypse by the Martyr Church of the first three centuries. In the Catacombs of Rome, there remains a profoundly interesting and touching reference to one of the opening and closing symbols of the Apocalypse in the oft recurring Monogram of the Name of Christ, in which the Greek letters Alpha and Omega, the first and the last of the Alphabet, are inserted on either side of the brief sign standing for Χριστος or Christ; the whole being enclosed in a circle, the symbol of eternity.

The following are the passages in the Apocalypse forming the foundation of the monogram. "I am Alpha and Omega, the beginning and the ending, saith the Lord, which is, and which was, and which is to come, the Almighty."[17]

"I am Alpha and Omega, the first and the last, and what thou seest write in a book."[18]

"I am Alpha and Omega, the beginning and the end, the first and the last... I Jesus."[19]

"The two letters of Greece, the first and the last," says Tertullian, "the Lord assumes to Himself, as figures of the beginning and end which concur in Himself: so that, just as Alpha rolls on till it reaches Omega, and again Omega rolls back till it reaches Alpha, in the same way He might show that in Himself is both the downward course of the beginning on to the end, and the backward course of the end up to the beginning; so that every economy, ending in Him through whom it began, — through the

---

17   1 Ch. 1:8.
18   Ch. 1:11.
19   Ch. 22:14, 16.

Word of God, that is, who was made flesh, — may have an end corresponding to its beginning."[20]

Such was the faith that overcame the world!

The place and power of the Apocalyptic prophecy as sustaining in the Martyr Church, the hope of the speedy advent of Christ, and thus strengthening that Church for its warfare and victory over the persecuting pagan Empire of Rome, were of the highest practical importance. The historian Gibbon recognizes the immense influence of the hope of Christ's speedy coming on the early Church. "The ancient Christians," he says, "were animated by a contempt for their present existence, and by a just confidence of immortality, of which the doubtful and imperfect faith of modern ages cannot give us any adequate notion... It was universally believed that the end of the world and the kingdom of heaven were at hand. The near approach of this wonderful event had been predicted by the apostles;" a view "productive of the most salutary effects on the faith and practice of Christians, who lived in the awful expectation of that moment when the globe itself, and all the various races of mankind, should tremble at the appearance of their divine Judge. The ancient and popular doctrine of the millennium was intimately connected with the Second Coming of Christ. As the works of creation had been finished in six days, their duration in their present state, according to a tradition which was attributed to the prophet Elijah, was fixed to six thousand years. By the same analogy it was inferred that this long period of labor and contention, which was now almost elapsed, would be succeeded by a joyful Sabbath of a thousand years; and that Christ, with the triumphant band of the saints and the elect who had escaped death, or who had been miraculously revived, would reign upon earth till the time appointed for the last and general resurrection."[21]

While correct in its historical principle and leading features, the interpretation of the Apocalypse by the early Church was necessarily deficient in scope. It foreshortened the prospect to a

---

20 Tertullian, Vol. III, p. 29.
21 "Decline and Fall," Ch. XV.

narrow margin. It knew nothing of the long centuries which were destined to elapse before the dispensation had run its course. It knew nothing of the great Apostasy which was to darken the earth by its long and terrible eclipse; and nothing of the glorious reformation which was to follow, although all these were foretold in the far-seeing prophecy. Rome Pagan, in her declining dominion, and proximate doom, filled the scene on which the early Christians gazed. One bright star shone in their sky, burning with intense and pristine splendor, the hope of the speedy coming of Christ. For that great event they watched and waited. They believed that to suffer with Christ was the prelude to reigning with Him, and that His kingdom was at hand. And this conviction nerved them to endure the utmost torments which heathen Rome had power to inflict. In this conviction they lived and died, "more than conquerors."

The following index to the numerous quotations from, or references to the Apocalypse, in the writings of the Ante-Nicene Fathers has been compiled from the separate indexes in the twenty-four volumes of the "Ante-Nicene Christian Library."

Quotations of the Apocalypse in the Writings of the Ante-Nicene Fathers

Quotations of the Apocalypse in the Writings of
the Ante-Nicene Fathers   '

Revelation, Chapter and Verse.	Book.	Vol.	Page.
1 : 1, 2.	Gregory Thaum Dionysius Alex.		166
1 : 3.	Victorinus. (under Tertullian.)	III.	416
1 : 5.	Irenæus.	I.	362
1 : 5.	Methodius.		168
1 : 6.	Tertullian.	III.	11, 35
1 : 7.	Apostolic Fathers Ep. Ignatius to Smyr.		243
1 : 7.	Tertullian.	II.	308
1 : 7.	"	III.	268
1 : 8.	Hippolytus.	I.	207
1 : 8.	"	II.	57

1 : 8.	Tertullian.	II.	372
1 : 8.	Clement of Alexandria.	I.	138
1 : 8.	Origen.	I.	29
1 : 9.	Dionysius Thaum.		167
1 : 10.	Tertullian.	II.	426
1 : 12.	Irenæus.	I.	448
1 : 13.	Tertullian.	III. 243, 256, 392
1 : 14.	Cyprian.	I.	345
1 : 15.	Irenæus.	I.	418
1 : 16.	Tertullian.	III.	230
1 : 16.	" against Marcion.		147
1 : 17.	Irenæus.	I.	448
1 : 20.	Tertullian.	III.	95
2 : 1, 8, 12, 18.	"	III.	96
2 : 4.	"	I.	271
2 : 5.	"	I.	306
2 : 5.	Cyprian.	I. 47, 78, 145 } 270, 363
2 : 6.	Tertullian.	III.	262
2 : 6.	Hippolytus.	I.	305
2 : 6.	Irenæus.	I.	98
2 : 7.	Cyprian.	II.	155
2 : 7.	Methodius.		23
2 : 7.	Tertullian.	I.	278
2 : 7, 11, 17, 29.	"	I.	271
2 : 9.	Tatian.		324
2 : 10.	Tertullian.	I. 254, 409
2 : 10.	Cyprian.	I. 21, 132
	"	II. 65, 155
2 : 12.	Tertullian.	III.	230
2 : 13.	"	I.	409
2 : 14.	"	II.	40
2 : 14, 15.	"	I.	271
2 : 17.	Irenæus.	II.	79
2 : 18, 20, 22.	Tertullian.	III.	108
2 : 20.	"	I.	271
2 : 23.	Cyprian.	I. 36, 401, 463
	"	II.	176
2 : 24.	Tertullian.	I.	143
2 : 26, 27.	"	I.	170
2 : 27.	"	I.	263
2 : 28.	Cyprian.	I.	370
2 :	Lactantius.	I.	468
3 : 1, 7, 14.	Tertullian.	III.	95
3 : 2.	"	I.	271
3 : 4.	"	II.	262
3 : 5.	"	II.	262
3 : 6, 13, 31.	"	I.	271
3 : 7.	Hippolytus.	I.	453
3 : 7.	Irenæus.	I.	440

Pre-Constantine, or Martyr Church Stage   43

3: 7.	Dionysius.		74
3: 10.	Tertullian.	I.	409
3: 11.	Cyprian.	I.	31, 63
3: 14.	Hippolytus.	I.	186
3: 17.	Tertullian.	I.	271
3: 17.	Cyprian.	II.	431
3: 18.	Tertullian.	III.	35
3: 19.	"	I.	223
3: 19.	Cyprian.	I.	361
3: 21.	"	I.	73
3: 21.	Tertullian.	I. 170. II. 405	
4: 3.	"	I.	311
4: 4.	"	I. 353. III. 393	
4: 4.	Clement of Alexandria.	II.	366
4: 5.	Tertullian.	III.	292, bis.
4: 6.	" Victorinus.	III.	389
4: 7.	Irenæus.	I.	293
5:	Hippolytus.	I.	454
5: 1–5.	Cyprian.	II.	110
5: 2.	"	II.	440
5: 5.	Hippolytus.	II.	7
5: 6.	"	II.	112
5: 6.	Irenæus.	I.	449
5: 6.	Clement of Alexandria.	II.	241
5: 6.	Tertullian.	III.	392
5: 6–10.	Cyprian.	II.	115
5: 7.	Tertullian.	III.	339
5: 8.	Irenæus.	I. 431. II. 176	
5: 8.	Origen.	II.	505
5: 9.	Tertullian.	II.	320
6: 2.	"	I.	354
6: 2.	Irenæus.	I.	452
6: 4, 8.	Tertullian.	III.	115
6: 9.	"	I. 409. II. 531	
6: 9, 10.	"	II. 258. III. 360	
6: 9–11.	"	II.	281, 426
6: 9–11.	Clement of Alexandria.	I.	259
6: 9–11.	Cyprian.	II.	37, 154
6: 10.	"	I.	364
6: 10.	Tertullian.	I.	183
6: 12–17.	Cyprian.	II.	444
6: 13.	Tertullian.	II.	104
6: 14.	"	II.	103
6: 14.	Hippolytus.	II.	123
7: 3.	Tertullian.	III.	309
7: 3–7.	Irenæus.	II.	137
7: 4.	Methodius.		57
7: 9.	"		11
7: 9–17.	Cyprian.	II.	155
7: 14.	Tertullian.	I.	410

44   History Unveiling Prophecy

Pre-Constantine, or Martyr Church Stage 45

16 : 15.	Cyprian.	II.	155
17 :	Tertullian.	I. 330. III.	229
17 : 1.	Cyprian.	I.	342
17 : 1-4.	"	II.	169
17 : 6.	Tertullian.	I.	410
17 : 8.	Apostolic Fathers. (Pastor of Hermes.)		345
17 : 8.	Irenæus.	II.	138
17 : 9.	Hippolytus.	II.	18
17 : 10.	"	I.	447
17 : 12.	Irenæus.	II.	125
17 : 14.	Tertullian.	I.	250
17 : 15.	Cyprian.	I. 216. II.	432
17 : 18.	"	II.	11 ?
17 : 18.	Hippolytus.	II.	22
18 :	Tertullian.	II.	258
18 : 2.	"	II.	253
18 : 4.	"	I.	351
18 : 4.	Cyprian.	I.	358
18 : 4-9.	"	II.	169
19 : 6.	Hippolytus.	I.	456
19 : 6, 7.	Cyprian.	II.	119
19 : 11-13.	"	II.	101
19 : 11-13.	Hippolytus.	II.	66
19 : 11-16.	Cyprian.	II.	129
19 : 11-17.	Irenæus.	I.	449
19 : 12.	Lactantius.	II.	125
19 : 13.	Cyprian.	II.	325
19 : 15-21.	Tertullian.	III.	230
19 : 20.	Irenæus.	II.	131
20 :	Justin Martyr.		201
20 : 2.	Tertullian.	II.	258
20 : 3.	"	II.	71
20 : 3, 4.	"	III.	309
20 : 4, 5.	"	II.	258
20 : 4, 5.	Cyprian.	II.	76
20 : 6.	Irenæus.	II.	149
20 : 6.	Methodius.		97
20 : 6.	Hippolytus.	II.	39
20 : 10, 13-15.	Tertullian.	II.	323
20 : 11.	Irenæus.	II.	153
20 : 11.	Tertullian.	II.	103
20 : 11.	Hippolytus.	II.	127
20 : 11-13.	Cyprian.	II.	445
20 : 12, 14.	Irenæus.	II.	154
20 : 12, 14.	Tertullian.	II.	258
20 : 13.	Methodius.		167
20 : 15.	Apostolic Fathers. (Pastor of Hermes.)		326
20 : 15.	Irenæus.	I.	154

46   History Unveiling Prophecy

2. The Post-Constantine, Or Imperial Church Stage

THE GREAT HISTORIC EVENT which immediately succeeded the Diocletian era of persecution was the fall of Paganism, and the establishment of Christianity as the religion of the Roman Empire.

In its internal character and far-reaching effects this revolution is one of the greatest and most remarkable that has ever taken place in the history of the world.

The ruin of Paganism, as Gibbon has pointed out, is perhaps "the only example of the total extirpation of any ancient and popular superstition." During the long period of a thousand years the dark shadow of Paganism had covered the city and empire of Rome. Its temples were innumerable and adorned with the utmost magnificence. Its wealth, the accumulation of ages, was fabulously great. Its priesthood was established and endowed by government, the Roman Emperor himself occupying the position of the supreme pontiff of the hierarchy. In the fourth century this monstrous system was brought to ruin. Working upwards from the lowest strata of society, the belief in the unity of the Godhead, and the divinity of the Christian religion, a belief commended by the lives, and sealed by the blood of the martyrs, had gradually reached the highest classes in the community, and effected the conversion of the Roman Emperor. The conviction that "the idolatrous worship of fabulous deities, and real demons, is the most abominable crime against the Supreme Majesty of the Creator," led to the subversion of the temples of the Roman world, and the total suppression of

27

Paganism. Maxentius, the last persecuting Pagan Emperor, was overthrown by Constantine at the memorable battle of Milvian Bridge, and his legions drowned in the waters of the Tiber. The Christian religion, liberated from persecution, became the religion of the State. The suppression of Paganism gradually followed, and within less than a century its "faint and minute vestiges were no longer visible."

In this memorable event Apocalyptic prophecy was strikingly fulfilled, a fact clearly recognized and openly confessed by the leading Christian writers of the period, and even celebrated by Imperial Enactment.

The fall of Paganism shed a flood of light on the Apocalyptic vision in which the issue of the deadly conflict between the Christian Church and the Imperial Roman power is represented by the casting down of the seven-headed Satanically inspired dragon from his lofty position of rule and authority.

The conflict and its issue are thus symbolically described in Revelation 12: "And there was war in heaven: Michael and his angels fought against the dragon; and the dragon fought and his angels, and prevailed not, neither was their place any more found in heaven, and the great dragon was cast out, that old serpent called the devil, and Satan, which deceiveth the whole world: he was cast out into the earth, and his angels were cast out with him. And I heard a loud voice saying in heaven. Now is come salvation, and strength, and the Kingdom of our God, and the power of His Christ, for the accuser of our brethren is cast down, which accused them before our God day and night. And they overcame him by the blood of the Lamb, and by the word of their testimony, and they loved not their lives unto the death."

Several points in this most remarkable prophecy should be especially noticed.

[1.] The dragon is the ten-horned wild beast power of the Apocalypse[22] whose identity with the fourth or ten-horned wild

_____
22 Revelation 12:3.

beast of the prophecies of Daniel was recognized by the Church of the second, third, and fourth centuries. Of the fourth beast "dreadful and terrible" Hippolytus says "who are these but the Romans... the kingdom which is now established?" "John in the Apocalypse," says Irenaeus, "teaches us what the ten horns shall be which were seen by Daniel."

[2.] This ruling power, under a sevenfold succession of heads, is represented as Satanically inspired. In a later vision[23] the sixth head is identified with the form of Roman rule which existed in St. John's own time, that of the Pagan Roman Caesars.

[3.] The dragon is described as "great." The power of heathen Rome was then the greatest in the world. It had conquered and crushed the nations.

[4.] As "red"; red with much bloodshed of war and persecution.

[5.] As wearing the "crowns" which symbolized its rule, not on the ten horns, which had not then arisen, but on its previous succession of "heads."

[6.] As first standing before the "woman," who represented as the Fathers clearly saw the Judeo-Christian Church,[24] to devour her child as soon as it was born, and then warring against her, and "her seed."

[7.] The conflict is described as a fierce and obstinate "war."

[8.] The army of the just, under its Heavenly Leader, is victorious over the dragon.

[9.] The victory is celebrated by a song of praise in which the great event is regarded as a signal triumph of the Kingdom of God. "Now is come salvation and strength, and the Kingdom of our God, and the power of His Christ."

[10.] The victors are declared to have "overcome by the blood of the Lamb, and by the word of their testimony": not by sword and

---

23 Ch. 17:10.
24 Hippolytus, "Christ and Antichrist," Sec. 25.

spear, as in a mere carnal conflict, but by moral, spiritual, and Christian weapons.

[11.] The martyr character of the conquerors is touchingly described in the concluding sentence "they loved not their lives even unto the death."

In connection with the application of this remarkable prophecy, it should be observed that the figure of the dragon was used as an ensign by the armies of heathen Rome. Ammianus Marcellinus thus describes this heathen Roman standard: "The dragon was covered with purple cloth, and fastened to the end of a pike gilt and adorned with precious stones. It opened its wide throat, and the wind blew through it; and it hissed as if in a rage, with its tail floating in several folds through the air." It was first used as an ensign near the close of the second century of the Christian era. "In the third century it had become almost as notorious among Roman ensigns as the eagle itself; and is in the fourth century used by Prudentius, Vegetius, Chrysostom, Ammianus, etc., in the fifth by Claudian and others."[25]

Two stages in the casting down of Roman Paganism should be distinguished; first its primary dejection when headed by Maximin and Licinius; and secondly, its final overthrow as headed by the apostate Emperor Julian. The persecution under Diocletian was the most prolonged and severe of those endured by the early Church. Under Maximin this persecution reached its climax. "Before the decisive battle," says Milner, "Maximin vowed to Jupiter that, if victorious, he would abolish the Christian name. The contest between Jehovah and Jupiter was now at its height, and drawing to a crisis." "The defeat and death of Maximin," says Gibbon, "delivered the Church from the last and most implacable of her enemies."

The effort of the apostate Emperor Julian thirty years later to restore Paganism throughout the Roman Empire was similarly

---

25 Elliott, III, p. 15.

defeated by the wonder working hand of God. It was "the design of Julian," says Gibbon, "to deprive the Christians of the advantages of wealth, of knowledge and of power." They were condemned to rebuild at enormous cost, the Pagan temples which had been destroyed. By these rash edicts "the whole empire, and particularly the East, was thrown into confusion." The persecution which broke forth afresh against the Church was terminated by the tragic death of Julian on the field of battle, in A.D. 363.

Theodoret tells us that "as soon as the death of Julian was known in Antioch (followed by the accession of the orthodox Jovian) public festivals were celebrated. And not in the churches and martyr chapels only, but even in the theaters the victory of the cross was extolled, and Julian's oracles held up to ridicule... They exclaimed as with one voice, 'Where are now thy predictions, O foolish Maximus? God and His Christ have gotten the victory.'"[26]

Bishop Gregory Nazianzen in a public discourse delivered on the occasion says, "Hear this, all ye nations... all that are now, and all that shall be hereafter. Hear every power in heaven, even all ye angels, whose office was the destruction of the tyrant: not of Sihon, King of the Amorites, nor of Og, King of Bashan, rulers of little importance, and their afflicted Israel, a small people only of the habitable earth; but the destruction of the dragon, the apostate, the man of great mind, the common enemy and adversary of all; who madly did and threatened many things on the earth, and spoke and devised great wickedness against the height above... Who shall worthily celebrate these things? Who shall declare the power of the Lord, and speak all His praise? Who shivered the armor, the sword and the battle, and broke the heads of the dragon in the water? ...It is the Lord mighty and powerful; the Lord mighty in battle."

Later on, alluding to the frustration of Julian's attempt to rebuild the temple of Jerusalem, and to destroy the very name of Christians, he says: — "What will be the end of the heathen if they turn not to Christ now? Would that they would consent to be

---

26 Elliott, III, p. 37.

ruled not with the rod of iron, but with that of the Good Shepherd."[27]

To commemorate the fall of Paganism, the Emperor Constantine caused medals to be struck representing that event under the semblance of a dragon precipitated into the abyss. "As we see on the coins of Constantine," says Ranke, "the Labarum with the monogram of Christ above the conquered dragon, even so did the worship and name of Christ stand triumphant above prostrate heathenism."[28] In his Epistle to Eusebius and other bishops concerning the re-edifying and repairing of churches, Constantine said that "liberty being now restored, and 'that dragon' being removed from the administration of public affairs by the providence of the Great God, and by my ministry, I esteem the great power of God to have been made manifest, even to all."[29]

The Emperor Constantine, says Eusebius, "caused to be painted on a lofty tablet, and set up in the front of the portico of his palace, so as to be visible to all, a representation of the salutary sign placed above his head; and below it that hateful and savage adversary of mankind, who by means of the tyranny of the ungodly, had wasted the Church of God, falling headlong, under the form of a dragon, to the abyss of destruction. For the sacred oracles in the books of God's prophets have described him as a dragon and a crooked serpent, and for this reason the Emperor there publicly displayed a painted resemblance of the dragon beneath his own and his children's feet, stricken through with a dart, and cast headlong into the depths of the sea."[30]

This triumphant celebration of the victory of the early Church over Roman Paganism was anticipated in the words of the Apocalyptic prophecy, tl Now hath come the salvation, and the

27 Compare Apocalypse, 12:5.
28 "History of the Popes," I, p. 9.
29 Eusebius, "Life of Constantine," 6, II, Ch. 46; Socrates, Hist. Eccles., I, Ch. 9; Theodoret, 6, I, Ch. 16.
30 Eusebius, "Life of Constantine," Book III, Ch. III.

power, and the Kingdom of our God, and the authority of His Christ... therefore rejoice ye heavens, and ye that dwell in them."

"The very word," says Elliott, "ευφραινεσδε, used in the Apocalyptic prophecy to wish the Christian professors joy, was the identical word addressed more than once to them in the Imperial Edict of Constantine."[31]

The exaltation of the Christian religion to the position of the religion of the State under Constantine, while productive of great advantages, especially in the cessation of persecution, led to serious declension, not only in the spiritual life of the Church, but also in her views as to the teachings of prophecy concerning her relations to the Roman Empire, and to the world. The divine weapon placed in the hand of the Church to preserve her from apostasy fell from her grasp. She lost the remembrance of her position as a pilgrim and a stranger on earth seeking a celestial city which hath foundations, whose Builder and Maker is God. The transformation of the Martyr Church of the early centuries into the Christendom of the Middle Ages involved the change of Apocalyptic interpretation as to the reign of Christ and His saints in a post-advent kingdom, into a prediction of a Romanized Christianity ruling after the fashion of the Caesars, the peoples of the world.

"The great Constantine revolution," says Elliott, "could hardly fail of exercising a considerable influence on Apocalyptic interpretation. A revolution by which Christianity should be established in the prophetically-denounced Roman Empire, was an event the contingency of which had never occurred apparently to the previous exponents of Christian prophecy; and suggested the idea of a time, mode, and scene, of the fulfillment of the promises of the latter-day blessedness that could scarcely have arisen before; viz. — that its scene might be the earth in its present state, not the renovated earth after Christ's coming (and the conflagration); its

31 *Horae*, III, p. 36.

time that of the present dispensation; its mode by the earthly establishment of the earthly Church visible. For it does not seem to have occurred at the time that this might in fact be one of the preparations, through Satan's craft, for the establishment, after a while, of the great predicted antichristian ecclesiastical empire, on the platform of the same Roman world, and in a professing but apostatized Church."[32]

This revolution of interpretation is strikingly visible in the case of Eusebius, who, though he seems in early life to have received the Apocalypse as inspired Scripture, and interpreted its seals in harmony with the method of Victorinus, was led, after the Constantine revolution, and the establishment of Christianity, to doubt the apostolic authorship of the prophecy. He continued, however, to apply the symbolic prefigurations of the Apocalypse to the changed events of the period; the casting down of the seven-headed dragon from its high and ruling position represented in the twelfth chapter seemed to him to agree in a marvelous manner with the dejection of Paganism, and of the Pagan Emperors, which had just taken place, from the supremacy which they had for ages exercised in the Roman world. The prophecies of Isaiah respecting the latter-day glory of the redeemed, and the Apocalyptic vision of the New Jerusalem, were applied by him to the Christian Church as newly established by Constantine. The millennial day of the glory and prosperity of the Church seemed to have dawned, and the language of the period was filled with the loftiest anticipations.

During the thousand years which followed, the Mediaeval period of history, the Church believed she was living in the millennium. The commencement of this millennium, or period during which Satan is bound, was variously dated; first with Augustine from Christ's ministry, when the Redeemer beheld Satan fall as lightning from heaven; and later on, when the lapse of time had proved the error of this view, from the Constantine revolution; the binding of Satan being taken to represent the restriction of Satanic power at the fall of Paganism. This

---

32 *Horae*, Vol. IV, p. 310.

extraordinary view continued to prevail up to the time of the Reformation in the sixteenth century, the Reformers supposing themselves to be living in the "little season" during which Satan was to be "loosed" at the close of the millennium.

To carry out the view that the millennium had come, and that the Church, as Eusebius supposed, had reached the stage of existence represented by the latter-day glory predicted by Isaiah, and the new Jerusalem foretold by John, "must soon have been felt most difficult: the Arian and other troubles which quickly supervened, powerfully contributing to that conviction. It resulted, perhaps not a little from this cause, that the Apocalypse itself became for a while much neglected; especially in the Eastern Empire, where the Imperial seat was now chiefly fixed."[33]

The sad effect of this neglect became evident in the dark apostasy which speedily followed. The Harlot Church denounced in the Apocalypse was magnified as the Bride of Christ, enriched with the privileges and adorned with the glories of the millennial state. The reign of Satan was mistaken for the reign of Christ. The solemn warnings of the Word of God intended to preserve the Church from the apostasy were forgotten; and the "falling away" foretold took place, carrying with it the whole of Christendom, with the exception of a small and feeble remnant of faithful witnesses to New Testament truths.

The growing perception of this apostasy led the prophetic interpreters of the fourth and fifth centuries to the view which had presented itself to the pre-Constantine Fathers, that the scene of the manifestation of Antichrist would prove to be the professing Christian Church. Thus Athanasius taught that the Antichrist of prophecy would prove to be a heretical ruler of the Roman Empire, making a Christian profession; and that Antichrist would come with the profession, "I am Christ," assuming Christ's place and character, like Satan transformed into an angel of light. Hilary, Bishop of Poictiers, in France, the contemporary and friend of

---

33 Elliott, IV, p. 312.

Athanasius, asked when the flood of Arianism swept over the western part of the Roman Empire, "Is it a doubtful thing that Antichrist will sit in Christian Churches?" He denounced the Emperor Constantine as a precursor of Antichrist; and speaks of Bishop Arius, and Bishop Auxentius as Antichrists. Cyril, of Jerusalem, says of Antichrist, "This man will usurp the government of the Roman Empire, and will falsely call himself the Christ." "He will sit in the temple of God: not that which is in Jerusalem, but in the Churches everywhere."[34] Jerome, in interpreting Paul's Man of Sin, declares that he "is to sit in the temple, that is in the Church." He adds, "It is only by assuming Christ's name that the simpler ones of believers can be seduced to go to Antichrist; for thus they will go to Antichrist, while thinking to find Christ."

---

34 Elliott, *Horae*, IV, p. 316.

3. The Mediaeval Stage

WITH THE GOTHIC INVASION and the break-up of the western Roman Empire into ten kingdoms, came the predicted rise of Antichrist.

The incipient fulfillment of the foretold partition of the empire began to be recognized as early as the fourth century. "In our time," said Jerome, "the clay has become mixed with iron. Once nothing was stronger than the Roman Empire, now nothing weaker, mixed up as it is with, and needing the help of barbarous nations." "He who withheld is removed, and we think not that Antichrist is at the door!" On the unthinking Church, blind to the meaning of the events occurring around her, came the predicted "Man of Sin," to take his foretold place and sit supreme for long disastrous centuries in the very Temple or Church of God.

The Rise of the Papacy to Universal Dominion

"A mighty and majestic figure," says Pennington, "comes upon our view in the Middle Ages. Its feet rest upon the earth, while its head towers towards the stars. A triple tiara, rich with the most costly gems, glitters on its brow. It is clothed in the sacred robes of the priesthood, but bears in its hand the golden sceptre of temporal dominion. The nations of the earth crouch at its feet. Around it clouds of incense roll upwards from innumerable altars. The ground on which it stands is whitened with the bones of God's

37

saints.[35]

The rise of this power was gradual. The removal of the Imperial Government from Rome to Constantinople, and the break-up of the empire by invading hordes of barbarians, liberated the Bishop of Rome from the bonds which had confined his activities, and hindered the attainment of the supremacy to which he aspired. Rome had in earlier times sat queen among the nations. Why should not the Bishop of Rome be accorded the proud position of Head of the Churches of Christendom? Why should he not become their spiritual dictator? Applications for assistance and advice came to him from every quarter. His letters, first mild and moderate in tone, gradually assumed the form of arbitrary mandates. Encroachments were made on the spiritual jurisdiction of other bishops. Appeals addressed to him by bishops or presbyters, and applications from monarchs to interfere in their quarrels, led to his asserting the right to decide by his own arbitrary will the disputes of individuals and the controversies of the Church. Additional powers were gradually obtained. The Bishop of Rome was the alleged successor of St. Peter, the prince of the apostles, to whom Christ had committed the keys of the kingdom of heaven. In the fifth century the lineal descent of the Popes from St. Peter was an accredited article of Christianity. Claiming to have been bestowed as a divine gift, the supremacy of the Bishop of Rome over all other bishops was established by a law of the Roman Emperor. In the year 607 the Emperor Phocas, a blood-stained usurper, placed the crown of universal supremacy in the Christian Church on the brow of Boniface III. The temporal dominion of the Popes speedily followed. In the next century the usurper Pepin bestowed upon the Pope the city of Rome, and the exarchate of Ravenna, which he had wrested from the Lombards. Charlemagne, crowned by the Pope in the year 800 as Emperor of the Romans, enlarged the Pope's dominions; and the Roman Empire, which had been overthrown by the barbarians, restored by Charlemagne, took officially the title of the *Holy Roman Empire*.

35　Pennington, "Epochs of the Papacy," p. 1.

King and priest stood side by side at the summit of this empire. Which stood highest? That question which took centuries to settle, ended by the exaltation of the Papal power in 1268 to supremacy over the Imperial power. A large space in the history of the Middle Ages is filled by the struggle between the empire and the papacy. Its termination witnessed the subjection of the temporal to the spiritual dominion.

In the Donation of Constantine — a forged document on which Papal supremacy was largely built — the emperor transfers the diadem from his own head to the head of the Pope of Rome, and says "in our reverence for the blessed Peter, we ourselves hold the reins of his horse, as holding the office of his stirrup-holder; and we ordain that all his successors shall wear the same miter in their processions, in imitation of the empire; and that the Papal crown may never be lowered, but may be exalted above the crown of the earthly empire. Lo, we give and grant not only our palace, as aforesaid, but also the city of Rome, and all the provinces and palaces and cities of Italy, and of the western regions, to our aforesaid most blessed Pontiff and universal Pope." The famous Decretal Epistles in the ninth century, now condemned as forgeries by the voice of Christendom, containing the "alleged judgment of the Popes in former ages, in unbroken succession from St. Peter, supplied them with everything they could require to establish the sovereignty of the Popes over the monarchs of the earth, and their authority over the doctrines and practices of the Churches of Christendom." In the exercise of his supremacy the Pope exalted or deposed monarchs, absolved subjects from their oaths of allegiance, declaring in the synod of 1080 "we desire to show the world that we can give, or take away at our will, kingdoms, duchies, earldoms, in a word, the possessions of all men, since we can bind and loose." Gratian's work, the Decretum, in the middle of the twelfth century, deciding questions relating to the Canon law of the Church of Rome, quoting as authority sixty-five of the forged Decretal Epistles, gave to the papacy a legal and long unquestioned standing. "This work was always the authority for the Canon law of the

Church of Rome, which was received into every nation before the Reformation. No book has ever exercised so much influence in the Church. In fact, this system of law constitutes the papacy."[36]

The subjection of the Bishops to Papal supremacy was followed by the destruction of the independence of Councils. "The only business of Bishops at a Council was considered to be to inform the Pope of the condition of their dioceses, and to give him their advice in spiritual matters. The Pope in fact appropriated to himself all the rights and institutions of the Church... National churches now found themselves subject to an irresistible despotism. Legates were appointed to represent the Majesty of the Pope in remote territories, who lived in splendor at the expense of the victims of their tyranny, deposing Bishops, holding Synods, promulgating Canons, and pronouncing sentences of Excommunication against those who dared to resist their arbitrary decrees."

In the year 1268 the Popes "blotted out the name of the House of Hohenstaufen from under heaven." The execution of Conradin, the grandson of Frederick II, the last heir of the House, leaving "another stain of blood on the annals of the papacy, marked the termination of the struggle for two hundred years between the Emperors and the Popes for supremacy over the nations. The latter now reigned without a rival in Christendom."

It only remained for the Popes to assume Divine honors. In the person of Boniface VIII, whose accession took place in 1294, the Pope sat "as God in the temple of God." Human ambition could rise no higher. The Pope boldly laid claim to the attributes and prerogatives of Deity. He represented the Father, the Son, and the Holy Ghost. He claimed to rule in three worlds, Heaven, Earth, and Hell; and in token thereof was crowned with a triple crown. He paraded himself before the world as the infallible Teacher of faith and morals. Exalted above bishops, above councils, above kings, above conscience, from his decisions there was no appeal. He was the supreme Judge of mankind. Lifted up to sit on the high

---

36 Pennington, "Epochs of the Papacy p. 71.

altar of St. Peter's, the chiefest Church in Christendom, he was publicly adored, cardinals, the princes of the Church, kissing in turn his feet; bishops bending low before him in deepest reverence; and nations worshiping him as the visible representative of the Godhead, possessed of power to pardon sins on earth, to canonize saints in heaven, to loose souls from the pains of purgatory in the world beneath; to judge, to govern, to bless, to save mankind; whose sentences, clothed with the authority of God, were inherently irreversible, irrevocable, final and everlasting.

And for what ends, and with what effects has the Godlike power of this great Usurper been employed?

Let history answer. Let the stake reply. Let the Inquisition speak. Let the Waldenses, the Wickliffites, the Lollards, the Hussites, the Huguenots sound forth the answer. Let Italy, let France, let Spain tell what they have witnessed. Let Roman Catholic lands in their notorious degradation, and Protestant lands deluged with blood by Papal wars and massacres, bear their testimony. The Bible prohibited; idolatry enforced; the gospel denied; Christianity caricatured; millions deluded; millions led to destruction; who can estimate the world-wide effects of this diabolical travesty of the religion of Jesus Christ? The cup of salvation changed into the cup of death; revealed religion, God's greatest, highest gift to man, transformed into a snare, an instrument of delusion, tyranny, and eternal ruin to countless souls, and generations of mankind.

Parallel Development of Prophetic Interpretation

Did the prophetic expositors of the Middle Ages, after the breaking up of the old Roman Empire, and the rise of the Papal power to supremacy over the Gothic kingdoms, recognize, on his appearance, the predicted "Man of Sin," or Antichrist?

Not at first. The comprehension of the character of Romanism and the papacy was a gradual growth. In its slow development the doctrinal errors of the Church of Rome were recognized as unscriptural long before the antichristian character of the papacy was perceived. Not until the papacy reached the monstrous height of self-exaltation and depravity which it attained in the twelfth and thirteenth centuries, was it seen to fulfill the predictions relating to the "Man of Sin," or Antichrist.

From the middle of the seventh century the Paulikians in Eastern Christendom, "bore a continuous and unvarying protest against the grosser superstitions of saint mediatorship, image worship, and other kinds of idolatry, as well as against the established system of priestcraft which supported them."[37] In Western Europe, Claude, Bishop of Turin, "was a true, fearless, enlightened, and spiritual witness for Christ's truth and honor, and against the superstition and wickedness of the age,"[38] and earned the title of "the Protestant of the ninth century." "When sorely against my will, I undertook at the command of Louis the Pious the burden of a Bishoprick," says Claude, "and when contrary to the order of truth I found all the Churches of Turin stuffed full of vile and accursed images, I alone began to destroy what all were sottishly worshiping. Therefore it was that all opened their mouths to revile me. And forsooth, had not the Lord helped me, they would have swallowed me up quick."[39] From the works of Claude, and the treatises written against him, it appears that he protested against the "worship of saints, relics, and the wooden cross, as well as of images; against pilgrimages, and all the prevailing Judaic or formal and ceremonial system of religion; against masses for the dead; against what was afterwards called transubstantiation in the Eucharist; against the supremacy of the Pope of Rome; and the authority of tradition in doctrines of religion. The written Word was made by him the one standard of truth."[40]

Agobard, archbishop of Lyons, from A.D. 810 to 841, was a determined enemy of all superstition. With reference to the

37 Elliott, *Horae*, II, p. 298.
38 Ibid., II, p. 235.
39 Ibid., II, p. 235.
40 Ibid., II, p. 236.

invocation of saints, he held that "there is no other Mediator to be sought for but He that is the God-Man." "He combats the idea of merit in human works with as much zeal and force," says Leger, "as Calvin himself."[41] Gottschalc, a monk of the abbey of Fulda, left his monastery with missionary purposes, and after preaching the gospel agreeably with Augustine's views of it, in Dalmatia, Pannonia, Lombardy, and Piedmont, was condemned as a heretic, degraded from the priesthood, beaten with rods, and cast into prison, where he lingered refusing retractation till his death in 868.[42] Treatises from the Lyonnese Church of this period exhibit "the same decided adhesion to the doctrines of Augustine." A reference occurs in the letters of Atto, Bishop of Vercelli near Turin, A.D. 945, to "certain false teachers, known among the common people by the name of prophets, under whose teaching certain persons in his diocese had been induced to forsake their priests, and their Holy Mother the Church."[43] In 1028 the archbishop of Milan discovered on a visitation a sect of so-called heretics whose central point and refuge was "the castle of Montfort, in the near neighborhood of Turin, its chief teacher there being one Gerard." When taken and imprisoned at Milan these heretics "spoke of their High Priest in contradistinction to the Roman High Priest." "In vain offers of life were made to them on condition of recantation. Gerardus especially, with happy countenance, seemed eager for suffering. The most continued steadfast; and so were burned, on the Piazza of the Cathedral."[44]

At the Council of Arras, heretics from the confines of Italy, who had been summoned before their Bishop in 1025, admitted their rejection of "the whole doctrines, discipline, and authority of the Romish Church." Berenger, in the year 1045, Principal of the Public School at Tours, and afterwards Archdeacon of Angers, combated the received doctrine of transubstantiation. His teaching was "condemned in Councils held at Rome, Vercelli, and Paris, in

---

41 Elliott, *Horae*, II, p. 233.
42 Ibid., II, p. 240.
43 Ibid., p. 243.
44 Elliott, *Horae*, II, p. 246.

the year 1050, and he was deprived of the temporalities of his benefice."[45]

Peter de Bruys, originally a presbyter of the Church, "became a missionary and protester against what he denounced as the superstitions of the day in the French provinces of Dauphiny, Province and Languedoc. His success was great, and a sect formed of his followers, vulgarly called after him Petrobrussians, but who called themselves Apostolicals. At length in the year 1126, after nearly twenty years of missionary labor, he was seized by his enemies, and burned to death in the town of St. Giles, near Thoulouse."[46]

The so-called heresies of Peter de Bruys "were propagated after his death by a monk named Henry." Beginning from Lausanne, in 1116, he preached in Paris and Languedoc "with eloquence such as to melt all hearts, and a character for both sanctity and benevolence such as to win all admiration. He was the Whitfield of the age and country, and with success that to a Catholic eye was fearful." He was seized in the year 1147, convicted and imprisoned. "Soon after he died, whether by a natural death or by the flames, is a point disputed." In the same year heretics were discovered and burned at Cologne. Maintaining their doctrines in opposition to the Church of Rome "from the Words of Christ and His apostles," they suffered martyrdom, "and what is most wonderful," says Evervinus, "they entered to the stake, and bore the torment of the fire, not only with patience, but with joy and gladness."[47]

The Henricians, or followers of Henry of Italy (called also Boni Homines) who were examined and condemned at the Council of Lombers, in 1165, rejected the characteristic doctrines of the Church of Rome, basing their beliefs on the Word of God alone.

Peter Waldo, or Valdes, a man eminent among Mediaeval witnesses to the gospel of Christ, sold all he had in the year 1170,

---

45 Ibid., II, p. 278.
46 Ibid., II, p. 282.
47 Elliott, *Horae*, II, p. 286.

distributed to the poor, and became the leader to "certain missionary bands known thenceforth under the name of Waldenses, as well as"Poor Men of Lyons" Before the close of the next century they were "well known as sectaries that had an intimate local connection with the Alpine valleys of Piedmont and Dauphiny." Perpetuated from the time of Claude of Turin, the separatists in Piedmont appear to have commingled later on with the sectaries of Lyonnese origin under the common name of Waldenses.

Driven by persecution from the plain of Lombardy, the Waldenses took refuge in the valleys of the neighboring Alps, where for many centuries they maintained, in opposition to the Church of Rome, their witness to New Testament teachings. An ancient manuscript copy of their treatise, "The Noble Lesson," exists in the library of Geneva, and another in the library at Cambridge. The date of this famous composition is A.D., 1100.

The record of the date of "The Noble Lesson" is preserved in the opening lines of the composition:

> "O Frayres entendè une noble Leyçon
> Souvent devèn veglar e star en oreson
> Car nos veen aquest mont esser pres del chavon.
> Mot curiòs deorian esser de bonas obras far
> Car nos veen aquest mont de la fin apropiar.
> Benha mil et cent an compli entierement
> Que fo scripta lara, que sèn alderier temp."

Leger's translation of this ancient Waldensian confession is given as follows in the antiquated French of 230 years ago.[48]

> "O Freres écoutés une noble Leçon,
> Souvent devons veiller et étre en oraison.
> Car nous voyons ce monde étre pres de sa fin.

---

48 Jean Leger, "Historic generale des Eglises Evangeliques des Vallees de Piedmont, ou Vaudoises," A.D., 1669, Vol. I, p. 26.

Bien soignens devrions étre à faire bonnes oeuvres,
Car nous voyons ce monde de sa fin approcher:
Il y a mil et cent am accomplis tout a fait
Que fut écrite l'heure qu'estions és derniers tems."

In this remarkable composition "the following doctrines are drawn
out with much simplicity and beauty: — the origin of sin in the fall
of Adam, and its transmission to all men; the offered redemption
through the death of Jesus Christ, who"underwent agonies, such
that the soul separated from the body, to save sinners; "the union
and cooperation of the three Persons of the blessed Trinity in man's
salvation; the obligation and spirituality of the moral law under the
gospel; the duties of prayer, watchfulness, self-denial,
unworldliness, humility, love, as"the way of Jesus Christ"; their
enforcement by the prospect of death and judgment, and the
world's near ending; by the narrowness too of the way of life, and
the fewness of those that find it; as also by the hope of the coming
glory at the judgment and revelation of Jesus Christ. Besides which,
we find in it a protest against the Romish system generally, as one
of soul-destroying idolatry; against masses for the dead, the
doctrine of purgatory, the confessional, priestly absolution, and
priestly mercenariness; and"the suspicion is half hinted, and
apparently half formed, that, though a personal Antichrist might
perhaps be expected, yet popery itself, with its followers was
probably one form of Antichrist."[49] The astounding development
of papal ambition in Innocent III, and the papal war of
extermination which followed against the Albigenses and
Waldenses, led the latter, early in the thirteenth century, to accept
as an article of their creed the doctrine"That the papacy and
Church of Rome were to be regarded as the Apocalyptic Harlot
Babylon, and by consequence Antichrist," a doctrine to which they
held unalterably ever afterwards."[50] This doctrine they embodied in
their Treatise on Antichrist, and other works. The idea of
Antichrist as a person or power professedly Christian in character is

49 Elliott, *Horae*, II, p. 394.
50 Ibid., II, p. 371.

seen slowly dawning on the mind in the Apocalyptic commentaries of the Middle Ages. Primasius, Bishop of the Carthaginian province, whose name appears in a Council held at Constantinople in 553, in his"Commentary on the Apocalypse " (discovered with his other works in the monastery of St. Theuderic, near Lyons, in the sixteenth century) lays stress on Antichrist's affected impersonation of or substitution of himself for Christ; and blasphemous appropriation to himself of Christ's proper dignity. He seems to view the second two-horned beast of Revelation 13, as ecclesiastical rulers, "hypocritically feigning likeness to the Lamb, in order the better to war against him: and by the mask of a Christian profession, under which mask the devil puts himself before men, acting out the Mediator."[51]

The venerable Bede, whose death in a Northumbrian monastery took place A.D. 735, similarly interprets in his "Commentary on the Apocalypse," the lamb-like beast of Revelation 13, as meaning "Antichrist's pseudo-Christian false prophets." "He shews the horns of a lamb, that he may secretly introduce the person of the dragon. For by the false assumption of sanctity, which the Lord truly had in Himself, he pretends that a matchless life and wisdom are his. Of this beast the Lord says, 'Beware of false prophets'which come to you in sheep's clothings but inwardly are ravening wolves."[52]

Ambrose Anspert, a Latin expositor whose era was A.D. 760 or 770, and dedicated his Apocalyptic commentary to Pope Stephen, interpreted the second beast of Revelation 13 as "signifying the preachers and ministers of Antichrist; feigning the lamb, in order to carry out their hostility against the Lamb; just as Antichrist too, the first beast's head wounded to death, would, he says, exhibit himself pro Christo, in Christ's place."[53]

Andreas, Bishop of Caesarea in Cappadocia, an expositor in the Greek Church during the latter part of the fifth century, explains

---

51 Elliott, *Horae*, IV, p. 342.
52 Bede on the Apocalypse, Ch. XIII, p. II.
53 Elliott, *Horae*, IV, p. 351.

after Irenaeus the two-horned beast as Antichrist's false prophet, "exhibiting a show of piety, and with pretense of being a lamb when in fact a wolf." "With regard to the harlot seated on the beast in Revelation 17, he observes that Rome had been judged by certain earlier writers to be the city intended, because of its being built on seven hills; but he objects its having then for some time lost its imperial majesty: unless indeed, he adds, very remarkably, this should in some way be restored to her,"a supposition involving the fact of a previous overthrow of the city now ruling," i.e., Constantinople.[54]

Berengaud, a Latin expositor of the Apocalypse, towards the close of the ninth century, explains the beast-riding harlot of Revelation 17 as Rome, and her predicted burning and spoiling by the ten kings, as the destruction of ancient Rome by the Gothic barbarians, with reference, however, as Rome was professedly Christian at that time, to the reprobate in her.[55]

Before the conclusion of the eleventh century, the papacy under Gregory VII "had risen to such a height of power as well as of pretension, and abused it to the enforcement of such unchristian dogmas, albeit in the professed character of Christ's vicar, as to force on the minds of the more discerning, surmisings about the Popes and Papal Rome, and their possible prefiguration in Apocalyptic prophecy, scarce dreamed of before. Already, just before the year 1,000, Gherbert of Rheims had spoken in solemn council of the Pope upon his lofty throne, radiant in gold and purple; and how that if destitute of charity, he was Antichrist sitting in the temple of God. And Berenger, in the eleventh century, as if apocalyptically instructed, and with special reference to the Pope's enforcement of the antichristian dogma of transubstantiation, declared the Roman See to be not the apostolic seat, but the seat of Satan."[56] Joachim Abbas, elected abbot of the monastery of Curacio in Calabria, about the year 1180, who had a

---

54 Elliott, *Horae*, IV, p, 363.
55 Ibid., IV, p. 377.
56 Elliott, *Horae*, IV, p. 380.

greater repute as an expounder of prophecy than any other in the Middle Ages, taught in his valuable "Commentary on the Apocalypse," that as Christ is both King and Priest, Satan would "put forth the first beast of Revelation 13, to usurp His Kingship, and the second to usurp His Priestly dignity: the latter having at its head some mighty prelate, some universal pontiff, as it were, over the whole world, who may be the very Antichrist of whom St. Paul speaks as being extolled above all that is called God, and worshipped; sitting in the temple of God, and showing himself as God."[57]

Thus gradually the idea of the professedly Christian character of the predicted Antichrist penetrated the minds of leading expositors in the Middle Ages, and the view that the professing Christian Church would be the sphere of his manifestation. The notion that the foretold break up of the Roman Empire had not taken place, because the Greek Byzantine ruler was still, after the Gothic catastrophe, called the Roman Emperor, and that therefore the rise of Antichrist should still be regarded as a future event, long hindered the application of the prophecies concerning Antichrist to the papacy: as also the supposition entertained in the Middle Ages that the period in which they lived was part of the Apocalyptic millennium precursive to the three-and-a-half-years' season of Satan's loosing, and the manifestation of Antichrist. "The passing away of the millennial year 1,000 without any such awful mundane catastrophe, loosing of Satan, and manifestation of Antichrist, as had been popularly expected, tended to make men earnestly reason and question both on the long received millennial theory, and on that of the Antichrist intended in prophecy, more than before. Moreover, the incoming of the twelfth century from Christ, promised (should the world last through it) to open to expositors the first possible opportunity of some way applying the year-day principle (which had never been recognized) not to the smaller three-and-a-half-days' prophetic period only, but also to the great prophetic period of the 1,260 days, without abandonment of

---

57 Ibid., IV, p. 409.

the expectation, ever intended, of Christ's second advent being near."

4. The Dawn Of The Reformation Stage

The Identification of Babylon and Antichrist.

IN the three centuries which preceded the Reformation the papacy was seen by men in a new light, and with growing clearness. The development of the "Man of Sin" reached its culmination, and the veil of professed sanctity which had concealed his real character fell from his shoulders. The papacy stood self-revealed.

Victorious over the imperial power in the middle of the thirteenth century, the popes of Rome "displayed far more ambition, arrogance, cruelty, and rapacity, than the kingdoms of this world with which they had struggled for the mastery." "Self-constituted vicegerents of the Almighty, the popes now sat 'as God in the temple of God,' and compelled the nations of the earth to crouch in vassalage before them. They had enslaved alike the souls and bodies of their fellow creatures."[58] Boniface VIII who ascended the pontifical throne in 1294 "surpassed even Innocent III in the arrogance of his pretensions, launching his spiritual thunderbolts against states and empires, summoning princes to his tribunal that he might as an infallible judge settle their controversies, and laying claim to supreme dominion over the monarchs of the earth."[59] During the period of seventy years which began in 1305, a fierce struggle for the papacy was carried on between rival factions. A set of popes and anti-popes, in Rome and Avignon, fought for the

58 Pennington, "Epochs of the Papacy," p. 145.
59 Ibid., p. 162.

tiara; pope hurled against pope the thunderbolts of anathemas and excommunications. The wealth of the papacy was enormous; the extortion and appropriation of benefices, the sale of bishoprics, of sacraments, of indulgences, yielded a golden tide of riches, "swelling the pomp, and augmenting the retinue of the pretended successors of the fisherman of Galilee."[60] All efforts to reform the Church proved abortive. "The vices, flagrant sins, and public crimes of the popes of the last half of the fifteenth century, and the early part of the sixteenth, gave them a conspicuous place in the annals of infamy. Paul II (1464— 1471) was a great drunkard, put up all offices to sale, and spent all his days in weighing money and precious stones. He also directed an infamous war against the Hussites; oppressed his subjects, tortured the members of a literary institution because he affected to discover in it a dangerous conspiracy against the Pope, and died in the possession of a large treasure. Sixtus IV was not only guilty of conspiracy, and of kindling the flames of war, but he was also dissolute, avaricious, intemperate, ferocious and bloodthirsty. Innocent VIII established a bank at Rome for the sale of pardons. Each sin had its price which might be paid at the convenience of the criminal. Alexander VI, and his son Caesar, were literally monsters in human shape. In early life, after he had become a cardinal, he was publicly censured for his gross debauchery. Afterwards he had five acknowledged children by a Roman matron, named Vanozia. After the death of Innocent in 1492, he succeeded by the grossest bribery in securing for himself the triple crown. He had become rich through his preferment, and through inheritance from his uncle Calixtus III. Of twenty-five cardinals, only five did not sell their votes. He is known to have sent four mules laden with silver to one, and to have given to another a sum of five thousand gold crowns. After his elevation he plunged without scruple and remorse into the practice of every vice, and the perpetration of every crime. His bastards were now brought forward and acknowledged as his children. The papal palace became the scene of Bacchanalian orgies. Licentious songs swelled by a chorus of revelers, echoed through its banqueting hall.

---

60 Pennington, "Epochs of the Papacy," p. 151.

Indecent plays were acted in the presence of the pontiff. He himself quaffed large draughts of wine from the foaming goblet. He indulged in licentiousness of the grossest description... Venality prevailed in the papal court. The highest dignities in the Church were conferred without shame upon the best bidders. He committed the greatest crimes for the advancement of his children. One of them, Caesar Borgia, was a fiend incarnate. The assassin's dagger, and the poison bowl were the constant instruments of his vengeance. Almost every night some assassination which he had ordered took place in the streets of Rome. The inhabitants were in constant terror of their lives. He caused the murder of his brother, of whom he was jealous, because he was preferred by a mistress with whom they were both intimate. These deeds were possible only in the spot where the highest temporal and spiritual authority were united in the same person. The palace of the popes was, in fact, a pandemonium. At length the reign of Alexander came to a sudden termination. He perished by a poisoned draught which Caesar had prepared for one of the cardinals whose wealth excited the cupidity of the Borgias. Multitudes which gazed on that livid corpse as it lay in state in St. Peter's Church, breathed a fervent thanksgiving to Almighty God for deliverance from the tyranny of an execrable monster, whose crimes had polluted the land, disgraced human nature, and placed him on a level with the very beasts that perish."[61]

The crimes, impurities, cruelties and tyrannies of these and other popes of the period opened the eyes of the nations, while the contemporaneous intervention of printing, and revival of learning, poured a blaze of light on these deeds of darkness. "The world stood aghast with horror at the contemplation of deeds as bad as those perpetrated in the darkest period of pagan antiquity."[62] A distinguished Roman Catholic historian, whose testimony on this subject is not likely to be questioned, acknowledges the corrupt state of the Church of Rome before the Reformation in emphatic

---

61 Pennington, "Epochs of the Papacy," p. 252.
62 Ibid., p. 256.

terms: "For some years" says Bellarmine, "before the Lutheran and Calvinistic heresies were published, there was not (as contemporary authors testify) any severity in ecclesiastical judicatories, any discipline with regard to morals, any knowledge of sacred literature, any reverence for Divine things, there was not almost any religion remaining." [63]

Recognition Of The Fulfillment Of The Prophecies Relating To The "Man Of Sin," Or Antichrist

History had interpreted prophecy, and justified the predictions in the Word of God. Men's eyes were opened. This then was what apostles and prophets had foretold. The thing predicted, the thing unexpected, the incredible thing, had come to pass. Antichrist was come. The "Man of Sin" was there, clothed in scarlet and purple, adorned with gold, and precious stones, and pearls; crowned with the priestly miter, and the proud diadem of the tiara; the Vice-christ; an enemy of the gospel; a persecutor of the saints; a monster of iniquity; he was there, lifted up at his coronation to sit on the high altar of St. Peter's; worshipped by cardinals; adored by superstitious multitudes; a usurper of the place and prerogatives of God; a false idol; covetous, cruel, blood-stained, "drunken with the blood of the saints and martyrs of Jesus." He was there in the seven-hilled city; he was there in the temple of God. Yes, this was he. Such were the convictions and confessions of God's faithful saints and servants of those days.

In examining their testimony one cannot but be impressed by the spirit which animated the Mediaeval witnesses to gospel truth; for such they were, their whole contention against the system of Rome being on the ground of its antagonism to "the truth as it is in Jesus"; "the faith once delivered to the saints." The seriousness of their spirit, their whole-hearted earnestness, their depth of

63 Ibid,p. 264.

conviction, the simplicity and singleness of their aim, the unflinching courage, the boldness of their attitude and tone, recall the confessors of Apostolic days, "the men who had been with Jesus." In the presence of this long line of "witnesses," one seems to hear a voice as from heaven saying, "Put off thy shoes from thy feet, for the place whereon thou standest is holy ground." As the eyes of the mind are opened, we come to see that the spirit which animated and upheld these noble men and women, was none other than the Spirit of Jesus; that He Himself was in them, and that that was the profound secret of their utter unworldliness, their bold antagonism to error and superstition, their deep humility, their sanctity and strength. In these His servants and followers Jesus Christ walked on earth during those long dark centuries. Risen from the dead, He repeated in them the testimony He had borne to the truths of "the Everlasting Gospel" in the days of His earthly life.

And the three and a half years of His own sackcloth clothed testimony had their parallel in the three and a half "times" of their sackcloth clothed witnessing; the twelve hundred and sixty literal days of the one answering to the twelve hundred and sixty years of the other; whilst His death and resurrection "on the third day," were paralleled by their death and subsequent resurrection after that three years' interval during which their enemies pronounced their testimony extinct. Thus did the Lord of Glory pass twice through analogous terrestrial experiences; first, in His own person, and next in the persons of His saints and followers, the members of His body, His flesh and His bones; first in the briefer period, and then in the longer; the one period answering to the other, on the prophetic scale of "a day for a year." Here is one of the principal keys to the times and visions of the Apocalypse. Here is the key to the story of the Church of the Middle Ages, and it is furnished by the word of prophecy as compared with the facts of history.

When with our understanding thus opened to the meaning of this long central period of the history of the Christian Church, intervening between the fall of Paganism in the fourth century, and the Reformation of the sixteenth and seventeenth centuries, we examine the records relating to the Paulicians, the Albigenses, the Waldenses, the Wycliffites, the Lollards, and the Hussites, who in Eastern and Western Europe, in Armenia, in Bulgaria, in the South of France, in the Alps of Piedmont, in Lombardy, in England, and Bohemia, kept the lamp of gospel testimony burning all through the Middle Ages, unextinguished by the superstitions, apostasies, and persecutions of those dismal times, and handed it on to the firm grasp of the Reformers, to be lifted up and set on a candlestick in the midst of Europe, and in the eyes of the nations, to shine as the great luminary of modern days, we recognize the unbroken continuity of the testimony of the true and living Church of Christ, and the fulfillment of His promise that against the Church He founded eighteen hundred years ago upon a Rock, the gates of hell should never prevail; that the living Church should continue, and its witness continue, unconquered and unchanged, from age to age; the very gospel sounded forth by His lips, and by those of His apostles, sounding still as an undying testimony, from century to century, in the utterances of His faithful saints, until triumphant over all opposition, it should fill the world as the voice of many waters and mighty thunders, and as the music of harpers harping with their harps.

And so we turn, though it be but for a brief and superficial examination, to the records of those days before the Reformation, and open the histories of the Albigenses, Waldenses, Lollards, and Hussites; the story of Constantine, of Sylvanus the Paulician, of Sergius; of Claude of Turin, of the Publicani in England; of the ancient Leonists, of the French Vallenses, and Peter Valdo; of Wycliffe and Huss, and Jerome of Prague.

The memorable story is told in such works as Sismondi's history of the crusade against the Albigenses; in Allix on the Churches of the Albigenses; in Faber's valuable book on the history and theology of the ancient Vallenses and Albigenses; in Jean Leger's folio on the history of the Vaudois; in the "authentic details of the Valdenses" by Bresse; in Gilly's "Waldensian Researches"; in

Dr. Alexis Muston's "Israel of the Alps"; in the "Historical defense of the Waldenses" by Jeane Rodolphe Pegran; in the valuable volume on "The Churches of Piedmont," by Moreland, Cromwell's commissioner; in the illustrated book on the Protestant Valleys of Piedmont, Dauphiny, and the Ban de la Roche by Dr. Beattie; in Foxe's "Acts and Monuments of the Martyrs"; in the writings of Wycliffe; in the voluminous works of John Huss; in the history of "The Reformation and Anti-reformation in Bohemia"; in McCree's history of the progress and suppression of the Reformation in Italy, and in Spain; in Limborch's massive work on the history of the Inquisition; in Llorente's history of the Inquisition in Spain from its establishment to the reign of Ferdinand VII, an author who had been "Secretary of the Inquisition"; and in Elliott's Horae Apocalypticae on "The Witnesses" of the Middle Ages; works which cast a flood of light on the history of the long line of Christian confessors in pre-Reformation times, and the noble army of martyrs of those never to be forgotten days.

And in the forefront of these testimonies we boldly place Bossuet's scornful work on the "Variations of the Protestant Churches" in which he pours forth the vials of contempt and obliquy on those despicable heretics the Waldenses, and Albigenses, and their predecessors the Paulicians of Armenia, and Bulgaria, the poor men of Lyons, the Bohemian Brethren, the impious and pernicious English arch-heretic Wycliffe, the Taborites, the Calixtines, and others "of whom the world was not worthy." As we turn over the pages of the eloquent Bishop of Meaux, the friend of Louis XIV, and persecutor of Madame Guyon and the Huguenots, we realize the truth of the Apocalyptic description of the Mediaeval "witnesses" to the gospel, which depicts them as "sackcloth clothed," for there in the pages of Bossuet's work these men of God stand dressed in the sackcloth of opprobrium. They are accused of ignorance, of error, of Manicheism, of schism, of hypocrisy, of presumption, of vain pretensions; they are treated as the scum of the earth, and "the offscouring of all things." The learned and noble Leger, "one of the Vaudois Barbes (or pastors) and their most celebrated historian" is stigmatized "as unquestionably the most bold and ignorant of all mankind!" Wycliffe, the blessed translator of the Bible into the English tongue, "subverted all order in the Church and State, and filled both with tumult and sedition." The poor men of Lyons were "obstinate heretics." Though St. Bernard testified of the "Thoulousian heretics" that "their manners are irreproachable, they oppress none, they injure no man; their countenances are mortified and wan with fasting; they eat not their bread like sluggards, but labor to gain a livelihood," yet "their piety is but disguise. Inspect the foundation, it was pride, it was hatred against the clergy, it was rancor against the Church; this made them drink in the whole poison of an abominable heresy."

These heretics "never ceased inveighing against human inventions, and citing the Holy Scriptures, whence they always had a text on hand on all occasions." This was their crime, and it was the crime which later on produced the Reformation, and gave birth to the temporal and spiritual liberties of the modern world.

We pursue Bossuet no further. Faber has answered him in his learned work on the true history and doctrines of the ancient Vallenses and Albigenses; and in "The Variations of Popery," Edgar has turned the tables on the Bishop of Meaux, and has shewn that it is the Church of Rome that has swerved from the teachings of the Apostles, not the Waldenses, Wycliffites, Hussites and Reformers, and that in all her leading and characteristic doctrines Rome has declined and departed from the faith of Apostolic times.

And now we reach the question, as to how this long line of Mediaeval witnesses to gospel truth interpreted the predictions in the Apocalypse, and kindred prophecies, with reference to the Antichrist, or "Man of Sin." Did they recognize the fulfillment of these prophecies in the papacy? Rome stood before them, revealed in her thousand superstitions, her proud pretensions, her persecuting actions. The head of that Apostate Church stood forth before their eyes crowned with the glittering tiara of a triple sovereignty, in heaven, earth, and hell, claiming to be the Vicar of Christ, and a Vice-God on earth. Did they recognize his portrait in the Word of God? Did they write his name beneath that portrait, and leave their testimony for the enlightenment of later years? They did. And having written it, they sealed the testimony with their blood.

Two hundred and fifty years before Wycliffe stood forth as the champion of Protestant truth; three hundred years before Huss and Jerome confronted the Council of Constance; four hundred years before Luther published his ninety-five theses in Wittemberg, the Waldenses wrote their treatise on Antichrist, a copy of which is contained in Leger's folio volume, dated A.D. 1120. That treatise whose doctrine is the same as their catechism dated A.D. 1100, and was the doctrine they faithfully maintained century after century, thus begins — "*Antichrist es falseta de damnation aeterna cuberta de specie de la Verita... appella Antichrist, O Babylonia, O quarta Bestia, O Meretrix, O home de pecca, filli de perdition.*" The treatise is given in full, with a French translation in Leger's work, pp. 71-83. In it is taught "that the Papal or Romish system was that of Antichrist, which from infancy in Apostolic times had grown gradually, by the increase of its constituent parts, to the stature of a full-grown man: that its prominent characteristics were to defraud God of the worship due to Him, rendering it to creatures, whether departed saints, relics, images, or Antichrist, i.e. the antichristian body itself; — to defraud Christ, by attributing justification and forgiveness to Antichrist's authority and words, to saints' intercessions, to the merit of men's own performances, and to the fire of purgatory; to defraud the Holy Spirit, by attributing regeneration and sanctification to the *opus operatum* of the two sacraments; — that the origin of this antichristian religion was the covetousness of the priesthood; its tendency to lead men away from Christ; its essence a vain ceremonial; its foundations the false notions of grace and truth."[64]

---

64 Elliott, *Horae*, II, p. 397.

"Antichrist," says this treatise, "is covered with the appearance of truth and righteousness," is "outwardly adorned with Christ's name, offices, scriptures, and sacraments," but though "covered and adorned with the semblance of Christ, His Church, and faithful members, opposes himself to the salvation wrought by Christ." He "perverts unto himself" the worship "properly due to God alone," "he robs and deprives Christ of His merits, with the whole sufficiency of grace, righteousness, regeneration, remission of sins, sanctification, confirmation, and spiritual nourishment; and imputes and attributes them to his own authority, to his own doings, or to the saints and their intercession, or to the fire of purgatory. Thus he separates the people from Christ, and leads them away to the things already mentioned."[65] "He attributes the regeneration by the Holy Spirit to a dead outward faith": "on which same faith he ministers orders and the other sacraments": "he rests the whole religion and sanctity of the people upon his Mass": "he does everything to be seen, and to glut his insatiable avarice." "He allows manifest sins without ecclesiastical censure and excommunication"; "he defends his unity not by the Holy Spirit, but by secular power"; "he hates, persecutes, and makes inquisition after, and robs and puts to death the members of Christ." "These are the principal works of Antichrist." And this "system" of iniquity "taken together is called Antichrist, or Babylon, or the fourth beast, or the Harlot, or the 'Man of Sin,' the son of perdition."

Such also, was the belief of the Albigenses. "All agreed," says Sismondi, "in regarding the Church of Rome as having absolutely perverted Christianity, and in maintaining that it was she who was designated in the Apocalypse by the name of the whore of Babylon."[66]

Even in the Romish Church the same view began to make its appearance towards the close of the twelfth century. The celebrated

---

65 Elliott, *Horae*, II, p. 336.
66 Sismondi, "History of the Crusades Against the Albigenses in the Thirteenth Century," p. 7.

Joachim Abbas in his "Commentary on the Apocalypse," written in 1183 declared that the harlot city reigning over the kings of the earth undoubtedly meant Rome, and that the false prophet foretold in the Apocalypse would probably issue out of the bosom of the Church; and that Antichrist might even then be in the world though the hour of his revelation had not yet come. Joachim was an abbot of the Roman Catholic Church in Calabria, learned in the Holy Scriptures, a deep student of the prophetic word. A few years later Almeric and his disciples taught that Rome was Babylon, and the Roman Pope Antichrist. Jean Pierre D'Olive, "another professed follower of Joachim, and leader in Languedoc of the austerer and more spiritual section of the recently formed Franciscan body, in a work entitled"Postils on the Apocalypse,' affirmed that 'the Church of Rome was the whore of Babylon, the mother of harlots, the same that St. John beheld sitting upon a scarlet colored beast, full of names of blasphemy, having seven heads and ten horns,' and the chief and proper Antichrist a pseudo-Pope; also very remarkably, that some reformation, with fuller effusion of Gospel light might be expected prior to Rome's final predicted destruction, in order that, through its rejection of that light, God's destruction of it might be the rather justified before the world."[67]

In the following century, Robert Grosthead, Bishop of Lincoln (A.D. 1235-1253), boldly proclaimed the Pope to be Antichrist. "Christ came into the world to save and win souls," said he, "therefore he that feareth not to destroy souls, may he not worthily be called Antichrist?" He foretold on his deathbed, with tokens of the deepest emotion that "the Church should not be delivered from her Egyptian servitude but by violence, force, and the bloody sword."[68]

In the same century the immortal Dante (A.D. 1265- 1321) denounced the Church of Rome as the Babylon of the Apocalypse,

---

67 Elliott, *Horae* IV, p, 428.
68 Foxe, "Acts and Monuments," Vol. II, pp. 523, 532, and Matthew Paris's English History, for year 1253.

painting the papacy in his poem on Hell, Purgatory and Paradise, in vivid colors, as the world beheld it then.

> "Woe to thee, Simon Magus. Woe to you
> His wretched followers, who the things of God
> Which should be wedded unto goodness, them
> Rapacious as ye are, do prostitute
> For gold and silver.
>   Your avarice
> O'ercasts the world with mourning, underfoot
> Treading the good, and raising bad men up.
> Of shepherds like to you the evangelist
> Was ware, when her, who sits upon the waves,
> With kings in filthy whoredom he beheld;
> She who with seven heads towered at her birth.
> And from ten horns her proof of glory drew,
> Long as her spouse in virtue took delight
> Of gold and silver ye have made your God,
> Differing wherein from the idolater.
> But that he worships one, a hundred ye?
> Ah, Constantine, to how much ill gave birth
> Not thy conversion, but that plenteous dower
> Which the first wealthy Father gained from thee."

In his poem on Paradise he says: —

> "My place he who usurps on earth hath made
> A common sewer of puddle and of blood.
> No purpose was of ours that the keys
> Which were vouchsafed me should for ensigns serve
> Unto the banners which do levy war
> On the baptized: nor I for vigil mark
> Set upon sold and lying privileges.
> Which makes me oft to bicker, and turn red.
> In shepherd's clothing, greedy wolves below

Range wide o'er all the pastures. Arm of God
Why longer sleepest thou?"

At the end of his poem on Paradise, he refers to the Apostle John
as: —

"The seer
That e'er he died, saw all the grievous times
Of the fair bride, who with the lance and nails
Was won."

Dante died in 1321. Petrarch, who was crowned with the laurel of
poetry by the Roman Senate in 1341, drew in eloquent words the
same picture of the papacy.

Three years after Dante's death, or about the year 1324, Wycliffe
was born, the Morning Star of the Reformation. Grand and
solitary witness, he stood forth, Bible in hand, 150 years before the
days of Luther, a light shining in the darkness of the Middle Ages;
like some mountain-top, while all the rest of the world lies in
darkness, illuminated with the glory of the unrisen sun. He wrote a
library of learned and powerful disquisitions, but his great work
was the translation of the Bible into the English language. "The
Scripture only is true," was his golden maxim, and he circulated as
well as translated the priceless Word of God.

Roused to concern about his soul in his twenty-third year, at
the time of the fearful pestilence which cut off so large a
proportion of the population of the world in 1345, he reached
spiritual conviction which was deep and abiding. "The pestilence
subsided in England in 1348. The earliest of the works attributed to
Wycliffe bears the date 1356, eight years later. This piece is
entitled"Last age of the Church." The end of the world seemed to
be approaching, and the coming of Antichrist at hand. In support
of this view Wycliffe cites among others the Abbot Joachim, whose
work on the Apocalypse he had read.

Later on Wycliffe came to regard the Pope of Rome seated in his blood-stained garments on the high altar in the Central Church of Christendom as the "Man of Sin," sitting in the temple of God, the true Antichrist of prophecy. Opening his English Bible, whose facsimile in black letter print, lies before us, we turn with interest to the "secounde pistel to tessalonicentes," and read the words bearing on the papacy as he wrote them in 1380, "that no man deceyve you in any maner for no but departynge aweye schal come firste: and the man of synne schal be schewide, the sone of perdicionne... so that he sitte in the temple of God: shewynge hymself as he be God... the mysterie (or pryvete) of wickednesse worchith nowe."

In his translation of the seventeenth chapter of the Apocalypse, he writes concerning Babylon the great: "I siye a womman sittynge on a reed beast ful of names of blasfemye: havynge sevene hedis, and ten horns... a womman drunken of the blood of seyntis and of the blood of martiris of Jhu. (Jesus), and when I siye hire I wondride with greet wondrynge."

Yes, Wycliffe beheld her, as did John the blessed disciple of our Lord; the one in the visions of prophecy, the other in the facts of history. Seeing Rome in her true character, Wycliffe wrote his treatise "Speculum de Antichristo" (Mirror of Antichrist) in which he unveils "the deceits of Antichrist, and his clerkes." It is said openly, he observes, "that there is nothing lawful among Christian men without leave of the Bishop of Rome though he be Antichrist, full of simony and heresy. For commonly of all priests he is most contrary to Christ, both in life and teaching, and he maintaineth more sin by privileges, excommunications, and long pleas, and he is most proud against Christ's meekness, and most covetous of worldly goods and worships." To subject the Church to such a sovereignty, he says, must assuredly be to subject her to the power of Antichrist.

Sedulous to maintain the preaching of God's pure Gospel, in his tract entitled, "Of good preaching priests," he says: — "The first general point of poor priests that preach in England is this — that the law of God be well known, taught, maintained, magnified. The second is — that great open sin that reigneth in divers states be destroyed, and also the heresy and hypocrisy of Antichrist and his followers." He calls the ravening prelates and their officers "the clerks of Antichrist," and argues "that Christian men of the realm should not be robbed by simony of the first-fruits, to go to the Bishop of Rome... that Christian men should give more heed to Christ's gospel and His life than to any rules from the sinful bishops of the world, or else they forsake Christ, and take Antichrist and Satan for their chief governor.[69]

"Worldly clerks show themselves traitors to God, and to their liege lord the king, whose law and regalia they destroy by their treason in favor of the Pope, whom they nourish in the works of Antichrist, that they may have their worldly state, and opulence, and lusts maintained by him."[70]

"Antichrist and his clerks travail to destroy Holy Writ," teaching "that the Church is of more authority and more credence than any gospel."[71] Writing on Indulgences, Wycliffe says, "This doctrine is a manifold blasphemy against Christ, inasmuch as the Pope is extolled above his humanity and deity, and so above all that is called God — pretensions which according to the declaration of the apostle agree with the character of Antichrist."[72]

"The same may be said concerning the fiction of the keys of Antichrist... as might he expected from Antichrist, he sets forth new laws, and insists under pain of the heaviest censure, that the whole Church militant shall believe in them, so that anything determined therein shall stand as though it were a part of the gospel of Jesus Christ." "...Arise," he cries, "O soldiers of Christ. Be wise and fling away these things, along with the other fictions of the prince of darkness, and put ye on the Lord Jesus Christ, and confide undoubtedly in your own weapons, and sever from the

---

69 "Tracts and Treatises of Wycliffe," p. 30.
70 Ibid., p. 37.
71 Tracts and Treatises of Wycliffe, p. 60.
72 Ibid., p. 197.

Church such frauds of Antichrist, and teach the people that in Christ alone, and in His law, and in His members, they should trust; that in so doing they may be saved through His goodness, and learn above all things honestly to detect the devices of Antichrist."[73]

Summoned to appear before his judges at Oxford, Wycliffe stood alone and unfriended. The Archbishop of Canterbury, the Bishops of Lincoln, Norwich, Hereford, Worcester, Salisbury, and London were there, sitting in judgment, together with the Chancellor of the University, and many of the inferior clergy. Forty years had passed since Oxford had first become the home of the Reformer. He was now gray with age and toil, but full of mental activity and divine illumination. Like another Elijah, he stood alone amid the generation of his countrymen, witnessing in clear, uncompromising terms to the eternal truths of God's Holy Word. Banished from Oxford he continued to write in defense of the gospel to the end of his days. His closing years were passed in full expectation of imprisonment and martyrdom. Seized with paralysis in December, 1384, on the last day of the month and of the year, his noble spirit passed into the world of rest, and everlasting reward.

Wycliffe's doctrines spread, not only over England, but to the continent, where they were the means of the enlightenment of John Huss. They were branded with condemnation by the Council of Constance, and the remains of the Reformer, by the command of the Pope, taken up and burned. His ashes were cast into the brook of Lutterworth, whence they were conveyed to the Avon, the Severn, and the sea; fit emblems of his doctrine now dispersed over the world.

A notable work entitled "The Plowman's Complaint" written by an unknown author about the time of Wycliffe, and subsequently reprinted by Tyndale and Foxe, the martyrologist, after declaring that none is more against Christ than he that "maketh himselfe Christe's Vicar in earth," terminates with the

---

73 Ibid., p. 198.

prayer, "Lord, gene our king and his lords hart to defenden Thy true shepheardes and Thy sheepe from out of the wolves' mouthes, and grace to know Thee that Thou art the true Christ, the Son of the heavenly Father, from the Antichrist that is the source of pride. And, Lord, gene us Thy poore sheepe patience and strength to suffer for Thy law, the cruelness of the mischievous wolves. And, Lord, as Thou hast promised, shorten these days. Lord, we axen this now, for more need was there never."[74]

The followers of Wycliffe took the same ground. Boldly they tore away the mask from the pretended vicar of Christ. Among them Walter Brute occupies a place of prominence as a faithful witness to the truth, whose testimony is "detailed to us by the venerable Foxe from original documents."

Brought up in the University of Oxford, Walter Brute, then a graduate, was accused of declaring that "the Pope is Antichrist, and a seducer of the people, and utterly against the law and life of Christ." In speaking thus he had blasphemed against the High Priest of Christendom. He had blasphemed Christ in the person of His sole representative. What had he to say? Walter Brute stands there solitary, defenseless, but courageous. He dares to speak the truth before these scarlet-cloaked doctors of the Church. Familiar with Wycliffe's New Testament, a student of the Word of God, he grounds his defense on the inspired words of prophecy. Did not the Pope answer to the Man of Sin prophesied by St. Paul? Was he not the chief of the false Christs, prophesied by Christ, who were to come in His name? Was not Rome the Babylon of the Apocalypse? Let it be admitted that this had been a mystery long hidden. "But if so, and only recently revealed, it would not be unaccordant with God's dealings and revelations. 'Make the heart of the people fat, that seeing they may not see,' was said by Isaiah of long-permitted judicial blindness in the Jews; and again by Daniel it was written, 'seal up the vision till the time of the end.' Now had come the time when the veil of mystery should be removed."[75]

---

74 Foxe, "Acts and Monuments," Vol. II, p. 747.
75 Foxe, "Acts and Monuments," Vol. II, p. 432.

"Very vain," he says, "had been the usual and long received ideas about Antichrist: ideas as of one that was to be born in Babylon of the tribe of Dan, to give himself out as the Messiah come for the Jews' salvation, and preach three and a half years where Christ preached; to kill Enoch and Elijah, and be himself finally slain by lightning." The times of Daniel and the Apocalypse, he argues, connected with the Antichrist, were symbolical of larger periods; and should be interpreted as the "seventy weeks" extending to the past advent of Messiah on the year-day scale. As the seventy "weeks" after which Christ was slain meant weeks of years, not days, so the 1,290 days of prophecy meant 1,290 years; a period which he noticed extended from the placing of the desolating idol by Hadrian in the Holy Place, to the "revealing, or in other words the exposure of Antichrist," in these latter days. As to that woman seated on the persecuting wild beast in Revelation 17, expounded by the angel to mean the city on seven hills, reigning over the kings of the earth, whose power was to continue forty-two months, or 1,260 days, this was Rome, whose duration was 1,260 years. Did not the ten days of Smyrna's suffering signify the ten years of Diocletian's persecution? Thus then, the 1,260 days represented 1,260 years. As to the Popes, "with their assumed kingly and priestly power, speaking like a dragon, and allowing none to sell their spiritual pardons but such as bore their mark, his name, identical with his number, 666, was Dux Cleri."My counsel is," says Walter Brute, "let the buyer be aware of those marks of the beast. For after the fall of Babylon,"If any man hath worshipped the beast and his image, and hath received his mark on his forehead, or on his hand, he shall drink of the wine of God's wrath, and be tormented with fire and brimstone in the sight of the holy angels, and of the Lamb; and the smoke of their torments shall ascend evermore."

John Huss and Jerome of Prague were contemporaries of Walter Brute, and bore the same testimony, for which they were burned at the stake by the Council of Constance in May, 1416. In a letter to Lord John de Clum, Huss declares that the Church of Rome is the Harlot Babylon "whereof mention is made in the Apocalypse."

Writing to the people of Prague, he warns them to be "the more circumspect," because "Antichrist being stirred up against them deviseth divers persecutions."

When cast into prison for the Word of God, he wrote thus to his friends and followers: — "Master John Huss, in hope, the servant of God, to all the faithful who love Him and His statutes, wisheth the truth and grace of God... Surely even at this day is the malice, the abomination, and filthiness of Antichrist marked in the Pope and others of this Council... Oh, how acceptable a thing should it be, if time would suffer me to disclose their wicked acts, which are now apparent; that the faithful servants of God might know them. I trust in God that He will send after me those that shall be more valiant; and there are also at this day that shall make more manifest the malice of Antichrist, and shall give their lives to the death for the truth of our Lord Jesus Christ, who shall give, both to you and me, the joys of life everlasting."

This epistle was "written upon St. John Baptist's Day, in prison and in cold irons. I having this meditation with myself that John was beheaded in his prison and bonds for the word of God."[76]

The year following that of the martyrdom of Huss and Jerome, witnessed the burning of Lord Cobham, at Smithfield. When brought before King Henry V and admonished to submit himself to the Pope as an obedient child, this was his answer: — "As touching the Pope, and his spirituality, I owe them neither suit nor service, forasmuch as I know him by the Scriptures to be the great Antichrist, the son of perdition, the adversary of God, and an abomination standing in the Holy Place."

For this testimony Lord Cobham was drawn on a hurdle to St. Giles' Fields, and "hanged there by the middle in chains of iron and so consumed alive in the fire, praising the name of God as long as life lasted."

---

76 Foxe, "Acts and Monuments," Vol. Ill, pp. 502, 503.

II. The Pre-Reformation War Against the Protestant Witnesses.

Not in a merely metaphorical sense was the persecution waged against the Albigenses, the Waldenses, and the Hussites, a "war," but in stern reality. It commenced by a crusade against the Albigenses in A.D. 1208. In his history of the period Sismondi tells us that "Innocent III, impelled by hatred, had offered to those who should take up the cross against the Provincials the utmost extent of indulgence which his predecessors had ever granted to those who labored for the deliverance of the Holy Land. As soon as these new Crusaders had assumed the sacred sign of the Cross, which to distinguish themselves from those of the East, they wore on the breast instead of the shoulders, they were instantly placed under the protection of the Holy See, freed from the payment of the interest of their debts, and exempted from the jurisdiction of all the tribunals; whilst the war which they were invited to carry on at their doors, almost without danger or expense, was to expiate all the vices and crimes of a whole life... Never, therefore, had the Cross been taken up with a more unanimous consent."

The first to engage through the commands of their pastors in this war which was denominated sacred were Eudes III, Duke of Burgundy, Simon de Montfort, Count of Leicester; the Counts of Nevers, of St. Paul, of Auxerre, of Geneve, and of Forez.

The Abbot of Citeaux with the Bernardines appropriated the preaching of the Crusade as their special province. "In the name of the Pope, and of the Apostles St. Peter and St. Paul, they promised to all who should perish in this holy expedition plenary absolution of all sins committed from the day of their birth to the day of their death." St. Dominic and his followers were sent by Innocent III to travel on foot, two by two, through the villages, to obtain full information about the so-called heretics, and to stir up persecution against them. Thus began the mission of the Dominicans, in subsequent times the terrible agents of the papacy in the work of the Inquisition. Descending the valley of the Rhone, by Lyons and Avignon, the principal army of the Crusaders began their dreadful work in Languedoc. "Men and women were all precipitated into the flames amidst the acclamations of the ferocious conquerors." The cities of Beziers and Carcassonne had been armed by Raymond Roger against the advancing papal army, but were unable to resist the attack. When asked how the Catholics were to be distinguished from the heretics in the slaughter which followed, Amalric, Abbot of Citeaux answered, "Kill them all; the Lord will well know those who are His."[77] This command was carried out.

Vainly did the persecuted inhabitants of Beziers take refuge in the churches. In the great Cathedral of Saint Nicaise all were slaughtered; in the Church of the Magdalen seven thousand dead bodies were counted. The city was then fired, and reduced to a grand funeral pile. "Not a house remained standing, not a human being alive." This dreadful crusade was continued until the greater part of the Albigenses had perished. "During the six hundred years which followed these events, invariably as far as occasions have served, the Church of Rome has avowed the same principles, and perpetrated or stimulated the same deeds. As soon as the war against the Albigenses was terminated the Inquisition was brought into full and constant action, encouraged and supported by the Romish Church to the utmost of its power."[78]

We turn from the Albigenses and the South of France to the Vaudois in Piedmont.

From the top of the famous Cathedral of Milan there is a magnificent view of the Alps of Piedmont. East and west they are seen to stretch as far as the eye can reach. The sun at noon falls full upon their crowded peaks. Dark forests mantling their lower slopes, they stand in silent sublimity, their summits crowned with glaciers and eternal snows. To the west among these, beyond the city of Turin rises the vast white cone of Monte Viso. Among the mountains at its base lie the Waldensian valleys. Five in number,

---

77 Sismondi, preface.
78 Sismondi, p. 36.

they run up into narrow elevated gorges, winding among fir-clad steeps, and climbing to the region of the clouds which hover around the Alpine peaks. These valleys were the refuge and home of the "Israel of the Alps." Protestants before the Reformation, they constituted a faithful remnant of the Church who had never bowed the knee to Baal. The first combined measures taken by the secular authority at the instigation of Rome for the destruction of the Vaudois do not appear to date before 1209, during the period of the Pontificate of Innocent III, when the Archbishop of Turin was empowered to destroy them by force of arms. At the commencement of the fourteenth century (about 1308) the Inquisitors renewed their murderous warfare. In 1487, Innocent VIII fulminated against the Vaudois a bull of extermination. "Thousands of volunteers — vagabond adventurers, ambitious fanatics, reckless pillagers, merciless assassins — assembled from all parts of Italy to execute the behests of the pseudo-successor of St. Peter. This horde of brigands, suitable supporters of a profligate pontiff, marched against the valleys in the train of another army of 18,000 regular troops, contributed in common by the king of France and the sovereign of Piedmont." The Vaudois fled to the heights of the Alps, and sought to protect themselves against their foes. At the moment of their greatest danger they were sheltered by a thick fog; their enemies falling over the humid rocks into the fatal abyss below. The following year their assailants were more successful. The Vaudois had retired to the rugged slopes of Mont Pelvoux, 6,000 feet above the level of the valley. Here they had taken refuge in a huge cavern. Led by La Pelud, Cataneo's ferocious fanatics climbing above the cavern, descended on the Vaudois, and piling up wood at its entrance set fire to it; "those who attempted to issue forth were either destroyed by the flames, or by the sword of the enemy, while those who remained within were stifled by the smoke. When the cavern was afterwards examined, there were found in it four hundred infants suffocated in their cradles, and the arms of their dead mothers. Altogether there perished in this cavern more than 3,000 Vaudois — including the entire population of Val Louise."

We pause in the history of the Vaudois persecution to glance at the contemporaneous war waged against the Hussites in Bohemia. After the martyrdom of Huss and Jerome, their followers were subjected to the most cruel persecutions. "In the year 1421 the miseries of the Bohemians greatly increased. Besides the executions by drowning, by fire, and by the sword, several thousands of the followers of Huss, especially the Taborites, of all ranks, and both sexes, were thrown down the old ruins and pits of Kuttemburg. In one pit were thrown 1,700, in another 1,308, and in a third 1,321 persons."[79] A monument still marks the place. This warfare against the Hussites continued until their testimony was silenced, and their name almost erased from the earth.

In his histories of the progress and suppression of the Reformation in Spain and Italy, McCrie has traced the propagation of the gospel in these lands by the instrumentality of the Albigenses in the twelfth and thirteenth centuries. "Province and Languedoc were at that time more Arragonese than French." "In consequence of the connection between the two countries some of the Vaudois had crossed the Pyrenees, and established themselves in Spain as early as the middle of the twelfth century." From 1412 to 1425 a great number of persons who entertained the sentiments of the Vaudois were committed to the flames by the Inquisitors of Valencia, Rousillon, and Majorca. "In Italy many of the Vaudois and Albigenses established themselves in the year 1180. In 1231 Gregory IX published a furious bull against them, ordaining that they should be sought out and delivered to the secular arm to be punished. In 1370 the Vaudois from the valleys of Pragela emigrated to Calabria, and for awhile flourished in peace. The colony received accessions to its numbers by the arrival of their brethren who fled from the persecutions raised against them in Piedmont and France; it continued to flourish when the Reformation dawned on Italy; and after subsisting for nearly two centuries, it was basely and barbarously exterminated."[80]

---

79 "Reformation and Anti-Reformation in Bohemia," p. 13.
80 McCrie, "Reformation in Italy," p. 5.

The chief instrument in the suppression of the Reformation in these lands was the infamous Inquisition, whose infernal cruelties have made its name a horror to this day. That Satanic tribunal! What shall we say of it? Before us lie the two quarto volumes of Limborch's history of the Inquisition; together with Llorente's detailed and dispassionate account; also Rule's book, in two volumes, and other works on the Inquisition in English and Spanish. When the Quemadero was opened at Madrid in 1870, and the ashes of the martyrs who had been burned by the Inquisition brought to light, we were present, and saw that thick bank of human remains, and stood breast deep in the ashes. We have seen in Mexico skeletons of victims of the Inquisition who had been buried alive; have visited the Inquisition in Rome; have seen its prisons, and conversed with its Inquisitors. Cold blooded tribunal! *Ne plus ultra* of tyranny! Its history, written in tears and blood, fills next to the story of the Crucifixion of Christ, the darkest page in the records of humanity. Llorente, who was secretary of the Inquisition in Madrid from 1789 to 1791, and in whose hands its archives were placed at the date of its suppression in 1811, has lifted the veil of secrecy which hid its diabolical character; has described its processes, and confirmed the copious witness of its victims to the almost incredible account of its cruelties. By his aid we see its all-powerful judges sitting in secret, during long centuries, under a succession of forty-four Inquisitor-generals, who in denial of every principle of justice, never permitted the accused to know the accusations laid to his charge, to face his accusers, or "to know more of his own cause than he could learn of it by the interrogations and accusations to which he was compelled to reply;"who extracted the confessions they sought by the infliction of the most ingenious, the most prolonged and the most exquisite tortures the mind of man has ever invented; putting into operation "water, weights, fire, pulleys, screws, — all the apparatus by which the sinews could be strained without cracking, the bones bruised without breaking, and the body racked exquisitely without giving up the ghost:"renewing those tortures from day to day; alternating the dungeon and the rack; until pain and anguish had done their work on the wreck of body and mind which remained in their hands, and then committing the victim to the flames, to burn like a fagot in the fire, until nothing remained but his ashes encumbering the chain which hung around the blackened stake. The Holy Inquisition! The Holy Office! Foe of truth and justice; minister of Satan; thy name has yet to be invented, for no one word employed by human lips can adequately describe thee. Miscalled preserver of the faith, thou hast been the nurse of hypocrisy, the parent of fear, of falsehood, of slavery; mental and moral degradation and national ruin have followed in thy wake. Monster of mediaeval cruelty, thy black shadow flees from the light of modern days, pursued by the abhorrence and execration of the world.

The following is a numerical summary of victims who suffered during the years 1481 to 1498, under the Inquisition in Spain:

1. Burned alive in Seville, 2,000; burned in effigy 2,000; penitents, 17,000.
2. Burned alive, 88; burned in effigy, 44; penitents, 625.
3. About the same as in preceding year in Seville, and in Cordova; in Jaen and Toledo, burned alive, 688; burned in effigy, 644; penitents 5,725.
4. About the same in Seville; and in the other places, burned alive, 220; burned in effigy, 110; penitents, 1,561.
5. Seville, Cordova, as the year preceding. In Estramadeira, Valladolid, Calaborra, Murcia, Cuenza, Zaragoza, and Valencia, there were burned alive 620; burned in effigy, 510; and penitents, 13,471.
6. In Seville and Cordova as the year before. In other places burned alive, 528; burned in effigy, 264; penitents, 3,745.
7. About the same as the year before, and in Barcelona and Majorca many more, making in all, burned alive, 928; burned in effigy, 664; and penitents, 7,145.
8. In the thirteen Inquisitions, burned alive, 616; burned in effigy, 308; and penitents 4,379.
9. About the same as the preceding year.

10. Burned alive, 324; burned in effigy, 112; and penitents, 4,369.

•   1491 to 1498. At about the same rate.

"Torquemada, Inquisitor-General of Spain, during the eighteen years of his inquisitorial ministry, caused 10,220 victims to perish in the flames; burned the effigies of 6,860 who died in the Inquisition, or fled under fear of persecution; and 97,321 were punished with infamy, confiscation of goods, perpetual imprisonment, or disqualification for office, under color of penance; so that no fewer than 114,401 families must have been irrecoverably ruined.[81] And the most moderate calculation gathered from the records of the Inquisition by the laborious Secretary, Llorente, up to the year 1523, when the fourth Inquisitor died, exhibits the fearful aggregate of 18,320 burned alive, 9,660 in effigy, 206,526 penitents. Total number of sufferers, 234,506, under the first four inquisitors-general."[82]

The Witnesses Silenced

The Inquisition continued its career of persecution under its forty-four inquisitors-general till 1820, when it was finally suppressed. But as early as the Lateran Council in 1514 the whole of the pre-reformation witnesses to the gospel in France, Spain, Piedmont, Italy and Bohemia, by means of the sword, the rack, and the stake, had been crushed and silenced. In England the Lollards were extinct. None remained to witness to New Testament truth. The orator of the session, ascending the pulpit, addressed to the assembled members of the Lateran Council, the memorable exclamation of triumph: — "There is an end of resistance to the Papal rule and religion; opposers there exist no more"

---

81 Llorente, Ch. VIII, Art. 4.
82 Rule, "Martyrs of the Reformation," p. 39.

5. The Reformation Stage

"After three days I will rise again." — Matt. 27:63.

IT WAS on the 5th day of May, 1514, at the ninth session of the Lateran Council that the Papal Orator "pronounced his paean of triumph over the extinction of heretics and schismatics."

"Jam nemo reclamat, nullus obsistit."

"There is an end of resistance to the papal rule and religion: opposers there exist no more."

Three years and a half later on, to a day, on October 31st, 1517, Luther posted up his Theses at Wittemberg. "The voice of an obscure monk rang through Europe, like the mighty thunder peal; awakening men from the slumber of ages, and shaking to its foundation the usurped dominion of Romanism."[83] In Luther and the Reformers the slaughtered witnesses to the truth of the gospel, risen from the dead, stood once more upon their feet before Rome and the world.

This was what the martyr Huss, a hundred years before, had foretold. "I am no vain dreamer," he said, "but hold for certain that the image of Christ shall never be effaced. They wish to destroy it: but it shall be painted afresh in the hearts of gospel-preachers better than myself. And I, awaking as it were from the dead, and rising from the grave, shall rejoice with exceeding great joy."

83 Pennington, "Epoch's of the Papacy," p. 276.

Jerome of Prague, his fellow martyr, named the interval one hundred years, "after which their memory would be vindicated, their cause triumphant."

This double prophecy was fulfilled.

Pope Adrian, Leo X's successor, in a brief addressed to the diet of Nuremberg in 1523, wrote thus: "The heretics Huss and Jerome seem now to be alive again in the person of Luther." "Not in the compass of the whole ecclesiastical history of Christendom, save and except in the death and resurrection of Christ Himself, is there any such example of the sudden, mighty, and triumphant resuscitation of His cause and Church from a state of deep depression."[84] Their lofty and animated descriptions of this divine revival are clothed by the writers of the period in metaphors borrowed from the pages of the Apocalypse. Thus Milton wrote, —

"When I recall to mind at last, after so many dark ages, wherein the huge overshadowing train of error had almost swept all the stars out of the firmament of the Church: how the bright and blissful Reformation, by divine power, struck through the black and settled night of ignorance and anti-Christian tyranny, methinks a sovereign and reviving joy must needs rush into the bosom of him that reads or hears; and the sweet odour of the returning Gospel imbathe his soul with the fragrancy of heaven. Then was the sacred Bible sought out of the dusty corners where profane falsehood and neglect had thrown it; the schools opened, divine and human learning raked out of the embers of forgotten tongues, the princes and cities now trooping apace to the new-erected banner of salvation; the martyrs with the unresistible might of weakness, shaking the powers of darkness, and scorning the fiery rage of the old red dragon."

A new era had dawned upon the world: an era of Light, Liberty, Life, Progress; the Age of the Book. Then was the Bible translated into the vernacular languages of Europe, and later on into all the

---

84 Elliott, II, p. 457, 460.

leading languages of the world, its sacred pages opened in the eyes of the nations, its truths expounded in their ears, its records placed in their hands, yea, its teachings written in the hearts, and reflected in the lives of millions emancipated from the prison house of papal bondage.

Then, to use the language of the historian, Gibbon, "the lofty fabric of superstition, from the abuse of indulgences to the intercession of the Virgin, was leveled with the ground. Myriads of both sexes of the monastic profession were restored to the liberty and labors of social life. An hierarchy of saints and angels, of imperfect and subordinate deities, were stripped of their temporal power... their images and relics banished from the Church; and the credulity of the people no longer nourished with the daily repetition of miracles and visions. The imitation of paganism was supplanted by a pure and spiritual worship of prayer and thanksgiving... The chain of authority was broken... the popes, fathers, and councils, were no longer the supreme and infallible judges of the world; and each Christian was taught to acknowledge no law but the Scriptures, no interpreter but his own conscience."

Advance in Prophetic Interpretation

The advent of the Reformation shed a broad beam of light upon the very center and heart of Apocalyptic prophecy. It illuminated the visions in the tenth and eleventh chapters, removing the obscurity which had hitherto hung upon their meaning; and caused the trumpet call to God's people in the eighteenth chapter, to come out of Babylon, to sound forth as never before.

Now was the mighty cloud clothed, rainbow crowned angel of the vision in the tenth chapter seen as it were to descend from heaven holding in his hand a little book open y and setting his feet on land and sea, he was heard to cry aloud as when a lion roareth. Then were heard the seven thunders of Rome's anathemas, pealing forth their defiant reply. Then did the Reformers take from the hands of the angel the "little book" of the newly-opened Word of

God, and eating it themselves, as Ezekiel had done before them, renew their prophecy, "before many peoples, and nations, and tongues, and kings."[85] Then did the Reformers "rise and measure the temple of God," as commanded, "and the altar and them that worship therein," leaving out, or casting out, as bidden, "the outer court," as given to the Gentiles to remain unreformed, and continue trodden under foot. Then too, was "the great city which spiritually is called Sodom and Egypt" denounced as such;[86] and the prophesying of Christ's sackcloth clothed witnesses, like that of the Jewish prophets in the days of the Baalitical and Babylonian apostasies, clearly recognized: the "olive trees" or anointed ones, like the faithful reformers in the days of Ezra and Nehemiah, after the return of Judah from the ancient typical Babylon seen to be "candlesticks" or light bearers, "standing before the God of the earth."

Now was the mystery cleared up; now was the meaning of these wondrous visions revealed, and the testimony of prophecy confirmed the faith, and justified the position of the Reformers. What Ezra and Nehemiah, Joshua and Zerubbabel had been in the great work of the restoration of Judah from Babylonish captivity, of the rebuilding of the altar, and temple of God, and of the ruined walls of Jerusalem, such were the modern Reformers in the still more glorious work of the Reformation of the Church after her long captivity in the anti-typical "Babylon the Great"; and the visions of the Apocalypse based as to their symbolism, upon the history of Judah's restoration, stood forth explained by the events of modern history; a brilliant lamp lighting the Reformers' feet; a miracle of divine prescience; a seal of approbation upon the Reformation movement; a warrant for its work, a pledge of its success.

---

85 Revelation 10:9-11.
86 Ibid 11:8.

A Twofold Discovery

The Reformation was born of a twofold discovery; the discovery of Christ, and the discovery of Antichrist. This discovery was first developed in the mind of Luther; and from his mind it passed into the mind of Western Europe; from whence it has since gone forth throughout the world. It arose from Luther's finding a Bible. To the awakened monk God revealed through His word the glorious gospel of salvation. Profoundly convinced of sin, Luther embraced "the righteousness of God" revealed in the Scriptures, and justification by faith in contrast with justification by works became the thrilling theme of his testimony.

There followed the posting up in October, 1517, of Luther's ninety-five theses against indulgences, which he affixed to the door of the chief church at Wittemberg, boldly offering to maintain them against all impugners. "The truths most prominently asserted in them were the Pope's utter insufficiency to confer forgiveness of sin, or salvation, — Christ's all-sufficiency, — and the true spiritual penitent's participation, by God's free gift, independently altogether of papal indulgence or absolution, not merely in the blessing of forgiveness, but in all the riches of Christ. There were added other declarations also, very notable as to the gospel of the glory and grace of God, not the merits of saints,"being the true and precious treasure of the Church"; — a denunciation of the avarice and soul deceivings of the priestly traffickers in indulgences; — and a closing exhortation to Christians to follow Christ as their Chief, even through crosses and tribulation, thereby at length to attain to His heavenly kingdom. Bold indeed were the words thus published; and the effect such that the evening of their publication[87] has been remembered ever afterwards, and is ever memorable, as the Epoch of the Reformation."[88]

Following Luther's discovery of Christ came his discovery of Antichrist. In the month of June, 1520, the Pope hurled a

---

87 All Hallows E'en, October 31st.
88 Elliott, *Horae*, II, p. 100.

thunderbolt at Luther, condemning his doctrines in a bull, and ordering that "unless within sixty days he retracted his errors, he was to be seized and sent as a prisoner to Rome."

On December 20th, 1520, "a pile of wood was erected at the east gate of Wittemberg. One of the oldest members of the university lighted it. As the flames arose, Luther advanced arrayed in his frock and cowl, and amid bursts of approbation from the doctors, professors and students, hurled into the fire the Canon Law, the Decretals, and the Papal Bully"The defiance of Wittemberg was followed by the emancipation of half the nations of Europe from their spiritual and temporal bondage."[89]

Hidden from his persecutors in a lonely castle in the Wartburg forest, Luther now translated the New Testament into vernacular German. He prefixed to the Apocalypse, in his great edition of the German Bible, in 1534, an outline of his views as to the meaning of the prophecy. He considered it contained a prefiguration of the chief events in the history of the Christian Church. The woman clothed with the sun, and crowned with twelve stars, who flees to the wilderness from her persecutors, represents in his view, the true Church; and the two witnesses a succession of faithful witnesses for Christ. Of the opposing wild beast powers, the first beast represents the papal secular revived Roman Empire; and the second beast the Pope's ecclesiastical or spiritual empire. The number of the beast, 666, signifies according to Luther, the number of years that the beast may be destined to endure, measured, he says in his Table Talk, from Gregory, or perhaps Phocas. The Antichrist is, in his view, an ecclesiastical person. In his "De Antichristo," he says, "The Turk cannot be Antichrist, because he is not in the Church of God." "Whoever so came in Christ's name," he exclaims, "as did the Pope?"

As the Reformation advanced, the true meaning of the predictions in the tenth and eleventh chapters of the Apocalypse more and more forced itself upon men's minds. Bullinger, at

---

89 Pennington, "Epochs of the Papacy," p. 287.

Zurich, in his expository discourses on the Apocalypse, published in 1557, boldly explains the angel vision in Apocalypse 10, as representing Christ's intervention through the Reformers. The "little open book" in the hand of the angel he interprets as the gospel, opened to men by the Reformers, and given to the world with the aid of the newly invented art of printing. He says the oath in the tenth chapter alludes to the three and a half "times" of Daniel 12, and surmises that the redemption of the Church at Christ's coming, to raise the dead and transform the living was even then drawing nigh. As to the witnesses, the number two indicated that they were to be few, yet sufficient. The great city of their slaughter is the empire of Papal Rome. The falling of the tenth of the city represented the mighty defections already begun from the Papal Church and Empire. On the seventh trumpet he says, "It must come soon, therefore our redemption draweth nigh." He explains the second beast as the Papal Antichrist, rising under Gregory I, and his successor Boniface, to the position of Universal Bishop. "On the name and number of the beast he adopts Irenaeus' solution, dwelling on the Latinism of the Papacy, much like Dr. More afterwards."

Bale, Bishop of Ossory under Edward VI, published an Apocalyptic Commentary entitled "Image of Both Churches," i.e., the true and the false. He explains the vision of Apocalypse 10, like Bullinger, as representing the Reformation; the book opened being the Scriptures then newly translated into the vernacular languages, and expounded by gospel-preachers. The measuring rod in Revelation ii he explains as God's Word, "now graciously sent as out of Zion," the temple as God's congregation or Church, distinguished by His Word from the synagogue of Satan; the witnesses as faithful protestors for Christ that continue with God's people all through the time of the Church's oppression by her so-called "Gentile" foes. The fall of the tenth part of the city, represents the diminution of the Papal Church. We have here, says Bale, "what is done already, and what is to come under this sixth trumpet, whereunder we are now; which all belongeth to the second woe."

In David Chytraus' *Explicatio Apocalypsis*, published at Wittemberg, in 1571, the 1,260 days of the Gentiles treading down the holy city are explained as 1,260 years, to be calculated either from Alaric's taking of Rome in A.D., 412, or from Phocas' decree, A.D., 606; and thus to end in A.D., 1672, or in A.D., 1866. The resurrection of the witnesses he explains of their speedy revival "on each individual occasion of their temporary suppression by Antichrist." Augustin Marlorat's exposition of the Revelation of St. John, published in 1574, under Queen Elizabeth, "is professedly collected out of divers notable writers of the Protestant Churches, viz.: — Bullinger, Calvin, Gaspar Meyander, Justus Jonas, Lambertus, Musculus, AEcolampadius, Pellicanus, Meyer, Viret." On Apocalypse 10 he sets forth "the clear decisive explanation of its Angel-vision usual among the Reformers, as figuring the opening of the Scriptures and revived gospel preaching at the Reformation: also the exclusion of the outer court in Apocalypse 11, as signifying the exclusion of Papists."

Thus similarly the venerable martyrologist John Foxe in his exposition of the Apocalypse written in the year 1586, — a work interrupted by his death, — applies the magnificent vision of Christ in Apocalypse 10 to the restoration of gospel preaching, the book in the angel's hand representing God's Word. The temple of Apocalypse 11 he takes to be the Church; its inner court the true worshippers; its outer the false; the measuring of the temple its separation and reformation "as in our day," implying a previous corruption under Antichrist. All this had been done under the sixth, or Turkish trumpet, whose end he considered to be near. Under the seventh trumpet which would follow, the Church would have its time of blessedness accomplished, in Christ's coming, and the saints' resurrection.

Brightman's "Commentary on the Apocalypse" dedicated to "the holy reformed churches of Brittany, Germany and France," was published in A.D. 1600 or 1601, before the death of Queen

Elizabeth. In this remarkable work which was deservedly popular with the Protestant Churches of the time, Brightman rightly identifies the locust woe of the fifth trumpet with the Saracen invasion, and the Euphratean woe of the sixth trumpet with the Turkish. The casting down of the dragon in Apocalypse 12, and his restoration in a new form under the beast of Apocalypse 13, he applies to the casting down of the rule of heathen Rome under Constantine, and the subsequent revival of Roman rule under the Popes; the head of the empire being wounded to death by the Gothic invasions, and healed by Justinian and Phocas in the exaltation of the papacy in the restored empire.

Considering the Apocalyptic interpretation of the sixteenth century as a whole we recognize not only a considerable advance in the understanding of the prophecy, but a practical application and use of its leading predictions of the highest importance. The glorious work of the Reformation was built upon doctrinal, practical, and prophetic grounds. Apocalyptic prophecy was accorded a prominent position among the stately pillars of its foundation. To the reformers the Church of Rome was "Babylon the great" of the Apocalypse, clad in purple and scarlet, adorned with "gold, and precious stones, and pearls," a faithless harlot seated on a wild beast power, intoxicating the nations with the cup of her idolatries and superstitions, and drunken with "the blood of the saints and martyrs of Jesus." The duty of separation from the Church of Rome was boldly proclaimed on the ground of the divine command in Revelation 18, "Come out of her my people that ye be not partaker of her sins, and that ye receive not of her plagues." The duty to reform the Church was urged on the authority of the command in Revelation 11, "Rise, and measure the temple of God, and the altar, and them that worship therein." While Rome excommunicated the Reformers, the Reformers excommunicated Rome in obedience to the command in Revelation 11, "The court which is without the temple, leave out (or rather 'cast out') and measure it not." The Pope of Rome was resisted and condemned as "the Man of Sin," "the Antichrist," the "standard-bearer" as Calvin calls him, "of an abominable apostasy." The long line of pre-reformation martyrs, and the reformers and martyrs of the Reformation, were regarded as the sackcloth clothed and faithful witnesses of the Apocalypse, God's anointed "prophets," like Elijah and Elisha in the days of the Baalitical apostasy of Israel, and Ezra and Nehemiah in the time of the restoration of Jerusalem, and rebuilding of the temple, who, warred against and overcome by the wild beast power, had been figuratively raised from the dead, and exalted in full view of their amazed antagonists. To the Reformers of the sixteenth century the era of the seventh trumpet was at hand, when "The kingdoms of this world" would become "the kingdoms of our Lord and of His Christ." And they awaited the predicted and proximate hour when "like a great millstone" "that great city Babylon" should be "thrown down and found no more at all," and the "great voice of much people in heaven" should lift up the rejoicing utterance, with thrice repeated hallelujahs, "salvation, and glory, and honor, and power unto the Lord our God, for true and righteous are His judgments: for He hath judged the great whore which did corrupt the earth with her fornication, and hath avenged the blood of His servants at her hand." The prominence of Apocalyptic interpretation in the voluminous writings of the Reformers is one of their most marked features. They wielded the word of prophecy as the sharp two-edged sword of the Spirit, "piercing to the dividing asunder of soul and spirit." And while God sealed their testimony with lasting spiritual success, they, on their part, sealed their witness with their blood. They inaugurated an era of light and liberty such as the world had never seen before, which remains as the colossal confirmation of their testimony, as interpreters and teachers of "the Word of God which endureth forever."[90]

---

90 The view that the Church of Rome is the "Babylon" of the Apocalypse, and the succession of the Popes the predicted "Man of Sin," or Antichrist, seated in the Christian Church, was universally held by the Reformers in the sixteenth century. See the works of Luther, Knox, Tyndale, Latimer, Hooper, Ridley, Cranmer, Jewel, Coverdale, Foxe, Fulke, Grindal, Bale, Bradford, Beacon, Bullinger, Rogers, Sandys, Norden, Nowell, Hutchinson, Whittaker, Whitgift, Melancthon, Zwingli, Calvin, etc. One of the fullest statements of the view will be found in Jewel's eloquent and able

6. The Puritan, Or Seventeenth Century Stage

IN TRACING the development of the interpretation of the Apocalypse as ceaselessly following the unveiling of the plan of Providence by the events of history, we direct our attention at this stage to the fresh page of history which lay before the eyes of prophetic interpreters in the seventeenth century.

"Commentary on Thessalonians," and abundant references to it in Foxe's "Acts and Monuments of the Martyrs"; a view embodied in the confessions of faith of the Reformed churches.

Numerous references to the teachings of the Reformers on the subject are given in the Index Volume to the works of the Reformers published by the Parker Society. Thus on Babylon as Rome, see Ridley, 70, 415. Bullinger IV, 11. Bradford 1,443; II, 329, Fulke II, 371. Jewel IV, 881, 1,063. Latimer I, 173. Tyndale I, 188, Coverdale II, 586. Bale, 458, 517-524, 533. On the Pope as the Man of Sin, or Antichrist, see Bale, 38. Bradford I, 435, 441; II, 142. Fulke II, 269, 366. Hooper V, 44. Hutchinson, 304. Jewel I, 109; II, 903, etc. Ridley, 53, 263, 414, etc. Sandys, 11, 389. Tyndale I, 147, IA 185, 191, 208, 232-252, 266, 340; II, 178, 179, 181, 182, 196; III, 96, 102-107, 171. Marks or signs by which he may be known. Bale, 203. Hooper II, 44, 56, 512. Jewel II, 913, 921, 991, 992. Seated in the temple of God, i.e., the Church, Bale, 208. Bradford I, 505,; 523 529. Jewel II, 991; IV, 727-729. At Rome, Jewel II, 915; IV, 743, 744. How to be destroyed, Bullinger IV, 34, 162. Fulke II, 393. Jewel II, 927, 928. Tyndale I, 312. Types of his destruction, Jewel II, 928, 929. St. John's account of it, Ib., 930-932. His destruction begun already, Sandys, 389. The Pope proclaimed as Antichrist by the Council at Rheims, Rogers, 182, 347; by the returned exiles, Zurich Letters, I, 27; by the legislature of Scotland, Zurich Letters, 199. See also the antipapal applications of prophecy in Knox's "History of the Reformation in Scotland"; John Foxe's "Acts and Monuments of the Martyrs," and the "Homilies of the Church of England."

I. The Papal Reaction

The Reformation of the sixteenth century was succeeded by the great Papal Reaction of the sixteenth and seventeenth centuries; a movement which included the founding of the Order of the Jesuits, the Marian persecutions, the wars in France against the Huguenots; the *Auto-da-fés* of the Inquisition in Spain; the decrees and anathemas of the Council of Trent; the diabolical attempt of the Duke of Alva to exterminate the Protestants in the Netherlands, of whom 18,000 were slaughtered in six years; the fearful massacre of St. Bartholomew in 1572; the invasion of the Spanish Armada in 1588; the Jesuit attempts on the life of Queen Elizabeth; the Gunpowder plot in 1605; the sanguinary thirty years' war beginning 1618; the massacre of 20,000 Protestants in Magdeburg in 1631; the diabolical barbarities of Count Tilly in Saxony; the massacre of 40,000 Protestants in Ireland in 1641; and wholesale slaughter of the Waldenses in 1655; together with other wars, massacres, and persecutions too numerous to be mentioned. By these dreadful acts the papacy was revealed as the persecuting Antichrist, in colors so glaring and terrible as to compel universal recognition. It is noteworthy that while the Church of England in her Thirty-nine Articles drawn up at an earlier date, in 1562 — articles strongly Anti-Romish in character — refrains from identifying the Pope with the predicted "Man of Sin," the Confession of the Westminster Assembly of Divines in 1647 (a confession ratified and established by Act of Parliament in 1649), does so identify him; as witness the following article, — "There is no other Head of the Church but the Lord Jesus Christ. Nor can the Pope of Rome in any sense be head thereof but is that Antichrist, that Man of Sin, and son of perdition, that exalteth himself in the Church against Christ, and all that is called God." Thus also the Articles of the Church of Ireland, drawn up in 1615, declare "The Bishop of Rome is so far from being the Supreme Head of the Universal Church, that his works and his doctrines do plainly discover him to be that "Man of Sin" foretold in the Holy Scriptures, whom the Lord shall consume with the Spirit of His mouthy and abolish with the brightness of His coming." With these solemn affirmations of the Protestant Churches of the seventeenth century the voices of all the leading prophetic interpreters of the period agree. Their works are before us as we write. We have carefully examined their teachings, from those of Lord Napier's "Commentary on the Apocalypse,"[91] published in 1593, to Vitringa's, a century later, including Cressener's "demonstrations" of the principles of Apocalyptic interpretation in 1690; the works of Dent (1607), Taffin (1614), Forbes (1614), Brightman (1615), Bernard (1617), Cowper (1619), Taylor (1633), Goodwin (1639,) Mede (1643), Pareus (1643), Cotton (1645 and 1655), Roberts (1649), Holland (1650), Homes (1654), Tillinghast (1654), Stephens (1656), Guild (1656), Durham (1680), More (1680), Jurieu (1687), Marckius (1689), Cressener (1690), Vitringa (1695), Cradock (1697), and others. All these seventeenth century writers are agreed as to the historical principle of interpretation, and as to the general outline of events fulfilling Apocalyptic prophecy. Their views on the thirteenth chapter of Revelation are especially important in their clear recognition of the papacy as heading the second, or revived stage of the wild beast power; and its persecution of the saints during the forty-two prophetic "months," or 1,260 years, of its domination. Cressener's works may be especially mentioned as containing a powerful demonstration of this view.

II. Events In Easter Christendom

Turning now to events in eastern Christendom we note that the capture of Constantinople, and overthrow of the Eastern Roman Empire by the Turks in 1453 was too near in point of time to the opening of the sixteenth century to be properly judged of by the Reformers. The event was one of such enormous magnitude as to require a more distant standpoint for its correct appreciation. But in the course of the sixteenth century its full character and effects became plainly visible. The Saracenic and Turkish conquests in the

---

91 The inventor of Logarithms.

time of Solomon the Magnificent, and the Amaraths and Achmets of the age were seen in their true colors. The House of Othman was "lord of the ascendant, and numerous and fair provinces had been torn from the Christians, and heaped together to increase its already ample dominions." The fulfillment of the locust and Euphratean woes of the fifth and sixth trumpets, in the conquests of the Saracens and Turks was now clearly recognized. In 1615 Brightman explained the 150 days ravages of the Locust horsemen as the 150 years of Saracenic conquests reckoned from their first ravages of Syria about A.D. 630. The year, month and day of Turkish conquests he reckons as 396 years (365+30+1), measuring it from the revival of the Othmans A.D. 1300, to the then future date of 1696. It is remarkable that the peace of Carlowitz in 1699, terminating seventeen years of war with Turkey, marked a closing crisis of Turkish power. cc From that time forth," says Sir Edward Creasy, "all serious dread of the military power of Turkey ceased in Europe." The prophetic period may be reckoned as 391 years (360+30+1),[92] and as extending from the reign of Alp Arslan (1063-1072 according to Gibbon) to the fall of Constantinople in 1453. Under Alp Arslan the Turks crossed the Euphrates, and invaded Europe. "The myriads of Turkish horse," says Gibbon, "overspread a frontier of 600 miles from Tauris to Erzeroum, and the blood of 130,000 Christians was a grateful sacrifice to the Arabian prophet." The story of the Turks in Eastern Europe is that of a succession of dreadful massacres without a parallel in the history of the world. With the capture of Constantinople, when Constantine XIV, the last Christian Emperor of the East fell and was "buried under a mountain of the slain," Gibbon terminates his history of "the Decline and Fall of the Roman Empire."

Goodwin (1639), expounds the fallen star of the fifth trumpet as Mahomet, fallen from the profession of Christianity; and the smoke issuing from the pit as the false religion of the prophet." Of the sixth trumpet, or Euphratean woe, he says, "No prophecy doth or can more punctually describe any nation or event than this doth

---

92 "History of the Ottoman Turks," p. 321.

the Turks, and their irruption upon the Eastern Empire, who when they came first out of their native country, about the year 1040 after Christ, did seat themselves first by the River Euphrates, and were divided into four several governments or kingdoms," etc., and completed their conquest of the Roman Empire "in the year 1453, which is 186 years since, who possess that whole Eastern Empire unto this day." Mede (1643), reckons the Turkish woe from 1057 to 1453 and More (1680), does the same. There is perhaps no point on which historical interpreters of the Apocalypse from Mede and Goodwin onwards are more agreed than in the application of the fifth and sixth trumpets to the overthrow of the corrupt and apostate Eastern Empire by the Saracens and Turks.

III. Two Principal Prophecies

The recognition of the fall of the Western and Eastern Empires, under the six first trumpets, led Mede, to the view that the Apocalypse contains two principal prophecies; first the prophecy relating to the decline and fall of the Roman Empire in the West, and in the East, figured under the seals, and six first trumpets; and secondly, the prophecy concerning the fortunes of the Christian Church, beginning with the vision of the descent of the angel in Chapter 10, holding in his hand "a little book open." An analogous twofold feature certainly characterizes the prophecies of Daniel, which consist of an earlier series relating to the Thrones, or governments of the world, and a later series relating to the Temple, and people of God, and the approaching Advent of Messiah. Throne prophecies followed by Temple prophecies, — such is the twofold order both in the book of Daniel and in the Apocalypse.

IV. The Binding of Satan As A Past Event

From the fourth and fifth centuries up to the time of the Reformation the binding of Satan introducing the millennium was regarded as a past event. The Church of the Middle Ages imagined itself to be living in the millennium, and the Reformers considered that the outbreak of Papal persecution at the close of the Middle Ages was the fulfillment of the loosing of Satan for "a little season," prior to the Great Day of Judgment.

By the middle of the seventeenth century the imagined "little season" of Satan's loosing had so lengthened out as to prove the error of this interpretation. Mede was the first to appreciate the fact. His demonstration of the futurity of the millennium was an immense advance, and created an era in Apocalyptic interpretation. Elliott truly describes it as "a mighty step of change from the long continued explanation of the symbol as meant of Satan's 1,000 years' binding from Christ's time, or Constantine's." The futurity of the millennium has held its ground as a Canon of interpretation from Mede's time to the present day.

V. The First Resurrection

In harmony with this view, Mede, like the oldest Patristic Expositors, Justin Martyr, Irenaeus, etc., interpreted the first resurrection as a literal resurrection of the Saints to be accomplished at the time of Antichrist's destruction, at the commencement of the Millennial Age. In this Mede was followed by an imposing array of Puritan Expositors. This was a return to primitive doctrine resulting from the abandonment of the false millennium of the Middle Ages. Dr. Twisse, then prolocutor of the Westminster Assembly of Divines, in an admirable and appreciative preface to Mede's "Commentary on the Apocalypse," gives a summary outline of the Apocalyptic interpretation of this learned Puritan, and says of him "many interpreters have done excellently, but he surmounteth them all."

VI. Mede's Synchronisms

Mede's Synchronisms form the leading feature of his "Key to the

Apocalypse." He laid down the principle that in order to the correct understanding of this mysterious prophecy, it is necessary in the first place to fix the order of its principal visions, apart altogether from the question of their interpretation. In doing this he gives central prominence to the five times recurring period of 1,260 days, forty-two months, or three and a half "Times"; and locates the chief visions of the prophecy by their relation to this period, as preceding it, cotemporizing with it, or succeeding it.[93]

The first synchronism established by Mede is that of what he calls "a noble quaternion of prophecies," remarkable by reason of the equality of their times: —

1. The woman remaining in the wilderness three and one-half "Times," or 1,260 "days."

2. The revived Beast ruling forty-two "months."

3. The outer court trodden down forty-two "months."

4. The witnesses prophesying in sackcloth 1,260 "days."

These periods, Mede shows, are not only equal, but begin at the same time, and end together; and therefore, synchronize throughout. As the various Apocalytic visions are connected with this central period, as introducing it, cotemporizing with it, or succeeding it, their place in the Apocalyptic drama is clearly indicated.

VII. The 1,260 Years of Prophecy

The lapse of time now led to a further important development of the historic interpretation. Sixteen and a half centuries had rolled by since the commencement of the Christian era *, thirteen and a half centuries from the fall of Paganism in the days of Constantine; and twelve and a half centuries since the invasion of the Roman

---

93 Mede's work, written in Latin was translated into English by Richard More, one of the burgesses in the English Parliament; and the House of Commons authorized its publication in 1641.

Empire by Alaric, the initial act of its Gothic overthrow.

The principle of the "year day interpretation" of the prophetic times was already recognized, and the fulfillment of the great prophetic period of 1,260 years now forced itself on general attention, — a period occurring in different forms no less than seven times in Daniel and the Apocalypse.

Room at last existed in Christian history for the location of this great prophetic period, and from the beginning of the seventeenth century onwards it was accorded a prominent place in the historical interpretation of prophecy.

Naturally, with the lapse of time, and the progressive fulfillment of the predictions relating to the Papal downfall, the location of the period was shifted forward from earlier to later dates. The fall of the Papacy has been gradual, like its rise; and the period in question was found to measure with remarkable accuracy the intervals which extended from the principal dates connected with its commencement, to corresponding dates in its decline and overthrow.

Lord Napier in his "Commentary on the Apocalypse," published in 1593, places the first commencement of the 1,260 years "between the year of Christ 300 and 316," and its corresponding end "about the year 1560," at which date "the tenth part of the Papistical Empire was reformed. He indicates a second possible fulfillment of the period in the interval extending from the accession of Justinian — a notable date in the rise of the Papacy — to the then future year 1786; which was a remarkable anticipation for the time, of the date of the French Revolution. Had Lord Napier dated the 1,260 years from the decree of Justinian in 533, constituting the Bishop of Rome"head of all the holy Churches and of all the holy priests of God," he would have correctly anticipated its primary termination in the central year of the French Revolution, 1793, — the year of the execution of Louis XVI, and of the reign of terror, in which the Papal Church and State were overthrown as if by the explosion of a volcano.

Mede in 1642, placed the commencement of the 1,260 years at Alaric's irruption, in 395; the date according to his view of the sounding of the first of the four trumpets connected with the overthrow of the Western Empire. Reckoning it thus, the termination fell in the then future year 1655, the year of the great massacre of the Protestant witnesses in Piedmont of which Milton wrote his memorable sonnet.

> "Avenge O Lord, Thy slaughtered saints, whose bones
> Lie scattered on the Alpine mountains cold."

This location of the 1,260 years is prominent in Mede's Chart of the Visions in the Apocalypse.

Pareus, whose valuable "Commentary on the Apocalypse" was published in 1643, shortly after Mede's, places the beginning of 1,260 years in A.D. 606, when Boniface III was exalted by a decree of the Emperor Phocas to "the chaire of universal pestilence." "From the yeare of Christ therefore 606, until this time the holy citie hath been trodden under foot by the Romane Gentiles, which is the space of 1,073 yeeres, and is yet to be trodden down 223 yeeres more, to wit, until the yeere of Christ 1866 ." We have lived to see the correctness of this remarkable anticipation.

In the year 1866 the overthrow of Papal Austria by Protestant Prussia took place, and the Papal invitation to all Catholic bishops to "celebrate the eighteenth century of the martyrdom of Peter and Paul" was sent forth: 599 bishops were present at the Allocution delivered by the Pope in 1867. The Pope's encyclical letter summoning the Vatican Council was issued in 1868, and the decree of Papal infallibility coinciding with the outbreak of the Franco-German war, together with the fall of the French Empire and the Papal Temporal Power took place in 1870. In the four years 1866-1870 Papal power was overthrown in Austria, Spain, France, and Italy; and since 1870 the Pope has ceased to possess even a shadow of political sovereignty.

Pareus was not the first to point out 1866 as the termination of the 1,260 years. David Chytraus in A.D. 1571 indicated Alaric A.D. 412, and the decree of Phocas, A.D. 606, as possible starting points of the period. But the anticipation of Pareus was more definite in character; and he takes a leading place in the list of prophetic interpreters who during the last two hundred years have fixed on A.D. 606 and 1866 as the chief termini of the 1,260 years period of Papal rule.[94]

It is a noteworthy fact that the historic interpretation of prophecy, constantly developing century by century with the unveilings of Providence, assumed in the sixteenth and seventeenth centuries, as to its leading outlines, a definite form from which it has never since departed. One has but to compare Mede's diagram of the historical fulfillment of the Apocalyptic visions (1641), and that of Whiston (1706), with that of Elliott (1844-1862), to be convinced of the fact.

---

94 The Papal and Mohammedan powers rose together in the years 606- 610.
    The Magdeburg Centuriators in their monumental history of the Christian
    Church published in 1559-1574, point out the fact and fix on the year 606, as
    that of the rise of the Papacy.
Paulus Diaconus, and Anastasius ("Historia Ecclesiastica et de Vitis Pontificum,"
    p. ii, ch. 3) indicate 600 as the date of this event; a date memorialized by the
    Pillar of Phocas (A.D. 607), still standing in the Forum at Rome.

7. The Revocation Of The Edict Of Nantes, And English Revolution Stage

HERE WE REACH the beginning of the last act of the Papal tragedy.

Louis XIV sat on the throne of France at Versailles. At his side was Madame de Maintenon. Behind her stood the Jesuit Confessor Pere la Chaise. Behind him again the Pope, and his inspirer the Prince of Darkness.

In Piedmont the trembling remnant of Protestants left by the great massacre of 1655 still clung to their native rocks, and Alpine fastnesses.

In England James II was struggling to restore Papal supremacy, and enslave the children of the Puritans who had bought their liberties at so great a price.

Behind the scene historically lay ages of darkness; before it ages of light.

O thou who wouldst draw near to behold this sight — the bush that burned with fire and was not consumed, take thy shoes from off thy feet, for the place on which thou standest is holy ground.

Clear away the mists of ignorance which hide the great tragedy from thine eyes. Thou art the heir of freedom purchased by the sufferings and sacrifices of these martyr days. Gaze then upon the sublime and touching spectacle, and let it fix itself in thy memory forever.

Fear not to enter this gloomy region for light shall spring from the sepulchral darkness; life from the ashes of the dead.

Hark! a wail bursts forth from the lips of thousands of Protestant parents robbed of their children. That wail is the prelude of the last great Papal persecution of the Huguenots; a persecution which was followed by the French Revolution, inaugurating the modern era of civil and religious liberty.

"A terrible law strikes dismay into the hearts of fathers and mothers — a law that will bring us to the determination to go and cast ourselves at the feet of the king; begging him to grant us either death, or freedom of conscience for us and for our children; or permission, leaving behind us our property, to forsake the nation, and drag out a languishing existence, scattered in every country of the globe." It is Pierre Jurieu who utters this bitter cry in his "Last Efforts of Afflicted Innocence," relating to the effects of the statute of Louis XIV, of June, 1681.

And what was this law? It was a law which struck at the existence of the family; which authorized the wholesale compulsory conversion of all the children of the Protestants throughout France to the Roman Catholic Church. It authorized children of the tender age of seven years to renounce the religion of their Protestant parents, and gave freedom to the Romish priests and population to ensnare them into an enforced confession of the Romish faith; a mere sentence, a word expressing admission of some popish doctrine sufficing; forbidding the poor innocent to take back its words; and thus tearing the child from its parents and its home, and hurrying it, in spite of frantic protests from the father and the mother, into some nunnery or other place, to be there immured until "conversion" was complete.

A refinement of cruelty this, unmatched even in the persecutions of old heathen Rome.

Institutions spring up at once all over France, *Nouveaux Catholiques* for boys; *Nouvelles Catholiques* for girls; they are quickly crowded. Bereaved Protestant parents sit in their desolated homes, weeping over the children who have been torn away from them. "All the torments that have heretofore been inflicted upon us are as nothing," say they, "in comparison with this." It is, however, but the beginning of the tragedy. The parents are not yet converted. Unreasonable parents! The elder brothers and sisters still remain Protestants. They dare to hold prayer-meetings in their desolated homes. They bow down on their knees, and hide their weeping faces in their hands. They cry to the Father in heaven. What infamy! A stop must be put to this.

But how? Had Satan ingenuity equal to the occasion? How were the parents and elder sons and daughters to be compelled to come wholesale into the Catholic fold? By a new method. By *Dragonnades*. The army of Louis XIV was vast and powerful; his soldiers unscrupulous, ungodly, superstitious, lustful, intolerant, ready instruments for any abomination. Quarter the soldiers in the homes of the Protestants. Commission these "booted evangelists" to convert them; give them leave to do as they will in these homes with the women, as well as the men; with the mothers and the daughters. Set them to work. Let them stable their horses in the parlors; break the furniture; devour the provisions; tie the fathers hand and foot, and violate in their presence the wives and daughters. Let them prevent the wretched Huguenots from closing their eyes in sleep until they have renounced their Protestantism.

Keep the heretics awake; beat them; drag them about. Shout at them, walk them up and down the rooms all night long. Keep up this fiendish treatment day and night till they submit. Cursed heretics, what right have they to resist the will of Louis XIV, and the almighty Pope of Rome?

And these horrors were done; done throughout all France. The soldiers quartered on the Protestants "pinched them, prodded them, hung them up by ropes, tormented them in a hundred other ways, until their unhappy victims scarcely knew what they were doing." "They spat in the faces of women, made them lie down on burning coals, made them put their heads into ovens whose hot flames stifled them." The new mission went forward rapidly, Louis XIV directing. "From Guyenne and Upper Languedoc the Dragonnades extended to Saintonage, Aunis, and Poitou on the west, and to Vivarais on the East. Next came the turn of the province of Lyonnaise, of the Cevennes, of Lower Languedoc, of Province, of Gex. Later still the rest of the kingdom became a prey to the hideous work of the"booted mission" as it was called — Normandy, Burgundy, and the central provinces, even to far-off Brittany, and to Paris itself."[95]"The horrors the dragoons inspired, the crimes they perpetrated, the sufferings the wretched victims endured," who shall describe? But this was only the beginning of the tragedy.

A statute still remained — the Edict of Nantes — protecting the lives and liberties of the Huguenots. By one fell stroke this last protection was swept away. The Edict was revoked. The floodgates were opened, and persecution in its worst form rolled over the Protestant population of France.

The fatal day of the revocation of the Edict of Nantes was the 17th of October, 1685.

The first article of the new law recalled all legislation favorable to the Huguenots.

The second forbade all gatherings of Protestants for the services of their religion.

The three following had reference to Protestant ministers. All these were commanded to leave France within fifteen days from the publication of the Edict, on pain of the galleys.

The seventh article abolished all private schools for the instruction of Protestant children.

The eighth prescribed that all children hereafter born of Protestant parents should be baptized by the parish priests, and

---

95 Baird, "The Huguenots and the Revocation of the Edict of Nantes," Vol. I, p. 565.

brought up in the Roman Catholic religion. Recalcitrant parents incurred a fine of five hundred livres or more.

In the tenth article the king issued "very express and repeated prohibitions to all his Protestant subjects against leaving his kingdom, or allowing their wives or children to leave it, and against exporting their goods and chattels. The penalty was the galleys for men, and confiscation of body and goods for women."

All the Protestant churches throughout France were shut or pulled down. Nothing but ruins remained. The pastors were exiled, and the flocks forbidden to follow them. An entire people, the best and noblest of the land, lay crushed under the cruel heel, the iron hoof, of the relentless Papal persecutor.

Then followed the great Exodus. Nothing could arrest it. Thousands on thousands of Huguenots fled from France. The frontiers were guarded in vain. Disguised in all manner of ways, their faces disfigured, their garments rent, in the darkness of night, by sequestered paths, through forests, across mountains, and over the seas in open boats, they fled, and still fled, until half a million had escaped. They fled to Switzerland, to Holland, to England, and other countries. Four hundred thousand perished in the effort to escape. The prisons were crowded. The homes of the Protestants emptied, their houses left tenantless.

Thousands of Protestants had broken down under the strain, and professed submission to their Roman Catholic persecutors; but the great mass of the Huguenots had remained faithful. No power could conquer their convictions, or compel them to deny their Lord. Chained to the oars in the horrible galleys, and brutally beaten and bastinadoed by their captors, they remained faithful. Crammed into filthy jails, left to rot in dungeons, they remained faithful. Broken on the wheel they remained faithful. Aged pastors lay bound by their limbs to that cruel instrument, while through a long agony, protracted sometimes for hours, every bone in their body was broken. Stroke followed stroke while life remained.

Groans went up from the galleys, from the prisons, from the lands of exile.

In The Tower of Constance Huguenot women were immured without hope of release. The walls were nearly ninety feet high, and eighteen feet in thickness. It contained two great circular vaulted chambers one above the other. High and narrow loopholes admitted a feeble light. By that ray one of the noble women imprisoned there wrote on the wall "Resistez" Yes, they "resisted unto blood" in that awful strife. Who were the victors in that struggle? Louis XIV and the Pope and priests of Rome, or the suffering Huguenots? Was not the Crucified the Conqueror? Is not the martyr the Victor? So they overcame. "When young Chamier underwent his horrible torture, for the scene of which, by a refinement of cruelty, the street in front of his paternal home had been selected, it was his mother that chiefly urged him to fortitude in suffering for the faith."I have yet," said she, "three children whom I shall cheerfully give up, if they be called to die for religion's sake."

Like the noble martyrs of primitive times "they loved not their lives unto the death." They overcame; for greater is He who was in them, than he who was in the opposing world. Rome believed and boasted that she had triumphed. She rang her joybells. She struck Commemoration ' Medals. On one of them the crowned monarch stands on the steps of the altar, and extends to France, represented by a kneeling suppliant the sceptre of his mercy; while around are inscribed the words *Sacra Romana Restituta.* — "The Roman religion restored."

The Queen of Sweden received and sheltered some of the refugees. "I pray with all my heart," said she, "that the false joy and triumph of the Church may not someday cost her tears and sorrows." What it did cost France history has since related.

In the Vaudois valleys at this same period the wave of persecution had reached its highest altitude. "In thy book," cried Milton,

> "record their groans
> Who were thy sheep, and in their ancient fold
> Slain by the bloody Piedmontese, that rolled
> Mother with infants down the rocks. Their groans
> The vales redoubled to the hills, and they
> To heaven."

The Vaudois Protestants were cut up alive, roasted over fires, impaled on stakes, disemboweled, torn limb from limb, tortured in ways too horrible to describe. Leger's volume contains pictures of all these horrors, and gives the names and numbers of the sufferers.

In 1686 Louis XIV sent 14,000 men under the Marquis de Catinat to join the Piedmontese army, to enforce the submission of the Vaudois. Following his victory over the Protestants of the Valleys the Duke condemned 14,000 of them to the prisons of Turin: of these 11,000 perished by heat, cold, hunger, and thirst in their imprisonment. The remaining three thousand on emancipation from prison fled over the mountains to Switzerland and Brandenburg. The republic of Geneva extended to the exiles a touching welcome.

In England James II had opened negotiations with the Pope. Papists were in full patronage and Jeffreys was holding his "bloody assizes." In the army Protestant officers were replaced by Romanists; the Papal Nuncio was received at Windsor, and the seven Bishops sent to the Tower, the people venting their feelings in tears and prayers.

A storm was brewing, and a dark cloud hung over the land.

This closing crisis of Papal persecution had long been expected. Students of prophecy in the days of the Reformation and of the Puritan Revolution had forecast its advent and sought to calculate the period of its occurrence. They knew that the Protestant religion would be suppressed in some unprecedented way before the final judgments of God were poured forth on their persecutors.

They believed that the Protestant "witnesses" were yet to be slain; that they were to lie unburied for three and a half years, and then to be raised from death, and exalted to power and supremacy.

Peter Jurieu, one of the exiled Huguenot ministers wrote a book in 1687, a copy of which lies before us, entitled, "The accomplishment of the Scripture prophecies on the approaching deliverance of the Church, proving that the present persecution may end in three years and a half; after which the destruction of the Antichrist shall begin, which shall be finished in the beginning of the next age, and then the Kingdom of Christ shall come upon earth."

It is a volume of six hundred pages, and remarkable for the clearness and force of its argument.

Was Jurieu mistaken?

The Revocation of the Edict of Nantes took place on the 17th of October, 1685.

The English Revolution followed in 1688, and the coronation of William of Orange and Queen Mary took place on the 11th of April, 1689.

From October, 1685, to April, 1689, the interval is three and a half years.

The English Revolution marked the end of Papal supremacy in England, and Papal persecution on any widely extended scale in the world. It was the first stage in the inauguration of a new era.

In 1688, James II, the last Popish King of England, abandoned his throne, and fled. The victories of William of Orange in Ireland and on the continent followed; including those of Marlborough over the armies of Louis XIV, in the nine years' war with France from May, 1689, to January 1697.

The almost unexampled series of English victories of this war was succeeded by the Treaty of Ryswick in September, 1697, and the full establishment of civil and religious liberty.

Encouraged by the English Revolution in 1689, the Vaudois refugees in Switzerland resolved to attempt to return to their country. Embarking at Nyon on the 16th of August, 1689, they crossed the Lake of Geneva, ascended the opposite heights, crossed the bridge of Marni, passed the towns of Cluse and Sallenches; crossed Mount Haute Luce, Mount Bon Homme, and the River Isere; crossed Mount Tisserand and Mount Cenis, Mount Tourliers, the Valley of Jaillon, by Chamont above Suza, Mount Sei, and descended into the Valley of Pragela, the most northern of the Vaudois valleys. In this long and perilous journey across the Alps, they were led by Henry Arnaud. Though opposed by 10,000 French and 12,000 Piedmontese, they cut their way through, losing only thirty of their number in their numerous encounters with their enemies.

Climbing the precipitous Alps, crossing the snows, sleeping on the bare ground: subsisting only on bread and herbs, they escaped or put to flight their foes, preserved as by a miracle from all the perils of the way. Their return to their native valleys celebrated as "La Rentree Glorieuse" was effected three and half years after their total dissipation.

We have said that Jurieu published a work on the "Approaching deliverance of the Church," in 1687, in which he anticipated that the Restoration of Protestantism would follow three and a half years after its overthrow at the Revocation of the Edict of Nantes in 1685.

Another work on the Apocalypse written in 1685 by an exiled French minister contains the same anticipation. Copies of both of these works are lying before us. The latter contains the following reference to its authorship on the title page, — "written by a

French minister in the year 1685, and finisht but two days before the Dragoons plundered him of all except this Treatise."

It is a small volume of about 300 pages. Fallen to pieces with age, with broken binding, and separated leaves, my copy is tied together with string to preserve it from destruction; an eloquent witness to the last great Papal persecution, and the anticipation based on the sure word of prophecy, of the speedy restoration of Protestant liberties. The author tells us that he was unacquainted with Jurieu's view when he wrote. "There were divers of the refugees," says he, "who had the sight of this discourse when they were in France. For the author had finished it near the end of August, 1685, about two days before the arrival of the new missionaries, the Dragoons, who plundered him of all he had. So that this was the whole that he was able to save out of that doleful shipwreck; which since his arrival at a place of security he hath reviewed and corrected, in several places. And having met with"the Accomplishment of Prophecies," written by the famous Monsieur Jurieu, the author was exceedingly pleased to find that he had explained the eleventh chapter (of Revelation) as promissory of the reestablishment of the Reformed in France, according as that great man hath done."

Not in France, however, but chiefly in England whither great numbers of the refugees had come, and in the Waldensian Valleys, was the restoration of Protestantism to be effected. It came at the expected time. A darker experience awaited France, the execution of terrible judgments in retribution for her cruel and long continued persecution of the Huguenots. Regarded in its widest aspects, the English Revolution under William of Orange marked the commencement of the modern era of full Protestant liberties, and the political ascendancy of Protestant power in Europe, and throughout the world.

8. The Eighteenth Century New Era Stage

FOLLOWING THE ESTABLISHMENT of Protestantism in the Revolution of 1688, came the Expansion of England; the rise of America; the great Revival of Religion; and the dawn of modern world-wide missions.

The siege and heroic defense of Londonderry, the battle of the Boyne, and the victories of Marlborough marked the termination of the struggle led by William of Orange against the Papal foe. On the 15th of September, 1697, William signed the Peace of Ryswick — a peace between Great Britain, the United Provinces, France, Spain, and the Emperor Leopold I. Under this Treaty, concluding the nine years' war with France, Louis XIV acknowledged the Prince of Orange as King of Great Britain without condition or reserve; Strasbourg was restored to the empire, Luxembourg to the Spaniards, together with other places taken by the French since the treaty of Nimeguen; and all places in the Low Country taken by France were abandoned. Concluded on as fair terms as England could exact, this pacification, as far as the prospects of the continent were concerned, was but "a preliminary armistice of vigilance and preparation." In England, however, the effect was of a more important character, and signalized the commencement of a new era of full civil and religious liberty.

On his return to England, William appointed the 2nd December, 1697, a day of solemn thanksgiving for the conclusion of the general peace. On that day, the Cathedral of St. PauFs, the magnificent work of Sir Christopher Wren, was first opened to the public.

The period thus inaugurated has seen the expansion of England to world-wide dimensions.

I. Wars With France in the Eighteenth Century

"The great English Navy," says Seeley, "first took definite shape in the wars of the Commonwealth, and the English army, founded on the Mutiny Bill, dates from the reign of William III. Between the Revolution and the Battle of Waterloo, it may be reckoned that we waged and won seven great wars, of which the shortest lasted seven years, and the longest about twelve. Out of a hundred and twenty-six years, sixty-four years, or more than half, were spent in war.

"Let us pass these wars in review. There was first the European war in which England was involved by the Revolution of 1688. It is pretty well remembered, since the story of it has been told by Macaulay. It lasted eight years, from 1689 to 1697.

"There was then the great war called from the Spanish succession, which we shall always remember, because it was the war of Marlborough's victories. It lasted eleven years, from 1702 to 1713.

"The next great war has now passed almost entirely out of memory, not having brought to light any very great commander, nor achieved any definite result. This war lasted nine years, from 1739 to 1748.

"Next comes the seven years' war in which we have not forgotten the victories of Frederick. In the English part of it we all remember one grand incident, the battle of the Heights of Abraham, the death of Wolfe, and the conquest of Canada. And yet in the case of this war also it may be observed how much the eighteenth century has faded out of our imaginations. We have quite forgotten that that victory was one of a long series, which to contemporaries seemed fabulous, so that the nation came out of the struggle intoxicated with glory, and England stood upon a pinnacle of greatness which she had never reached before. This is the fourth war. It is in sharp contrast with the fifth, which we have tacitly agreed to mention as seldom as we can. What we call the American war which from the first outbreak of hostilities to the peace of Paris lasted eight years, from 1775 to 1783, was ended ignominiously enough in America, but in its latter part spread into a grand naval war in which England stood at bay against almost all the world, and in this, through the victories of Rodney, came off with some credit.

"The sixth and seventh of the two great wars with Revolutionary France which we are not likely to forget, though we ought to keep them more separate in our minds than we do. The first lasted nine years from 1793 to 1802, the second twelve from 1803 to 1815.

"Now probably it has occurred to few of us to connect these wars together, or to look for any unity of plan or purpose pervading them. But look a little closer. Out of these seven wars of England five are wars with France from the beginning, and both the other two, though the belligerent at the outset was in the first Spain, and in the second one our colonies, yet became in a short time and ended as wars with France... I say 'these wars made one grand and decisive struggle between England and France.' On the continent, in Canada, and in India, England overcame the armies of France. England, as a result, became a great world power.

"The Expansion of England in the New World and in Asia is the formula which sums up for England the history of the eighteenth century."[96]

The second great feature of the period is the

II. Rise of the United States of America.

The Puritans who after a warfare against arbitrary power in

96 Seely, "The Expansion of England," pp. 24-33.

England subverted the monarchy and overturned the church, laid in America the foundation of the most mighty Republic the world has ever known.

Exiled from England during the reign of Mary, the Puritans returned on the accession of Elizabeth "bent upon the great design of extirpating from the constitution of the church what they deemed the last degrading vestiges of popery, and remodeling it after the doctrines and practices of the Continental Reformers." "Now commenced a stern and unrelenting struggle. The High Church party resolved to admit no compromise. The Puritans, on the other hand, exposed to the utmost rage of persecution, could only oppose to it an indomitable firmness and tenacity. The Puritan ministers ejected from their livings, driven from their pulpits and their homes began to travel the country, and disseminate their views, by preaching and issuing pamphlets, in defiance of fine and imprisonment."

When James I came to the throne "the Puritans lost no time in presenting to the king a petition signed by 825 ministers, praying for the removal of superstitious usages and other abuses which deformed the Church." The celebrated Hampton Court Conference was the reply, a conference in which James I brow beat the unfortunate Puritan ministers in the coarsest manner, "encouraged by the sycophantic smiles of the prelates and courtiers." "If," said he, "you aim at a Scottish Presbytery, it agrees as well with Monarchy as God with the devil. I will none of that. I will have one doctrine and one discipline." Rising from his chair, he added, "I shall make them conform themselves, or I will harry them out of the land, or yet do worse."

Denied the religious liberty they sought in England, many of the Puritans fled to Holland, and from that country made their way to America. Their voyage in the Mayflower marked the commencement of the mighty development of civil and religious freedom existing in America today. After tossing on the Atlantic in their small and crowded vessel, for more than two months, the Pilgrims landed on Plymouth Rock on the 25th December, 1620.

"Here the low sandhills of Cape Cod covered with scrubby woods that descended to the sea, seemed at the first glance, a perfect paradise of verdure to the poor sea-beat wanderers." Before entering the harbor they subscribed their names to a covenant in which they stated that "having undertaken for the glory of God, and advancement of the Christian faith, and honor of our king and country, a voyage to plant the first colony in the Northern part of Virginia," we "do solemnly and mutually, in the presence of God, and of one another, covenant and combine ourselves together into a civil body politic, for our better ordering and preservation... and by virtue hereof to enact, constitute and frame such just and equal laws, ordinances, acts, constitutions, and offices, from time to time, as shall be thought most meet and convenient for the general good of the colony, unto which we promise all due submission and obedience."

American writers have denominated this voluntary agreement "the birth of popular constitutional liberty," and though it was no intention of the Pilgrims to cast off subjection to England, they did practically, by giving every man the right of voting and choosing officers to draw up and carry out the laws of the colony, "lay the foundation of a totally new system of government upon the basis of a democratic equality and practical independence, over which the nominal sway of a distant power could never exert any efficient permanent control."

A further settlement of Puritan Pilgrims in Massachusetts in the time of Charles I, formed a later stage in the planting of American colonization. Like the Pilgrims of 1620, these had been "driven forth from their native country by the intolerable burdens of enforced conformity." But the Puritan settlers had not completely shaken off the spirit of intolerance from which they had suffered. For announcing the principle that the civil magistrate had no right of control in the sacred sphere of conscience, Roger Williams was banished from the colony. Driven forth in the depths of winter, under storms more fierce than those that assailed the Pilgrim Fathers when they landed from the Mayflower, he had to skulk for many weeks amid the intricate wilds of the leafless forest, glad when he discovered a hollow tree to shelter him from the pitiless blasts of the north wind laden with ice and snow. "But the ravens," said he, "fed me in the wilderness." The wild Indians protected the outcast, and through his long life, he never forgot the debt of gratitude. Williams removed at length to Rhode Island. Five companions who shared with him the large views of liberty for which he had endured these sufferings, followed him thither; and there, with the advice of the benevolent governor of Boston, and beyond the reach of the Charter of Massachusetts, the pioneer of liberty founded a new settlement, to which he gave the name of "Providence."

Thus was planted that sapling which has since grown into the mighty tree of the United States of America. The American Declaration of Independence in 1776 marks one of the most important stages in the New Era of civil and religious liberty which broke on the world at the commencement of the eighteenth century. The hand of a Higher Power is here seen, guiding events to nobler issues than had been contemplated by even the best of men. From the Pilgrims of the Mayflower to Roger Williams, and from Roger Williams to Washington, the path exhibits a continuous ascent to the lofty level of freedom attained by the American people. The discovery of the New World was the prelude to the Reformation and the completion of the edifice of civil and religious liberty in the New World has been the crown of the new era inaugurated by the doctrines of the Reformers, and the deeds of the Puritans.

III. The eighteenth century witnessed a revival in England and America of spiritual life.

Liberty is not the chief possession needed by mankind. Spiritual life is still more essential, and God, who gave in this era enfranchisement and enlargement to oppressed Protestant peoples, granted also a deep and widespread revival of spiritual religion, whose effects have since extended throughout the world.

Like the Reformation of the sixteenth century, this revival began in Germany. August Herman Franke, a professor of Divinity at Halle in Saxony, filled with faith and love, placed an alms box at his study door, into which contributions were thrown for the purchase of books for the instruction of the poor. The erection of schools for poor children followed, and then the building of his great orphan home. A wonderful revival of the spirit of piety in the city and University of Halle accompanied the movement, whose influence extended to other places in Germany.

In 1710 Zinzendorf was sent to the seminary of Halle, where he became a pupil of Franke, and experienced the quickenings of spiritual life. Devoting himself to the service of God, Zinzendorf formed at Halle a society of like-minded persons called the "order of the grain of mustard seed. After studying in the University of Wittemburg, and traveling in Holland and France, Count Zinzendorf went to reside at Bertholdsdorf, in Lusatia, on the borders of Bohemia. A few members of the Moravian Church, driven by persecution from their native country, sought refuge with him in 1722, and were permitted to form a settlement on his estate, which received the name of Herrnhut,"The Lord's guard," or "Watch of the Lord." Other Moravian refugees joined the settlement, which grew under the fostering care of Zinzendorf to an important center of religious life and missionary operations. In 1727 the Church of the United Brethren was established at Herrnhut. The Moravian brethren were the direct descendants of the ancient Hussites of Bohemia, among whom the Reformation had been crushed by cruel and prolonged persecution. It may be said that the slain Hussites were revived in the Moravians of Herrnhut.

From Zinzendorf John Wesley received the clear knowledge of the gospel. At that time religion in England was in a dreadfully low and dead condition. A few young men at Oxford University, of whom Wesley was one, formed a company knit together by ties of religious sympathy. By their fellow students they were derided as

"Sacramentarians," "Bible Bigots," "Bible Moths," "The Godly Club." Whitfield was drawn towards them, and defended them from the revilings of opponents. Thus began the great Methodist movement, which has since grown to such gigantic proportions. In 1737 Wesley sailed for America, in company with some Moravian missionaries. After his return from Georgia, he connected himself more closely with Zinzendorf. Differences afterwards arose which led the Methodists and Moravians on diverging paths, but in spirit they were one. Baptized by the power of the Holy Spirit, Whitfield and Wesley did a glorious work of evangelization in the eighteenth century. Crossing the Atlantic repeatedly, they were the first great preachers in both hemispheres, and were the means of the conversion of thousands.

Whitfield's ministry was one of unparalleled power. "Before Whitfield no one man had ever come into contact with so many minds; no one voice had ever rung in so many ears; no one ministry had touched so many hearts."

A most remarkable outpouring of the Spirit of God was manifested at the same time in New England in connection with the labors of "Jonathan Edwards."

The year 1741 witnessed a revival which seemed like the return of Pentecostal days. Edwards has left a full account of it. Deep convictions of sin, and transporting views of the excellency of Christ, and of the glory and sufficiency of the gospel, characterized this work, which was productive of numerous and widespread conversions, and unwonted growth in grace. In 1743 Edwards became acquainted with Brainerd, then a missionary to the Indians at Kaunaumeek, and subsequently wrote his memoir. From Brainerd may be dated the era of modern missions.

In Northampton, New England, the spot consecrated by the labors of Jonathan Edwards, the remains of David Brainerd and Jerusha Edwards lie side by side. Around their humble graves has sprung up a lovely and peaceful cemetery, whose inscriptions recall the history of the Puritan forefathers of America. The Puritans have passed away, but the spirit which inspired them still lives and operates, and is the mightiest influence of modern days. It has emancipated England, and given birth to America, and through these is transforming the religious beliefs and political institutions of surrounding nations.

The Anglo-Saxons number today more than a hundred millions, are in possession of a third of the earth, and rule over 400,000,000 of its inhabitants. Steam and electricity have given wings to the world-transforming movement; and it is evident to all thoughtful minds that the way is being everywhere prepared for the advent of a new and nobler order of things connected with the Kingdom of God.

IV. Apocalyptic Interpretation in the Eighteenth Century.

The advent of the new era which followed the English Revolution had a most marked and important effect on Apocalyptic interpretation. Fresh fulfillments of prophecy were recognized, and the attainment of an advanced and commanding position for the study of the subject. The progress in science, philosophy, and theology which marked the period was reflected in Apocalyptic literature. The age of Sir Isaac Newton, of Butler, and of Jonathan Edwards saw the production of works on prophecy of greater learning and breadth of view than any that had previously appeared.

Among the most important works on the Apocalypse produced in the interval between the English and French Revolutions are those of Cressener (1690), Sir Isaac Newton (1691, published in 1733 after his death), Vitringa (1695), Fleming (1701), Whiston (1706), Daubuz (1720), Lancaster (1730), Roberts (1730), Lowman (1737), Bishop of Clogher (1749), Bishop Newton (1754), Bengel (1757), Jonathan Edwards (1773), and Gill (1776).

To these we must add the work of the Swiss astronomer, Loys de Cheseaux, on the times of Daniel and the Apocalypse, published in 1754.

The following advances in prophetic interpretation are exhibited in these works:

1. The definite conclusion that the death of the Apocalyptic witnesses was past, and their resurrection accomplished.

In 1689, the year of the coronation of William of Orange as William III, Dr. Cressener published a volume on the "Judgments of God upon the Roman Catholic Church," with a dedicatory preface addressed to the king in which he holds forth the prospect of a "speedy revival of the Reformation where it has been extinguished," and hails the English Revolution as "the first opening of the glorious scene." "It may now be reasonably concluded," says Cressener, "that the death of the witnesses is already past, and that in all probability the point of time from which the three and a half years of its continuance did begin was at the Revocation of the Edict of Nantes by the king of France." In 1690 Cressener published "A demonstration of the first principles of the Protestant applications of the Apocalypse," in which he maintained that it was impossible that the death and resurrection of the witnesses could have taken place before the period then reached; and that their resurrection was "unexpectedly fulfilled by the return of the Protestants of Savoy," in spite of the opposition of their enemies to their own land, and the reestablishment of the Protestant religion in the Vaudois valleys where it had been suppressed three and a half years previously.

He remarks that the Vaudois were for many ages the only considerable party of Protestant witnesses, and are therefore not beneath the notice of the prophecy. Their return "may therefore be very well accounted as the first comfortable earnest of a more universal revival of the silenced churches in other places."

The celebrated Whiston, Sir Isaac Newton's successor in the chair of mathematics at Cambridge, maintained the same view in his work on the Apocalypse. Whiston calls attention to the interesting fact that the resurrection of the Vaudois a was foretold from this prophecy before it came to pass by the Lord Bishop of Worcester."[97] There is a mention in Evelyn's Memoirs of a visit paid by Mr. E. on the 18th of June, 1690 to Bishop Lloyd. Referring to the death and resurrection of the Apocalyptic witnesses the bishop mentioned"that he had persuaded two exiled Vaudois ministers to return home, when there was no apparent ground of hope for them, giving them £20 towards the expenses, and which return was wonderfully accomplished.[98]

The story of the Vaudois restoration is related as follows by Whiston: "The Duke of Savoy, the sovereign of these Vaudois, by an edict dated January 31, 1685-6, N. S., forbade the exercise of their religion on pain of death; and therein ordered their churches to be demolished, and their ministers to be banished. The edict for the banishment was dated Turin, April 9th; enrolled the 10th, and published in the valleys the nth, and an army sent against them of Savoy and French troops who attacked them on the 22nd of the same month, and totally subdued them in the following month of May; when many of the poor people were killed and barbarously slaughtered; great numbers cast into prison, and inhumanly used there, and the miserable remainder of them were at length released out of prison, and permitted to depart about the beginning of December, so that the total dissipation of them was not completed till that time, or the beginning of December the same year, 1686. In the meantime these poor Vaudois were very kindly received and succoured by the Protestant States, particularly those of Holland, Brandenburg, Geneva, and Switzerland, and so preserved from

___

97 "Whiston on the Apocalypse," p. 272.
98 See footnote in Elliott's *Horae*, IV, p. 497, and reference to Bishop Lloyd's act in Bishop Newton on the prophecies, p. 566.

ruin. Towards the latter end of the year 1689, about three years and a half after the publication of the Edict above mentioned, in the valleys, or the beginning of its execution, they passed the Lake of Geneva secretly, and entering Savoy with their swords in their hands they recovered their ancient possessions, and by the middle of April, A. D. 1690, established themselves in it, notwithstanding the opposition of the troops of France and Savoy; of whom they, who were comparatively but a few, slew great numbers with inconsiderable loss; till the Duke himself, who had now left the French interest, by his League, and an Edict signed June 4, 1690, just three and a half years after their total dissipation, recalled the rest of them and reestablished them, with liberty to the French refugees themselves to return with them also. So that on the whole, these Vaudois, when they were about to finish their testimony, or near the conclusion of their 1,260 years' prophecy in sackcloth, have been slain, i. e. in prophetic style, imprisoned, murdered, expelled and banished;. .. they have continued in that state of expulsion three years and a half, exactly according to this prophecy, and that in the public view of the Papists, and to their great joy. And after those three years and a half now over the Spirit of life from God has entered into them, and they have risen again from the dead, and stood upon their feet, i.e., recovered their old habitations, and obtained the pardon and protection of their prince; and so terribly defeated their numerous enemies that fear and terror could not but fall upon them thereupon; exactly also as their prophecy foretold of them. And this event is the more to be observed because it takes in the resurrection of both the witnesses, the Waldenses and the Albigenses, which have been a united people, and dwelt together in these valleys of Piedmont ever since the conclusion of the Crusades against the latter of them in the thirteenth century; and because it was from this prophecy expressly foretold before it happened by the most learned the Lord Bishop of Worcester, as is well known to many, and exactly come to pass accordingly. And thus far of the prophecy seems to me to have been already fulfilled, and that very remarkably."[99]

99 "Whiston on the Apocalypse," pp. 206, 208.

Various books on the Vaudois written since Whiston's time, tracing their history down to the present day, exalt the *Glorieuse Rentree* accomplished under Henri Arnaud, as the crisis of their restoration. After the treaty of 1690, their privileges were constantly confirmed, and perfect liberty of conscience accorded them. "The Protestant powers continued their protection, and particularly England; for a pension was granted by that country to the pastors under William and Mary, which was named the English Royal Subsidy; and this being found insufficient, in 1770 a general collection was made, the interest of which was paid under the name of the English National Subsidy."

In Switzerland "studentships were established at the Universities of Geneva, Lausanne and Basle for the young Vaudois intended for the ministry."[100] The Vaudois church which has of late years experienced a spiritual revival is now engaged in conducting a widespread work of evangelization in Italy.

Thus has God fulfilled His Word. The resurrection of the slaughtered witnesses, prefigured by the resurrection of their Lord, "the faithful and true witness," has been accomplished. The memorable prediction in relation to Him, "Thou wilt not leave my soul in Hades, nor suffer Thine Holy One to see corruption," has been fulfilled in a figurative sense in the experience of his slaughtered saints. On the third day He rose again from literal death — in the third year they rose from symbolical death. The powers of destruction were unable to retain their victims. The spirit of life proved victorious. Christ and His witnesses have arisen. He lives forever, and they too, live as witnesses to die no more.

---

100 "Authentic details of the Waldenses," pp. 389, 390.

2. The recognition of the fact that there have been several stages in the death and resurrection of the witnesses.

Some interpreters are of opinion, says Bishop Newton, that this prophecy of the death and resurrection of the witnesses was accomplished by the advent of the Reformation three and a half years after the complete suppression of the Waldenses, Hussites and Lollards celebrated in the Lateran Council in 1514. "Some again think this prophecy very applicable to the horrid massacre of the Protestants at Paris, and in other cities of France, begun at the memorable eve of St. Bartholomew's Day, 1572. According to the best authors there were slain thirty or forty thousand Huguenots in a few days."Their dead bodies lay in the streets of the great city," one of the greatest cities of Europe, for they were not suffered to be buried, being the bodies of heretics; but were dragged through the streets, or thrown into the river, or hung upon gibbets, and exposed to public infamy. Great "rejoicings" too, were made in the courts of France, Rome, and Spain; they went in procession to the churches, they returned public thanks to God, they sang Te Deums, they celebrated Jubilees, they struck medals; and it was enacted that St. Bartholomew's Day should ever afterwards be kept with double pomp and solemnity. But neither was this joy of long continuance, for in little more than "three years and a half," Henry III, who succeeded his brother, Charles IX, entered into a treaty with the Huguenots, which was concluded and published on the 14th of May, 1576, whereby all the former sentences against them were revised, and the free and open exercise of their religion was granted to them: they were to be admitted to all honors, dignities and offices, as well as the Papists; and the judges were to be half of one religion, and half of the other; with other articles greatly to their advantage. "Others again have recourse to later events, and the later indeed the better and fitter for the purpose. Peter Jurieu, a famous divine of the French Church at Rotterdam, imagined that the persecution then carried on by Louis XIV against the

Protestants of France, after the Revocation of the Edict of Nantes in October, 1685, would be the last persecution of the Church... Bishop Lloyd, and after him Mr. Whiston, apply this prophecy to the poor Protestants in the Valleys of Piedmont, who by a cruel Edict of their sovereign, the Duke of Savoy, instigated by the French king, were imprisoned and murdered, or banished and totally dissipated at the latter end of the year 1686. .. but reestablished by another Edict signed June 4, 1690, just three and a half years after their total dissipation... at the same time" with these massacres, "popery here in England was advanced to the throne, and threatened an utter subversion of our religion and liberties, but in little more than 'three years and a half' a happy deliverance was wrought by the glorious Revolution."

Though more than two hundred years have elapsed since the English Revolution, the Protestant religion continues dominant in England. No great persecution of Protestants has ever taken place since the suppression of the Huguenots and Waldenses in 1685-6. So far Jurieu's expectation has proved correct; the Papacy has manifestly lost the persecuting power it formerly possessed; it cannot now burn Protestants as heretics, or subject them to wholesale massacre. The inquisition has been abolished, and the reign of Papal tyranny brought to an end.

This accomplishment of the predicted "death and resurrection" of the witnesses in several stages is not an exceptional event, but has its parallel in the method in which other analogous prophecies have been fulfilled.

Thus the Babylonish captivity had several commencing dates, and corresponding termini; so also the "seventy weeks" of Daniel; and the great period of "seven times," connected with the duration of the four Gentile empires. The same thing is observable in the fulfillment of the three and a-half "Times," assigned to the duration of the Papal power, as shown in the "Calendar of the Times of the Gentiles," appended to the work I published in 1878, on "The Approaching End of the Age." All these prophecies have been accomplished "according to that latitude which is agreeable and familiar unto divine prophecies, being of the nature of the author, with whom a thousand years are but as one day, and therefore not fulfilled punctually at once, but have springing and germanent accomplishment throughout many ages, though the height of fullness of them may refer to some one age."[101]

---

101 Bacon, "Advancement of Learning," Book II. I have shown in "The Approaching End of the Age," and "Light for the Last Days," that the prophetic periods "seven times," and" three and a-half times," are fulfilled in history on the lunar scale as well as on the solar. Thus the duration of the four kingdoms of Babylon, Persia, Greece and Rome, from the era of Nabonassar, B. c. 747, to the deposition of Romulus Augustulus, and end of the western Roman Empire in A. D 476, was exactly 1,260 lunar years (1,222 solar). The interval from the fall of the Western Empire in A. D. 470 to the completion of the English Revolution movement at the Peace of Ryswick in 1697, commemorated at the opening of St. Paul's on December 2d of that year, and the almost contemporaneous Peace of Carlowitz (January, 1699), by which Turkey lost Hungary, Transylvania, the Morea, Dalmatia, Podolia, the Ukraine and Azof — the first great gap made in the Ottoman Empire, since which their power has ceased to be formidable to Europe — was also 1,260 lunar years; while the interval from the era of Nabonassar to A.D. 1774, the year of the accession of Louis XIV — the initial date of the French Revolution — is "seven times," or 2,520 solar years.
The "death and resurrection" of the witnesses at the termination of 1,260 years of sackcloth clothed prophesying could not have taken place at any earlier date than the commencement of the Reformation of the sixteenth century, reckoning the period even in its briefer lunar form. From the Era of Martyrs, A.D. 284, the earliest commencing point of the period, twelve hundred and sixty lunar years extended to Luther's conversion in 1506-7. This was the date of spiritual quickening in the soul of the reformer. Luther entered the monastery of St. Augustine on the 17th of August, 1505, being then twenty-one years and nine months old. His conversion took place "in the second year of his abode in the convent (D'Aubigne,"History of Reformation," p. 63). "From that moment light sprang up in the heart of the young monk of Erfurth."
From the fall of Paganism at the victory of Constantine at the battle of Milvian Bridge, October 28th, 312, 1,260 solar years extend to the massacre of St. Bartholomew, in 1572. The Papal Era of Indictions began September 1, 312, and the massacre of St. Bartholomew began on the 24th of August, and continued during September, 1572; the interval being exactly 1,260 solar years. The period from the end of the Western Roman Empire, August 22, 476, to January 26, 1699, the date when the peace of Carlowitz was signed, is just 1,260 lunar years. This and the almost contemporaneous Peace of Ryswick marked, as we have said, the inauguration of a new era, in relation to Papal

3. The prophetic interpreters of the eighteenth century recognized the fact that the woe of the sixth trumpet had terminated at the Peace of Carlowitz.

This date of the termination of the sixth trumpet, or Turkish "woe," had long been foreseen. "The end of it," says Whiston, "was foretold by Mr. Brightman about a century ere the time came; and by Dr. Cressener some years before; and both from the same prophecy, and all came to pass accordingly."

The duration of the Turkish "woe" of the sixth trumpet is limited in the prophecy to "a day, a month, and a year"; which on the year-day scale of fulfillment is either 360+30+1=391 years, or 365 30+1=396 years.

Whiston, who was an astronomer, takes it as the latter. The Ottoman Emperors, whose device is the crescent, the sign of aggressive Islam, began their reign in Europe in the year 1299. Ertoghrul, the father of Othman, had previously led the advance of the Turks from the Upper Euphrates. In the Turkish annals, Osman, or Orthoman, is looked upon by the sultans as the founder of their dynasty; hence the name Osmanlis. "Names come from heaven," says the Koran; Ottoman's signified "bone breaker," and well have the Ottomans deserved the name they bear. "In 1301," says Sir Edward Creasy, "Othman encountered for the first time a regular Greek army which was led against him by Muzaros, the commander of the guards of the Byzantine Emperor. This important battle took place at Koyounhissar, in the vicinity of Nicomedia. Ottoman gained a complete victory, and in the successful campaign of the six following years he carried his arms as

---

and Mohammedan domination.

A. D. 284. 1,260 lunar years. A. D. 1506-7.

A. D. 312. 1,260 solar years. A. D. 1572.

B. C. 747. 1,260 lunar years. A. D. 476 (August).

A. D. 476. 1,260 lunar years. A. D. 1699 (January).

B. C. 747. 2,520 solar years. A. D. 1774.

far as the Black Sea, securing fortress after fortress, and hemming in the strong cities of Bousa, Nice and Nicomedia with a chain of fortified posts." Under the reign of Alaeddin the corps of the Janissaries was created, so long the scourge of Christendom. The formation of cavalry, arrayed under banners in thousands and in hundreds followed, and speedily effected the conquest of the Danubian provinces. The Byzantine Empire, fallen to the lowest degree of abasement, cankered with anarchy, idolatry and corruption, became a prey to the inroads of the Turks. The conquest of the Greeks succeeded, and the memorable capture of Constantinople. Under Mahomet II, "one of the most detestable manslayers recorded in history," the Ottomans, who had been rather an army than a nation, were organized under a code of laws. The number four was taken "as the basis of the hierarchical government, in honor of the four angels who support the Koran, and of the four Khalifites, disciples of Mahomet."[102] Wallachia, Bosnia, Karamania, the Crimea, Rhodes, Cyprus, Egypt and Hungary were successively conquered by the Turks, against whom the Crusades launched in vain their enormous armies.

The disastrous defeat of the Turks in the attempt to capture Vienna marked the approaching downfall of the Mohammedan Empire in Europe. Under the "Holy Alliance" — a league of the Emperor of Austria, the King of Poland, and the Republic of Vienna, a successful war was waged against the common foe. Prince Eugene of Savoy was placed by the Emperor at the head of the Austrian army. A series of victories over the Turks was concluded by the Peace of Carlowitz, in 1699, and with the loss at that time of Hungary, Transylvania, the Morea, Dalmatia, Podolia, the Ukraine and Azof, the Ottomans ceased to be the terror of Christendom.

Under the sixth trumpet the Euphratean horsemen are loosed to slay "the third part of men," or overthrow the Eastern Roman Empire, on account of the "worship of devils, and idols of gold, and silver, and brass, and stone, and wood," and the "murders, sorceries, fornications and thefts" practiced by its inhabitants. But

---

102 Menzies, "Turkey Old and New," p. 102.

the judgment is limited to the period symbolically described as "a day, a month, and a year," 391 or 396 years. Brightman, writing in the year 1615 says that the commencement of the Ottoman ravages "falleth in the yeare 1300 by one consent of all the historians." Measuring thence the 396 years of the Turkish woe he adds that the period "shall expire at last about the yeare 1696."[103]

In his book on the "Judgments of God" published in the year 1689, Cressener says, "The grounds that I rely upon to make me apprehend that the 'second woe' will be at an end within these few years are these. The second woe is the Turkish Empire, and its invasions upon the Roman Empire: and the time of the continuance of that woe is determined by the prophecy to a set number of years, which if we count from the rise of the Ottoman Empire, about the year 1300, will expire soon after the year 1690."

The fulfillment of these anticipations is remarkable. Whiston, writing after the event reckons the period of the woe as 396 years, and shows its accurate termination at the Peace of Carlowitz in 16pp.

4. During the eighteenth century, Cressener, Turretine, and Vitringa set forth clearer and stronger demonstrations of the Protestant interpretation of prophecy than had ever before been made.

A mighty change had taken place in England with reference to Protestantism, during the reigns of Charles II and James II. "The religion of Rome had become, not only fashionable at Court, but the religion covertly, or avowedly, of the reigning kings themselves. Moreover, the sufferings of the Episcopal clergy during the fifteen

---

103 Brightman, "Commentary on the Apocalypse," p. 327.

years' ascendancy of Cromwell and the Puritans had tended to make them look on the latter as their nearest and chiefest enemy; and by a consequence not unnatural, to regard Popery with less of disfavor, and sometimes even with the thought and desire for friendly approximation and union. This feeling could not but have its effect on the current view of the prophecies in Daniel and the Apocalypse, which had been hitherto by the Reformers alike German, Swiss, and English, applied undoubtingly to the Roman Popedom. By the celebrated dutch scholar and politician, Grotius, and by our english Dr. Hammond, a preterist view was adopted of the Apocalyptic Beast, and his great city Babylon, very like Alcasar's, referring it all to the old Pagan Roman City and Empire." Bossuet traces the parentage of this view to the Jesuit Alcasar. "Le savant Jesuite Louis d'Alcasar, a fait un grand commentaire sur l'Apocalypse, ou Grotius, a prit beaucoup de ces idees."[104]

Cressener writing in the year 1690 says "the present age is so generally prepossest with the interpretations of these learned men that it is necessary to remind (the approvers) that these are great novelties in the doctrine of the Church of England... It is manifest by the Homilies, approved of in our articles as the faith of our Church, that the charge of Babylon on the Church of Rome is the standing profession of the Church of England: and it continued to be the current judgment of all the best learned members of it till the end of the reign of James I."[105]

Cressener's book entitled "A Demonstration of the first principles of Protestant Applications of the Apocalypse," as Elliott says "well answers its title... In a series of connected propositions he incontrovertibly establishes, against Alcasar and Bellarmine, that the Apocalyptic Babylon is not Rome Pagan, as it existed under the

---

104 Preface sur l'Apoc. 11:13.
105 A reference in the preface of Cressener's Commentary is given to the third part of the sermon against Idolatry, in the Homilies, and the sixth part of the sermon against rebellion. Of other writers he specifies Bishop Jewel, p. 373. Bishop Abbot, Antichrist Demonstratis, Archbishop Whitgrift, Tract 8, p. 349; Bishop Andrews Tortura Torti. Bishop Bilson, p. 527. Bishop Morton: and Hooker's Treatise on Justification. Sec 10, 57.

old Pagan Emperors, nor Rome Paganized at the end of the world, as Ribera and Malvenda would have it to be; but Rome Papal, as existing from the sixth century. For he argues it is Rome idolatrous and antichristian as connected with the Beast or Roman Empire in its last form, and under its last head, which last head is the seventh head revived, after its deadly wound with the sword: with and under which the Beast exists through all the time of the witnesses; in other words from the date of the breaking-up of the old empire into ten kingdoms, until Christ's second coming to take the kingdom"

The eminent Swiss theologian Turretine had published five years before in his "Theological Institutes," his most powerful proof of the truth of the interpretation which identifies the Church of Rome with idolatrous Babylon, and the Pope of Rome with the "man of sin," or Antichrist; and five years after the appearance of Cressener's Commentary the learned Dutch Theologian Vitringa, in answer to Bossuet, sent forth his standard work on the Apocalypse, Anakrisis Apocalypsios, with its copious and masterly demonstration of the same conclusion. Vitringa's work is deservedly associated by Dean Alford with those of Elliott and Bishop Wordsworth on this subject, as especially worthy of consideration.[106]

The works of Vitringa (1705), Daubuz (1720), and Sir Isaac Newton (1733),[107] viewed from the standpoint of learning, represent the high water mark of Apocalyptic interpretation in the eighteenth century.

Vitringa was Theological Professor in the academy of Franeker, and "from that petty Dutch town, near the mouth of the Zuyder Zee, sent forth those masterly and learned works on Isaiah and the Apocalypse which have always been regarded as placing him on a high rank among Biblical expositors."[108] He illustrated each subject he handled by "a wide ranging erudition alike in secular and

---

106 Alford, "Commentary on Revelation 17."
107 Published six years after his death.
108 Elliott, *Horae* IV, pp. 506, 513.

ecclesiastical, Hebraic and Greek literature; often applying a just and acute criticism to show the untenableness of opinions, more or less plausible, adopted by expositors of note before him."

The large folio commentary on the Apocalypse by Daubuz is "redundant with multifarious research and learning." He was by birth a French Protestant; one of the many who had taken refuge in England after the Revocation of the edict of Nantes. While Vicar of Brotherton near Ferrybridge in Yorkshire he wrote his "Perpetual Commentary on the Apocalypse," of which an abridgment was subsequently published by a writer named Lancaster, which however fails to give any adequate idea of "the research and learning of the original."[109]

Sir Isaac Newton's "Observations on the Prophecies of Daniel and the Apocalypse" was the outcome of many years of study, his attention having been turned to the subject as early as 1691, while his work was not published till forty-two years later, in 1733. Of the exalted genius of Sir Isaac Newton, of his mathematical, scientific, historical and chronological researches, it is needless to speak. His skillful tracing of the most intricate subjects, accuracy of statement, clearness of demonstration, and far-reaching comprehensiveness of view have never been surpassed. In their acceptance of the historical interpretation of the Apocalypse, and in the general outline of their views, Vitringa, Daubuz, and Newton were in agreement. They held that history was the true interpreter of prophecy. They held that the seals, the trumpets, and the vials of the Apocalypse portrayed the course of Christian history from the time of St. John down to the consummation. They regarded the Church of Rome as Babylon the great. They interpreted the wild beast power in its three successive Apocalyptic forms,[110] under its crowned heads, under its crowned horns, and as bearing and then casting oiF the Harlot Babylon, as the Roman Empire, first as united under its earlier chiefly pagan rulers; then as divided under its Gothic kings;

---

109 Elliott, *Horae*, IV, p. 513.
110 Revelation 12, 13, 17.

and lastly as submitting to and then casting off and warring against the corrupt and guilty Church of Rome.

To them the martyrs of the Apocalypse were the Christian martyrs who had suffered under pagan and papal persecution, and its witnesses the witnessing saints of Mediaeval and Reformation days. Their interpretations involved the rejection alike of the Preterist view which confines the fulfillment of the Apocalypse to the Neronic period in the first century, and the futurist view which relegates its fulfillment to an imaginary still future period, some brief crisis at the close of the Christian dispensation, as erroneous, and contrary to the testimony of history, and of holy writ. As to unfulfilled prophecy, Sir Isaac Newton who avoided speculation both in science and theology, wisely said, "Let Time be the interpreter." How great is the contrast between such interpreters of prophecy and the futurists of modern times; the interpreters who have forgotten history, and have rudely broken with the traditional interpretation of the past eighteen centuries. The fact that Rome has lost her persecuting power, and that infidelity looms largely in these modern days as the opponent of Revelation, explains in some degree, though it does not justify the abandonment of the traditional interpretation of the Apocalypse. To forsake the sober historical interpretation of that sacred prophecy, and substitute for it invented and imaginary fulfillments to take place at some future time, is unworthy of a rational and reverent mind. Instead of speculating uncertainly, or even wildly, on what is to be, let the modern student of prophecy turn his attention to what has been, and what is. Let him soberly compare the indisputable facts of history with the mysterious predictions in God's holy word, for in such a comparison, if anywhere, the truth on the subject is to be found.

5. Jonathan Edwards, the greatest theologian of the eighteenth century, ably exhibited the meaning and place of Apocalyptic prophecy in the Divinely revealed history of Redemption.

Jonathan Edwards who is generally regarded as "the most distinguished metaphysician and divine of America," exercised his ministry in New England from 1722 to 1750, and died as President of Princeton College, New Jersey, on the 28th of March, 1758. In his "essay on the writings and genius of Jonathan Edwards" Henry Rogers says, "By the concurrent voice of all who have perused his writings, he is assigned one of the first, if not the only first place, amongst the masters of human reason. The character of his mind was essentially logical; the dominant attribute was reason. He possessed probably in a greater degree than was ever before vouchsafed to man the ratiocinative faculty, and in this respect, at least, he well deserves the emphatic admiration which Robert Hall expressed when he somewhat extravagantly said, that Edwards was 'the greatest of the sons of men.'"

Edwards' "History of Redemption" appeared in the form of sermons preached by him in 1739, and published in 1773, fifteen years after his death. The date of the publication was remarkable as that of the inauguration of the French revolutionary era, with its woes on Papal Christendom. It was the year of the suppression of the Jesuits by Clement XIV.

The appalling death of the corrupt and profligate Louis XV, took place the following year, on the 10th of May, 1774; and on the same day the accession of Louis XVI, and Marie Antoinette, subsequently dethroned and executed in the French Revolution.

The design of Edwards in his "History of Redemption" was "to show how the most remarkable events in all ages from the fall to the present times, recorded in sacred and profane history, were adapted to promote the work of redemption; and then to trace by the light of scripture prophecy how the same work should be yet further carried on even to the end of the world."

It was a work which singularly suited the sublime and comprehensive character of his mind. To him the history of the world with all its changes and revolutions exhibited one great divine work, ceaselessly carried on from age to age, for the redemption or recovery of mankind. The Bible was the book of redemption. Its histories and prophecies were histories and prophecies of redemption. In his view the story of redemption falls into three parts; the first, that of the antecedents of redemption; the second, that of the accomplishment of redemption; the third, that of the application of redemption. The first, that of history before Christ; the second, that of the history of Christ; the third, that of subsequent history. Seventeen hundred years had elapsed of this third period, up to Edwards' time, exhibiting the progress of Christ's kingdom, and the fulfillment of the prophecies regarding the Christian dispensation. Those prophecies included not only Old Testament predictions, as those in the book of Daniel, but also the prophecies of our Lord; of St. Paul, and of the Apostle John, the favored seer of New Testament times. The Apocalypse, as the gift of the ascended Saviour, and the last great Scripture prophecy, held a place of preeminence. In its wondrous visions the story of the conflicts and triumphs of the Christian Church was told in advance; and its practical power as illuminating the perilous path the church was called to tread, sustaining her faith, inspiring her courage, nerving her efforts, and brightening her hopes, was of inestimable value. The views of Edwards as to the meaning of the Apocalypse were in harmony with those of the historical interpreters of pre-reformation, and reformation times. They were the views of the Puritans, and of the Pilgrim Fathers. The early Christian settlers of New England held these views. The men and women whose moldering tombstones stand today in the pine shadowed cemetery of Northampton, where the dust of David Brainerd sleeps, professed them. To Edwards they were no doubtful speculations. The testimony of innumerable saints and martyrs consecrated them. The glorious work of the Reformation which was built upon these views, justified them. History sealed them with its unerring testimony. Such was their self-evidencing light that they afforded an unanswerable argument for the inspiration of Scripture, doubly needed in those days of scornful deistic unbelief, and threatened darker infidelity. To hold fast, and hold forth the Word of God under these circumstances, was evident duty, for "prophecy came not in old time by the will of man, but holy men of God spake as they were moved by the Holy Ghost." And so in his most scriptural and comprehensive "History of Redemption," Edwards interweaves, in simple unaffected language, the facts of Christian history, and the predictions of Apocalyptic prophecy, the prophecy reading as history in his luminous expositions.

The reader is referred to Edwards' "History of Redemption" in which, among others, the following themes are dealt with.

- I. The two ways in which the story of Redemption is narrated in Scripture, historic and prophetic.

  1. The terminal character of the Christian dispensation.
  2. The kingdom of heaven as the fifth and final kingdom of Daniel's prophecies.
  3. Rome, the persecuting Babylon of the Apocalypse.

- V. The warfare and casting down of the Satanically inspired great red dragon of the Apocalypse.

  1. Signification of the judgment of the sixth seal.
  2. Satan as the dragon casting out a flood of water to overwhelm the woman fleeing to the wilderness.
  3. Signification of the four first trumpets.
  4. The great apostasy and rise of Antichrist.

- X. Date, and gradual character, of the rise of Antichrist.

  1. The locust woe of the fifth trumpet.
  2. The horsemen woe of the sixth trumpet.
  3. The uninterrupted succession of gospel witnesses.

4. The persecuted woman hidden and sustained in the wilderness.
5. The company of pure and faithful Virgins.
6. The Harlot Babylon drunken with the blood of saints and martyrs.
7. The persecuting little Horn of Daniel 7.
8. The saints warred against and overcome by the revived wild beast of Revelation 13.
9. The glorious fulfillment of the prophecy that the gates of hell should not prevail against the church.
10. The marvelous fulfillment of the prophecy concerning Antichrist.
11. Strong encouragement to expect the fulfillment of prophecies which are as yet unaccomplished.

6. By various interpreters of prophecy in the eighteenth century it was clearly shown that the outpouring of the vials remained unfulfilled; and that their accomplishment as following speedily after the conclusion of the sixth trumpet was then at hand.

The futurity of the vials was intelligently maintained in the work we have referred to entitled, "a new Systeme of the Apocalypse, written by a Huguenot minister in the year 1685, and finished but two days before the Dragoones plundered him of all except this treatise."

While Jurieu asserted that the six first vials had already been poured out, and that the seventh had been pouring forth since Luther's Reformation, the anonymous author of the above remarkable treatise maintained in opposition to Jurieu that the seven vials belong to the period of the seventh trumpet, or "Third woe," since they are the "last plagues"; that the "second woe" (that of the sixth trumpet), is expressly said to terminate before the "Third woe" begins; that the death and resurrection of the witnesses precede the seventh trumpet, and the whole order of the vials; and that under the seven vials Popery and Mohammedanism, together with all opposition to the gospel, will be brought to an end.

In this view of the vials the exiled Huguenot minister followed Launay, or Launeus, who wrote a Commentary under the name of Jonas le Buy, Sr. de le Perie. Vitringa refers with approval to the view of Launeus that the seven vials answered to the seven compassings of Jericho on the seventh day. Whiston also definitely held that the seven vials were contained in, and are the evolution of the seventh trumpet; and that the sounding of the seventh trumpet was still future in his time, but would occur shortly.

Bishop Newton maintained that the vials were future; and so did Dr. Gill in his "Commentary on the Apocalypse." The expectation was general that the outpouring of these vials was at hand; an expectation strongly confirmed by the declaration occurring at the end of the "second woe," that "the third woe cometh quickly" (Revelation 11:14).

7. In his "Observations on the Prophecies of Daniel and the Apocalypse," Sir Isaac Newton expressed the view that only under the seventh trumpet would the time come for a perfect understanding of their mysteries.

"The event," he said, "will prove the Apocalypse; and the prophecy thus proved and understood will open the old prophets, and all together will make known the true religion, and establish it. For he that will understand the old prophets must begin with this; but the time is not yet come for understanding them perfectly, because the main revolution predicted in them is not yet come to pass. In the days of the voice of the seventh angel when he shall begin to sound the mystery of God shall be finished, as he hath declared to his servants the prophets, and then the kingdoms of this world shall become the kingdoms of our Lord, and His Christ, and He shall reign forever."[111] There is already so much of the prophecy fulfilled that as many as will take pains in this study may see sufficient instances of God's providence: but then the signal revolutions predicted by all the holy prophets will at once both turn men's eyes upon considering the predictions, and plainly interpret them. Till then we must content ourselves with interpreting what has been already fulfilled." He adds, "Amongst the interpreters of the last age, there is scarce one of note who hath not made some discovery worth knowing; and thence I seem to gather that God is about opening these mysteries."[112]

8. A century before the French Revolution Sir Isaac Newton anticipated that the prevalence of infidelity would in all probability be an instrument in the hand of God for the overthrow of the tyrannical supremacy of the Church of Rome.

"Sir Isaac Newton had," says Whiston, "a very sagacious conjecture, when he told Dr. Clarke, from whom I received it, that the overbearing tyranny and persecuting power of the antichristian party, which hath so long corrupted Christianity, and enslaved the Christian world, must be put a stop to, and broken to pieces, by the prevalence of infidelity for some time before Christianity could be restored;"which, adds Whiston, writing A.D. 1744, "seems to be the very means that is now working in Europe for the same good and great end of Providence."

---

111 Apocalypse 10:7; 11:15.
112 Newton, "Observations." pp. 252, 253.

9. In the year 1701, Fleming, in his work on "The Rise and Fall of Rome Papal," pointed out that the years 1794 and 1848 would be marked as crises in the overthrow of the Papal power.

Those dates were reached by reckoning the 1,260 years of Papal duration, first, from Justinian's Pope exalting Edict, in A.D. 533; and secondly, from the similar decree of Phocas in A.D. 606. In the latter case 1,260 calendar years extend to 1848; and 1,260 solar to 1866. The year 1793 did prove the most central in the French Revolution, that of the Reign of Terror; while 1848-9 and 1866-7 were marked years of crisis in the downfall of Papal sovereignty.

Dr. Gill, in his "Commentary," A.D. 1746, maintained that the date when the Bishop of Rome was made Universal Bishop, or Pope, should be considered that of the decree of the Emperor Phocas in the year 606; "if to this," he says, "we add 1,260, the expiration of his reign will fall in the year 1866, so that he may have upwards of a hundred and twenty years yet to continue; but of this we cannot be certain; however, the conjecture is not improbable."

Events proved this remarkable "conjecture" to be correct. The years 1866-1870 were those of the wars between Germany, Austria, and France, resulting in the overthrow by Protestant Germany of the two chief Catholic powers in Europe; they also witnessed the Antipapal Revolution in Spain, the Vatican Council in which the Pope was decreed to be infallible, the downfall of the Papal Temporal power, and the liberation and unification of Italy.

11. The astronomical confirmation of the year-day theory.

While the celebrated German theologian, John Albert Bengel who held the historic fulfillment of the Apocalypse, was working out his curious and fantastic theory as to the significance of the prophetic times, a Swiss astronomer, Lays de Cheseaux, little known to fame, discovered their astronomic value, viewed as periods measured on the year-day scale.

It seems strange to think of these two gifted men, so different in character and occupations, working unknown to one another, at the same time, on the same problem, that of the true measure of the prophetic times, and reaching conclusions so opposite; those of the theologian doomed to disappear as time demonstrated their falseness; and those of the man of science destined to endure as founded, not on speculation, but on indubitable chronological facts.

Assuming as a fundamental principle the position that the Beasts number 666 construed as years must equal the Beasts' numerical period forty-two months, Bengel shortened the prophetic "months" to suit his theory, and fitted them to historical events in an arbitrary manner, supposing the forty-two "months" to extend from A.D. 1143 to A.D. 1810.[113] A second similar period of 666-7 years extends from the fall of the Western Roman Empire, in A.D. 476 to A.D. 1143. That Bengel was bordering on a correct view as to a double, or even treble fulfillment of the number 666, viewed as years, in the rise, reign, and decline of the great antichristian power seems to me evident. His error was (1) in the location of the 666 years, and (2) in arbitrarily shortening the prophetic forty-two months to agreement with 666 years.

Bengel's mistake reminds us of the fact that there is commonly an element of truth in error; that our errors are often half truths; and therefore not to be wholly rejected, but rather corrected by the separation of their dross, or the addition of omitted elements.

A copy in manuscript of the work of Loys de Cheseaux lies before me. I had it made from the original in the library of the British Museum. It is entitled "Memoires Postumes de Monsieur

---

113 Bengel, "Gnomon of the New Testament," Vol. V, p. 347.

Jean Philippe Loys de Cheseaux, Correspondant de l'Academie Royale des Sciences de Paris, Associe etranger de celle de Gottingen; sur divers sujets d'astronomie, et de mathematiques, avec de nouvelles tables tres exactes des moyens movements du Soleil, et de la lune."

Its date is 1754. In the chapter on "the discoveries of M. de Cheseaux," in "The Approaching End of the Age," pp. 399-406, I have given an account of this remarkable work; and referred to it in "Light for the Last Days," p. 186; and in "Creation Centered in Christ," Vol. I, pp. 324-330, have given a translation of M. de Cheseaux' account of his discovery of the astronomic character of the 1,260 and 2,300 years prophetic periods. I have added in these books accounts of further discoveries made by myself in the same line of investigation, and have furnished in Vol. II of "Creation Centered in Christ" full tables of solar years and lunar months for 3,555 years, calculated to days, hours and minutes from the prophetic periods contained in the prophecies of Daniel and the Apocalypse of John, interpreted on the year-day scale.

These tables which extend to 627 pages contain 101,217 Solar and Lunar dates. Copies of the tables exist in all the principal astronomical observatories in the world, where they are in practical use, having been accepted by astronomers as correct and trustworthy. The confirmation afforded by these tables of the year-day theory is complete.

12. Towards the close of the interval between the English and French Revolutions Gibbon wrote his monumental work on the Decline and Fall of the Roman Empire.

It was in Rome, as he tells us, on the 15th day of October, 1754, as he sat "musing among the ruins of the Capitol, while the barefooted friars were singing vespers in the temple of Jupiter" that "the idea of writing the Decline and Fall of the City" first started in his mind. "My original plan," he says, "was circumscribed to the decay of the city, rather than of the empire." Gradually the idea widened until it embraced the larger subject. For twenty years this work occupied the labors of his life. During this period the vision of the slow decline and ultimate fall of the Western and Eastern Empires of Rome, the mightiest and most enduring political fabric the world has ever beheld, passed before his mind; the "various causes and progressive effects" connected with the vast and awful movement; "the artful policy of the Caesars who long maintained the name and image of a free republic; the disorder of military despotism; the rise, establishment and sects of Christianity; the foundation of Constantinople; the division of the monarchy; the invasion and settlement of the barbarians of Germany and Scythia; the institution of the civil law, the character and religion of Mahomet, the temporal sovereignty of the popes; the restoration and decay of the Empire of Charlemagne in the west; the crusades of the Latins in the East; the conquests of the Saracens and Turks; the ruin of the Greek Empire; the state and revolutions of Rome in the middle age." On that history he continued to labor throughout all the eventful years of the second half of the eighteenth century, from the 18th of October, 1764, to the 27th of June, 1787, when "between eleven o'clock and midnight" he wrote the last line of his great work in the summer-house of his garden at Lausanne, on the shores of Lake Leman. More than once have I visited that spot, and sought to realize the circumstances and the emotions of the historian on completing his gigantic task. He tells us that on that memorable night as he paced the walk beneath the "acacias, which commands a prospect of the country, the lake, and the mountains, the sky was serene, the silver orb of the moon reflected from the waters, and all nature was silent." One wonders what were then the thoughts of higher intelligencies in the invisible world as they beheld from their loftier standpoint, and with clearer vision, the wonderful retrospect of the long decline and tragic fall of that Empire which they knew to be destined to be the last of human monarchies before the advent of the Eternal Kingdom of God?

Had the work of the historian no interest in their eyes? Did they not recognize its value as giving for the first time a connected view of the course of events which prophecy had long before portrayed; and did they not note the fact that whereas the historian had brought down his narration only to the fall of the Eastern Empire in 1453, preceding the Reformation, and had but glanced at the latter event as almost foreign to his subject, the inspiring spirit of prophecy, overpassing these limits, had taken in the yet further stage in the history, that of the awful impending revolution which was destined to lay in ruins the still existing empire of Papal Rome; the ten kingdomed Western Empire under its Papal head, the proud possessor of temporal and spiritual sovereignty, and of a dominion over the minds of millions such as the Caesars in the centuries of their loftiest elevation had never attained. For what but this, and the brighter scenes which should succeed it, was the theme of the Apocalypse, that last prophetic revelation of the course of human history, conveyed by angelic intervention? What was its theme but the decline and fall of earth's greatest empire, and the rise and establishment of the Kingdom of God? What was its theme but that twofold conflict of Rome Pagan, and Rome Papal with the early martyrs and later witnesses of Christian history, and the long succession of judgments by which the might of the iron Empire was to be broken and brought to nought to make way for the kingdom of the Son of Man, and of the Saints of the Most High, whose kingdom is an everlasting kingdom, and of whose dominion there shall be no end?

Suspense, expectation, review, such were the characteristics of the period which immediately preceded the great revolution which changed the face of the continent and of the world. Interpreters of prophecy had clearly recognized the fact that the pouring out of the predicted vials of Divine wrath and judgment on the papal power was still a future event; and one which would speedily occur. The shortness of the interval between the second woe y whose termination had taken place at the Peace of Carlowitz, and the third woe, that of the seven vials, had been foretold in the words, "the second woe is past, and behold, the third woe cometh quickly."[114] No long interval, therefore, was to be expected before the outbreak of the coming judgment, and one interpreter of prophecy, the great Sir Isaac Newton, had anticipated the rise of infidelity as a power destined to overthrow the vast structure of tyranny and superstition which still encumbered and oppressed the world; and even then, in those closing decades of the century, his expectation seemed to be in process of accomplishment, for such a tide of infidelity had set in as never before had been witnessed, threatening to engulf all things in its destructive flood.

Yes, the time seemed short, and even calculable. Had not the prophetic word limited the duration of the Papal power to 1,260 years, and did not the rise of that power take place when the Emperors Justinian and Phocas conferred on the Bishop of Rome the title of Universal Bishop of the Christian Church, or Head of Christendom, the former in the year 533; the latter in the years 606 or 607; and calculating the period of 1,260 years from those dates, would it not terminate in the years 1793 and 1866-7?

And taking the period in its calendar form of 1,260 years, of 360 days each, would not the period as reckoned from the decree of Phocas terminate in the year 1848-9? So had Fleming pointed out in 1701, and a long series of prophetic interpreters from Pareus in 1643, to Gill in 1776 had similarly indicated these dates. But were these expectations destined to disappointment? Were they idle dreams? Was the papacy after all to continue for centuries to corner and were the foretold vials to be delayed to some still distant date? No; that could hardly be. The inspiring Spirit had declared the interval would be short between the end of the second, or Turkish woe, and the advent of the third woe; and the prophetic times seemed to fix a proximate boundary to the continuance of the dominion of the Papacy.

---

114 Revelation 11:14.

And so the students of the prophetic word watched the course of events, and waited for the fulfillment of the judgments on the Papal power foretold in the Book of God.

9. The French Revolution Stage

SUDDENLY the storm burst on France, and on the world. The elements of destruction had long been gathering. The skies were already dark. There was a restless heaving of the nations. The throes of a terrible convulsion were felt to be at hand. It came like the bursting of a volcano. Thrones and temples went down in the wreck. France was covered with carnage; Europe thrown into war; the world revolutionized.

Never was there anything more terribly majestic in human history — never will there be — till the last judgment day.

Viewed in relation to the past and to the future, to all that it destroyed, to all that it inaugurated, the French Revolution stands alone, without a parallel.

Viewed in itself as an explosion of infidelity, immorality, massacre and war, there is nothing in the range of the world's history to compare with it.

Before the tremendous forces which it unchained, thrones, temples and institutions which had stood forages were overturned as trees by a tempest, and swept away as straws by a whirlwind.

> "Give unto the Lord, O ye mighty,
> Give unto the Lord glory and strength:
> The voice of the Lord is upon the waters,
> The God of glory thundereth;
> The Lord is upon many waters.
> The voice of the Lord is powerful,

The voice of the Lord is full of majesty;
The voice of the Lord breaketh the cedars;
Yea, the Lord breaketh the cedars of Lebanon.
The Lord sitteth upon the flood;
Yea, the Lord sitteth King forever."

The history of the French Revolution is the history of Europe for more than a century; the history of the modern world.

Alison, who entitled his voluminous history of the French Revolution, "The history of Europe since the accession of Louis XVI," begins by declaring that "There is no period in the history of the world which can be compared with it, in point of interest and importance," and that "in no former age were events of such magnitude crowded together, or interests so momentous at issue between contending nations. From the flame which was kindled in Europe the whole world has been involved in conflagration, and a new era has dawned upon both hemispheres from the effects of its extension."

On the 10th of May, 1774, the corrupt and profligate Louis XV died. On the same day Louis XVI came to the throne of France; the Louis, who nineteen years later was executed on the scaffold.

At this point — the accession of Louis XVI in 1774 — Carlyle, like Alison, begins his history of the French Revolution, written as with a pen of fire.[115]

In France at this time, France of the many massacres of the Huguenots, "Faith had gone out, skepticism had come in."

"In such a France," says Carlyle, "as in a powder-tower, where fire unquenched and now unquenchable is smoking and smoldering all around, has Louis XV lain down to die;" a "portentous hour." His reign had been, to use the words of Alison,

---

115 It is worthy of remark that from the Nabonassar era, B. c. 747, the starting point of the kingdom of Babylon, "seven times" in solar measure, or 2,520 solar years, extend to the year 1774, the initial year of the French Revolution. See Calendar of the times of the Gentiles in the author's work on "The Approaching end of the Age."

"the most deplorable of French history. The whole frame of society seemed to be decomposed... all that we read in ancient historians, veiled in the decent obscurity of a learned language, of the orgies of ancient Babylon, was equaled, if not exceeded, by the nocturnal revels of the Regent Orleans, the Cardinal Dubois, and his other licentious associates... nor were manners improved on the accession of Louis XV, who fell under the government of successive mistresses each more dissolute and degraded than her predecessor, until at length decorum was so openly violated at court that even the corrupted circles of Versailles were scandalized by the undisguised profligacy which was exhibited."

On the doings of Madame Pompadour, Madame Du Barry, and the Parc aux Cerfs we drop the veil.

Embarrassment in the national finances, involving an annual deficit of seven and a half millions of money was a further feature of the period. The Church was "richer than Golconda," while the poor of the land groaned like wild animals under the load of oppression, and the lash of cruelty. The process of "stripping barer," which men "called governing," was coming to a crisis. The despised masses in their "clay houses, and garrets, and hutches," consisted as Carlyle reminds us, of "units," every one of which had "his own heart and sorrows;" a "miraculous man with a spark of the Divinity, what thou callest an immortal soul, in him." "Untaught, uncomforted, unfed, they pine stagnantly in thick obscuration, in squalid destitution and obstruction, — the lot of millions." Some rioted and were hanged the following days. "O ye poor naked wretches," says Carlyle, "and this, this is your inarticulate cry to heaven, as of a dumb tortured animal, crying from uttermost depths of pain and abasement. Do these azure skies, like a dead crystalline vault, only reverberate the echo of it on you? Respond to it only by hanging on the following days? — Not so: not forever. Ye are heard in heaven. And the answer too will come, — in a horror of great darkness, and shakings of the world, and a cup of trembling which all the nations shall drink."

Here then, was a kingdom full of oppressions, superstitions, immorality, and infidelity. The salt of the land had been cast out. The Huguenots had been expelled; the Jansenists crushed. The Huguenots had striven to produce a Reformation outside the Romish Church; the Jansenists a Reformation within it. Both had been defeated and suppressed with the utmost tyranny and cruelty. What histories theirs! Let the great library of Huguenot works in Paris, and the Jansenist works collected in New York[116] bear witness.

France had got rid of Huguenots and Jansenists; only the crimson blood stains of the tragedy remained. Pope and king had it all their own way. Side by side they stood, with their feet planted on the necks of a prostrate people* whose bodies and souls they had enslaved. But that people could still see, and feel, and think. They were millions in number, and began at last to turn under the heel of tyranny. Why should they be forever trodden on, they asked; by what right, human or divine were they, the people, sacrificed to crowned and mitred dignities? Had not the individual man his rights? The tyranny which trampled on them was consecrated by religion. What then was the religion worth? It claimed to be the only authorized, the only divine religion in the world, but it was an imposition. Let its mask be torn away. Thus did superstition make men infidels; while tyranny made them rebels. Infidel revolutionists know no restraint. As a force they can only destroy.[117]

---

116 Private Library collected by Dr. Williams.
117 The contrast between the French and the English Revolutions, should here be noted, that the English Revolution sprang from faiths the French Revolution from infidelity. In England, m Switzerland, in America, great democratic movements have arisen, which have prospered, for their foundations were laid on the rock of Divine truth and righteousness. The fear of God is the beginning of wisdom. Men must learn to obey God before they can govern. "He that ruleth over men must be just, ruling in the fear of God." The Puritans of England, and of New England, were such; they were men who feared God, and feared none beside. But these French infidels, who turned all things sacred into mockery;, who knew no self-restraint; who respected nothing in heaven or on earth j how could they wisely and justly govern their fellow men; how could they regenerate the world? All they could do was to destroy the corrupt government, and dominant superstition of the age, and they did it.

First then, in the list of the destructive agencies which produced the French Revolution, should be placed infidelity. A revolution in the inner realm of mind preceded the revolution in the outer social realm.

Marvelous in their adaptation to its accomplishment were the instruments of this work. Of these Montesquieu, Voltaire and Rousseau were among the chief. Montesquieu was born on the 18th of January, 1689, the year of the completion of the English Revolution; Voltaire on the 20th of February, 1694; Rousseau on the 28th of June, 1712.

In the profound quiet of his retreat Montesquieu, who was a philosopher, compared the leading governments of the world, and analyzed their abstract rights, in works which have become famous, and produced an immense and lasting influence on public opinion in France. His greatest work, "*L'Esprit des Lois*" undermined the existing government without directly attacking it. It destroyed its foundations in the minds of men. Rousseau's numerous and eloquent works, especially his "*L'inegalité parmi les hommes*" and "*Contrat social*" poured light on the injustice of the existing order of things; while Voltaire's satires held up all that had been reverenced to contempt and mockery. For the better part of a century he wrote, and wrote; sending forth a stream of essays, tragedies, comedies, Actions, histories, and poems in Seventy Volumes, which from first to last were "one continued sneer at all that men do hold, and all they ought to hold sacred." Didero and D'Alembert in their infidel Encyclopedic, attacked both faith and superstition in the name of science. A host of writers of similar principles sprang up, and through the popular press poured forth a flood of infidelity. Under its influence the old bonds were loosened; the old landmarks swept away.

Writing from Paris, December 25, 1753, Lord Chesterfield said, "All the symptoms I have ever met with in history, previous to great changes and revolutions in government, now exist, and daily increase in France." There was "a monarchy all but absolute, a feudal nobility with oppressive powers, and invidious privileges; a burdensome official aristocracy, with its own privileges and exemptions; an exacting royal administration; injurious monopolies; and an oppressed and suffering people without political rights."

There was a Church which had crushed the Huguenots and Jansenists; a society utterly corrupt in morals, and literature propagating infidelity, and sowing the seeds of revolution.

Now was seen the marvelous spectacle of a nation which had silenced her noble Protestant teachers, had cast out the salt which might have preserved her from corruption; a Church which had triumphed over truth, and trampled religion beneath her feet; and a monarchy which denied rights and liberty to its subjects, "confronted by a new clan of thinkers;" hostile alike to state and religion; men who were the direct product of the system they opposed; clever, satirical, resolute, unsparing, bold in their assaults; followed, flattered, worshipped by the multitude; idolized even by those whom they had taught to dethrone the vain idols their fathers had adored.

Following the change of public thought, came a change of action. With the pressure of financial distress the Parliament of Paris demanded "that the states-general should be assembled to devise means for the relief of the country." Nearly two hundred years had elapsed since this "disused and almost forgotten body" had been called into existence. The king, "distracted by divided counsels, but leaning to a liberal policy" consented to "this hazardous venture, and convoked the states-general." The *tiers-etat* were to be double the number of the other orders; by this arrangement power was at once transferred to the lower classes, which up to that time, had been without political influence.

The famous Mirabeau cast in his lot with the commons; a "body intent upon reforms, and a steady foe to privileges. Its mission was to satisfy the complaints of the people; and it was burning to resist the pretensions of the nobles and the Church." "The two higher orders sat apart in their respective churches, leaving the Commons as the largest body in possession of the great hall... the Commons insisted that the verification of the powers of the three estates should be conducted by the entire body, and awaited the coming of the two other orders... after five weeks of fruitless negotiations the Commons took a bolder step and declared themselves the National Assembly. It was an act of usurpation which marked the commencement of the Revolution."

They followed up the act by "decrees designed to secure their own authority. The king, influenced by the court, closed the doors of the hall against the assembly." "The Commons at once adjourned to the racket court where they swore not to separate until they had given a constitution to France." On the racket court being closed against them, they adjourned to the Church of St. Louis. Threatened and commanded to separate they refused to move.

"This defiance of the king's authority was submitted to by the court, and from that day power passed into the hands of the Assembly."[118] In the struggle which followed, two popular parties strove for the ascendancy, the Girondists and the Jacobins, The former, the representatives of the people in the Gironde, near Bordeaux, endeavored to obtain "the sovereignty of right over force; of intelligence over prejudices; of people over governments; they sought equality; the substitution of reason for authority; the reign of the people; they called the principles they proclaimed"a gospel of social rights, a charter of humanity." Lamartine has written their history in three eloquent volumes. The Jacobins, so called from the convent of Jacobins in which the deputies from Brittany first met, under the name of the "Club Breton," were of a different character. Distinguished by the violence of their proceedings, prepared for the commission of every crime, they attracted "the most audacious and able of the democratic party."

"Fifteen hundred members usually attended their meetings; a few lamps only lighted the vast extent of the room; the members

118 Sir Erskine May, "Democracy in Europe," Vol. II, pp. 135-139.

appeared for the most part in shabby attire, and the galleries were filled with the lowest of the populace. In this den of darkness were prepared the bloody lists of proscription and massacre; the meetings were opened with revolutionary songs, and shouts of applause followed each addition to the list of murder, each account of its perpetration by the affiliated societies. Never was a man of honor — seldom a man of virtue — admitted within this society; it had an innate horror of every one who was not attached to its fortunes by the hellish bond of committed wickedness. A robber, an assassin, was certain of admission — as certain as the victim of their violence was of rejection. The well known question put to the entrant: —"What have you done to be hanged if the ancient regime is restored?" exemplifies at once the tie which held together its members. The secret sense of deserved punishment constituted the bond of their unholy alliance. Their place of meeting was adorned with anarchical symbols, tricolor flags, and busts of the leading revolutionists of former times. Long before the death of Louis XVI, two portraits, adorned with garlands, of Jacques Clement and Ravaillac, were hung on the walls: immediately below was the date of the murder which each had committed, with the words, "He was fortunate, he killed a king."

The leaders of this party were Danton, Marat, Robespierre, Billaud Varennes, St. Just, and Collot d'Herbois — names destined to acquire an execrable celebrity in French annals, whose deeds will never be forgotten so long as the voice of conscience is heard in the human heart. Into the hands of these wretches came the government of France.

Among them, Danton gained the ascendancy. "Nature seemed to have expressly 'created him for the terrible part which he played in the Revolution... His figure was colossal, his health unbroken, his strength extraordinary; a countenance ravaged by the smallpox, with small eyes, thick lips, and a libertine look, but a lofty commanding forehead at once fascinated and terrified the beholder. A commanding air, dauntless intrepidity, and a voice of thunder fitted him to be what Mirabeau described as "a huge blast bellows to inflame the popular passions."[119]

"Marat was the worst of this band. Nature had impressed the atrocity of his character on his countenance, hideous features, the expression of a demon, revolted all who approached him; ... for more than three years his writings incessantly stimulated the people to cruelty; ... so complete a fanatic had he become in this respect that he scrupled not to recommend torture to the captives, burning at the stake, and branding with red hot iron, as a suitable means of satisfying the public indignation... But all the leaders of the Jacobins sink into insignificance before their ruler and despot, Robespierre... a sanguinary bigot, a merciless fanatic, with talents of the highest order, his reasoning powerful, his intellect cool, his sagacity great, his perseverance unconquerable. He adhered steadily to principle. He maintained that the multitude can do no wrong." "He strove to destroy all the higher classes of society," and "wellnigh annihilated the whole intellect and virtue of France... Napoleon did not prosecute savage warfare for the external glory of the republic with more vigor and perseverance than Robespierre did internal massacre to exterminate its domestic enemies, and the extraordinary success and long-continued power of both proved that each had rightly judged the popular mind in his own day — that they both marched, as Napoleon said, "with the opinion of five millions of men."[120] He had great designs in view in the reconstruction of the social edifice after three hundred thousand heads had fallen. His visions were of an innocent republic, with equal fortunes, arising out of the sea of blood. He never abandoned a principle, but he never saved a friend. It was hard to say whether his supporters or his enemies fell fastest beneath the scythe of his ambition.

Our limits forbid us to give any full account of the tragic events of the Revolution, which beginning with the convocation of the

---

119 Alison, "History of Europe from the commencement of the French Revolution,"II, p. 13.
120 Alison, II, p. 19.

states-general in 1789, and the establishment of a Republic in 1793, advanced to the strife between the Girondists and Jacobins, and after the fall of the former, entered on the era of the Reign of Terror, the period of general massacre; and culminated in the rise of military despotism, and all the terrible wars of Napoleon. History tells us "how the infidel democracy suddenly uprose in its might, destroyed the Bastille, issued its declaration of the rights of man; assaulted the king and queen by night, at Versailles, and murdering some of their body-guard, forced them to proceed as prisoners to Paris, the bloody heads carried on pikes before the royal carriage. How the people confiscated all the vast revenues of the Church, all the domains of the crown, and all the estates of refugee nobles, for the use of the State; subjected to themselves all ecclesiastical, civil, and judicial power throughout the country; murdered the royal guard, and some five thousand leading royalists; dethroned, imprisoned, tried, condemned, and murdered the king, and then the queen; declared war against all kings, and sympathy with all Revolutionists everywhere; how the"reign of terror" witnessed the slaughter of one million and twenty-two thousand persons, of all ranks and ages, and of both sexes, till the streets of Paris ran with blood, and the guillotines could not overtake their work. How thousands were mowed down by grapeshot fusillades; drowned in "*noyades*," where in loaded vessels, hundreds of victims were purposely sunk in the rivers; roasted alive in heated ovens, or tortured to death by other infernal cruelties. How Christianity was publicly renounced, and a prostitute enthroned as "goddess of reason" at Notre Dame, and worshipped by the National Convention, and by the mob of Paris, with the wildest orgies of licentiousness (morality as well as mercy having perished with religion); how the most horrid mockery of the solemn rites of Christianity was publicly enacted, an ass being made to drink the sacramental wine; how the Sabbath itself was abolished, and the decade substituted for the week; and how hundreds and thousands of priests were massacred or driven into exile, and the churches and cathedrals turned into stables and barracks. Taken as a whole, the French Revolution was a convulsion, in which the angry passions of men, set free from all restraint, manifested themselves with a force and fury unprecedented in the history of the world, against monarchical, aristocratic, ecclesiastical, and religious institutions."[121]

Five features in this marvelous course of events demand recognition.

[1.] The complete overthrow of the corrupt and tyrannical government of France.

On the 21st of January, 1793, between the Gardens of the Tuileries and the Champs Elysees, surrounded by an innumerable multitude as far as the eye could reach, standing on the scaffold, his hands bound, his words lost in the roar of the drums being beaten, Louis XVI, King of France, laid his head upon the block, and the descending axe terminated his existence. With the execution of the king, and the murder of the queen, fell the government of France, laden with the crimes of centuries of oppression, corruption, and cruelty.

[2.] The complete overthrow of the Roman Catholic Church in France.

On the 23rd of November, 1793, "atheism in France reached its extreme point, by a decree of the municipality ordering the immediate closing of all the churches, and placing the whole priests under surveillance." The services of religion were now universally abandoned. The pulpits were deserted throughout all the revolutionized districts; baptism ceased; the burial service was no longer heard; the sick received no communion; the dying no consolation. A heavier anathema than that of papal power pressed upon the peopled realm of France — the anathema of heaven, inflicted by the madness of her own inhabitants. The village bells were silent; Sunday was obliterated. Infancy entered the world without a blessing; age left it without a hope. In lieu of the services of the Church, the licentious fêtes of the new system were performed by the most abandoned females; it appeared as if the

---

121 Author's work, "The Approaching end of the Age," pp. 358, 359.

Christian worship had been succeeded by the orgies of the Babylonian priest, or the grossness of the Hindu theocracy. On every tenth day a revolutionary leader ascended the pulpit, and preached atheism to the bewildered audience; Marat was universally deified; and even the instruments of death were sanctified by the name of the "Holy Guillotine." Throughout the whole of France the Roman Catholic Churches were desecrated; Notre Dame in Paris was converted into the "Temple of Reason": 24,000 priests were massacred, and 40,000 Churches "turned into stables."[122]

[3.] The complete overthrow of the Papacy in Italy.

On the invasion of Italy by the French Revolutionists, the government of the Pope was overthrown. Berthier "marched upon Rome, set up a Roman republic, and laid hands upon the Pope. The sovereign pontiff was borne away to the camp of the infidels... from prison to prison, and finally, carried captive into France. Here he breathed his last at Valence, in the land where his priests had been slain, where his power was broken, and his name and office were a mockery and byword, and in the keeping of the rude soldiers of the unbelieving commonwealth, which had for ten years held to his lips a cup of such manifold and exceeding bitterness."[123]

The spoliation of Rome accompanied the overthrow of the Papacy. "Long before the Pope had sunk under the persecution of his oppressors, Rome had experienced the bitter fruits of republican fraternization. Immediately after the entry of the French troops, commenced the regular and systematic pillage of the city. Not only the churches and the convents, but the palaces of the cardinals and of the nobility, were laid waste. The agents of the Directory, insatiable in the pursuit of plunder, and merciless in the means of exacting it, ransacked every quarter within its walls, seized the most valuable works of art, and stripped the Eternal City of those treasures which had survived the Gothic fire, and escaped the rapacious hands of the Spanish soldiers in the reign of Charles V.

122 Alison, II, p. 22.
123 Gill, "Papal Drama," Book X.

The bloodshed was much less, but the spoil collected incomparably greater, than at the disastrous sack which followed the storm of the city, and death of the Constable Bourbon. Almost all the great works of art which have since that time been collected throughout Europe, were then scattered abroad. The spoliation exceeded all that the Goths or Vandals had effected. Not only the palaces of the Vatican and the Monte Cavallo, and the chief nobility of Rome, but those of Castel Gandolfo, on the margin of the Alban Lake, of Terracina, the Villa Albani, and others in the environs of Rome, were plundered of every article of value which they possessed. The whole sacerdotal habits of the Pope and cardinals were burned, in order to collect from the flames the gold with which they were adorned. The Vatican was stripped to its naked walls; the immortal frescoes of Raphael and Michael Angelo, which could not be removed, alone remaining in solitary beauty amidst the general desolation. A contribution of four millions of francs in money, two millions in provisions, and three thousand horses, was imposed upon a city already exhausted by the enormous exactions it had previously undergone. Under the directions of the infamous commissionary Haller, the domestic library, museum, furniture, jewels, and even the private clothes of the Pope were sold. Nor did the palaces of the Roman nobility escape devastation. The noble galleries of the Cardinal Braschi, and the Cardinal York, the last relic of the Stuart Line, underwent the same fate. Others, as those of the Chigi, Borghese, and Doria palaces, were rescued from destruction only by enormous ransoms. Everything of value that the treaty of Tolentine had left in Rome became the prey of republican cupidity; and the very name of freedom soon became odious from the sordid and infamous crimes which were committed under its shelter.

"Nor was the oppression of the French confined to the plunder of palaces and churches. Eight cardinals were arrested, and sent to Civita Castellana; while enormous contributions were levied on the Papal territory, and brought home the bitterness of conquest to every poor man's door. At the same time, the ample territorial possessions of the Church and the monasteries were confiscated, and declared national property; a measure which, by drying up at once the whole resources of the affluent classes, precipitated into the extreme of misery the numerous poor, who were maintained by their expenditure, or fed by their bounty. All the respectable citizens and clergy were in fetters; and a base and despicable faction alone, among whom, to their disgrace be it told, were found fourteen cardinals, followed in the train of their oppressors; and at a public festival, returned thanks to God for the miseries they had brought upon their country."[124]

[4.] The Wholesale Revolutionary Massacres in Paris, and throughout France.

The great massacre of St. Bartholomew was cast into the shade by "the St. Bartholomew of five years," as the massacre of the Revolution has been called. More than 30,000 were massacred in the city of Lyons; at Nantes, 27,000; in Paris, 150,000; in La Vendee, 300,000. In all France about two millions of persons were massacred, of whom 250,000 were women; 230,000 children; and 24,000 priests. The massacre of the priests "was but the prelude to a general massacre in the Abbaye, the horrors of which exceeded anything hitherto witnessed in the Revolution. Wearied at length with the labor of hewing down so many victims, they fell upon the plan of instituting a mock tribunal, with the murderer Maillard for its president, in which, after going through the form of a trial, they turned them out to be massacred by the people who thronged the prison doors, loudly clamoring for their share in the work of extermination. The cries of these victims, who were led out to be hewn to pieces by the multitude, first drew the attention of the prisoners in the cells to the fate which awaited themselves; seized separately and dragged before an inexorable tribunal, they were speedily given over to the vengeance of the populace. Reding was one of the first to be selected. The pain of his broken limbs extorted cries even from that intrepid Swiss soldier, as he was dragged along from his cell to the hall of trial; and one of the

---

124 Alison, IV, pp. 132, 133.

assassins, more merciful than the rest, drew his sword across his throat, so that he perished before reaching the judges. His dead body was thrown out to the assassins. The forms of justice were prostituted to the most inhuman massacre. Torn from their dungeons, the prisoners were hurried before a tribunal, where the president Maillard sat by torchlight with a drawn sabre before him, and his robes drenched with blood; officials with drawn swords, and shirts stained with gore, surrounded the chair. A few minutes, often a few seconds, disposed of the fate of each individual. Dragged from the pretended judgment-hall, they were turned out to the populace, who thronged round the doors armed with sabres, panting for slaughter, and with loud cries, demanding a quicker supply of victims. No executioners were required; the people dispatched the condemned with their own hands, and sometimes enjoyed the savage pleasure of beholding them run a considerable distance before they expired. Immured in the upper chambers of the building, the other prisoners endured the agony of witnessing the prolonged sufferings of their comrades; a dreadful thirst added to their tortures, and the inhuman jailers refused even a draught of water to their earnest entreaties. Some had the presence of mind to observe in what attitude death soonest relieved the victims, and resolved when their hour arrived, to keep their hands down, lest, by warding off the strokes, they should prolong their agonies."[125]

"Similar tragedies took place at the same time in all the other jails of Paris, and in the religious houses, which were filled with victims."[126]

This was the era of the guillotine. Fixed first on the Place St. Antoine, and soon after at the Barriere du Trone, in the Faubourg St. Antoine, that terrible instrument of decapitation was in daily and ceaseless use.

In its victims' first the nobles and ecclesiastics only were included: by degrees the whole landed proprietors were

---

125 Alison, II, p. 71.
126 Ibid., II, p. 73.

reached; but now the work of destruction seemed to be approaching every class above the lowest. On the lists of the Revolutionary Tribunal, in the latter days of the Reign of Terror, are to be found tailors, shoemakers, hairdressers, butchers, farmers, mechanics, and workmen, accused of anti-revolutionary principles. From the loth of June to the 17th of July, that court had sentenced twelve hundred and eighty-five persons to death. The people felt pity for these proscriptions, not only from their frequency, but their near approach to themselves. Their reason was at length awakened by the revolutionary fever having exhausted itself; humanity began to react against the ceaseless effusion of human blood, after all their enemies had been destroyed. It was impossible that pity should not at length be awakened in the breast of the spectators, for never had such scenes of woe been exhibited to the public gaze. 'The funeral cars,' says the republican historian, Lamartine, 'often held together the husband, wife, and all their children. Their imploring visages, which mutually regarded each other with the tender expression of a last look, the heads of daughters falling on the knees of their mothers, of wives on the shoulders of their husbands, the pressure of heart against heart, both of which were so soon to cease to beat — now gray hairs and auburn locks cut by the same scissors, now wrinkled heads and charming visages falling under the same axe; the slow march of the cortege, the monotonous rolling of the wheels, the hedge of sabres around the procession, the stifled sobs of the victims, the hisses of the populace, the cries of the furies of the guillotine — all impressed a mournful character on these assassinations, which seemed to be provided for no other purpose but to serve for the pastime of the people.'"[127]

"At Lyons the scaffold opposite the Hotel de Ville, where the trials were conducted, was kept in ceaseless

---

127 Alison, III, p. 91.

employment. Around its bloody foundations large
quantities of water were daily poured; but they were
inadequate to wash away the ensanguined stains, or remove
the fetid odor. So noxious did they become, that
Dorfeuille, the functionary entrusted with the executions,
was obliged to remove it to another situation; where it was
placed directly above an open sewer, ten feet deep, which
bore the gore away to the Rhone. The washerwomen there
were obliged to change their station from the quantity of
blood which became mingled with its waters. At length
when the executions had risen to thirty or forty a day, the
guillotine was placed in the middle of the bridge at Morand
in the center of the Rhone, into which the stream of blood
at once fell, and into which the headless trunks and severed
heads were precipitated. Yet even this terrible slaughter,
which went on without intermission for three months,
appeared insufficient to the Jacobins."[128]

"At Nantes a Revolutionary Tribunal was formed under
the direction of Carrier, and it soon outstripped even the
rapid progress in atrocity of Danton and Robespierre.
'Their principle,' says the Republican historian, 'was, that
it was necessary to destroy, *en masse*, all the prisoners. At
their command was formed a corps called the Legion of
Marat, composed of the most determined and bloodthirsty
of the Revolutionists, the members of which were entitled,
of their own authority, to incarcerate any person whom
they chose. The number of their prisoners was soon
between three and four thousand, and they divided among
themselves all their property. Whenever a fresh supply of
captives was wanted, the alarm was spread of a counter
revolution, the *generale* beat, the cannon planted; and this
was immediately followed by innumerable arrests. Nor
were they long in disposing of the captives. The miserable
wretches were either slain with poniards in the prisons, or

---

128 Ibid., Vol. II, p. 339.

carried out in a vessel and drowned by wholesale in the
Loire. On one occasion, a hundred "fanatical priests," as
they were termed, were taken out together, stripped of
their clothes, and precipitated into the waves. The same
vessel served for many of these *noyades*; and the horror
expressed by many of the citizens for that mode of
execution, formed the ground for fresh arrests and
increased murders. Women big with child, children eight,
nine and ten years of age, were thrown together into the
stream, on the banks of which, men armed with sabres
were placed to cut them down, if the waves should throw
them undrowned on the shore. The citizens, with loud
shrieks, implored the lives of the little innocents, and
numbers offered to adopt them as their own; but, though a
few were granted to their urgent entreaty, the greater part
were doomed to destruction. Thus were consigned to the
grave whole generations at once — the ornament of the
present, the hope of the future.' So immense were the
numbers of those who were cut off by the guillotine, or
moved down by fusillades, that three hundred men were
occupied for six weeks, in covering with earth the vast
multitude of corpses that filled the trenches which had
been cut in the Place of the Department at Nantes, to
receive the dead bodies. Ten thousand died of disease,
pestilence, and horror, in the prisons of that department
alone."[129]

"The *noyades* at Nantes alone amounted to twenty-five, on
each of which occasions from eighty to a hundred and fifty
persons perished; and such was the quantity of corpses
accumulated in the Loire, that the water of that river was
infected so as to render a public ordinance necessary,
forbidding the use of it by the inhabitants. No less than
eighty thousand perished in these ways, or by the
guillotine, in Nantes alone, during the administration of

---

129 Alison, Vol. II, pp. 279, 280.

Carrier; and the mariners, when they heaved the anchors, frequently brought up boats charged with corpses. Birds of prey flocked to the shores, and fed on human flesh; while the very fish became so poisonous as to induce an order of the municipality of Nantes, prohibiting them to be taken by the fishermen."[130]

"From Saumur to Nantes, a distance of sixty miles, the Loire was for several weeks red with human blood; the ensanguined stream, far at sea, divided the blue waves of the deep. The multitude of corpses it bore to the ocean was so prodigious that the adjacent coast was strewed with them; and a violent west wind and high tide having brought part of them back to Nantes, followed by a train of sharks and marine animals of prey, attracted by so prodigious an accumulation of human bodies, they were thrown ashore in vast numbers. Fifteen thousand persons perished there under the hands of the executioner, or of diseases in prison, in one month: the total victims of the Reign of Terror at that place exceeded thirty thousand."[131]

[5.] The overthrow of Roman Catholic governments, and enormous destruction of life connected with the wars of Napoleon.

The reign of the guillotine was followed by the reign of the sword. With the rise of Napoleon, the French Revolution took a new character, and became the scourge of Europe. The armies of France were now led on an unparalleled career of conquest by that man who was the most "gigantic manifestation of mental power and despotic will" the world had ever seen. Arrogant, unscrupulous, selfish, remorseless, ambitious, self-reliant, with indomitable vigor, unwearying energy, marvelous military genius, surpassing administrative ability, uniting a lofty comprehensive intellect with utter disregard for moral considerations, Napoleon

---

130 Ibid, Vol. II, pp. 280, 281.
131 Alison, Vol. II, p. 281.

sacrificed the lives of millions, overturned the thrones of Europe, revived the Empire of Charlemagne, and strove to obtain the monarchy of the world.

His career as a ruler and conqueror consists of two chief periods: the first, that of his seizure of the reins of power as First Consul, followed by his Italian, German, Egyptian, and Syrian campaigns; secondly, that commencing with his assumption of Imperial power in 1804, and extending to his fall in 1815, embracing the campaigns of Austerlitz, Jena, and Friedland; the long Peninsular war, the later wars in Italy, leading to the extinction of Papal authority; his struggle with Austria, his disastrous invasion of Russia; his last fatal war with Germany, and his final defeat by the Allied Powers at the Battle of Waterloo.

Career of Napoleon

Born on the 15th of August, 1769, Napoleon was five years old at the accession of Louis XVI in 1774. After a military training, Napoleon, as an officer of Artillery, began his career by dispersing the National Guard of 30,000 men in Paris with grapeshot in October, 1795.

In 1796 he was sent to Italy by the French Directory, where he took Piedmont, Milan and Lombardy, quartering his troops on the unfortunate inhabitants, who were forced to pay the expenses of the war, including 20,000,000 francs exacted from Lombardy. On Pavia resisting, he took the town by storm, and abandoned it to plunder by his troops. The Duke of Parma was compelled to pay 1,500,000 francs, and the Duke of Modena 6,000, 000; and 2,000,000 more in provisions, cattle, etc. He took Leghorn, where the merchants paid 5,000,000 for ransom, and 50,000,000 francs was forwarded from these wars of plunder in North Italy to the French Directory. Milan having been evacuated by the Austrians, Napoleon seized from the Pope Bologna and Ferrara, and compelled Pius VI to pay 15,000,000 livres in gold, 6,000,000 more in goods, and to permit the spoliation of works of art and manuscripts which were sent to Paris. On Austria preparing a fresh army for the recovery of Lombardy of fifty to sixty thousand men, Napoleon in six weeks destroyed it in detail. A third army was sent into Italy by Austria, the same year (1796), of 50,000 men, which Napoleon succeeded in dividing and conquering. He then regulated internal affairs in North Italy, forming a republic. The Pope, after paying 5,000,000 livres, stopped payment, while Austria, reinforcing her army by 50,000 men, continued the struggle, but was defeated with immense loss. The condition of North Italy was miserable in the extreme, both armies treating the nation as enemies. On all hands the people were plundered, and when they resisted, killed.

Secure from the Austrians, Napoleon turned against the Pope, and invaded Ancona, the Marches, and Tolentina. Pius VI sued for peace, and was forced to pay 15,000,000 livres within a month, and as much more in two months. He was permitted to remain in Rome a little longer.

The Austrians now raised a new army, chiefly recruits. General Bernadotte, with 20,000 men from the Rhine Provinces, reinforced Napoleon, who conquered the Austrians, and advanced through the Tyrol and Upper Styria to within eight days' march of Vienna. The Austrian Emperor sued for peace, and ceded to Napoleon the Austrian Netherlands and Lombardy, who promised him, by a secret treaty Venice, in part compensation. The Doge resigned. Thus ended the republic of Venice after fourteen centuries of existence, and with it the naval power of Italy became extinct. Genoa paid 4,000,000 livres to the Directory in Paris, and had her constitution remodelled to a republic. All Italy, excepting Naples, was now in subjection to France.

In December, 1797, Napoleon, returning from his wars in Italy, was received with acclamation in Paris.

1798. In pursuance of his plan of world conquest, Napoleon made an expedition to Egypt. Malta surrendered, and the spoliation of its churches took place. On March 29th, 5,000

Mamelukes were defeated by Napoleon at Alexandria. The French fleet was destroyed by Nelson. The Sultan declared war against France. In Cairo there was a terrible massacre of Mussulmans by French troops. With 10,000 men Napoleon crossed the desert, by Suez, to Palestine. Jaffa was given up to plunder, with frightful horrors, and the Turkish prisoners were massacred wholesale. The defense of Acre followed. After fifty-four days from opening the trenches, Napoleon was compelled to raise the siege, and return to Egypt. He reached Cairo 14th June.

1799. "With 10,000 men on the banks of the Euphrates," said Napoleon, "I might have gone to Constantinople or to India, and have changed the face of the world. I should have founded an Empire in the East, and the world would have run a different course."

Towards the end of July, the Turkish fleet landed 18,000 men at Aboukir, near Alexandria. Napoleon attacked them, and 10,000 Turks perished by the bayonet, or the sea. The victory of Aboukir on the 17th of June, 1799, closed the Egyptian campaign, and Napoleon returned to France.

In Paris he arbitrarily dissolved the Assembly of 500, and was made first of three Consuls. He reopened the Roman Catholic Churches, which had been closed in the Revolution.

1800. Crossing the St. Bernard pass with his troops, Napoleon defeated the Austrians at Marengo; Piedmont and Genoa were given up to France.

1801. Napoleon appoints the Bishops of the Roman Catholic Church in France; and arranges that the incumbents should be approved by civil authority. All convents were abolished.

1802. Napoleon was appointed Consul for life. He immediately reduced the number in the Senate. Switzerland supplied 16,000 men for the service of France, and Napoleon became Mediator of the Helvetic League. The Civil Code Napoleon was drawn up.

1804. Tragedy of the Duke D'Enghein. — On the 18th of May, Napoleon was crowned as Emperor. Pius VII was compelled to be present at the coronation, and blessed the crown, while Napoleon put it on his own head. He then changed the Italian republics into monarchies. At Milan he crowned himself with the iron crown of the Lombard kings.

1805. Napoleon's campaign in Germany. A new coalition of England, Russia, Austria and Sweden was formed against him. On the 2nd of December, 1805, he gained the great battle of Austerlitz, the loss of the allies was tremendous. Multitudes perished in a frozen lake. Austria gave up the Venetian provinces to Italy, and the Tyrol to Bavaria.

Napoleon then united the provinces of Germany as the Confederation of the Rhine, placing himself at the head. He dissolved the old German Empire. Thus ended the "Holy Roman Empire," after an existence of 1,000 years. In October of 1805 was fought the battle of Trafalgar.

1806. Having made his brother Joseph king of Naples and Sicily, Napoleon attacked the Prussians, defeating them at Anerstadt and Jena. The Prussians gave up the fortresses of Magdeburg, Spandau, and others. Napoleon entered Berlin 21st October. Turning to Poland, he occupied Warsaw. A winter campaign against Russia followed. At the battle of Friedland he defeated the Russians, and agreed that Russia should take Finland. He then sent Junot to take Portugal. In Italy Napoleon annexed the Marches, or Adriatic provinces, to his kingdom of Italy. His troops invade Rome; Napoleon telling the Pope that he regarded himself as the successor of Charlemagne, and therefore King of Italy.

Invading Spain, Napoleon occupied Madrid, where he made his brother Joseph " King of Spain and the Indies."

The seven years Peninsular war followed. Six hundred thousand French troops enter Spain; only 250,000 return to France. Loss of Spaniards incalculable.

1809. New Austrian war. Napoleon conquers in the battle of Eckmaul, and enters Vienna. He wins the battle of Aspem. In the great battle of Wagram, he defeats the Austrians, great loss on both sides.

Napoleon divorcing his lawful wife, Josephine, marries the daughter of the Emperor Francis of Austria.

The Pope was taken as a prisoner to Savona, and thence to Fontainbleau, and the Papal territory divided.

1810-1811. Period of Napoleon's greatest power. French Empire extends from Denmark to Naples. Population of France 42,000,000. Population of the new French Empire of Napoleon 80,000,000.

At that period Austria and Russia were Napoleon's allies. In Sweden he placed his General Bernadotte on the throne. Spain was bleeding at every pore from the effects of the Peninsular war. Britain alone defied the power of the great conqueror.

1812. Napoleon's Russian campaign. With an enormous army, consisting of 270,000 French; 80,000 Germans from the Rhine Confederation, 30,000 Poles, and 20,000 Prussians, Napoleon invaded Russia, advancing as far as Moscow, which the Russians evacuated and burned. The disastrous French retreat succeeded, in which 125,000 were slain; 132,000 died of fatigue, hunger, disease and cold; 193,000 were made prisoners, the loss including 3,000 officers, and forty-eight generals. The Russians lost 308,000 men.

Returning with the remnant of his troops to Germany, Napoleon won the battle of Lutzen, against Prussians and Russians united. A series of battles at Dresden followed, and a disastrous defeat of the French army at Leipsic: 25,000 French were made prisoners of war. Napoleon reached the Rhine with seventy or eighty thousand out of an army of 350,000. Returning to France, he issued a new conscription for 300,000 men. But the allied armies entered Paris before he could reach it, and compelled Napoleon to abdicate on the 4th of April, 1814; assigning to him the Island of

Elba. A conspiracy for his restoration to France followed. Napoleon escaped from Elba, assembled rapidly an army of 125,000 men, of which 25,000 were cavalry. He attacked Blucher.

1815. The Battle of Waterloo. Napoleon defeated by the allied armies; great loss on both sides. Thus closed a series of wars which had lasted twenty-three years. During ten years, Napoleon raised by conscription two millions, one hundred and seventy-three thousand men (2,173,000), of whom two-thirds perished in foreign lands, or were maimed for life.

On Napoleon's second abdication, on the 22d of June, 1815, he was sent as a prisoner to the Island of St. Helena, where after an imprisonment of nearly six years, he died of cancer in the stomach. May 5, 1821. On the night of his death there was a terrible storm in the island, trees being tom up by the roots.

Reviewing the career of Napoleon "it may safely be admitted that not only in his power of combination — of embracing in one harmonious plan a great number of distant and independent elements, — but also of watching over and directing, at one and the same time, the complicated movements of mighty armies, the tone of the public press, the operations of foreign and domestic commerce, in addition to the endless intricacies and details of his system of policy, and the great measures of his government, not merely in France, but through the whole extent of his vast empire — he was unequaled by any commander or sovereign that ever lived... No other sovereign of whom history makes mention, ever maintained himself, even for a single day, against such a combination of gigantic powers: yet Napoleon not only maintained himself, but for twelve years, was constantly adding to his dominions in the face of an opposition as was never before or since arrayed against any single ruler... with all his sagacity, he committed the stupendous error, of supposing that he could, in the nineteenth century, hold Europe in subjection by the mere force of his intellect and will, without the exercise of any strictly moral attributes, and without laying the foundations of his power in the affections of his people."[132]

Summary. Retributive character of the French Revolution.

Viewed as a whole, the French Revolution presents in its destructive effects, a spectacle of Divine Judgment without a parallel in human history. Terrible as was the destruction of Jerusalem by the Romans, even it sinks into a secondary place when compared with the wholesale slaughter by massacre and war which accompanied this fearful modern judgment, affecting not only the whole of France, but all the surrounding nations of Europe.

In letters of flame across the movement, is written the word Retribution.

France, the France of St Bartholomew, of the wars of the Huguenots, of the siege of La Rochelle, of the Revocation of the Edict of Nantes, of the suppression of the Jansenists, of the destruction of Port Royal, the France which had cast out with sublime folly and inhuman cruelty, the gospel and the Saints of God, was visited with a plague of infidelity and immorality, like an ulcerous sore, covering the nation from head to foot. The proud and tyrannical monarchy, which had persecuted and banished the Huguenots was overthrown and abolished in a national convulsion of revolutionary crime and excess in which all restraints of law and order, human and divine, were relaxed and dissolved; government delivered into the hands of sanguinary wretches; monarchy brought to the scaffold; aristocracy abolished, estates confiscated or plundered; the nobles slain or exiled; youth, talent, beauty ruthlessly sacrificed: prisons glutted with victims; rivers choked with corpses; churches desecrated; priests slaughtered; religion suppressed; an infidel calendar substituted for the week with its sabbath; and the worship of a harlot as the goddess of Reason for

---

132 Thomas, "Dictionary of Biography," Vol. I, p. 394.

the worship of the host on the altars of the Church of Rome. In France was beheld the reign of infidelity, anarchy, and the guillotine; while from France were communicated to surrounding Europe the fires of revolution and an anti-ecclesiastical mania that has never since been allayed. Nor was this all, for democratic revolution was succeeded by military despotism; the horrors of massacre by the horrors of war. All Europe was involved in the far-reaching conflagration. Italy, Austria, Germany, Poland, Spain, Portugal, and Russia were one after another invaded by the bloodthirsty armies of France, led by a resistless conqueror, eclipsing in his military powers the Alexanders and Caesars of antiquity. The Catholic nations which had warred for centuries against the Reformed faith were successively crushed under the feet of this ruthless despot; thrones overturned, crowns trampled in the dust; armies scattered; cities pillaged; provinces wasted with war; and reduced to desolation.

The Holy Roman Empire and the Holy Catholic Church were prostrated by the tornado; the Imperial and Papal powers overthrown in common ruin. Side by side they had stood supreme for a thousand years; and both were abolished. The Holy Roman Empire which had risen with Charlemagne, which had revived the Imperial power of the Caesars — combined Germany, Italy and France in a single empire, and maintained its existence under a long succession of rulers, with varying fortunes through the Middle Ages, and the succeeding centuries of the Reformation; the empire which had warred against and crushed the Hussites with barbaric cruelties; which had stood as the pillar of the Papacy in the days of Luther; which had inflicted on Germany the horrors of the thirty years* war in the time of Gustavus Adolphus; was now in a series of sanguinary conflicts stripped of its Italian territories, driven back bleeding at every pore from the plains of Lombardy, and then, as an Imperial power, totally suppressed, and brought to nought. In Germany, divided into a host of petty principalities, the "Confederation of the Rhine ** was formed, which, contrary to all that was intended by Napoleon, was destined, together with the contemporaneous growth of Prussia, to lead to the rise of the German Em pire y and to the subsequent victories over Roman Catholic Austria and France of Sadowa and Sedan.

Piedmont, in northern Italy, which had all but exterminated the Waldenses, and turned their wild and lonely valleys into a slaughter-house, was overrun by merciless invaders, and filled with the horrors of ruthless spoliation and bloodshed. The Pope of Rome, stripped of his possessions, his temporal government abolished, was carried captive to die in a foreign land, and Rome given up to plunder and desecration.

Spain, which had crushed the Reformation within in her own borders, and in other lands, by the horrors of the Inquisition, and the Auto da Fe, was delivered over to the dreadful bloodshed and miseries of the seven years Peninsular war: the Inquisition suppressed; and a revolutionary spirit awakened which has made the Country since the theatre of endless strife, disaster, and decay.

And then the guilty powers which had wrought the widespread havoc were arrested and destroyed. All the revolutionary leaders in France came to miserable ends. The nations of Europe combined against the military despot who sought to become the master of the world; the powers of Nature fought against him; the sands of the Syrian desert, the snows of Russia, the waves of the ocean rose up to arrest his progress; his armies scattered, his fleets destroyed, he was compelled to abdicate, and chained like an eagle to a rock in mid ocean, was left to contemplate the ruin of all that he had planned and wrought, and the triumph of the powers he had once defeated and despised. "The Lord is known by the judgment which He executeth; the wicked are snared in the work of their own hands."

Influence of the French Revolution on the Interpretation of Prophecy.

The effect of the French Revolution on prophetic interpretation has been profound and lasting. It has inaugurated a new era in the interpretation of the Apocalypse. Men have lived to see the accomplishment of the judgments on Papal Christendom so long foretold, and so long expected; and, while trembling at the view, have had new hopes kindled within them, respecting the nearness of the promised kingdom of God. In studying the works on prophecy written since the commencement of the Revolution by Bichino, Galloway, Faber, Cunninghame, Frere, Irving, Fuller, Croly, Habershon, Keith, Bickersteth, Brooks, Birks, Elliott and many others, one seems to hear the prolonged reverberation of the seventh trumpet of the Apocalypse — the great trumpet of Judgment and of Jubilee.

In 1794, the year following that of the Reign of Terror, Bichino published his work on "The signs of the times, or the overthrow of the Papal tyranny in France, the prelude of destruction to popery and despotism, but of peace to mankind" The preface is dated January 19, 1793, only two days before the execution of Louis XVI. Three leading conclusions dominate Bichino's treatise: (1) that the persecuting wild beast power of the Apocalypse is chiefly represented by the French monarchy; (2) that this power had slain the Witnesses by the Revocation of the Edict of Nantes, while God had raised them from the dead in the persons of their successors; (3) that the prophetic period of 1,260 years measuring the domination of the Papacy had been fulfilled. Reckoned from its commencing point at Justinian's decree, conferring on the Bishop of Rome the universal oversight of the Christian Church in the year 529, the period had expired in 1789, the opening year of the French Revolution. More correct computations adopted since Bichino's time place Justinian's decree in the year 533, and make the 1260 years terminate in 1793, the central year of the Reign of Terror. "My mind has of late," says Bichino, "been much affected with the appearance of things in the Christian world, and the occurrences which have, within these few years, burst upon us; occurrences which are unparalleled in the history of nations." He then refers to the striking fulfillment of Sir Isaac Newton's conjecture "that the overbearing tyranny and power of the antichristian party which hath so long corrupted Christianity, and enslaved the Christian world, must be put a stop to, and broken to pieces by the prevalence of infidelity, for some time before primitive Christianity could be restored;"and refers to Whiston's observation in 1744, that the infidelity Sir Isaac Newton expected seemed to be "the very means now working in Europe for the same good and great work of Providence." In turning over the pages of Bichino's work, one seems to see the awful sufferings and hear the heartrending groans of the persecuted Huguenots under Louis XIV. The noble French preachers, Saurin and Claude, tell us of the horrors their eyes had seen; "now," says Saurin, as quoted by Bichino, "we were banished, then we were forbidden to quit the kingdom on pain of death. Here we saw the glorious rewards of those who betrayed their religion; and there we beheld those who had the courage to confess it haled to a dungeon, a scaffold, or a galley. Here we saw our persecutors drawing on a sledge the dead bodies of those who had expired on the rack, there we beheld a false friar tormenting a dying man, who was terrified on the one hand with the fear of hell if he apostatized, and on the other with the fear of leaving his children without bread if he should continue in the faith." When the arguments of priests failed, cruel soldiers were quartered in their houses, to exert their skill in torments to compel them to become Catholics. "They cast some," says Claude, "into large fires, and took them out when they were half roasted, they hanged others with ropes under their armpits and plunged them into wells till they promised to renounce their religion; they tied them like criminals on the rack, and poured wine with a funnel into their mouths, till, being intoxicated, they promised to turn Catholics. Some they slashed and cut with pen-knives; some they took by the nose with red-hot tongs, and led them up and down the rooms till they promised to turn Catholics. These cruel proceedings made eight hundred thousand persons quit the kingdom." This system of persecution remained more or less in force till it was overthrown in 1789.

My eyes fall while I write on a venerable witness to the truth of these accounts. A grand old Huguenot Bible lies before me, a folio volume printed in La Rochelle in 1606. Its antiquated French title is as follows: "*La Bible, qui est Toute la saincte escriture du Vieil et du Nouveau Testament; autrement L'ancienne et la Nouvelle Alliance, le tout reveu et confere sur les textes Hebrieux et Grecs par les Pasteurs, et Professeurs de l'eglise de Geneve.*" A figure of a winged woman adorns the title page. She is represented as leaning on a cross, trampling on a prostrate skeleton, and upholding in her hand a book with the title "*Religion Chrestiene.*" The Huguenot metrical version of the Psalms, with their tunes printed in square shaped semibreves, is appended to the volume, and also a simple and scriptural Liturgy. The leather binding is almost black with age, and seems to show by its look, and that of the discolored edges, that the book must have been long concealed in some Huguenot chimney, and embrowned by smoke. On opening the venerable Book, my eyes fall on the verses relating to the Witnesses: "*Et quand ils auront acheve leur tesmoignage, la beste qui monte de l'abisme fera guerre cont'eux, et les vaincra, et les tuera. Et leur corps morts seront gisans es places de la grand cite, qui est appelee spirituellement Sodome et Egypte, la ou aussi nostre Seigneur a este crucifie... mais apres ces trois joursla et demi, l'esprit de vie venant de Dieu entrera en eux, et ils se tiendront sur leurs pieds, et grande crainte saisira ceux qui les auront veus... Le second malheur est passe, et voici, le troisieme malheur viendra bientost. Le Septienne Ange donc sonna de la trompette, et furent faites grandes voix au ciel, disans, Les royaumes du monde sont reduits a nostre Seigneur et a son Christ, et il regenera es siecles des siecles.*" Did you behold from your heights of glory, O ye Huguenot sufferers, the inauguration of that great predicted event? Did you witness its awful commencement, you spirits of the just made perfect; you martyrs and confessors of that noble army of those who for the sake of Christ and the Gospel "loved not their lives even unto death?" Did you behold the judgments of God poured forth on that Papal France which had been guilty of your blood? Ye knew her prisons well; did you rejoice to see that terrible Bastille overthrown, where stands today the lofty column with the golden Statue of Liberty shining on its summit? France would have none of you; she shed your blood in torrents; she forced you into exile; what thought ye of the tremendous overthrow of her monarchy and Church in the French Revolution? Were ye of those holy beings, those victors over "the beast, and his image, and his mark," who stood on "a sea of glass mingled with fire" having "the harps of God," and who when the golden girded angels were sent forth from the Temple of God's glory and power, to pour out the vials of his wrath on the beast, and his worshippers, and on Babylon the great, drunken with the blood of saints, and martyrs, sang the triumphant song of Moses, the servant of God, and the song of the Lamb, saying, "Great and marvelous are Thy works, O Lord God Almighty; just and true are Thy ways, Thou King of Saints; who shall not fear Thee, O Lord, and glorify Thy name? For Thou only art holy: for all nations shall come and worship before Thee, for Thy judgments are made manifest."

Surely you were there in that shining host of victors, ye blessed, martyred witnesses of the Lamb.

With many deep emotions I handle the venerable and sacred volume which remains as a visible memento of your faith and sufferings. Turning to its last page, written on the inside of the iron-bound cover, I decipher the record of a baptism, containing the names of the baptized, — the near relations, and the officiating "*Ministre de Pevangile*," with the touching words, "*fait aux desert*," celebrated in the wilderness — and the date 1745; the time of the *Eglise du desert*. Sweet and simple record of suffering experiences at the close of those days during which the Woman clothed with the sun, and crowned with stars, was hidden in the wilderness from her persecutors, fed there, like Elijah, by the Providence of God; and sustained by the words of the Book, its words of consolation and Eternal Life. One wonders what that woman shall be like, when she comes forth from the wilderness, leaning on the arm of her Beloved, arrayed in the pure linen of spotless righteousness, "having the glory of God"; with the Father's name shining on her forehead, prepared as a bride adorned for her husband? Shall she remember her past in that day of gladness, and bless "the hand that guided, and the heart that planned, when throned where glory dwelleth, in Immanuel's land?" Yes; nought shall be forgotten. Ye shall "remember all the way" by which God led you through the wilderness, to bring you to the better land. And all the bitter tears of your earthly sorrows shall be wiped away. O wondrous music of your gladness; methinks even now I can catch from afar some faint sounding of its thrilling strain.

"The Seventh Trumpet Sounded"

They had reached this glorious and dread event. Such was the conviction of the Apocalyptic interpreters at the time of the French Revolution. Its terrible thunders could be heard rolling in the dark Armament overhead. Surely this was the end of the great apostasy; the end of the gigantic fabric of antichristian power now falling on every side, like the ruins of some vast structure held in the grasp of roaring and relentless flames.

What was to follow? Did the Apocalyptic interpreters, who witnessed these great and terrible events, expect the immediate advent of the Kingdom of God? They did not, for they knew that the destruction of the Apostate Papal Empire was to be accomplished, not by one single act, but by a series of judgments under the outpouring of the seven vials, contained in the seventh trumpet; vials which were the evolution of the "third," and "last woe." Bichino, for example, in his "Signs of the Times," says as regards the contents of the seventh trumpet, "we are not to understand that on the sounding of the seventh trumpet, the kingdom of universal righteousness, peace and happiness is instantly to commence; but that that great scene now opens which is to prepare the way for it."

An old copy of Galloway's work on the Apocalypse lies before me. Its date is 1802. The author had witnessed the horrors of the French Revolution, and writes as profoundly affected by what he had seen. He recoils from it as from some hideous spectre. "This monster," he says, speaking of the Jacobin Club, "directed all the operations and explosions of the revolution. It everywhere appointed the most active leaders, and as instruments employed the profligates of every country. Its power far surpassed that which has been attached to the Inquisition, and other fiery tribunals, by those who have spoken of them with the greatest exaggeration. Its center was at Paris, whilst clubs in every town, in every little borough, overspread the surface of the whole kingdom. The constant correspondence kept up between these clubs, and that of the capital, was as secret and as speedy as that of freemasonry. In a word, the Jacobin Club had prevailed in causing themselves to be looked up to as the real national representative. Under that pretense they censured all the authorities in the most imperious manner. And whenever their denunciations, petitions, or addresses failed to produce immediate effect, they gained their point by insurrections, assassinations, and fire."

At its nod a horde of banditti started up in the several provinces, plundering, prostrating and burning the castles and archives of the seignoral nobility, and the mansions of men of all ranks. At its nod the most bloody civil wars were kindled, in which no quarter was given on either side, whilst France became a field of blood — and was made "one great tomb" Galloway sees in these judgments the outpouring of the earlier vials of the Apocalypse. An awful gloom overspreads his pages, only relieved by the hope that the year 1866 would witness the end of Papal power, the termination of its 1,260 years as reckoned from the decree of Phocas in A.D. 606-7; and the advent of a better order of things destined to usher in the Kingdom of God.

From Galloway's work I turn to Faber's "Dissertation on the Prophecies," published in 1805. He too, writes as an eyewitness of the French Revolution. On the 12th of August, 1792, he tells us, the Jacobins, who counted 300,000 adepts, and were supported by 2,000,000 men scattered through France, armed with torches and pikes, and all the necessary implements of revolution," overthrew the French monarchy, and inaugurated the reign of Terror. "On this memorable day," he says, "I conceive the Third woe trumpet to have begun its tremendous blast." "As the first of these days witnessed the abolition of all the distinctions of civil society, so the second beheld the establishment of atheism by law. A decree was then passed ordering the clergy to leave the kingdom within a fortnight after its date, but instead of allowing them the time specified, even by their own decree, the Jacobin tyrants of France employed the whole of that period in seizing, imprisoning, and putting them to the most cruel deaths."

The very treatment which Louis XIV had given to the ministers of the French Protestant Church in 1685, was now inflicted by the infidel Jacobins in 1792 on the priests of the French Roman Catholic Church: — they were ordered to leave the kingdom in a fortnight, and massacred by the way. We know not how many of the Huguenot pastors perished at the Revocation of the Edict of Nantes, but we know that 24,000 priests were massacred in the French Revolution, and 2,000,000 persons murdered in France. Thus had the vengeance of God begun to "destroy them that destroy the earth," to bring to an end the tyrannical and persecuting rule of Rome. Faber's book seems to vibrate with the earthquake shocks of the Revolution it describes. In reading it one seems to feel the throes of the awful convulsion of which the author had been the witness.

From Faber we turn to Cunninghame. The sounding of the seventh trumpet in the French Revolution is the principal theme of his remarkable work on the Apocalypse, written in 1812. "There have been," says Cunninghame, "only three great Revolutions of the Roman Empire in the west, from the ascension of our Lord to the present period. The first was that in the age of Constantine, whereby the religion of the state was changed from Paganism to Christianity. The second was at the period of the Reformation, and it shook Europe to its foundations. The third is the Revolution which began in France in the year 1789, and having by its first vibration overthrown the monarchy of the Bourbons in the year

1792, has from that period to the present continued to agitate Europe." "The seventh trumpet sounded at the fall of the French monarchy in 1792." "This trumpet comprises within itself the whole of the seven vials of wrath, which are the constituent parts of the third woe."

Cunninghame gives an extract from a letter which he had received from the celebrated Andrew Fuller, of Kettering, who says, "I am fully persuaded that this is the period of the pouring out of the vials. The seventh trumpet seems to me to have sounded about the time of the French Revolution, and to wear a double aspect: 1st, of wrath towards Antichrist, I mean the grand Papal apostasy in all its branches; 2nd, of mercy towards the Church, and even the world, inasmuch as it was the signal of" the kingdoms of this world becoming those of the Lord and His Christ." Hence I conceive the period of the vials is also a period to be distinguished by the spread of the gospel. This view is more fully developed in Andrew Fuller's posthumous work on the Apocalypse, published in 1815. In its preface he says, "The manuscript has lain by me between four and five years, during which I have frequently examined its contents, and availed myself of any further light which by reading or reflection has appeared on the subject." On page 192 he says, "If the sounding of the seventh angel form an era in the Christian Church, it requires that we pause, and pay particular attention to it. The contents of this trumpet are of deeper interest than any that have preceded it, both to the enemies of the Church, and to the Church itself. It wears a twofold aspect. Towards the enemies of the Church it is a trumpet, and a signal of mighty vengeance: towards the Church itself it is a harbinger of joy, a kind of jubilee-trumpet, announcing the year of enlargement; for when the seventh angel sounded, there were great voices in heaven, saying," The kingdoms of this world are become the kingdoms of our Lord, and of His Christ, and He shall reign forever and ever."

Under the first of these aspects it includes the seven last plagues, which are but so many subdivisions of it... under the last aspect it comprehends all the success of the gospel previous to y and during the Millennium, with all the glorious results of it as described in the remainder of the prophecy. We are not to consider it, however, under either of these aspects as being more than a signal of things which are to follow. As the vengeance will not all be poured forth at once, so neither will the kingdoms of this world at once become the kingdom of our Lord, and of His Christ; but from the sounding of this trumpet both shall have a commencement, and both be singularly progressive under it."

Frere, a gifted contemporaneous writer, whose "Combined View" of the prophecies was published in 1815, states in its preface that he had "for about seventeen years been increasingly impressed with a sense of the importance of the period of the world in which we live." Though differing in some respects from the views of Faber and Cunninghame, he was at one with them in considering that the seventh trumpet had sounded in the French Revolution, that the seven vials were included under it, and that their outpouring was for the purpose of the destruction of the Roman Empire as a preparation for the advent of the Kingdom of Christ. This he shows in a historical and chronological diagram at the commencement of his work. He divides the history of the Roman Empire into three periods: "First, the period of its strength as a republic, and under its emperors. Secondly, the period of its weakness, when divided into ten kingdoms. Thirdly, the period of its destruction;"and considers that "the three successive periods in the history of the Church during the same space of time are those in which it is opposed by its three great enemies, the Pagan, Papal, and Infidel powers"; and that "the period of the destruction of the empire is the same as the period of Infidelity in the history of the Church." Broad and comprehensive views these, and well deserving our consideration.

The celebrated preacher, Edward Irving, published in the year 1826 a work on "Babylon and Infidelity Foredoomed of God," which he dedicated to Frere. In the preface he acknowledges that it was through Frere's teachings he was led to the view M that the Apocalypse is a narrative of events running on in regular historical order." There is so much of humility, and such a tone of deep conviction in Irving's words that we cannot refrain from quoting them.

"To my beloved friend and brother in Christ, Hatley Frere, Esq.:

"When I first met you, worthy sir, in a company of friends, and, moved I know not by what, asked you to walk forth into the fields, that we might commune together, while the rest enjoyed their social converse, you seemed to me as one who dreamed, while you opened in my ear your views of the present times, as foretold in the book of Daniel and the Apocalypse. But being ashamed of my own ignorance, and having been blessed from my youth with the desire of instruction, I dared not to scoff at what I heard, but resolved to consider the matter. More than a year passed before it pleased Providence to bring us together again, at the house of the same dear friend and brother in the Lord, when you answered so sweetly and temperately the objections made to your views, that I was more and more struck with the outward tokens of a calm and sincere believer in truth. And I was again ashamed at my own ignorance, and again resolved to consider the matter. After which I had no rest in my spirit, until I waited upon you and offered myself as your pupil, to be instructed in prophecy according to your ideas thereof. And for the ready good will with which you undertook, and the patience with which you performed this kind office, I am forever beholden to you, most kind and worthy friend.

"As becometh one that is ignorant towards his teacher, I received without caviling, and endeavored to comprehend the whole scheme and substance of your interpretation, both of Daniel and the Apocalypse; and then withdrew to consider and try the matter by the two great criterions, — the structure of the books themselves, and the correspondence with the events which had been fulfilled; adding a careful consideration of the discursive prophecies also, which cast many cross-lights upon the subject. Now I am not ashamed to confess, that, at first, my mind fell away from the system of interpretation, which, with Mede and Moore, and other exact interpreters, you have followed, and inclined to the simple idea, that the Apocalypse is a narrative of events running on in regular historical order. Nor was it till after your system of interpretation had decomposed itself in my mind, that it gradually recomposed itself, under a more patient and assiduous consideration of the subject. Which I mention, because I believe it to be the true way in which this or any other subject ought to be studied, and in which I wish this discourse to be read; with the humility of one who desireth to comprehend the whole matter, then to be weighed apart from the authority of a teacher, and the forms of his arguments, and so expect the approval or disapproval of the conscience expected and waited for. I mention it, moreover, in order publicly to declare my acknowledgments to you, most kind and generous friend. For I am not willing that anyone should account of me, as if I were worthy to have had revealed to me the important truths contained in this discourse, which may all be found written in your treatise on the prophecies of Daniel: only the Lord accounted me worthy to receive the faith of those things, which He had first made known to you, his more worthy servant. And if He make me the instrument of conveying that faith to any of His Church, that they may make themselves ready for His coming, or to any of the world, that they may take refuge in the ark of His salvation from the deluge of wrath which abideth the impenitent, to His name shall all the praise and glory be ascribed by me, His unworthy servant, who, through mercy, dareth to subscribe himself,

"Your brother in the bond of the Spirit, and the desire of the Lord's coming.

"Edward Irving."

To Irving the conviction that, to use his own words, "the ending of the 1,260 years was in the year 1792, the year of the French Revolution," and that at that date the seventh trumpet had sounded, was one which profoundly affected him, and one which he embodied in eloquent and moving sermons on the prophecies which sometimes lasted as much as two and a half hours. All London flocked to listen to his orations, and an interest was awakened in prophetic studies whose effects have never ceased. There was a want of balance in his temperament, and "a prodigious want of tact" in his lengthy prayers and sermons, but the strength of his convictions, and his singular eloquence, were unquestionable. "Irving," says Chalmers, "is very impressive, and I do like the force and richness of his conversation." There can be no doubt that he was a witness of important truths to his day and generation; but a warnings too, of the dangers attending speculation on coming events, and reliance on interior impressions as a source of divine revelation. The rock on which he struck is indicated by the wreck that remains of his work and influence, but his life was given to the service of Christ, and his death was hallowed by a sacred sense of his Master's presence. The last utterance which fell from his lips was a quotation of the words of the great apostle of the Gentiles, "Whether we live, we live unto the Lord, or whether we die, we die unto the Lord." Faintly came the parting sentence, "If I die, I die unto the Lord. Amen."

Irving died in December, 1834. In the same year Habershon published his "Dissertation on the prophetic Scriptures, chiefly those of a chronological character, showing their aspect on the present times, and on the destinies of the Jewish nation."

His sober mind sought to build on the *terra firma* of historical and chronological facts, and his chart of scripture history and prophecy is in advance of any that had previously appeared. In his view the sounding of the seventh trumpet indicates "the fall of Mohammedanism and Popery." The terminal period of the prophetic times was in his judgment the interval extending from the French Revolution in 1793 to the yet future year 1918-9.

The excellent Edward Bickersteth, who published the first edition of his valuable and often reprinted "Guide to the Prophecies," as early as 1823, held like Habershon "that the first great blow to Popery was in 1793, the French Revolution, and the date of the first close of the 1,260 days." "Daniel gives us," he says, "two further periods of thirty and forty-five years longer. At the close of the thirty years, 1822-3, the first French Revolution having ended, the sixth vial began in the independence of Greece, and the wasting of the Turkish Empire. At the close of the seventy-five years we reach 1868." The year thus indicated proved to be that of the summoning of the (Ecumenical Council, which met in December, 1869, and affirmed the Infallibility of the Pope on the 18th of July, 1870. The Franco-Prussian war, and the fall of the Papal Temporal Sovereignty followed that event with startling suddenness. It was the long-predicted end of the Papal Temporal power.

The prophetical works of Cunninghame and Bickersteth had a marked effect on the mind of that great and good man, Dr. Chalmers. The following letter from him to Edward Bickersteth written on February 17, 1836, "is interesting in itself, and still more for the sympathy it discovers between two men so variously gifted, and honored above most in their own day, in the diffusion of Divine truth."[133]

"February 17th, 1836.

"My dear Sir,[134]

"I should have acknowledged much sooner the receipt of your kind note, and of the precious volume which accompanied it. I am now reading it with great interest, and think I shall accord more fully with its views than with those of any author I have yet read, who has ventured on the field of unfulfilled prophecy. I lately finished the perusal of all Mede's, and of all Cunninghame's prophetical works, and certainly have been much impressed by them. I sympathize, however, far more with your doubts, than I do with his decision, on the subject of a personal reign. But of this, on

133 Birks, "Life of Bickersteth," Vol. 2, p. 93.
134 Bilks, "Life of Bickersteth," Vol. 2, pp. 94, 95.

the general, I am well satisfied, that the next coming (whether in person or not, I forbear to say) will be a coming, not to the final judgment, but to precede and usher in the millennium. I utterly despair of the universal prevalence of Christianity, as the result of a pacific missionary process, under the guidance of human wisdom and principle. But without slackening in the least our obligation to help forward this great cause, I look for the conclusive establishment through a widening passage of desolating judgments, with the utter demolition of our present civil and ecclesiastical structures.

"Let me advert to the practical character and unction of your work, as stamping an additional virtue upon it; being throughout a powerful address to the conscience, instead of a mere entertainment, which too many of our works of prophecy are, to the curiosity of men.

"I am, my dear sir,

"Yours most gratefully and respectfully,

"Thomas Chalmers."

The Rev. S. W. Brooks, the author of "Abdiel's Essays on the Advent and Kingdom of Christ," wrote, at Bickersteth's suggestion, a work on the "Elements of Prophetical Interpretation," in which he advocates with great force the view that the French Revolution inaugurated the period of the outpouring of the seven vials destined to destroy the Apocalyptic beast, and Babylon the great. He also edited in the years 1831-6 a valuable prophetic journal entitled the Investigator and Expositor of Prophecy; containing important articles by Cunninghame and Birks on the prophetic times, and reviews of works on prophecy, etc. Appended to the fifth volume is a most comprehensive "dictionary of writers on the prophecies," occupying more than 100 pages.

In 1843, the Rev. T. R. Birks, Fellow of Trinity College, Cambridge, published his "First Elements of Sacred Prophecy," followed by many other valuable works on prophetic subjects. For clearness of statement and cogency of argument, I know of no writings in the whole range of prophetic literature to be compared with those of Mr. Birks. In his later years he occupied the position of Knightbridge Professor of Moral Philosophy at Cambridge.

Like Bickersteth, whose eldest daughter he married, and whose memoir he wrote, he held that the outpouring of the seven vials had commenced with the French Revolution, and that we have reached the era of the destruction of the fourth and last Gentile Empire, and are rapidly approaching the period of the Lord's Second Advent.

In 1844 the Rev. E. B. Elliott of Brighton, Fellow of Trinity College, Cambridge, published the first edition of his "*Horae Apocalypticae*," a learned and laborious commentary on the book of Revelations in four volumes, dedicated to the Earl of Shaftesbury. For twenty years Mr. Elliott had studied the subject, and he produced a work of standard value, which for more than half a century has remained without a rival in its own peculiar field.

The late Dr. Candlish, of Edinburgh, who had a wide acquaintance with theological literature, and was no mean judge of such matters, in a lecture on "The Pope the Antichrist of Scripture," named in "a host of modern authorities" "as among the most learned, profound and able expositors any of the body of Scripture have ever had, — Elliott in England, and Gaussen in Geneva." Dr. Cumming, of London, whose numerous works on prophecy are widely known, stated it as his view that Elliott's "Horae" occupied a place in reference to prophetic exposition parallel with "that which Newton's 'Principia' has occupied in reference to science." Albert Barnes, of America, in his valuable commentary on the Apocalypse, has reproduced the views of Elliott, with illustrations drawn from the writings of the historians, Gibbon and Alison. While differing from Cunninghame, Faber, Frere, and Birks, on certain secondary details, Elliott is at one with them in considering that the French Revolution is the opening of the seventh trumpet era of the Apocalypse, and that we are living now in the period of the outpouring of the seven vials destined to destroy the Papal and Mohammedan powers.

Interpretation of the Seven Vials.

The Apocalyptic vision which introduces the outpouring of the seven vials is full of glory and sublimity. A sea of glass mingled with fire is beheld, and standing upon it those who have "gotten the victory over the beast, and over his image, and over his mark, and over the number of his name," "having the harps of God," singing "the song of Moses the servant of God, and the song of the Lamb, saying, Great and marvelous are Thy works, Lord God Almighty; just and true are Thy ways, Thou King of saints; who shall not fear Thee O Lord, and glorify Thy name, for Thou only art holy; for all nations shall come and worship before Thee; for Thy judgments are made manifest." Seven angels then issue from the temple "having the seven last plagues, clothed in pure and white linen, and having their breasts girded with golden girdles; and one of the four living creatures gives to the seven angels seven golden vials, full of the wrath of God, who liveth forever and ever." And the temple is filled with smoke from the glory of God, and from His power; and no man is "able to enter into the temple till the seven plagues of the seven angels" are "fulfilled."

The outpouring of the seven vials, on Babylon and the beast, brings about the climax of the Apocalyptic Drama.

Their imagery is drawn from the plagues inflicted upon Egypt and the judgments poured forth on Babylon by the Euphrates. The sevenfold order of the vials as falling under the seventh trumpet is typified by the events at the fall of Jericho, when during seven successive days the city was compassed about by the warriors of Israel, led in their march around the city by seven priests blowing "seven trumpets of rams' horns before the ark of the Lord," "and on the seventh day compassing the city after the same manner seven times." At the seventh time Joshua directed the people to shout, — "shout for the Lord hath given you the city"; on the rising of which great shout the wall of Jericho "fell down flat," and Israel entering in "utterly destroyed all that was in the city," and "burnt the city with fire." And with this fall of Jericho which introduced and in principle comprehended the victories of Joshua over the Canaanites, did Israel enter into their Canaan inheritance and rest.

And now we hear "a great Voice out of the temple saying to the seven angels, Go your ways, and pour out the vials of the wrath of God upon the earth."

Then in succession on the earth, on the sea, on the rivers, and on the sun, the vial judgments are poured forth; and thus on the totality or entire realm of the antichristian world power.

The earth is smitten with a plague falling on the worshippers of "the beast"; the sea and the rivers become blood; the sun scorches with destructive fire.

Thus did the four first trumpet judgments fall on the earth, the sea, the rivers, and the celestial luminaries. But mark the difference. For whereas the judgment of the first trumpet was that of a storm of hail and fire, that of the first vial was a grievous sore, like the sixth plague of Egypt, "the boil breaking forth with blains upon man and beast" (Ex. 9:10), and that, too, inflicted by "ashes of the furnace,"" sprinkled up towards heaven." So were ashes of the" smoking furnace" seen by Abraham in his dread vision of the Egyptian bondage of his seed. "Sprinkled up towards heaven!" Like the cry of Abel's blood rising to the skies.

And then, whereas at the sounding of the second trumpet a mountain burning with fire was cast into the sea, at the pouring out of the second vial the sea itself became a sea of blood.

And whereas, at the sounding of the third trumpet, the waters of the rivers were embittered, and became like wormwood, at the pouring out of the third vial, the streams and fountains of water were, as of old in Egypt, changed to blood. The worshippers of the beast and persecutors of the saints and martyrs are given blood to drink, "for they are worthy" (Rev. 16:6).

And whereas at the sounding of the fourth trumpet, the third part of the luminaries of heaven were darkened as by a dread eclipse, at the pouring out of the fourth vial y the sun blazes with scorching heat upon the inhabitants of the earth, so that men" scorched with great heat blasphemed the name of God who has power over these plagues," and "repent not to give Him glory."

The fifth, sixth, and seventh vials are poured forth on the throne of the beast, on the River Euphrates, and into the air. Under the fifth vial the kingdom of the beast is filled with darkness, as in the ninth plague of Egypt. Under the sixth vial the waters of the Euphrates are dried up, as at the taking of ancient Babylon. Under the seventh vial great Babylon is destroyed, while the solemn final sentence sounds from heaven, "It is done."

It should further be observed that while under the sixth trumpet the destroying army of Euphratean horsemen were loosed for their career of destruction, as a judgment on idolaters worshiping the work of their hands, "idols of gold, and silver, and brass, and stone, and wood, which neither can see, nor hear, nor walk; who under the dreadful infliction repented not of their murders, nor of their sorceries, nor of their fornications, nor of their thefts;"that under the pouring out of the sixth vial the waters of the Euphrates are dried up" that the way of the kings of the east might be prepared."

The seventh trumpet, like the seventh vial is final. As the third and last of three woe trumpets it contains the "seven last plagues" of the vials. Such are the resemblances, and such the differences, of the trumpets and vials.

Interpretation of the Seven Vials

And now, behold, the growth of light and understanding as to the meaning of these last judgments of the Apocalypse.

For as the light of approaching morn is first dim and faint, then waxes stronger, and becomes more evident, and then gaining intensity gilds the eastern clouds with touches of brightness, and sends up rays to the zenith, to herald the rising of the star of day, so has it been with the growth of light and understanding in relation to these sacred prophecies. Far back in past ages they shed a dim light upon the minds of men, who scarce comprehended more than the existence of some mysterious woes in reserve for the closing days of the Christian dispensation; but as the centuries rolled on the meaning of the strange predictions became localized in place and time; erroneous conceptions one after another were cast off, and at length a full persuasion of the character and sphere of these final judgments took possession of the minds of those who pondered the meaning of the oracles of God, and a solemn hush of expectation fell upon their spirits as they awaited the fulfillment of the things foretold. At last the hour arrived; the dreaded tempest broke; and as the vials of wrath were poured forth upon apostate Christendom, the saintly watchers, trembling at the things they beheld, recognized the fulfillment of the predicted woes, and were awakened to expect that great event to which these judgments are but the introduction, the return in glory and majesty of the King of Righteousness, and Prince of Peace, of whose kingdom there shall be no end.

Earlier Interpretations of the Vials

For first, in the centuries preceding the Constantine Revolution the seven vials were thought to be plagues inflicted on some short-lived infidel antichrist who should rise up at the end of the world, as a Satanic apparition, and blazing for a few brief years, like a disastrous comet, should plunge again into darkness, and disappear from the astonished scene. Then in Mediaeval times some thought as did Joachim Abbas, that the seven vials were judgments which ran parallel with the seven seals, and seven trumpets, thus extending the period of the vials to the entire interval between

Christ's departure and His return. When, later on, the Papal head was recognized as the predicted Man of Sin, and Papal Rome as the foretold Babylon, students of prophecy began to apply the vials to the long series of woes inflicted on the Papacy and Church of Rome, from those of the great schism towards the close of the middle ages, to those of the wars attending the Reformation, and the Puritan Revolution, in which the supremacy of Rome was over a large extent of Europe overthrown. But when the eighteenth century began it was seen by the most intelligent students of prophecy that the period of the seven vials was still future; and some were able to fix the very time of their fulfillment with correctness; while others anticipated with wonderful insight the nature of the judgments the vials were destined to bring. At length the fulfillment came, and came at the hour which had been indicated in the prophetic times. Then, one after another, as the vials of wrath were poured forth, they were seen to accomplish the prophecies of God's Holy Word; and men bowed their heads, and worshipped Him who liveth forever and ever, whose word is true from the beginning, and standeth fast for evermore. The fabric of heaven and earth may be dissolved, and pass away like the vision of a night, but His word shall not pass away, but be fulfilled in its season; not one thing failing of all that had been foretold.

For in the first place it was recognized from the beginning that the Babylon of chapters 17 and 18, is none other than Rome; and thus the sphere of the vials was localized. Victorinus in the third century, says of Rev. 17:9, "The seven heads are the seven hills on which the woman sitteth, that is, the city of Rome"

So Tertullian, Jerome, Augustine, and all the early fathers. The vision in the nineteenth chapter which closes the vial series Victorinus says represents "our Lord coming to His kingdom with the heavenly army." The contemporaneous judgment of the winepress he says represents "the nations that should perish on the advent of the Lord." But further light on the symbolism of the seven vials he lacks. Primasius, Bishop of the Carthaginian province in 553, says that the fall of Babylon under the vials is that of Rome.

Bede, in the seventh century, recalls the fact that God declares repeatedly in Leviticus "and I will smite you with seven plagues." "And these," he adds, "are to be the last when the Church shall have come forth from the midst of it," thus connecting the outpouring of the vials with a previous exodus of the Church from the scene of judgment, according to the words, "Come out of her, my people, that ye be not partakers of her plagues." Such an exodus was the Reformation of the sixteenth century, and such in a different way was the exodus forced on the Huguenots of France before the fall of those woes which covered the country which banished them with bloodshed.

Ansbert in 770 interprets the first vial as symbolizing the plague of infidelity; a remarkable anticipation of the truth.

The Albigenses and Waldenses, the Wycliffites and Hussites all applied the judgments on Babylon under the vials to Papal Rome. The Reformers did the same, and interpreted the seven vials of a series of judgments inflicted chiefly on Rome. Thus Bullinger in 1573 applies the third vial to Popes and Papal princes, "stirring up bloody wars in which themselves were slain." Foxe in 1587 thought the first five vials were poured on ancient Rome, and the sixth and seventh on Papal Rome.

Brightman in 1615 considered that the vials had been poured out, the first in the later Reformation days, in the time of Queen Elizabeth; the second in the time of the Council of Trent; the third he connected with the Jesuits; the fourth with the contentions arising from the light shining from the newly opened scriptures; the fifth on Rome, the throne of the beast; the sixth had past reference to the Turks from the Euphrates; the seventh completed the overthrow of Papal and Mohammedan power.

Pareus in 1615 thought the first vial represented "the ulcerous sores which fell on the Papists from Luther's Reformation; the second and third deadly decrees of the Council of Trent; and judgments on Papal bishops and doctors for shedding saints' blood; the fourth, fresh heat and light from the Scriptures enraging the Papists; the fifth, the darkening of Rome; the sixth, the drying up the resources of the anti-typical Babylon; the seventh, atmospheric pestilence, followed by universal destruction.

Mede in 1643 held that the vials related to the destruction of Antichrist; the first at the time of the secession of the Waldenses, Wycliffites, and Hussites; the second at Luther's secession; the third at the secession and protest in the time of Elizabeth; the rest of the vials he thought future; of these the fourth might fall on "the German emperor as the chief luminary of the Papal system," the fifth on Rome; the sixth on the Turkish Empire; the seventh on Satan's kingdom as the prince of the power of the air. Here we recognize an advance in interpretation. furieu in 1685 maintained that the vials were the "steps by which the Babylonian or Papal Empire comes to its ruin/' The first vial he thought was poured out in the tenth century; the second and third in the earlier and later crusades; the fourth Papal despotism in the eleventh to the fourteenth centuries; the fifth the woes on the Papacy leading to the transference of the Papal seat from Rome to Avignon; the sixth the overthrow of Constantinople by the Turks; and the seventh the earthquake of the Reformation; so blind was this great man to the judgments which were yet to fall on the Papal and Mohammedan powers. But now came a notable advance in the interpretation; Launeus, living at the same time with Jurieu noted the fact his predecessors had overlooked, that the seven vials were the"seven last plagues," and that the seventh trumpet was the last, or finishing woe. The vials, therefore, belonged to a future period. The banished Huguenot minister to whom we have referred who wrote a book entitled "A New System of the Apocalypse," "finished but two days before the dragoons plundered him of all except this treatise," followed Launeus in his interpretation, and opposed the views of Jurieu as to the past fulfillment of the vials.

"Seeing," he says, "the vials contain judgments yet to come, I design not to speak otherwise of them than by way of conjecture." The first vial may then represent the rage and miseries of prelates and priests at the diminution of their revenues, their blind zeal and superstition... The sea of the second vial is "the Papal kingdom." Under the third vial the members of the Church of Rome who had shed the blood of Protestants shall turn their arms against themselves "and tear one another. And by that means like shall be returned unto them for like." The fourth vial will probably be poured on the Ottoman Emperor, as the sun of the Eastern Empire. The fifth on the city of Rome; the sixth on the Turkish Empire preparing the way for the conversion of the Jews; the seventh a final and universal judgment on antichristian power. How truly remarkable are some of these anticipations. Sir Isaac Newton, living at the same time, laid stress in his work on the Apocalypse on the predicted sealing up of the meaning of these prophecies, till the time of the end. This period he thought that of the seventh trumpet, at whose sounding "the mystery of God should be finished." That "main revolution" when all would be explained was "near at hand."

Whiston as we have seen tells us it was Newton's persuasion "that the antichristian, or persecuting power of the Popedom which had so long corrupted Christianity would be put a stop to and broken to pieces by the prevalence of infidelity for some time before primitive Christianity could be restored." Whiston in 1706 strongly advocated the view that the seven vials were contained in the seventh trumpet, and were all future. Vitringa, whose learned work on the Apocalypse belongs to the same period, acknowledged the plausibility of the opinion of Launeus that the vials were the development of the seventh trumpet, but puts forth the view that the earlier vials were already fulfilled in Papal history. Fleming, whose book on the rise and fall of the Papacy was published in 1701 deeply studied the question of the vials, and thought the fourth vial was poured on the sun of the Papal kingdom, the "houses of Austria and Bourbon." He regarded it as partly fulfilled, and to be more so afterwards. As France was made use of to vex and scorch the Austrian family" so might it be hereafter. "The present French king takes the sun for his emblem, and this for his motto, *Nec pluribus impar* (not equaled by many)." "As to the expiration of this vial, I do fear it will not be until the year 1794. The reason of which conjecture is this, that I find the Pope got a new foundation of exaltation when Justinian upon his conquest of Italy, left it, in a great measure, to the Pope's management, being willing to eclipse his own authority to advance that of this haughty prelate." Reckoning the 1,260 years from Justinian, Fleming reaches 1794. He adds the notable conclusion that as the Pope received the title of Supreme Bishop in A.D. 606, 1,260 years from that date in prophetic or calendar measure (— 1,242 solar years) would expire in 1848, at which date the vial judgment of 1794 he thought would reach its terminus. A wonderful anticipation of the truth! "But yet we are not to imagine" he adds, "that this vial will totally destroy the Papacy (though it will exceedingly weaken it) for we find this still in being and alive when the next vial is poured out." Whiston, in a later edition of his "Commentary on the Apocalypse," published in 1744, expressed the view that the infidelity which was destined to overthrow the Papal Babylon had begun to reveal its presence. In this he was indisputably correct.

Bishop Newton in 1754 declared that the symbolism of the fourth vial might represent "a most tyrannical and exorbitant exercise of arbitrary power by those who may be called the sun in the firmament of the beast, pope, or emperor ," adding, "time must discover."

Dr. Gill in 1776 said in regard to the question whether the vials had been poured out, "I am ready to think they are not, because they seem to me to refer to the seventh trumpet." He thought the first vial would be probably not physical, but moral in character. Under the second vial he anticipated a judgment on the maritime powers of Spain and Portugal; under the third woes on the Papal lands of Italy and Savoy; the fourth might be poured on the ruling house of Austria, or the Pope; the fifth would fall on Rome; the sixth on the Turkish power, the seventh would bring to an end the kingdom of Satan.

Two years before Gill's Commentary was published, Louis XVI came to the throne of France, the monarch who lost his life in the

French Revolution. How near was the interpreter to the events of which he wrote, while all unconscious of their close proximity.

Reckoning from the decree of Phocas, Gill considered that the Papal power would fall in 1866. In 1866-70 came the crisis of its termination as a Temporal Government; but what great events had to precede that momentous close of an apostate dominion which had lasted for more than a thousand years.

Thirteen years later than the publication of Gill's Commentary, on the 14th of July, 1789, began the French Revolution with the destruction of the Bastille, and four years later, in 1793, came the Reign of Terror. In August, 1792, 40,000 priests were exiled. In September took place the massacre in Paris. On the 20th of January, 1793, Louis XVI was condemned to death, on the 21st he was executed. In March followed the war in La Vendee; on the 23d of June the proscription of the Girondists. On the 16th of October the execution of Queen Marie Antoinette. On the 10th of November the worship of the goddess of Reason in Notre Dame; on the 24th the adoption of the New Republican Calendar. In 1794 Robespierre was president. On the 28th of July he and seventy-one others were guillotined. Bonaparte's campaign followed; then his dictatorship as first consul; and then his coronation as emperor. In the twenty years of his wars most of the kingdoms of Europe were overthrown; millions perished by the sword; the Papacy was stripped of its revenues and temporal dominion, and the Pope carried into captivity. In the brief space of a quarter of a century the whole face of Europe was changed by a Revolution, which for crime, bloodshed, and world-wide effects, was without a parallel in human history.

To the students of prophecy it was now no longer a question what the vials signified. They beheld them poured forth. And with what terrific rapidity and dire effects!

In the infidelity and corruption in France which preceded and led to the Revolution they beheld the first vial fulfilled; in the unexampled bloodshed of the Revolution they saw accomplished the second and third vials; in the dreadful wars of Napoleon the fourth vial; in the deposition and captivity of the Pope y and spoliation of Rome, the fifth vial; in the decline and wasting away of Turkish power the sixth vial; and in the consummation of Babylon's destruction which they still await, the seventh and concluding vial.

The First Vial

It had long been acknowledged that the grievous sore of the first vial must represent either a physical or a moral plague, and the probability admitted that it represented the latter, especially as considered in the light of that passage in Isaiah I, in which the hateful moral condition of apostate Israel is described under the same figure, — "from the sole of the foot even unto the head there is no soundness in it, but wounds and bruises, and putrifying sores." And what for a century had been the moral state of France but this? A plague rendered more acute and deadly by the venom of infidelity which had taken possession of the entire nation, loosening every moral tie, and preparing the totally apostate people to dethrone God Himself, if it had been possible, substituting the worship of a licentious harlot, as the goddess of Reason, for the worship of the living and true God.

The French Revolution Stage

The thing foretold had come to pass. The moral monstrosity was an accomplished fact. On the worshippers of the Papal Power were plainly seen the hateful plague blotches. They were marked men, like the plague-smitten Egyptians in the days of old; men to be shunned with aversion and horror.

Writing in 1813 Cunninghame says that atheism and anarchy were chief blotches in the dreadful plague. "On the Continent these dreadful principles have had their full sway, and in the devoted country of France /fend its immediate dependencies they have at length produced a degree of moral turpitude, perhaps unequaled hitherto in the history of our species."

Faber saw in the delusive spirit of atheism which had sway in the Revolution the darkest form of Antichristian apostasy; that of the open and blasphemous denial of the Father, and of the Son.

Elliott, taking a more comprehensive view of the actual facts sees the fulfillment of the Apocalyptic symbol in "that tremendous outbreak of social and moral evil of democratic fury, atheism, and vice, which characterized the French Revolution; that of which the ultimate source was in the long and deep-seated corruption and irreligion of the nation; its outward vent, expression and organ in the Jacobin Clubs, and their seditious and atheistic publications; its result, the dissolution of all society, all morals and all religion, with acts of atrocity and horror accompanying scarce paralleled in the history of man; and suffering and anguish of correspondent intensity throbbing throughout the whole social mass, and corroding it: — that which from France, as a center, spread like a plague, through its affiliated societies, to the other countries of Papal Christendom, and proved, wherever its poison was imbibed, to be as much the punishment as the symptom of the corruption within."[135] The commencement of this moral plague in France was certainly earlier than 1792, the date at which Bichino, Faber, Cunninghame and Frere had thought the seventh trumpet sounded, and the vial judgments began.

Faber points out that on the 26th of August, 1792, the denial of God in France "was for the first time formally established by law." Let it be granted that this was a crisis in the plague, but let it be also admitted that the plague in question was raging in 1755 when Rousseau published his "*Discours sur l'origine et les Fondements de TInegalite parmi les hommes*," and Diderot and D'Alembert were issuing their infidel "Encyclopaedic."

---

135 *Horae*, III, p. 359.

Of Voltaire Vinet says "*a partir de 'lan A.D., 1750, il fut encore le plus populaire et le plus puissant des ecrivains. .. 'lan 1750, ou plutot 1746, marque le point essentiel dans la carriere et dans la direction du siecle." "De Pan 1750 a l'an 1780, epoque ou bt publication complete de l'ouvrage de Raynal, est comme le dernier eclat d'une incendie, a qui rien ne reste a devorer.*"

Ascending still earlier in the century we recall the facts that in 1727 the Church of the United Brethren was established by Count Zinzendorf at Herrnhut; that in 1731 Whitfield and Wesley commenced their evangelistic labors so marvelously blessed on both sides of the Atlantic: and that in 1740-44, the Glorious Revival took place at Northampton in New England, in connection with the labors of Jonathan Edwards, who thought the work of God which he witnessed, and has so fully described, was the dawn of the Millennial Day. May we not hear in the voices which sounded forth in this great and remarkable awakening, alike in Germany, in England, and in America, the seventh trumpet of the Kingdom of Christ, already commencing to peal forth its glad note of jubilee?

For surely that trumpet is primarily the trumpet of the kingdom, and only in a secondary sense the trumpet of woes and judgments sent to prepare the way for the establishment of the Kingdom. Viewed in this light, may not the going forth of the angel of the everlasting gospel just before the fall of Babylon (Rev. 14:6, 8), coincide with the sounding of the seventh trumpet of Jubilee?

Sir Isaac Newton said most correctly, "An angel must fly through the midst of heaven with the everlasting gospel to preach to all nations before Babylon falls, and the Son of Man reaps His harvest."

Did not this flight of the angel of the Everlasting Gospel begin in the Great Revival in the time of Zinzendorf, Wesley, Whitfield, and Jonathan Edwards? Are not modern missions in all their world-wide range the evolution of the Revival which then began?

If this be so, how cheering the view presented of the mode in which the seventh trumpet era was inaugurated. It broke upon the world, not as the mere messenger of woes and judgments, but as the herald of mercies prepared for all mankind. Its trumpet note was primarily one of triumphant joy; its thrilling proclamation liberty for the captives, and salvation for the lost.

The Second Vial

And now returning to the vials we recall the fact that the first vial has been poured out on Papal France, where the worshippers of the beast are covered with its predicted "noisome and grievous sores"; and that the plague has been recognized by the interpreters of the prophetic word.

They note the universal massacres and dreadful wars which followed. "France," says Cunninghame, "became drenched in its own blood, and the whole territory converted into a vast slaughter-house. It has been computed that two millions of men perished in that devoted country within three years after it became a Republic.

"Long after the Revolutionary massacres had ceased, French blood still continued to flow in torrents, and from the accession of Napoleon to the Consular and Imperial powers, till his overthrow by the combined forces of Europe, it successively fertilized the soil of every country from the banks of the Tagus to the deserts of Poland and European Russia in the series of dreadful wars carried on to glut the ambition of a ferocious usurper. In particular during the late awful campaigns in Russia, Germany and France, this and the following vial have received a fearful accomplishment in a destruction of. the human race without example in the annals of modern times."

The "sea" on which the second vial is poured out turning it to blood, is understood by Cunninghame to represent primarily the French nation. Elliott and other interpreters consider that the sphere of this judgment was in a special sense a maritime one; that its effects fell on "the maritime power, and commerce, and colonies of Papal Christendom."

The democratic revolutionary spirit of France and the naval force of England contributed to effect the purpose of Divine Providence. First, the Isle of Hayti or St. Domingo, the most flourishing of the French colonies, being infected by the like infidel principles, was lost after a servile war of twelve years, in which 60,000 blacks were slaughtered.

Then, for twenty years, the fleet of England (preserved and directed by the same good providence of God) wasted in all directions the ships, commerce, and maritime colonies of France, and of her allies, Holland and Spain. Their fleet was destroyed in 1793, at Toulon, by Lord Hood; by whom also Corsica, and nearly all the Spanish and West Indian Islands were taken in 1794. In 1795 followed the naval victory off L'Orient, and the capture of the Cape of Good Hope.

The victory in 1797 off Cape St. Vincent was quickly succeeded by that of Camperdown over the Dutch fleet.

Then followed Lord Nelson's three mighty victories of the Nile in 1798, of Copenhagen in 1801, and in 1805 of Trafalgar.

Viewing the losses suffered by France from 1793 to the end of 1815, we find that nearly 600 vessels of war, besides numerous ships of commerce, were destroyed, together with a large proportion of their officers and men.

The world's history does not furnish such a period of naval war and bloodshed. "The sea became as the blood of a dead man." Finally, when the maritime power of the papal nations bad been swept away by English victories, the Spanish colonies of South America threw off their allegiance, after another scene of carnage, only paralleled by those before described; the Brazils also were separated from Portugal, and so the prediction was complete: as regarded the papal European colonies, they became "dead."

Doubtless the judgments on many of these colonies might be considered as being retributive for the cruelties practiced in their exercise of the slave trade.

The Third Vial

Slaughters in papal lands watered by the Alpine fountains and streams, and by the boundary rivers, the Rhine and Upper Danube, followed. It seems natural to apply the third vial to this dreadful retributive judgment.

Albert Barnes notices that four points as to this vial are clear: (1) "That it would succeed the first mentioned, and apparently, at a period not remote. (2) That it would occur in a region where there had been persecution. (3) It would be in a country of streams, and rivers, and fountains. (4) It would be a just retribution for the bloody persecutions which had occurred there."

In this interpretation of it he follows Elliott, who says, "During the year 1792 war was declared by France against Germany, and the next year against Sardinia; consequently all those towns watered by the Rhine and Alpine streams became scenes of carnage. Metz, Worms, Spires; the towns formerly desolated by Attila, suffered. Another French army entered upon the countries situated on the Meuse, a branch of the Rhine; a third advanced into Piedmont, the Alpine frontier. In 1793 and 1794 war still raged in the same quarters. The French advanced to Holland. In many places the success fluctuated, but in most instances they were victorious. At last Charles of Austria drove their generals, Moreau and Jourdan, and their armies back to the Rhine.

In A.D. 1797 Bonaparte attacked the Sardinians and Austrians. The course he tracked was from the Alpine rivers through Northern Italy, till he reached Venice. Every river was a scene of carnage, and he crossed seven in succession. The Alpine rivers were turned to "blood."

It was in 1797 that Bonaparte uttered the remarkable threat, "I will prove an Attila to Venice."

Before peace could be restored Austria was forced to submit; and the treaty of Campio Formio stipulated that the valley of the Rhine, one part of the prophetic scene, together with the Austrian Netherlands and Palatinate on one side of the Rhine, and Wurtemberg, Bavaria, Baden and Westphalia on the other, should all be made over to France.

Again in 1799 the "fountains of waters" were dyed with blood, the French having suffered reverse and been driven out of all the places they occupied in North Italy with much bloodshed.

The war soon recommenced. In 1800 that terrible and decisive battle of Marengo was fought, and the Danube became the scene of judgment. One victory after another succeeded, till the memorable battle of Austerlitz completed the overthrow of the Austrian power.

The reason given by the angel for the judgment is remarkable — "They are worthy, for they have shed the blood of saints and prophets, and thou hast given them blood to drink."

Was it not so that the cruelties — of the French and Piedmontese, and the rulers of Savoy, against the Waldenses and Albigenses, the Huguenots and Calvinists, from the end of the thirteenth to the end of the eighteenth century, and of Austria against the Hussites, the Waldenses and Lutherans in Lombardy, Moravia, and the Netherlands already related —did call out for retributive justice?"How long, O Lord, holy and true, dost Thou not avenge our blood on them that dwell on the earth."

The Fourth Vial

"In regard to the application of this vial," Barnes the Commentator, who follows Elliott, says, "the following things may be remarked: (a) That the calamity here referred to was one of the series of events which would precede the overthrow of the 'beast/ and contribute to that — for to this all these judgments tend. (b) In the order in which it stands, it is to follow, and apparently to follow soon, the third judgment — the pouring of the vial upon the fountains and streams, (c) It would be a calamity such as if the sun, the source of light and comfort to mankind, were smitten, and became a source of torment. (d) This would be attended by a great destruction of men, and we should naturally look in such an application for calamities in which multitudes of men would be, as it were, consumed, (e) This would not be followed, as it might be hoped it would, by repentance, but would be attended with reproaches of God, with profaneness, with a great increase of wickedness.

Now, on the supposition that the explanation of the previous passages is correct, there can be no great difficulty in supposing that this refers to the wars of Europe following the French Revolution; the wars that preceded the direct attack on the papacy, and the overthrow of the papal government. For these events had all the characteristics here referred to. (a) They were one of a series in weakening the papal power in Europe — heavy blows that will yet be seen to have been among the means preliminary to its final overthrow, (b) They followed in their order the invasion of Northern Italy — for one of the purposes in that invasion was to attack the Austrian power there, and ultimately through the Tyrol to attack Austria itself. Napoleon, after his victories in Northern Italy, above referred to, (comp, chapter xx of Alison's 'History of Europe'), thus writes to the French Directory: 'Coni, Ceva, and Alexandria are in the hands of our army; if you do not ratify the convention, I will keep their fortresses and march upon Turin. Meanwhile, I shall march tomorrow against Beaulieu, and drive him across the Po; I shall follow close at his heels, overawe Lombardy, and in a month be in the Tyrol, join the army of the Rhine and carry our united forces into Bavaria. The design is worthy of you, of the army, and of the destinies of France.'[136] (c)

136 Alison, i, 401.

The campaign in Germany in 1796 followed immediately this campaign in Italy. Thus, in chapter xx of Alison's History, we have an account of the campaign in Italy; in chapter xxi we have the account of the campaign in Germany; and the other wars in Europe that continued so long, and that were so fierce and bloody, followed in quick succession — all tending, in their ultimate results, to weaken the papal power, and to secure its final overthrow, (d) It is hardly necessary to say here that these wars had all the characteristics here supposed. It was as if the sun were smitten in the heavens, and power were given to scorch men with fire. Europe seemed to be on fire with musketry and artillery, and presented almost the appearance of the broad blaze of a battlefield. The number that perished was immense. These wars were attended with the usual consequences — blasphemy, profaneness, and reproaches of God in every form. And yet there was another effect wholly in accordance with the statement here, that none of these judgments brought men to 'repentance, that they might give God the glory.' Perhaps these remarks, which might be extended to great length, will show that, on the supposition that it was intended to refer to those scenes by the outpouring of this vial, the symbol was well-chosen and appropriate."[137]

Elliott says the "scorching with fire" we may refer to the sufferings of the countries which were exposed to these fearful troubles. The accounts which we have received enable us to appreciate the point and truth of Napoleon's own observation, — "The genius of conquest can only be regarded as the genius of destruction." Conscriptions, taxation, loss of life, pillage of property, devastation, and ruin, marked his course, and sullied the glory of his exploits. Men were "scorched with great heat."[138]

The Fifth Vial

The fifth vial is poured out on "the seat of the beast." "We have

---

137 Barnes, "Commentary on the Apocalypse," pp. 479-80.
138 Elliott, *Horae*, pp. 323-4.

already seen," says Elliott, "how in the Revolution the Romish clergy suffered. Their means of support was withdrawn by the abolition of tithes, the confiscation of the Church lands, and the destruction of monastic houses. This was followed by the national abolition of the Romish religion, and the razing the churches to the ground. So was the whole French ecclesiastical establishment broken up. Twenty-four thousand of the clergy were massacred with horrid atrocities; the terrified remnant fled.

"So much had the anti-papal spirit increased, that the French army urged their march against Rome itself, and the Pope only saved himself by the surrender of several towns, and the payment of a large sum of money, and the best treasures of the Vatican.

"At length the decree went forth for the humbling of the beast himself. In 1809 Napoleon declared the Pope's temporal dominion at an end. The estates of the Church were annexed to France; and Rome was degraded to be the second city of the French Empire. Surely on 'the seat of the beast' the vial of wrath had been poured out.

"Subsequently the Pope was brought prisoner to France, and there, as a pensioner, he received a stated salary. True he afterwards gained back the privilege of fixing his seat at Rome. But the world had seen his weakness, and a precedent was established for the benefit of future generations.

"In France the Romish religion continued only to be tolerated on an equality with other religions; in Portugal and Spain church property has been lately confiscated; and in Italy still later events have shown that the papal authority, if unsupported by temporal power, has not any longer in itself that which can maintain its supremacy."

The Sixth Vial

The drying up of the Euphrates flood under the sixth vial had long been understood to refer to the wasting away of the Turkish or

Mohammedan power, which according to prophecy, was to follow the judgments of the French Revolution.

The Turks who had overthrown the corrupt Eastern Empire of Rome had come into Europe "from the upper stream of the River Euphrates.¹³⁹ All over Southeastern Europe the flood had extended as far as Venice. It had been a fearful 'woe' on Eastern Christendom. In 1820 a formidable insurrection against the Turkish power began in Greece, which quickly spread to Wallachia, Moldavia, and the Aegean isles.

"In 1826 Turkey was obliged to surrender to Russia all its fortresses in Asia, and frightful civil commotions distracted Constantinople, ending in the slaughter of the Janissaries, when 4,000 veteran but mutinous and unmanageable soldiers were shot or burned to death by order of the Sultan himself in their own barracks in the city, and many thousands more all over the country. The empire had for centuries groaned under their tyranny, and Mahmoud II was resolved to organize a fresh army on the military system of western Europe, and saw no other way of delivering himself from the tyrannical Jannissaries than this awful massacre, which, while it liberated Turkey from an intolerable incubus, at the same time, materially weakened her strength. Before a fresh army had been matured, Russia again attacked the Turkish Empire, and backed up by England and France, secured the independence of Greece, after the great naval battle of Navarino, in which the Ottoman fleet was totally destroyed. In 1828 and 1829 Russia again invaded Turkey; her armies crossed the Balkans, and penetrated as far as Adrianople where a treaty, more disastrous to the Porte than any previous one, was concluded. The freedom of Servia was secured, and no Turk was permitted to reside in future north of the Danube, while Russia obtained one of the mouths of that river, and territory to the south of it. The large Turkish province of Algeria in North Africa was lost to the Sublime Porte, and became a French colony in the following year.

---

139 Sir Edward Creasy, "History of the Ottoman Turks."

"In 1832 Turkey was brought to the verge of dissolution in consequence of the successful rebellion of the powerful pasha of Egypt, Mehemet Ali. He attacked and conquered Syria, and defeated the Turkish armies in three great battles, and he would have taken Constantinople had not the western nations intervened. A second rebellion on the part of Egypt took place in 1840, when Ibrahim Pasha defeated the Turks at Nezib. The Turkish fleet was betrayed into the power of Mehemet Ali, and taken to Alexandria; and Europe was obliged again to interfere to protect the Sultan from the rebellion of his vassal, who could at that time have easily overthrown the Turkish empire. In the following year the British Admiral took Sidon, Beyrout, and St. Jean d'Acre; and, in order to restore the Turkish rule, which had been completely lost, drove Mehemet Ali out of Syria. Egypt has been, however, virtually independent ever since, and her present rulers bear the title of Khedive, or king, in recognition of the fact. They are now far more under the power of England than under that of Turkey.

"In 1844 the Porte was compelled by the Christian nations of Europe to issue an edict of religious toleration, abolishing forever its characteristic and sanguinary practice of execution for apostasy, that is, for the adoption of the Christian faith. As this was entirely against its will, because against the precepts of the Koran, and contrary to the practice of all the ages during which Mohammedanism had been in existence, it was a most patent proof that Ottoman independence was gone, as a matter of fact, though often mentioned still as a plausible fiction of diplomacy, and that henceforth it had to shape its conduct in accordance with the views of its neighbors, the Christian nations of Europe. It was a compulsory sheathing of the sword of persecution, which had been relentlessly wielded for over twelve centuries, a most marked era in the overthrow of Mohammedan power."[140]

---

140 Author's work, «"Light for the Last Days," pp. 90, 91, 92.

The Seventh Vial

This is the greatest of the vials, and the last. On its outpouring is heard "a great voice out of the temple of heaven, from the throne, saying, It is done." As this is the vial of the destruction of "Babylon the great," the detailed descriptions of that event in Rev. 17, 18, and 19 belong to it, and will be fulfilled in its course. The scope of the seventh vial in apocalyptic prophecy is greater than that of all the preceding vials. To it belongs the solemn and sublime description of the issuing forth from the opened heaven of the rider on the white horse, in chapter 19, to "judge and to make war," whose eyes are as a flame of fire; on whose head are many crowns; whose garment is a vesture dipped in blood; whose name is "Faithful and True," the "Word of God," the "King of Kings and Lord of Lords"; whose followers are "the armies in heaven," seated upon white horses, clothed in fine linen, white and clean; from whose mouth goes a sharp sword that with it he should smite the nations; who shall rule the nations with a rod of iron; and who "treadeth the winepress of the fierceness and wrath of Almighty God."

This is He who, in the language of Old Testament prophecy, "comes from Edom, with dyed garments from Bozrah, glorious in His apparel, traveling in the greatness of His strength, mighty to save"; concerning whom the question is asked, "Wherefore are Thou red in Thine apparel, and Thy garments like him that treadeth the winefat?" and who Himself replies, "I have trodden the winepress alone, and of the people there was none with Me; for I will tread them in Mine anger, and trample them in My fury; and their blood shall be sprinkled upon My garments, and I will stain all My raiment. For the day of vengeance is in Mine heart, and the year of My redeemed is come!"[141]

And as the final treading of "the great winepress of the wrath of God" is described at the close of the parenthetical visions in Rev. 14, that judgment also belongs to those of the seventh vial, in which according to Rev. 19, "the winepress of the fierceness and

---

141 Isaiah 63.

wrath of Almighty God" is trodden. If the winepress is not trodden twice over, both passages must refer to the same event. And hence the destruction of "the vine of the earth," or Harvest of the Vintage in chapter 14 takes place under the seventh vial. Its prediction is as follows, — "And another angel came out of the temple which is in heaven, he also having a sharp sickle. And another angel came out from the altar, which had power over fire, and cried with a loud cry to him that had the sharp sickle, saying, Thrust in thy sharp sickle, and gather the clusters of the vine of the earth; for her grapes are fully ripe. And the angel thrust in his sickle into the earth, and gathered the vine of the earth, and cast it into the great winepress of the wrath of God. And the winepress was trodden without the city, and blood came out of the winepress even unto the horse bridles, by the space of a thousand and six hundred furlongs."

And further, to the judgment of the seventh vial belongs the Armageddon conflict and its issues of the nineteenth of Revelation, under which "the beast" and "the kings of the earth, and their armies," are "gathered together to make war against him that sat on the horse, and against his army"; when "the beast is taken, and with him the false prophet that wrought miracles before him," and both are "cast alive" into the lake of fire. This final destruction of the anti-Christian hosts is that of" the supper of the great God," to which" all the fowls that fly in the midst of heaven" are called to come, that they" may eat the flesh of kings, and the flesh of captains, and the flesh of mighty men, and the flesh of horses, and of them that sit on them, and the flesh of all men, both free and bond, small and great."

The events of the seventh vial as described in Rev. 16, are as follows, —

[1.] The preliminary warning, "Behold I come as a thief. Blessed is he that watcheth, and keepeth his garments, lest he walk naked, and they see his shame."

[2.] The gathering together of the anti-Christian hosts" into a place called in the Hebrew tongue, Armageddon."

[3.] The pouring out of the seventh vial into the air; not as previous vials on "the earth," on "the sea," on" the rivers and fountains of waters," and on" the sun," all of which spheres are local and restricted; but" into the air," a universal judgment on the sphere of Satan's government, as" the prince of the power of the air" (Eph. 2:2).

[4.] The great voice out of the temple of heaven, from the throne saying, "It is done" a terminal sentence analogous to the "It is finished" of Calvary, and "It is done" of the New Creation in chapter 21:6.

[5.] The voices, and thunders, and lightnings.

[6.] The "great earthquake, such as was not since men were upon the earth, so mighty an earthquake, and so great."

[7.] The tripartite division of the great city Babylon; "the great city was divided into three parts"; the" great city" of chapter 11, "which spiritually is called Sodom and Egypt, where also our Lord was crucified"; the city whose "tenth part" had fallen by the "great earthquake" which followed the death, resurrection, and ascension of the witnesses; the "great city Babylon" of the judgment described in chapter 18, at the smoke of whose burning ascends the cry "What city is like unto this great city?" "That great city that was clothed in fine linen, and purple, and scarlet, and decked with gold, and precious stones, and pearls;"that mighty city" whose merchandise of all precious things includes "the bodies and souls of men" which as "a great millstone cast into the sea" shall be "thrown down," and "found no more at all"; the city by whose "sorceries were all nations deceived"; and in which "was found the blood of prophets, and of saints, and of all that were slain upon the earth."

8.   The fall of "the cities of the nations."

9. The coming of "great Babylon" "in remembrance before God to give unto her the cup of the wine of the fierceness of his wrath."

10. The convulsion in which "every island fled away, and the mountains were not found."

11. The great hailstorm falling on men out of heaven, "every stone about the weight of a talent"; men blaspheming "because of the plague of the hail, for the plague thereof was exceeding great."

10. The Present Stage [1905]

THE PERIOD which has elapsed since the fall of Napoleon or the end of the French Revolution era, has witnessed: —

[1.] The denial of the historic and Protestant interpretation of the Apocalypse.

[2.] Its defense.

[3.] Its confirmation.

We propose in this closing section to trace these three steps in the story of the interpretation of the Apocalypse on historic lines.

Chapter 1. The Modern Denial Of The Historic And Protestant Interpretation Of The Apocalypse

IN A LECTURE on "The Pope, the Antichrist of scripture," the late eminent Dr. Candlish, of Edinburgh, thus refers to the modern twofold denial of the historic and Protestant interpretation of prophecy.

"Two schools of interpretation have sprung up," in recent times, "in opposition to the almost unbroken harmony of the Reformed Churches; but neither their numbers nor their impartiality entitle them to much consideration.

"I. The first is that which owes its origin to Germany, and the rationalist theologians of that country. It is patronized by Moses Stuart in America, and by Dr. Davidson in England. It holds that the prophecies in the Revelation, and of course those also in the other passages connected with it, have been long ago fulfilled, having all had reference to the fall, first of Jerusalem, and then of Pagan Rome. Moses Stuart advocates this view chiefly on the ground that the suffering Christians in John's day could not be expected to take much interest in the events of a remote futurity, and that what John wrote for their consolation must have related more nearly to their present circumstances. To us it seems clear, on the other hand, that to believers smarting under pagan persecution, and ready almost to despair of Christ's cause, nothing could be more encouraging than to see, however dimly, drawn out in long perspective before their eyes, the entire course of the eventful voyage through which the church had to pass, among troubled and tossing billows, until she reached at last the desired haven of rest. Moses Stuart's reason, therefore, for antedating the fulfillment of the Apocalyptic predictions, has evidently no force in it, but the reverse. And when we come to the details of his exposition, we find so much vagueness of application, and withal so much violence in torturing texts, and dates, and facts, that we are rather driven at last to the idea of the late learned Dr. Arnold, that prophecy has no definite accomplishment at all; — that it is a sort of mystical description, by anticipation, of the prolonged conflict of good and evil principles that goes on continually in the world and in the Church; — and that it is designed to indicate no more than the general prevalence of good on the whole, amid partial and temporary victories of evil, and the complete triumph of the good over the evil at last.

"2. The other school of interpretation is that of certain modern expounders of unfulfilled prophecy, who, in their anxiety to magnify the grandeur of the scenes connected with the coming of Christ, would reserve all that is terrible, as well as all that is glorious, in the Apocalyptic visions, for that momentous era. Hence they will not allow that any of the Church's history already past, or anything in her position now, fulfills the predictions respecting Antichrist; and they look for some monster — some, I know not what, satanic incarnation — as yet to rise on the astonished world, that he may personally cope in arms with the Saviour coming in His glory, and be signally overthrown in the encounter. Of this school I content myself with speaking now, not in my own words, but in those of a profound student of prophecy, who on this point has rendered right good service to the Church of Christ; — I mean the late Mr. Cunninghame of Lainshaw.

"The truths which the Futurist desires to subvert, are not of secondary, but primary and vital importance. They are truths which martyrs have sealed with their blood, and which every genuine Protestant would still be ready to bear witness to, even unto death...

"In estimating the character of the Reformation and its transcendent importance, it is necessary to bear in mind that it was properly a testimony; and a testimony of a double nature. The Reformers, like the prophets of old, were to bear witness for the truth of God. This they did in their Confessions of Faith. But in the second place, as the ancient prophets were witnesses against Israel, so were the Protestants set as witnesses against Papal Rome, the great corrupter of the truth, and the slaughterer of the saints. This part of their testimony, like the former part of it, could only be fulfilled by their recurring to the written Word, for to men who are not themselves inspired by the Holy Ghost, it is not given to testify against the enemies of God, or the corrupters of His truth, in any other way, or with any other weapons, than the Sword of the Spirit, which is the Word of God. The Reformers did accordingly (as already observed), fulfill this part of their testimony by their perfectly unanimous denunciations of Rome, as Babylon, the Mother of Harlots, and the Pope, as The Man of Sin.

"Now from the last part of this testimony, it is manifest that the Futurists have entirely fallen; yea, they desire to destroy it root and branch, flattering themselves that they have thus risen to a higher degree of illumination, and have left us in the vale of darkness...

"No one who rejects the principles of interpretation affixing on Rome Papal and her bishop the characters of Babylon and the Man of Sin is truly a Protestant, seeing that he has denied that which all the Reformers held to be the testimony of the Spirit against that idolatrous Church."

Breaking Down the Barriers Against Romanism

An army of men is constantly employed on the coast of Holland in keeping up the barriers which prevent the ocean from invading the land. To neglect the barriers, or to permit them to be broken down at any spot, would be to bring certain and widespread destruction on life and property. Now the Word of God in its doctrinal, practical, and prophetic teachings, has erected strong barriers to keep out the errors and superstitions which tend, like a surrounding and devouring sea, to encroach on the Christian Church, overthrow her primitive faith and discipline, and conform her character to the world from which she has been delivered. The predictions and warnings of the Word of God relating to the Romish apostasy constitute a main part of these barriers.

This anti-Romish barrier has been broken down in England, by professedly Protestant ministers; clergymen of the Established Church, and the consequences of their act have been disastrous and appalling.

Three men stood forth as pioneers in this destructive work, the Rev. S. R. Maitland, Librarian to the Archbishop of Canterbury; Dr. James Todd, Fellow of Trinity College, Dublin; and the celebrated John Henry Newman, of Oxford. In the Donnellan Lectures preached by Dr. Todd before the University of Dublin in 1838, on "the prophecies relating to Antichrist in the writings of Daniel and St. Paul" the following inscription appears on the opening page. "To the Rev. Samuel Roffey Maitland, Librarian to His Grace the Archbishop of Canterbury, as an humble testimony to the great value of his writings in the interpretation of prophecy, and as an acknowledgment of the assistance derived from them in the composition of the following pages, this volume is inscribed by his sincere and affectionate friend the author."

Two years later John Henry Newman wrote his treatise on "The Protestant idea of Antichrist" (dated 1840). That treatise opens with the following sentence: — "The Discourses which Dr. Todd has recently given to the world are perhaps the first attempt for a long course of years in this part of Christendom to fix a dispassionate attention and a scientific interpretation upon the momentous 'Prophecies relating to Antichrist in the writings of Daniel and St. Paul.'"

In this treatise Newman quotes Dr. Todd's Lectures, and builds on his arguments from beginning to end. "We have pleasure," he says, "in believing that in matters of doctrine we entirely agree with Dr. Todd." Thus Todd derived his views from Maitland, while Newman drew his arguments from Todd.

What then, we enquire, were the views of these three men, and how did they originate?

Maitland had been a lawyer, was gifted with a remarkably acute intellect, and possessed the power of expressing his views in a clear and telling manner. Being trained for the Bar, his education had tended to develop argumentative power rather than historical and religious knowledge. The direction of his attention to prophecy was purely casual, and arose, as he tells us, from a chance remark made to him one day by a friend.

"Between nine and ten years ago," he says, "I chanced to be in company with a gentleman (not a lawyer) but one whose right to speak on the subject you must yourself allow — an Irishman bred to the Church, in Trinity College, Dublin. Happening in the way of civil discourse to say something of the 1,260 years, he took me up (as, by your leave, some of your countrymen are apt to do), rather smartly, but all in perfect good humor and asked me 'How I could believe that system.' I was a good deal startled, and such was my ignorance at that time that without considering the difference between our breeding I ventured to reply. We discussed the matter, and I soon found, as might have been expected, that my friend knew more of the matter than I did; and I was led to feel a strong suspicion that he was in the right. When he had left me, I pursued the enquiry almost in silence, for I knew scarcely any one who would have taken the trouble to talk about the matter, until after about three years, another gentleman, also bred to the Church, in Trinity College, Dublin, was kind enough to give me a visit. I found that he agreed with me; and he was the means of bringing me into a very interesting and instructive correspondence with a third gentleman, a Doctor of Divinity, and a Senior Fellow of the same College, and when I published my first enquiry I did not know that there were any men in the world but those three who were prepared to agree with me" Thus originated Maitland's attack on the Protestant Interpretation of prophecy.

For more than ten years Maitland continued to write on this subject; his works include treatises on the grounds on which the prophetic period of Daniel and St. John has been "supposed to consist of 1,260 years"; replies to reviews in The Morning Watch, "an attempt to elucidate the prophecies concerning Antichrist replies to the works of Digby and Cunninghame on the prophetic times; strictures on Faber's work on the ancient Waldenses and Albigenses" etc. No wide acquaintance with history, no deep sympathy with the great work of the Reformation, no spiritual insight into the Word of God, can be traced in these very polemical productions. From first to last they are occupied with captious objections to the interpretations of prophecy put forth by the Reformers, by Mede, Sir Isaac Newton, Bishop Newton, Bishop Hurd, and other Protestant writers. The view of the Church of Rome that prophecy is silent as to the great apostasy of the Middle Ages, and in its references to Antichrist only supplies warnings against some infidel apostasy to take place in future times, is that which Maitland advocates. To accuse the Church of Rome of having apostatized from the faith of the New Testament was to him an utter mistake. Rome held all the fundamentals of the Christian faith, and only erred in some matters of secondary importance. In his tracts and treatises he cleverly selects the weakest and most vulnerable points in the Protestant interpretation of prophecy as the objects of special attack. He parades the differences in the views of prophetic interpreters, and the mistakes which some of them have made as to the fulfillment of the prophetic times. He denies the honesty and good faith of Bishop Newton, who had, he maintains, misrepresented the views of Sulpicius Severus. Bengel had made some manifest errors in his chronological interpretations. Cunninghame had been mistaken in supposing the Jews would be restored in the year 1822. The "Man of Sin" was an infidel, yet to arise, and sit for 1,260 literal days in a literal temple, of brick or stone, proclaiming himself to be God. The Albigenses were heretics, and their blood, shed by the Church of Rome, was not the blood of saints. Thus carping and quibbling, building up nothing, but objecting and opposing, on secondary or side issues, personal and non-essential points, the Rev. S. R. Maitland, formerly lawyer, now librarian to an archbishop, proceeds in pamphlet after pamphlet to demolish the foundations of Protestantism, as built on the prophetic testimony of the Word of God. The fact that that testimony had been a central and principal factor in the production of the Reformation, and had been sealed by the blood of saints and martyrs weighs nothing with him. The purely hypothetical character of his interpretation of prophecy as unsupported by the facts of history does not in the least distress him; nor the fact that his views in these matters were identical with those of the Church of Rome. He has no fear of the ocean of Popish superstition which waited to invade the land when the barrier he sought to break down was removed. The real use and importance of the prophetic barrier never seems to have occurred to him. Pull it down, take it out of the way, destroy it; such was his constant cry; and most effectually that work was done. The times favored the act. An age more critical than spiritual had commenced, and a Rome-ward movement was already arising, destined to sweep away the old Protestant landmarks, as with a flood.

Dr. Todd in his Donnellan Lectures preached before the University of Dublin in 1838, proclaimed himself Maitland's follower, and boldly attacked the views of the Reformers as to the Church of Rome. He rashly rushed into the wide question of the interpretation of the prophecies of Daniel and St. John, and maintained that the fourth kingdom of Daniel's vision is not the Roman empire; that the three first beasts of Daniel 7 are not identical with the kingdoms represented by the gold, silver, and brazen parts of the image; that destructiveness was no characteristic of the Roman power; that the "stone cut out without hands" was not fulfilled by the preaching of Christianity; that Romanism is not properly an apostasy from the faith; that Paul's prophecies of "the Man of Sin" and the apostasy of the latter times, do not relate to the Church of Rome; that the study of history was not necessary in order to the comprehension of prophecy; and that the symbolical prophecies of Daniel and John, though divinely asserted to be full of mysteries, should be taken "in their plain and literal signification," as perfectly intelligible "without the need of any external aid to unfold a hidden meaning, or to discover in their visions a history of the Church and of the world." He maintained that to "endeavor to prove that the corruptions of the Church were foretold in Scripture" was a "vain and chimerical speculation," that the prophecies relating to the apostasy were none of them fulfilled, and that the whole Protestant Church, including the Waldenses, Lollards, Hussites, Lutherans, Calvinists, Huguenots, Puritans, and the great mass of Protestant interpreters of prophecy, the Protestant Confessions of Faith, the Westminster Assemblies Catechism, etc., were all in gross error as to the meaning of prophecy, and the character of the Church of Rome.

In his treatise on "the Protestant idea of Antichrist," written in 1840, and built on Dr. Todd's then recently delivered discourses, Newman plainly says "we take up Dr. Todd's position." Linking Maitland with Todd he says of the latter "pursuing the line of remark which the learned Mr. Maitland has opened, Dr. Todd has brought together a mass of information on this subject." Accusing the Albigenses of error, and belittling as far as possible the testimony of the Waldenses, Hussites and others before the Reformation, he asks with Dr. Todd: "Are these the expositors from whom the Church of Christ is to receive the true interpretation of the prophecies?"

The claims and admissions he makes in opposing "the Protestant idea of Antichrist," deserve the most serious consideration. "We observe," says Newman, "that the essence of the doctrine that there is 'one only Catholic and Apostolic Church' lies in this: — that there is on earth a representative of our absent Lord, or a something divinely interposed between the soul and God, or a visible body with invisible privileges. All its subordinate characteristics flow from this description. Does it impose a creed, or impose rites and ceremonies, or change ordinances, or remit and retain sins, or rebuke and punish, or accept offerings, or send out ministers, or invest its ministers with authority, or accept of reverence and devotion in their persons? All this is because it is Christ's visible presence. It stands for Christ. Can it convey the power of the Spirit? Does grace attend its acts? Can it touch, or bathe, or seal, or lay on hands? Can it use material things for spiritual purposes? Are its temples holy? All this comes of its being (so far) what Christ was on earth. Is it a ruler, prophet, priest, intercessor, teacher? Has it titles such as these in its measure as being the representative and instrument of the Almighty who is unseen? Does it claim a palace and a throne, an altar and a doctor's chair, the gold, frankincense, and myrrh of the rich and wise, an universal empire, and a never-ending succession? All this is so because it is what Christ is. All the offices, names, honors, powers which it claims depend upon the determination of the simple question: 'Has Christ, or has He not, left a representative behind Him?' Now, if He has, all is easy and intelligible, this is what churchmen maintain; they welcome the news; and they recognize in the Church's acts but the fulfillment of the high trust committed to her. But let us suppose for a moment the other side of the alternative to be true; supposing Christ has left no representative behind Him. Well then, here is an association which professes to take His place without warrant. It comes forward instead of Christ and for Him; it speaks for Him, it develops His words, it suspends His appointments, it grants dispensations in matters of positive duty; it professes to minister grace; it absolves from sin; and all this of its own authority. Is it not forthwith according to the very force of the word 'Antichrist'? He who speaks for Christ must either be His true ambassador, or Antichrist; and nothing but Antichrist can he be if appointed ambassador there is none. Let his acts be the same in both cases, according as he has authority or not, so is he most holy or most guilty. It is not the acts that make the difference, it is the authority for those acts. The very same acts are Christ's or Antichrist's according to the doer; they are Antichrist's if Christ does them not. There is no medium between a Vice-Christ and Antichrist."

Exactly so. Well and memorably said; and this the sin of Rome and the papacy. As destitute of warrant in the Word of God the Bishop of Rome claiming to be the vicar of Christ, is Antichrist.

We thank you, John Henry Newman, for so clearly stating the alternative in this great question. Either the Pope of Rome is what he claims to be, the vicar of Christ, or in making that claim he is Antichrist. What his doctrines are, what his acts are, what his self-exaltation is, what his usurpations, tyrannies and persecutions have been in past ages, we well know, and can never forget. To regard him as the representative of Christ, as His vicar upon earth, we cannot. Truth and conscience forbid us to do it. We reject and abhor his false and blasphemous pretensions. But they remain. They characterize him. They are the crown he wears; his proud title; the badge upon his brow. He claims to be the vicar of Christ. He is therefore Antichrist. Dread alternative! Vicar of Christ or Antichrist. Not the former, then the latter. A fact to be remembered, pondered, and boldly declared.

Before the close of his treatise on "The Protestant idea of Antichrist," Newman makes some remarkable admissions as to the character of what he calls "the Roman party," in the Christian church. "One more remark," he says, "shall we make, and that shall be the last. What is the real place of the Church of the Middle Ages in the divine scheme need not be discussed here. If we have been defending it, this has been from no love, let our readers be assured, of the Roman party among us at this day. That party, as exhibited by its acts, is a low-minded, double-dealings worldly-minded sets and the less we have to do with it the better."

This he says, "not against the Church of Rome," nor against "individual members of it," but against "that secular and political spirit which in this day has developed itself among them into a party, and at least in this country is that party's motive principle and characteristic manifestation."

With regard to this "Roman party" we readily agree with what Newman said before inconsistently entering the Church of Rome, "the less we have to do with it the better."

One concluding question is proposed by Newman. "If we must go by prophecy, which set of prophecies is more exactly fulfilled in the Church of the Middle Ages, those of Isaiah which speak of the evangelical kingdom, or those of St. Paul and St. John which speak of the antichristian corruption?" Without hesitation we reply the latter. The Church of the dark ages presents no fulfillment of Isaiah's glorious visions of the final results of redemption.

Having denied the Anti-Romish witness of prophecy, Newman proceeded to demolish the doctrinal barrier, which separated the teachings of the Church of England from those of the Church of Rome. In Tract XC he boldly maintained that "the Articles are not written against the creed of the Roman Church, but again# actual existing errors in it, whether taken into its system or not."

"Scripture," he said, "is not on Anglican principles the Rule of faith." The "pardons" condemned in the Articles are only "large and reckless indulgences from the penalties of sin obtained on money payments." In the thirty-first Article the Sacrifice of the mass is not spoken of, but the "Sacrifice of masses." "Bishop is superior to bishop only in rank, not in real power; and the Bishop of Rome, the head of the Catholic world, is not the center of unity except as having a primacy of order" On purgatory, pardons, the worshiping and adoration of images and relics, the invocation of saints, and the mass, the Articles do not contain any condemnation of the doctrines of the Church of Rome, but only of such absurd practices and opinions as intelligent Romanists would repudiate. The mode of interpretation advocated by Newman "reconciled subscription to the Articles with the adoption of errors they were designed to counteract."

As Dr. Arnold said about it "a man may subscribe to an article when he held the very opposite opinions — believing what it denies, and denying what it affirms." "I was embarrassed," says Newman, "in consequence of my wish to go as far as possible in interpreting the Articles in the direction of Roman dogma, without disclosing what I was doing to the parties whose doubts I was meeting."

In 1846 Newman left Oxford for Rome. On becoming a Catholic he accepted "those additional Articles which are not found in the Anglican creed," transubstantiation included. "People say," wrote Newman, "that the doctrine of transubstantiation is difficult to believe; I did not believe the doctrine till I was a Catholic. I had no difficulty in believing it as soon as I believed that the Catholic Roman Church was the oracle of God." To use the words of John Knox, Newman "mistook a harlot for the spouse of Jesus Christ." A fatal mistake, and one fraught with tremendous consequences in the perversion of thousands from the faith of the Gospel to "another gospel which is not another"; one which if Paul were on earth today he would anathematize as he did the false doctrine of the Galatian Church, yea, though even preached by "an angel from heaven."

The Rome-ward movement in the Church of England in whose inauguration Newman was so influential, has assumed the character of a widely extended "conspiracy" within that church against its doctrine, discipline and practice. It aims at the restoration of auricular confession, the worship of the mass,

Romish ceremonies, superstitions, and idolatries, and corporate reunion with the Church of Rome.

The movement has attained gigantic proportions, and seeks the conversion of England to Romanism, through the perversion of the established Protestant Church. "To restore the authority of the Holy See in England" is its aim.

A large part of the Church of England has already become Romanized in doctrine and ritual. In her sanctuaries the priest kneels at the altar, or sits in the Confessional, and the deluded flocks follow their false shepherds, the blind leading the blind.

So momentous have been the consequences which have followed the breaking-down of the barriers erected by Prophecy against the errors and superstitions of the Church of Rome.

Chapter 2. The Defense

AS THE MOST celebrated works in defense of Christianity have been called forth by attacks on the Christian religion, so the ablest works in defense of the Protestant interpretation of Prophecy have been evoked by the controversial war waged against it in recent times. Among these the works of Cunninghame, Faber, O'Sullivan, Birks, and Elliott occupy a foremost place. Of the masterly book written by the Rev. T. R. Birks in 1843, under the title "First Elements of Sacred Prophecy, including an examination of several recent expositions, and of the year-day theory," Faber says, "the attacks of 'modern speculatists' have called forth a most able and seasonable work in which they have been triumphantly exposed with a force of demonstration scarcely equaled, never excelled. The 'First Elements of Sacred Prophecy' I should pronounce to be a book henceforth indispensable to every honest and laborious student of the predictions of Daniel and St. John."[142] "By his masterly work on the First Elements of Prophecy, Mr. Birks," says Elliott, "has advanced the cause of truth, and shown himself its

---

142 "Sacred Calendar of Prophecy." Vol. 1, Introd.

martel and hammer, against what I must beg permission to call the reveries of the Futurist."[143]

The work of the Rev. Mortimer O'Sullivan, D.D., on "The Apostasy Predicted by St. Paul," published in 1842, is an able answer to Dr. Todd's lectures on the subject. Dedicated to "the Provost, the Fellows and the Students of the Dublin University," it is marked by candor and learning, by its Christian spirit, by the beauty of its style, and the strength of its argument.[144]

O'Sullivan writes as one who had deeply studied both the Word of God, and the character of Romanism. No tone of bitterness mars his pages. They pour their sunlight into the dark caverns of the papal system, and produce a profound conviction that that system is the great apostasy predicted in the Pauline prophecy of the "Man of Sin."

The "Horae Apocalyptica" of Elliott, which may well be considered as the most important and valuable commentary on the Apocalypse which has ever been written, was also called into existence by Futurist attacks on the Protestant interpretation of prophecy. In his preface to the fifth edition Elliott says: — "When I first began to give attention to the subject some twenty years ago, it was the increasing prevalence among Christian men in our country

---

143 *Horae Apoc.* IV, p. 557.

144 One sentence only can we quote from this admirable work on the way in which prophecy should be studied — a fair specimen of the whole.

"Prophecy," says O'Sullivan, "presents a mirror to the future, in which God constrains events, long centuries before they have a sensible being, to appear, and shew themselves undisguised, as they are seen by Him. It is a wondrous telescope which He Himself has framed, and disposed, and adjusted. Who shall dare to disturb this divine mechanism, or, in refuting its revelations to change them by addition or reserve? A careless, a cautious touch might disarrange the delicate disposition of some minute but essential part; the presence of a disturbing or darkening passion might confuse or hide the image in which futurity has been anticipated. He who would behold it must approach with reverence — must await and observe, with indrawn breath and motionless; he must hold himself disengaged from the power of sense and transitory things, and live the serene life of the soul. When patient, passionless, self-renouncing contemplation has been rewarded, and the vision has been given, it should be declared with the same fidelity and singleness of heart which had disposed the Spirit to receive it."

of the Futurist system of Apocalyptic interpretation — a system which involved the abandonment of the opinion held by all the chief fathers and doctors of our Church respecting the Roman Popes and Popedom as the great intended anti-Christian power of Scripture prophecy, — that suggested to me the desirableness and indeed necessity, of a more thoroughly careful investigation of the whole subject than had been made previously. For thereby I trusted that we might see God's mind on the question; all engaged in that controversy being alike agreed as to the fact of its being expressed in this prophecy, rightly understood: and whether indeed in His view Popery was that monstrous evil, and the Reformation a deliverance to our Church and nation as mighty and blessed, as we had been taught from early youth to regard them. Even yet more does the importance of the work strike us at the present time, when infidelity has become notoriously prevalent among our educated men, and even from ordained ministers in our own church a voice has been raised somewhat pretentiously, with questionings of the truth of Christianity as a religion supernaturally revealed from heaven, and denial of all supernatural inspiration of the Christian Scriptures. For supposing the evidence in proof of the fulfillment of the Apocalyptic prophecy in the history of Christendom since St. John's time to be satisfactory and irrefragable, we have herein a proof similarly irrefragable not only of the possibility but also of the fact of the divine supernatural inspiration of one book at least of Holy Scripture; — a fact annihilative of the skeptic's doctrine as to the impossibility in the nature of things of such inspiration, and rendering more than probable, c a priori ' the idea of divine supernatural inspiration in other of its prophetic books also."

Elliott's Commentary was practically the work of the lifetime of one of the most learned and laborious expositors of modern times. Like Gibbon's "History of the Decline and Fall of the Roman Empire," to which it frequently refers, it stands alone in its sphere, as a monumental work of surpassing value. The ten thousand references it contains to ancient and modern works bearing on the subject elucidated greatly enhance its value. We may safely say that during the half century which has elapsed since its publication, no other work on historic lines of interpretation has appeared of equal importance.

Chapter 3. Confirmation Of The Protestant Interpretation Of The Apocalypse

FROM THE DENIAL AND DEFENSE of the Protestant interpretation of the Apocalypse we now advance to its confirmation by the events which have taken place since the French Revolution.

To trace the fulfillment of apocalyptic prophecy in the period we have now reached it will be needful,

[1.] To consider the things foretold with reference to the period, and

[2.] The things which have come to pass.

On comparing the one series of things with the other, we shall see that the predictions have to a large extent been fulfilled; and that the fulfillment is such as to afford a strong confirmation of the historic interpretation of the Apocalypse; together with a clear indication of the nearness of those final judgments which mark the close of the present age.

I. Apocalyptic Predictions Relating to the Present Period.

In the events of the French Revolution we have already traced the fulfillment of the judgments of the earlier vials, from the first to the fifth; from the "grievous sore" inflicted on "the worshippers of the beast," or adherents of the papacy, to the judgments poured on "the throne of the beast," or the seat of Papal sovereignty.

These solemn judgments occupied in their fulfillment the century which terminated with the fall of Napoleon in 1815.

Beginning with the plague of infidelity and moral corruption which was the precursor of the French Revolution, these judgments included the overthrow of Monarchy, and abolition of the Roman Catholic religion in France, with attendant massacres and wars, appalling in character and world-wide in effects, and culminated in the spoliation of Rome, the captivity of the Pope, who died in exile, and the incorporation of Rome with France as the second city of the empire.

In the order of prophecy the judgments which follow these are those of the sixth vial.

Predictions Under the Sixth Vial

1. The sixth vial is poured out on the River Euphrates, and dries up its waters.

The meaning of the sixth vial is determined by that of the sixth trumpet. Under the "woe" of the sixth trumpet, a destroying army, vast in its numbers, issues from the River Euphrates as a judgment on idolatrous Christendom. With one consent historical interpreters have recognized the fulfillment of this "woe," in the overthrow of the Eastern Roman Empire by the Turks, whose myriads of horsemen came from the banks of the Euphrates. Hence the drying-up of the Euphrates which takes place under the sixth vial, has long been interpreted to mean a wasting away or notable diminution of Turkish power; involving the decline of its population, and the loss of its territories.

2. The Time Indicated

The time indicated in prophecy for this event is the close of 2,300 years measured from the advance of Persia, or the "pushing westward" of the Persian ram — the apparent starting point of the vision in Daniel 8, or the invasion of Greece by Persia B.C. 480.

Measured from that date, the prophetic period of 2,300 years terminated A.D. 1821. Bichino, writing in 1797, anticipated that the "cleansing" of the downtrodden eastern "sanctuary" would take place at the close of 2,300 years, reckoned from the starting of Xerxes from Susa in 481 B.C. But it is evident that the period should be reckoned from the actual invasion of Greece by Xerxes in the following year B.C. 480. Allowing for the necessary subtraction of one year (in adding B.C. to A.D. dates) the 2,300 years ran out in 1821. At this date, then, the foretold "cleansing" of the downtrodden "sanctuary" ought to have commenced, or some notable diminution of the resources, armies, population, and territories of Turkey, as representing the apostate Mohammedan power which has trodden down Palestine and Eastern Christendom ever since the fall of Constantinople in 1453.

3. The Drying Up Of The Euphrates

On the drying-up of the Euphrates, three "unclean spirits" like frogs, issue "from the mouth of the dragon, the mouth of the beast, and the mouth of the false prophet." Satanically inspired, for they are "the spirits of devils," and working in some sense "miracles" or wonders, they "go forth unto the kings of the earth and of the whole world to gather them to the battle of that great day of God Almighty." In connection with this terminal event it is added, "Behold, I come as a thief. Blessed is he that watcheth and keepeth his garments, lest he walk naked, and they see his shame. And He gathered them together into a place called in the Hebrew tongue Armageddon."

The dragon, in chapter 12, is interpreted to mean the Satanically inspired Paganism of Ancient Rome. The "beast" has been shown to be the eighth ruling head of the Roman Empire, or the papal power; while the "false prophet" is the minister of the beast; lamb-like in pretensions, but dragon-like in character, for he had "two horns like a lamb, and spake as a dragon" (ch. 12:11).

Heathen-like infidelity, Popery, and apostate priestcraft, would seem then, to be the three unclean spirits, whose noisy loquacity, symbolized by their being compared to "frogs," and delusive influence, bring about the final dreadful Armageddon conflict.

4. "...that the way of the kings of the east might be prepared"

The drying-up of the Euphrates "that the way of the kings of the east might be prepared," is an evident allusion to the drying-up of the literal Euphrates, which preceded the capture of Babylon, by Cyrus and Darius, kings of the east. As the literal Babylon is in prophecy the figure of the apostate Church of Rome, the drying-up of the Euphrates may well have a secondary reference to the wasting or consumption of the stream of wealth and prosperity by which that Church is supported. An analogous double reference of apocalyptic symbolism is seen in chapter 17, where the "seven heads" of the wild beast power represent both "seven mountains where the woman sitteth," and "seven kings," or ruling powers.

5. "...I come as a thief."

The warning under the sixth vial, "Behold, I come as a thief," and the blessing pronounced on those who "watch" and "keep their garments" in preparation for the Lord's coming, seem to point to the nearness at this juncture of the Second Advent, and to an awakening of watchfulness, and renewal of preparation among the Lord's faithful followers, for His coming.

II. Predictions with reference to the Fall of the Papacy.

The 1,260 years' duration of the papal power is properly measured from the era of its commencement, the brief period which extended from the edict of Justinian, in A.D. 533, to the edict of the Emperor Phocas in A.D. 607, constituting the Bishop of Rome, Pope or Universal Bishop in the Christian Church.

Measured from the first of these dates, the 1,260 years of papal domination ended in 1793, the time of the fall of the papacy, and abolition of the Roman Catholic religion in the French Revolution.

Measured from the second of these dates, the year 607, the 1,260 years extended: —

[1.] In calendar, or prophetic years of 360 days, to 1849.

[2.] In solar years to 1867.

Fleming, as will be remembered, pointed out in 1701 that the 1,260 years' papal duration should be reckoned In calendar or prophetic years, of 360 days • which would cut off eighteen years from the 1,260, making 1,242 years; and that so reckoning the period from the decree of Phocas, it would end in 1848-9.

It will also be remembered that numerous writers on prophecy during the last three hundred years have indicated 1866- 1868 as the last great terminus of the 1,260 years' papal domination.

According then, to these anticipations based on the prophetic times of Daniel and Revelation, and on the facts of history, the years 1848-9 and 1866-7 ought to have possessed a terminal character in relation to the papal power.

III. Predictions as to the Restoration of the Jewish People.

The Word of God, which foretells the "casting away" of the Jews, and their long exile from their land, foretells also their restoration. "He that scattered Israel will gather him." Every prophet from Moses to Malachi dwells upon the theme, and the Apostle Paul devotes the central section of the Epistle to the Romans to its elucidation.

The restoration of the Jews, according to the "sure word of prophecy," immediately follows the termination of "the times of the Gentiles." It was our Lord who said "Jerusalem shall be trodden down of the Gentiles until the times of the Gentiles are fulfilled."

Several stages are to mark this great restoring work. First, the scattered children of Israel are to be reunited, or unified as a people; secondly, while continuing in unbelief they are to return to their own land, and to be reconstructed as a nation; and thirdly, after passing through the deep trials which await them there, in order to compel them to judge their ways aright, as did Joseph's brethren in the trial which befell them in Egypt, they are to be led to repentance for their rejection and crucifixion of the Messiah, and converted by some manifestation of Christ; turned from darkness to light, and from the power of Satan unto God.

Time of Jewish Restoration

According to the prophecies in the last chapter of Daniel the commencement of Jewish restoration takes place at the close of 1,260 years, reckoned from the setting up of the desolating power by which Palestine has been long trodden under foot.

As the capture of Jerusalem by the Saracens A.D. 637, followed by the erection of the Mosque of Omar on the site of Solomon's temple, was the initial date of the last down-treading of the city, the expiration of 1,260 years reckoned from this date, first, in lunar years, and second, in solar years, should have led to initial stages connected with the restoration of the Jews.

[1.] One thousand two hundred and sixty lunar years, from A.D. 637, terminated in 1860.

[2.] One thousand two hundred and sixty solar years from the same date, ended in 1897.

The years 1860 and 1897 should therefore have witnessed the inauguration of some important movements for the unification of the Jewish people, and their restoration to Palestine.

Chapter 4. Fulfillment Of The Events Predicted Under The Sixth Vial

IN OUR CHAPTER on the seven vials we pointed out the wonderful fulfillment of the predictions under the sixth vial of the drying up, or wasting away of the Turkish power which has been taking place since 1821, the year of the Greek insurrection. The coincidence of this with the close of 2,300 years, the prophetic period in the eighth of Daniel which terminates with "the cleansing of the sanctuary," is remarkable. The eastward pushing of the Persian ram in Daniel's vision is the earliest commencement of the 2,300 years' period connected with the post Babylonian "treading down of the sanctuary." This great historical event, the invasion of Greece by the Persian Monarch Xerxes took place in the year B.C. 480. In the spring of that year the Persians commenced their march through Thrace and Macedonia against Greece; in the summer took place the famous battle of Thermopylae, and in the autumn the battle of Salamis. The great prophetic cycle of twenty-three centuries reckoned from B.C. 480 terminated in A.D. 1821,[145] the date of the general revolt of the Greeks in the Morea, Wallachia, Moldavia and the islands, from Turkish rule. This was followed the same year by the capture of Tripolizza, and the liberation of the Peloponnesus. The destruction of the Turko- Egyptian fleets in the battle of Navarino took place in 1827; since which the power of the Turks over their European, African, and Asiatic territories has ebbed as steadily as the tide.

Since the Syrian massacre of 1860, the government of the Lebanon district in Palestine has been transferred from Turkish to Christian hands. The Turk still holds Jerusalem and the larger part

---

145 In this reckoning one year is subtracted for the difference between B.C. and A.D. dates.

of Palestine in his grasp, but the movement for "the cleansing of the sanctuary" from Mohammedan rule is steadily progressing, and thus the preparation for the restoration of the Jews to their own land.

Contemporaneously with the drying up of the Euphratean or Turkish flood, under the sixth vial, there takes place according to Apoc. 16:13, 14, the issuing forth of "three unclean spirits like frogs," spirits of error which go forth throughout the world to gather together the antichristian hosts to the great and final battle of Armageddon.

As this prediction points to events of the most momentous character taking place in the present day, we ask for it the special attention of our readers.

I. Issuing forth of "The Three Frogs" — Meaning of the Symbol.

"And I saw (come) out of the mouth of the dragon, and out of the mouth of the beast, and out of the mouth of the false prophet, three unclean spirits like frogs. For they are the spirits of demons working signs, which go forth to the kings of the whole world, to gather them together to the war of that great day of God Almighty" (Apoc. 16:13,14).

"By this novel and very remarkable symbol," says Elliott, "which followed next after that of the drying up of the waters of the Euphrates, but ranged still evidently under the sixth vial, there seemed signified some extraordinarily rapid, widespread, and influential diffusion throughout the whole Roman, or perhaps the whole habitable world, of three several unclean or unholy principles, characteristic respectively of the Apocalyptic dragon, beast, and false prophet, from whom they appeared to emanate: all being alike directed and speeded on their course by spirits of hell; and all alike, in respect of the earthly agencies employed to propagate them, resembling frogs; the well-known type of vain loquacious talkers and agitators, deluding and seducing the minds of men. Now by the dragon we know to have been meant (for the evangelist tells us so) that old serpent the devil, as in earlier days animating and acting in the paganism of ancient Rome; the covering skin in which he had been primarily depicted, in a vision figurative of the final war of heathenism against Christianity, at the opening of the fourth century, being that of a seven-headed dragon, and the seven heads said to figure Rome's seven hills. Again, by the beast, or rather (according to the angel's definition of the thing intended in his description) the beast's eighth ruling head, we saw, on I think irrefragable evidence, that the Popes of Rome were meant, from and after the time of their occupying the dragon's throne and empire in Western Christendom. Once more, by the false prophet, at least when with the further characteristic attached to it, so as in Apoc. 19:20, of acting out its functions 'before,' or in subordination to, the beast (a characteristic which completely identifies it with the two-horned lambskin-covered beast of Apoc. 13), there is meant, we have seen, the apostate priesthood of the patriarchate of Western Europe, from and after the time of its subjection and official attachment to the Romish Popedom.

"And what then, if this be correct, the three spirits, or principles, that may be considered most fitly characteristic of these three several actors on the scene: — of the devil, in that character specially in which he had agitated and spoken against Christ's Church in the times of Pagan Rome; of the Roman Papal Antichrist, and of the priesthood of the apostate Romish Church? To myself, with reference to the two first, the answer seems sufficiently obvious: — viz., that the one from the dragon's mouth is the principle of heathen-like infidelity, with its proper accompaniment of blasphemy, and perhaps too of rebelliousness against rightful authority, when opposed to it, alike divine and human ('by which sin fell the angels'): — and the one from the beast the pure direct principle of Popery, based on its fundamental antichristian dogma of the Roman Pope being Christ's divinely appointed vicegerent on earth. But, on the question as to the third spirit intended, there is difficulty. For, as just defined, it seems hard to assign to the false prophet's spirit a sufficiently distinct character from the beast's spirit, seeing that the two-horned beast is described as the chief organ, agent, and mouthpiece, as well as supporter, of the papal beast, its principal. Yet on closer examination, the difficulty will, I think, vanish. The name here given to this agent of evil is simply that of 'the false prophet'; without any further adjunct, expressive of its subjection to the beast, so as in Apoc. 19. This seems not obscurely to suggest the solution. For 'the false prophet' is, by itself, the generic appellation of an apostate priesthood in the professing Church: and of an apostate priesthood what the most characteristic spirit but that of priestcraft? A spirit this of which the essence in professed Christianity, just as in heathenism, is to arrogate to its own peculiar order the distinction of being the appointed and necessary earthly mediator between men and God, the one effective deprecator of His wrath, and channel of his grace and salvation; and which is thus seen to be distinct from, and independent of, that of direct Popery; though naturally, and almost necessarily, its ally. In fact it acted thus independently ere the close of the fourth and through the fifth century, long before its organization under the particular form of the two-horned lambskin-covered beast of Apoc. 13, just as the preparer of the way for a heading sacerdotal earthly Antichrist; though afterwards, under the particular organization just spoken of, devoting itself to him as his most effective instrument and supporter. Still, however, with the full retention of its own essentiality of the spirit of priestcraft.

"Such, I say, — if the dragon, beast, and false prophet mean what I think it proved they mean, — appear to me clearly to be the three principles, or spirits, intended: — spirits in regard of which the prophecy intimates that they would act with unity of effect, if not of purpose, so as to gather the powers of the world (very much as Ahab was seduced by a lying spirit to Ramoth-Gilead) in antagonism against Christ's truth and people, introductorily to the great coming day of final conflict. And, if these be the spirits intended, — spirits to go forth, let it be remembered, after a certain progress made in the drying up under the sixth vial of the Turkman flood from the Euphrates, — it is only too obvious that within the last twenty or thirty years, the precise period marked out in the prophecy (for I will carry down my sketch, now on revising for my fifth edition, to the time present, A.D. 1861), there has been an outgoing of principles and spirits of error, both in England and over the world, which have most strikingly answered to each and every one of them."[146]

II. The three unclean spirits of delusion which have gone forth since the French Revolution.

The figure employed in the prophecy deserves careful consideration. It is drawn from two events in the prefigurative history of the Jewish people; the plague of frogs in Egypt, and the drying up of the Euphrates before the capture of Babylon. As the turning of the waters to blood in Egypt was followed by the plague of frogs, so the turning of the waters to blood under the second and third vials is followed by the plague of unclean frogs under the sixth vial. In the same way as the drying up of the Euphrates by its being turned out of its channel (foretold in Jer. 51:36) was immediately followed by the capture of Babylon, so the drying up of the antitypical Euphrates under the sixth vial is followed by the fall of "Babylon the great" under the seventh.

The connection between the drying up of the Euphratean flood and the issuing forth of the frogs is evident. While the river flowed in its fullness the frogs were hidden in its channel. But as the river was dried up the frogs issued from its bed and banks, and filled the air with their croakings. This relation between the drying up of the river, and the issuing forth of the frogs, points to a double significance in the Euphratean symbol. While the overflow of the

---

146 Elliott, *Horae*, III, pp. 492-496.

Euphrates under the sixth trumpet connects its drying up under the sixth vial with the diminution and wasting away of the Turkish power, the drying up of the river under the sixth vial just previous to the fall of Romish Babylon under the seventh, indicates a causative connection between the two events; that the fall of the modern Babylon (like that of the ancient Babylon) is brought about by the drying up of the river which had supplied it with its wealth. This connection casts light upon recent history, and the prospects of the future, linking as it does the notable drying up of the mighty stream of papal revenues in and since the French Revolution, with the approaching destruction of the papal power, and of Romish Christendom. And further the removal of the old order of things under which the Romish church possessed unbounded wealth and supremacy in the continent of Europe has created a void into which a host of new-fangled theories, philosophies, and constitutions, social, religious, or anti-religious have rushed. Worse than the frogs of Egypt their promulgators assail not the ear of sense merely, but that of mind and spirit. They fill the press with their publications, the schools and the senate with their vociferations. Their inharmonious and jarring voices accuse, attack, affirm, deny, boast and blaspheme, without cessation. Every day adds to their number and their noise. This they say is the age of reason, and free speech. All chains are broken, all tongues loosed. Of the new order of things they are the apostles and prophets; the founders of the philosophy, the politics, the science and the religion of the future.

III. The Croaking of French Frogs.

It is a curious physiological fact that frogs abound in France. It might almost be called the land of frogs. This arises from its numerous marshes. Thus the old French banners had three frogs as their device.

So noisy and troublesome are frogs in France that before the Revolution, the nobility and courtiers, when spending any time in the country, were in the habit of forcing the miserable peasants to flog the neighboring waters all night to keep the frogs quiet. The banishment of the Huguenots, by causing large tracts to become neglected and undrained, increased the plague of fevers and frogs. And the moral history of the country has been analogous with the physical. Unhappy France has become morally a land of fevers and of frogs, and a center from which they have spread throughout Europe, and more or less throughout the world.

Identification of the three "unclean spirits"

While not excluding the idea put forth by Edwards and Barnes that Heathenism, Popery and Mohammedanism are referred to under this symbol, we strongly incline to the view of Elliott and others, that the "dragon," the "beast," and the "false prophet" chiefly represent:

[1.] Satan, as inspiring heathenism and infidelity — the dragon of Revelation 12.

[2.] The Papacy — the eighth head of the revived wild beast power of Revelation 13.

[3.] An apostate priesthood — such as the minister to "the beast" in Revelation 13.

As proceeding from the "mouths" of these three powers the "unclean spirits" are instruments of speech. They are "spirits," not material forms; spirits inspiring multitudinous tongues; they are "unclean spirits," false, ungodly, immoral; they are "frog like," noisy, loquacious, unceasing in their vociferations; low in character while lofty in pretensions; drowning with their hoarse croakings the sound of nobler and more harmonious voices, and wearying the ear with persistent clamor.

As to the fulfillment of this remarkable symbol certainly no fact in modern history is more apparent, and none more appalling than the outburst of Rationalism, Romanism, and Ritualism which has succeeded the French Revolution. Infidelity has advanced in recent times to the utmost limit of its possible development; Romanism has assumed its highest pretensions; and Ritualism has undertaken to overthrow the Reformation, and to restore the apostate church of the middle ages. A common spirit animates these erroneous systems, which through the press have the ear of the civilized world. While divided in their doctrines they are united in their opposition to the Christianity of the New Testament. And their action is wide in its effects. It is fast transforming the philosophy, the literature, the policy, the science, and the religion, of the world.

IV. The Unclean Spirit from the Mouth of the Dragon.

That the voice of ten millions of people, said Coleridge, "calling for the same thing is a spirit, I believe. But whether it be a spirit of heaven, or of hell, I can only know by trying the thing called for by the prescript of reason and God's will."

That there has gone forth from the mouth of the dragon, the early antagonist of Christianity in the days of Roman Paganism (Apoc. 12) an unclean spirit of heathen-like infidelity during the period of the drying up, or wasting away of Turkish or Mohammedan power in the East, and the contemporaneous diminution, or gradual drying up of the secular privileges and resources of the Apostate Romish Church in the West, is a fact which must be evident to every observer of the course of modern history. In the sphere of politics, in science, in philosophy, in biblical criticism, in England and on the continent, an open attack has been waged against Christianity, against the word of God, and even against natural religion, unlike any attack of infidelity in preceding times. The Deism of the eighteenth century, and blasphemous Atheism of the French Revolution have given place to the materialism, pantheism, positivism, and agnosticism of modern times. In Mr. Balfour's recent work on "The Foundations of Belief," the creed of naturalism, which is the outcome of modern infidelity is exposed and condemned at the bar of reason. "The theory that 'dwarfs' and drags in the dust our estimate of the importance of man, that makes 'his very existence an accident,' his story only a passing episode 'in the life of one of the meanest of the planets'; that from some unknown origin, after infinite travail evolves through strife 'famine, disease, and mutual slaughter' a race 'with conscience enough to feel that it is vile, and intelligence enough to know that it is insignificant,' and then consigns that race with all its labors, genius, devotion, sufferings, and aspirations to the pit of everlasting oblivion, to be as though it had never been — such a theory does violence to the deepest instincts of reason, and destroys the foundations of morality. 'All that gives dignity to life, all that gives value to effort, shrinks and fades under the pitiless glare of a creed like this."

The late Herbert Spencer in a series of philosophic works designed to carry the theory of evolution to its utmost limits of development maintained that the great first cause is utterly and necessarily unknown; that God, if there be a God, is and will ever be "the unknown God"; and hence that there is no such thing as Revelation, and that all religion built upon the foundation of Revelation is worthless. On the continent, August Compte, the founder of the modern school of Positivists rejects not only religion, natural and revealed, but even philosophy; and as man is prone to worship something, proposes that he shall worship Humanity! Huxley, who calls himself an Agnostic, and was the inventor of that term, says "when the Positivist asks me to worship humanity, that is to say to adore the generalized conception of men as they ever have been, and probably ever will be — I must reply that I would just as soon bow down and worship the generalized conception of a 'wilderness of apes'."[147]

Agnostics, he says "have no creed, and by the nature of the case cannot have any."

---

147 Huxley, "Essays on Controverted Questions," p. 371.

The warfare in these modern days against Revelation and religion is waged not only by philosophy but also in the name of science. Charles Darwin the principal author of the theory of the development of species by the struggle for existence and survival of the fittest, confessed the completeness of his infidelity. "I do not believe," he says, "that there ever has been any Revelation." "Unbelief crept over me at a slow rate, but was at last complete." Nature had ceased to speak to him of God. Though once capable of "wonder, admiration and devotion" in the presence of the works of God, now he says not even the grandest scenes could "cause any such convictions or feelings to rise in my mind.[148] I am like a man," he confesses, "who has become color blind." Ceasing to believe in a future existence he abandoned faith in religion. To him man was but an improved animal. No spirit from on high had ever been breathed into him, and all his boasted knowledge of God and of futurity was a baseless imagination, and a fading dream. Since Darwin's day how marvelously has spread this spirit of scientific rationalism, how portentous has become its development! In Germany Hackel's "Pedigree of Man" has carried Darwinianism to fantastic and amazing conclusions. The ancestor of the human race was not Adam but "Homo primigenius," the "ape man." Man is an automaton. The freedom of the human will is an illusion. "Every atom is gifted with sensation and a will." All molecules have memory, which is a general function of organized matter. Every atom is provided with an "atom soul." The effective cause of everything is the "perigenesis of the plastidules"! "The blind unconscious forces of nature, working without end or aim, are the effective natural causes of all the complex forms of animal and plant life." "German science," says the Freethought Publishing Company, which has adopted Hackel's work as a textbook, "is one of the glories of the world: it is time that it should lend in England that same aid to free thought which in Germany has made every educated man a free thinker."

---

148 Life and Letters of Charles Darwin," Vol. I, pp. 307, 311.

The modern attack on Revelation from without has been accompanied by an attack from within. Inquiries have been conducted in the name of biblical criticism into the age, authorship, and history of the books of the Old and New Testament, and into the trustworthiness of the gospel narrative, whose rationalistic tendencies have been of the most marked description, and whose disastrous influence has been most widely felt. "Springing from the soil of German Rationalism and French infidelity the so called 'higher criticism' has 'spared nothing sacred or otherwise, and its progress has transformed the history of the past into a nebulous mist.'" Astruc and De Wette hazarded conjectures as to the structure of the Pentateuch; Ewald, Vatke, Graf, Kuenen and other critics carried the disintegrating process still further, applying the boldest hypotheses to the destruction of the sacred text; while Wellhausen, advancing beyond the mutilation of documents, the displacement of names, events and dates, strove to convert history to legend, and to reduce the riches of Old Testament Revelation to a medley of disordered facts, fictions, and immoralities. According to the wild theories of this lawless and arrogant critic, the Jehovah of the old Testament was a mere tribal deity; His servant Moses never prohibited the worship of images, while he sanctioned the worship of the brazen serpent; priests and prophets forged the books of the law, etc. On searching for the proofs of Wellhausen's theory they are not forthcoming. "It is all theory based on theory, and resulting in theory." "The narrative exists simply for the construction of the theory; the theory is not materially suggested by the narrative, nor is it in anyway dependent upon it, because as soon as any incident or statement is found inconveniently rigid for the requirements of the theory it is ruled out of court as unhistorical or spurious."[149] The "higher criticism thus developed in Germany has been transplanted to England and America, where however it appears in less startling and repulsive forms, and animated by a more reverent spirit. Thus Canon Driver's"Introduction to the Literature of the Old Testament," while arbitrarily cutting up the text of scripture into innumerable

---

149 Stanley Leathes, D. D., "The Law in the Prophets."

shreds and fragments, and assigning their sources with a dogmatic confidence which ill becomes one who has nothing to guide his judgment but the documents which he mutilates, acknowledges some sort of inspiration, and affirms that in revealing Himself to Israel God prepared the way for the manifestation of Himself in Jesus Christ. Still so complex does the problem of texual criticism become in the hands of this critic, as to make it practically impossible to teach the Bible to any man of ordinary intelligence."[150] The attacks on the gospel narrative, the very center of scripture, have been chiefly conducted by German and French Rationalists. Two celebrated Swabian critics, Strauss and Baur, led the attack, which was followed up by Renan in his"Vie de Jesus," a work which has been translated into all the languages of Europe. Space forbids us to follow the theories of these skeptical critics; a single sentence is all that we can quote from the writings of Strauss, a sentence which closes a volume of 784 pages, containing the most searching and unscrupulous attack on the gospel narrative which has ever been made. The following is the summary which Strauss gives of the results of his investigation.

"The results of the inquiry which we have now brought to a close have apparently annihilated the greatest and most valuable part of that which the Christian has been wont to believe concerning his Saviour Jesus; have uprooted all the animating motives which he has gathered from his faith, and withered all his consolations. The boundless store of truth and life which for eighteen centuries has been the aliment of humanity, seems irretrievably dissipated; the most sublime leveled with the dust; God divested of His grace; man of his dignity; and the tie between heaven and earth broken." And as if in bitter mockery all that Strauss proposes to substitute for the religion he claims to have destroyed, is "the idea of Humanity." Baur, Strauss and Renan have been answered, but the infidelity of Germany and France remains as a dark and settled cloud over these countries. It has spread throughout Europe; extended to America, India, and the

---

150 Author's work, "Creation Centered in Christ," pp. 26, 27.

colonies, and more or less affected the world. Bales of the works of Tom Paine, and other infidel revolutionary publications have been sent out to seduce and poison the newly awakened mind of India; the works of Spencer, Huxley and other agnostics are widely read by the English speaking students in the colleges and universities of India and Japan, and are producing their natural fruit in the growth of a philosophic skepticism which bars the entrance of Christianity. Truly in our days the spirit of infidelity has gone forth throughout the world, and gathered an uncounted host of opponents to Christianity to "the battle of that great day of God Almighty" which seems already to have begun, and is to signalize the end of the present age.

V. The "Unclean Spirit" from the Mouth of the "Beast."

The revival of Popery which has taken place since the French Revolution, and especially during the Pontificate of Pius IX, and his successor Leo XIII, is one of the most remarkable facts of modern history. The system seemed to have received its deathblow, but lo! it lifts its head again with higher pretensions than ever. It has restored the Jesuits who had been suppressed by Pope Clement XIV, in 1773; and under their inspiring influence the Romanism of the past has been transformed into the Popery of the present.

The modern transformation of Romanism into Popery is an event which should arrest the attention of every thoughtful mind. In the year 1850 a magazine was commenced in Rome at the instance and under the direction of the Jesuits bearing the title Catholic Civilization (*Civiltá Cattolica*). More than a hundred volumes of this magazine were published between 1850 and 1877. The Rev. William Arthur in his work on "The Pope, the Kings, and the People," says of this magazine, "considering the number of books, serials, and journals in different languages of which it is the inspiring force, and considering the modifications it has already succeeded in bringing about in the ideas, and even in the organization of the whole Catholic society, they can scarcely be charged with vain boasting who call it the most influential organ in the world. The Jesuit Fathers forming its editorial staff reside close to the Pope's palace, and work under his immediate direction."[151]

"To reconstitute society according to the Catholic ideal" is its avowed aim. In order to this it considers that "a salutory conspiracy, a holy crusade" is needed. That conspiracy brought about the council of the Vatican, with its decree of papal infallibility.

On the 18th of July, 1870, six archbishop princes, forty-nine cardinals, eleven patriarchs, six hundred and eighty archbishops, and bishops, twenty-eight abbots, twenty-nine generals of orders, eight hundred and three spiritual rulers, representing the Church of Rome throughout the world, solemnly decreed the blasphemous dogma that the occupant of the papal chair is, in all his decisions concerning faith and morals, infallible! "It is said that arrangements had been made to reflect a glory around the person of the Pope by means of mirrors at noon when the decree was made. But the sun shone not that day. A violent storm broke over Rome, the sky was darkened by tempest, and the voices of the council were lost in the rolling of thunder."

The following is the decree of papal infallibility promulgated by the Vatican Council: — "We teach and define that it is a dogma divinely revealed that the Roman Pontiff when he speaks ex cathedra, that is when in the discharge of his office of pastor and doctor of all Christians, by virtue of his supreme apostolic authority, he defines a doctrine regarding faith, or morals, to be held by the Universal Church, by the Divine assistance promised to him in blessed Peter, is possessed of that infallibility with which the Divine Redeemer willed that His Church should be endowed for defining doctrine regarding faith and morals; and that therefore such definitions of the Roman pontiff are irreformable of themselves and not from the consent of the Church. But if any

---

151 "The Pope, the Kings, and the People," Vol. 1, p. 14.

one, — which may God avert, — presume to contradict this our definition, let him be Anathema."

"The new Vatican doctrine," says Dollinger, "confers on the Pope the attribute of the whole fullness of power, (*totam plenitudinem potestatis*) over the whole Church as well as over every individual layman, — a power which is at the same time to be truly episcopal and again specifically papal, which is to include in itself all that affects faith, morals, duties of life, and discipline, and which can without any mediation whatever seize and punish, bid and forbid every one, the monarch as well as the laboring man. The wording is so carefully chosen that there remains for the bishops absolutely no other position and authority than that which belongs to papal commissaries or plenipotentiaries, as every student of history, and of the fathers will admit. The episcopate of the ancient Church is thus dissolved in its inmost being, and the Apostolic Institution to which, according to the judgment of the Church Fathers, the greatest significance and authority of the Church belongs, fades into an unsubstantial shadow."[152]

"In the future every Catholic Christian when asked why he believes this or that can and may give but the one answer: 'I believe or reject it because the infallible Pope has bidden if to be believed or rejected.'"

The Vatican decree erects an "Asian despotism" over conscience and the Christian Church. The authority which it creates is independent, inasmuch as it does not depend upon the Church, her bishops, or any living voice or power distinct from the papal personality; and "it is absolute inasmuch as it can be circumscribed by no human or ecclesiastical law." These words are not those of an opponent of the Church of Rome, but of Cardinal Manning himself.[153] The words are his, and his work *"Petri Privilegium"* was written to expound and sustain the principle they express.

---

152 Dollinger, "Declaration and Letters on the Vatican Council." p. 91.
153 "Petri Privilegium,"p. 113.

"It needs but a step further," says Janus, "to declare the Pontiff an incarnation of God."

The *Civiltá Cattolica* describes in the following words the exalted position of the Pontificate, regarded in the light of the Vatican decree: —

"The Pope is not a power among men to be venerated like another, but he is a power altogether divine. He is the propounder and teacher of the law of the Lord in the whole universe. He is the supreme leader of the nations, to guide them in the ways of eternal salvation; he is the common father and universal guardian of the whole human species in the name of God. The human species has been perfected in its natural qualifications by Divine revelation, and by the incarnation of the Word, and has been lifted up into a supernatural order in which alone it can find its temporal and eternal felicity. The treasures of Revelation, the treasures of truth, the treasures of righteousness, the treasures of supernatural graces upon earth, have been deposited by God in the hands of one man, who is the sole dispenser and keeper of them. The life-giving work of the Advent and Incarnation, work of wisdom, of love, of mercy, is ceaselessly continued in the ceaseless action of one man thereto ordained by Providence. This man is the Pope. This is evidently implied in his designation itself — the Vicar of Christ, for if he holds the place of Christ upon earth, that means that he continues the work of Christ in the world; and is in respect of us what Christ would be were He here below Himself visibly governing the Church...

It is then no wonder if the Pope in his language shows that the care of the whole world is his; and if, forgetting his own peril he thinks only of that of the faithful nations. He sees aberrations of mind, passions of the heart, overflowing vices; he sees new wants, new aspirations; and holding out to the nations a helping hand with the tranquility of one securely seated on the throne given him by God, he says to them, 'Draw nigh to me, and I will trace out for you the way of truth and charity, which alone can lead to the desired happiness."[154]

"Language like this," says William Arthur, "is not to be smiled at when it goes to the heart of perhaps half a million of Ecclesiastics, each one of whom transmits the impression through a wide circle."[155]

Now let the reader ponder the following coincidence — "On the very day following the culmination of papal arrogance and self-exaltation was declared that terrible Franco- German war in which the French Empire of Louis Napoleon — by the soldiers of which the Pope was maintained on his tottering throne — fell. The temporal sovereignty of the Pope fell with it. No sooner had the French troops been withdrawn from Rome and the French Empire collapsed than the Italian Government announced its intention of entering the Roman States, and did so. On the 20th of September, 1870, Rome was declared the capital of United Italy, and became the residence and the seat of the Government of Victor Emmanuel. The Times Summary for that year says —

"The most remarkable circumstance in the annexation of Rome and its territory to the kingdom of Italy is the languid indifference with which the transfer has been regarded by Catholic Christendom. A change which would once have convulsed the world, has failed to distract attention from the more absorbing spectacle of the Franco-German war. Within the same year the papacy has assumed the highest spiritual exaltation to which it could aspire, and lost the temporal sovereignty which it had held for a thousand years"

The Voice of the Vice God

"I am 'the Voice,'" said Pius IX, "for though unworthy, I am nevertheless the Vicar of Christ, and this Voice which now sounds

---

154 *Civiltá Cattolica*, Serie vii, v, iii, pp. 259-60.
155 The Pope, the Kings, and the People," Vol. I, p. 210.

in your ears is the Voice of Him whom I represent on earth." "He that is with me is with God. If you are united to me who am His Vicar you are united to Christ." Presented by the Belgian deputation in 1871 (the year following that of the Vatican decree) with a Tiara, "rich as ever it could be, ornamented with seventy-two large emeralds, as many agates and rubies, while brilliants formed the warp of all the web," the Pope said, "you offer me gifts, a tiara — a symbol of my threefold dignity in heaven, upon earth, and in purgatory." Thus does the Infallible Pope interpret the meaning of the triply crowned miter which he wears! Discoursing loftily on "the Patrimony of St. Peter," he says, "Those who ought to guard the Patrimony of St. Peter take it away. It is true that I cannot like St. Peter launch certain thunderbolts that reduce bodies to ashes, but I can none the less launch the thunders which reduce souls to ashes; and I have done it by excommunicating all those who have perpetuated and borne a hand in the sacrilegious spoliation."

This bad tempered blasphemy is glorified as "*Christo parlante.*"

"Most blessed Father," says the faculty of theology in Rome, "in obeying your Voice we are obeying our own conscience; devoted to the infallible authority of your teaching we shall ever venerate and diffuse it in expounding sacred doctrines. Let your blessedness deign to comfort us with your benediction." And then they bow down and worship their idol, "*l'idole qu'ils se sont erigeé au Vatican*"; as Montalembert said, "They offer up justice, truth, reason, and history in a holocaust to the idol they have set up at the Vatican." Concerning a volume containing one hundred and one speeches of Pius IX, the Romish editor says, "Let this divine volume of the angelical Pio Nono be received as from the hand of an angel!"

The degradation of Christ linked with this exaltation of the Pope strikingly appears in a sermon preached during the session of the Vatican Council in 1870. The discourse was under three heads:

—

(1) Jesus Christ in the manger.

(2) Jesus Christ in the Eucharist.

(3) Jesus Christ at the Vatican.

And the conclusion was that Christ was" a child at Bethlehem, a 'host' on the altar, and an old man at the Vatican." "Love the person of the Pope," said Manning, "not as an abstract principle, not as the Holy See, not as an institution, but the living breathing man who has upon him the dignity and unction of the Great High Priest. Be filially devoted to him; for the time is come when according to the prophecy he is the sign which shall be spoken against; he is set for the fall and for the rising again of nations. He is the test of the world." In the person of Pius IX, Jesus reigns on earth, and "He must reign until He hath put all enemies under His feet."

The Modern Advance of Popery

Following the reinstitution of the Jesuits there has taken place an alarming advance of Popery throughout the world. Rome has boldly invaded Protestant lands, imposed on them its hierarchy, alike in England, America, and the Colonies; multiplied its chapels, monasteries, nunneries, colleges, and schools; entrapped thousands of the children of Protestants in its educational institutions; secured large endowments from Protestant governments; introduced elements of division and distraction into the legislation of Protestant countries; multiplied Catholic reviews, magazines and newspapers; poured forth a flood of cheap religious controversial works; tracts for the masses, romances, novels, works on poetry, history, music and architecture, designed to help forward the Romanizing movement. Under the influence of this extensive propaganda conversions to the Church of Rome have become frequent, and the whole attitude of Protestant society towards that church has changed. The influence on the public press of England and America has been most marked. The self-exalting Pope of

Rome, the "Man of Sin" of Pauline prophecy, is systematically glorified as "His holiness." His doings and sayings are constantly kept in evidence. Having ceased to persecute, and adorned himself in the garments of superhuman sanctity, the Pope has been "transformed into an angel of light," and his ministers as "the ministers of righteousness" (2 Cor. 11:15). History is forgotten, the antichristian character of Popery ignored, or denied: and the seductive spirit of falsehood, superstition and idolatry, which has found a home within the professing church of Christ, spreads as a leaven of evil from class to class, and from country to country, in its effort to permeate with its poison the mass of modern society.

VI. The "Unclean Spirit" from the Mouth of the Fake Prophet.

This spirit, as we have already recognized, is that of priestcraft, whose essential characteristic is "to arrogate to its own order the exclusive dignity of being the earthly mediator between God and man; and necessary for the effective averting of his wrath, and communication of his favor and salvation."[156]

That such a spirit has gone forth since the beginning of the outpouring of the sixth vial on the Turkish Empire, and spread far and wide in Protestant lands, is a matter of common knowledge. The initial date of the modern drying up, or exhaustion of the Turkish Empire, was, as we have already seen, that of the Greek insurrection in 1821. The 14th of July, 1833, was kept by the late Cardinal Newman as the date of the start of the Tractarian movement; a movement which has developed into the Ritualism of the present day, with its conspiracy to Romanize England, through Romanizing the established Protestant church of the land.

The Rome-ward character of the ritualistic movement is evident not only from its doctrines and practices, as the saying of masses, the adoration of the elements, the claim of the ministry to be a

---

156 Elliott, *Horae*, III, p. 516.

sacrificing priesthood, the practice of auricular confession, and the use of Popish ceremonial, but from its effort to bring about the "corporate reunion" of the English church with the Romish, and from the number of ritualists, both lay and clerical who have joined the church of Rome. The founder of the movement, Newman, went over to the Romish church, and was made a cardinal. Ward, Faber, Hurrell Froude, Pusey, and others intimately associated with Newman in the Tractarian conspiracy, regarded Protestantism with abhorrence, and strove to restore in the English church Romish doctrines and practices cast out of it by the Reformation. In order to accomplish this the most dishonest methods were employed. When Newman was endeavoring to restore Popery he wrote against it, justifying the act by saying beneath his breath, "I am not speaking my own words"; "such (anti-Romish) views are necessary for our position."[157] Though he had long held that the Roman was the one true church, Ward retained his position as a clergyman of the Church of England, "because he believed he was bringing many of its members towards Rome."[158] He justified equivocation, saying as his son tells us "make yourself clear that you are justified in deception, and then lie like a trooper."[159] Hurrell Froude, as early as 1834 confessed that the Tractarian movement was "a conspiracy."[160]

The ritualistic "Society of the Holy Cross" consists of "bishops, priests, deacons, and candidates for Holy Orders, in the Church of England, all its members being pledged to secrecy, to the saying of masses, the adoration of the elements, the practice of auricular confession, and the use of Popish ceremonial.[161]; This was the society which made itself responsible for that abominable book written for the guidance of ritualistic father confessors, and known as the priest in absolution."[162] "The Order of Corporate Reunion is even more secret and mysterious than the Society of the Holy Cross, and is more unblushingly Popish, going the length of

157 Walsh, "Secret History of the Oxford Movement," p. 13.
158 Ibid., p. 15.
159 Ibid., p. 31.
160 Ibid., p. 46.
161 Ibid., p. 45.
162 Walsh, "Secret History of the Oxford Movement," p. 56.

acknowledging the Pope as the lawful head of the whole visible church on earth."[163] A high official of the order plainly said at its first synod that "as a church we must have some executive head, and as there is no other competitor, we believe the Pope to be that head." The order "actively pursues its labors," and has representatives "in almost every English diocese." The Roman Catholic Standard and Ransomer, in its issue for November 22, 1894, stated that "there are now eight hundred clergymen of the Church of England who have been validly ordained by Dr. Lee and his co-bishops, of the order of corporate reunion."[164] The solemn subscriptions and even the oaths of ritualistic clergymen are no longer to be depended on. Pusey taught that the confessor" may swear with a clear conscience that he knows not what he knows only as God.[165] He owned the abuse of the confessional, that it was "a sad sight to see confessors giving their whole morning to young women devotees, while they dismiss men or married women who have perhaps left their household affairs with difficulty to find themselves rejected with"I am busy, go to some one else."[166]

The Confessional in the Church of England

In a confessional book for children "edited by a committee of clergy," which has had a wide circulation, it is taught that little children from six and a half years old should go to confession, and they are instructed that "It is to the priest, and to the priest only, that the child must acknowledge his sins, if he desires that God should forgive him." [167] That gross immorality has arisen from the practice of auricular confession in the Church of England was shown by archdeacon Allen in the course of a debate in the Lower House of Canterbury Convocation, on July 4, 1877. "A venerable and wise high churchman," he said, "told me that in his own

---

163 Ibid., p. 147.
164 Ibid., p. 161.
165 Ibid., p. 82.
166 Ibid., p. 120.
167 Walsh, "Secret History of the Oxford Movement," p. 112.

experience he had known of three clergymen who practiced this teaching of habitual confession as a duty, who had fallen into habits of immorality with women who had come to them for guidance."[168] The dangerous tendency of the confessional is "proved beyond the possibility of refutation by the bulls of the popes themselves against solicitant priests." The congregation of the Inquisition at Rome was compelled in 1867 to put forth an instruction addressed to all archbishops, bishops and ordinaries complaining that the Constitution on the crime of solicitation "did not receive proper attention, and that in some places abuses had crept in, both as to requiring penitents to denounce guilty confessors, and as to the punishing of confessors guilty of solicitation" (i.e. of soliciting women while in the confessional to immorality).[169] Even Dr. Pusey speaking from experience said "you may pervert this sacrament (of penance) from its legitimate end, which is to excite an exceeding horror of sin in the minds of others, into a subtle means of feeding evil passions, and sin in your own mind"; and again "be assured that this is one of the gravest faults of our day in the administration of the sacrament of penance, that it is the road by which a number of Christians go down to hell." The father confessor is often while in the confessional "the murderer of souls." During the conference held at Fulham Palace on confession and absolution Canon Aitken said that the system of auricular confession was "full of danger. He had had two or three instances of the extreme danger of the practice recently brought before him. A friend of his who occasionally used sacramental confession told him that in conversation with a young lady something made him think that she was unhappy, and he told her so. They arranged an interview, and he found that she was living in sin with her confessor. She had been betrayed into sin by the very peril of this institution."[170] When Dr. Longley, afterwards Archbishop of Canterbury, held an official and public inquiry as to a confessional scandal connected with the church of St. Saviour in Leeds, he

---

168 Ibid., p. 117.
169 Ibid., p. 119.
170 Report of Conference, p. 96.

wrote, after investigating the facts to the Rev. H. F. Beckett, the Vicar, that "Mr. Rooke who was then a deacon having required a married woman, a candidate for confirmation, to go for confession to you as a priest, you received that female to confession under these circumstances, and that you put to her questions which she says made her feel very much ashamed, and greatly distressed her, and which were of such an indelicate nature that she would never tell her husband of them." Instead of trying to place the matter before Dr. Longley in a more favorable light Mr. Beckett's reply to the bishop seemed to make the case even darker against himself for he declared "your lordship cannot but see that Mrs. ——s not mentioning what had passed between her and myself to her husband is nothing at all to the purpose, since no woman would, I suppose, ever tell her husband what passed in her confession." Dr. Tait, Archbishop of Canterbury said before the House of Lords with reference to the ritualistic book entitled "The Priest in Absolution," "no modest person could read that book without regret j it is a disgrace to the community that such a book should be circulated under the authority of clergymen of the established Church. I cannot imagine that any right minded man could wish to have such questions (as it suggests) addressed to any member of his family; and if he had any reason to suppose that any member of his family had been exposed to such an examination, I am sure it would be the duty of any father of a family to remonstrate with the clergyman who had put the questions, and warn him never to approach his house again."[171] Of the ritualistic "Society of the Holy Cross" Mr. Ward says, "Its filthy confessional book has never been condemned by the society as a whole, though a few of its members have written and spoken against it."[172] The bishop of Carlisle, the late Dr. Harvey Goodwin, declared that the Society of the Holy Cross has "created a scandal in the church of almost unparalleled magnitude," and that the "only right course for wise and loyal churchmen was to wash their hands of it." But the society continues to spread the practice of auricular confession in the

---

171 Report of Conference, p. 98.
172 Ibid., p. 145.

Church of England, as part of the work of "leveling up" to the methods of the Church of Rome.

Real Nature of the Ritualistic Movement

The Rev. W. I. G. Bennett, late Vicar of Frome, in his plea for toleration wrote, "It is not for a chasuble or a cope, lighted tapers, or the smoke of incense, the miter or the pastoral staff, that we are contending, but as all who think deeply on either side of the question know full well for the doctrines which lie hidden under them." We "set the bulbs," said Dr. Pusey, "which were to bring forth the flowers." The real object of the movement is "the restoration of Romanism in England by means of the National Church, and the consequent overthrow of the Reformation." The extent to which the movement has grown may be partly gathered from the published list of 9,600 clergymen of the Church of England who have already joined it, with the names of the ritualistic societies to which they belong. How long shall these traitors be suffered to carry on their conspiracy, to multiply their secret societies, to spread their poisonous leaven, to teach Romish doctrines in Protestant pulpits, to subvert the foundations of the faith, to mislead multitudes to their eternal ruin; and to do this with Protestant money, with the connivance or support of Protestant bishops, and with the authority of a Protestant king and Parliament? — Is it not written "Purge out the old leaven." "Know ye not that a little leaven leaveneth the whole lump?" Already nearly half the clergy of the Church of England are engaged in the Rome-ward movement. By their means the venerable structure of the Protestant established church is burning with incendiary fires. The bishops sleep while the building blazes, or even cast fuel on the flames.

Spread of Ritualism to Other Lands

From England ritualism has spread with disastrous effects to

America, the continent, India, and the colonies. Nor is the climax of the movement reached. The spirit which inspires it is destined to carry it throughout the world. Its end will not be reached till the close of the great Armageddon conflict which marks with its lurid signal the termination of the present age.

Chapter 5. Termination Of The 1,260 Years Of Papal Dominion

THIS GREAT PROPHETIC PERIOD is mentioned no less than seven times in Daniel and the Apocalypse.

First as three and a half prophetic "times" in Daniel 7. The persecuting "little horn" arising among the ten horns of the divided Roman empire, and distinguished from them by his episcopal character as having "eyes" of intelligent oversight, "like the eyes of a man," and by his proud self-exalting utterances, having "a mouth that spoke very great things," was to exercise tyrannical "dominion" over the saints. They were to be "given into his hand" until "a time, and times, and the dividing of time."

Secondly, as the three and a half "times" of the scattering and subjugation of "the holy people in Daniel 12," "And I heard the man clothed in linen which was upon the waters of the river, when he held up his right hand and his left hand unto heaven, and swore by Him that liveth forever, that it shall be for a time, times, and a half; and when He shall have accomplished to scatter the power of the holy people, all these things shall be finished."

Thirdly, as "forty-two months," during which "the holy city" shall be trodden under foot, (Rev. 11:2), "The court which is without the temple leave out (or cast out) and measure it not; for it is given unto the gentiles; and the holy city shall they tread under foot forty and two months."

Fourthly, as the 1,260 days of the prophesying of the sackcloth clothed witnesses, (Rev. 11:3), 14 And I will give power unto my two witnesses, and they shall prophesy a thousand, two hundred, and threescore days, clothed in sackcloth."

Fifthly, as the 1,260 days during which the persecuted woman is hidden and fed in the wilderness, (Rev. 12:6), "And the woman fled into the wilderness where she hath a place prepared of God that they should feed her there a thousand, two hundred, and threescore days."

Sixthly, as "time, times, and a half" during which the woman is nourished from the persecuting dragon who had been cast down from his place of exaltation, (Rev. 12:13, 14), "And when the dragon saw that he was cast out unto the earth, he persecuted the woman which brought forth the man child. And to the woman were given two wings of a great eagle, that she might fly into the wilderness, into her place where she is nourished for a time, and times, and half a time, from the face of the serpent." "And the dragon was wrath with the woman, and went to make war with the remnant of her seed, which keep the commandments of God, and have the testimony of Jesus Christ."

Seventhly, as "forty-two months," during which the revived head of the ten horned wild beast power, the head which has" a mouth speaking great things and blasphemies," exercises dominion; finally "making war" with the saints, and overcoming them, (Rev. 13:5), "And there was given unto him a mouth speaking great things, and blasphemies; and power was given unto him to continue forty and two months." "And it was given unto him to make war with the saints, and to overcome them: and power was given him over all kindreds, and tongues, and nations."

As 1,260 days are equal to forty-two months of thirty days each, and as forty-two months equal three and a half years, it is evident that one and the same period is intended.

Should this period be interpreted on the day-day scale, or on the year-day scale? In other words are the 1,260 days to be taken as literal days of twenty four hours each, or as symbolical days, representing 1,260 years?

We have shown in our chapter on Prophetic Chronology in "The Approaching End of the Age" (pp. 300-322), that the wild beasts of Daniel and the Apocalypse with their heads, and horns, and times are miniature representatives of historic events and periods. Every feature is on a reduced scale, and therefore among the rest the times of their duration. "The reduction is on as enormous a scale as when our world is represented by a globe a foot in diameter." The fulfillment of one of these prophetic periods on the year-day scale supplies the key to all the rest. The "seventy weeks" of Daniel 9, extending from the decree of Artaxerxes to the advent and death of Messiah was fulfilled, not as seventy literal weeks, or 490 days, but as 490 years. Further both in the law and the prophets this scale is employed in relation to the times prophetically announced; in the law of Moses in the words "after the number of days in which ye searched the land, even forty days, each day for a year y shall ye bear your iniquities, even forty years" (Num. 14:34); and in the prophecies of Ezekiel in the passage "I have laid upon thee the years of their iniquity, according to the number of the days, three hundred and ninety days, so shalt thou bear the iniquity of the house of Israel. And when thou hast accomplished them, lie again on thy right side, and thou shalt bear the iniquity of the house of Judah forty days: I have appointed thee each day for a year."

Let these facts in relation to the prophetic times be duly considered, and especially the words "I have appointed thee each day for a year," and the conclusion will be apparent that the symbolic times of Daniel and the Apocalypse should be interpreted on the year-day scale; in other words that the 1,260 days, the 1,290 days and the 1,335 days of these prophecies represent 1,260, 1,290 and 1,335 years.

An exhaustive and masterly treatise on the year-day system from the pen of the Rev. T. R. Birks (Fellow of Trinity College, Cambridge, Professor of Moral Philosophy), appeared more than fifty years ago in his work entitled "First Elements of Sacred Prophecy"; a book now difficult to procure. The following is a

brief summary of the general scope of the argument. "The year-day theory," says Professor Birks, "may be summed up in these maxims:
—

"1. That the church, after the ascension of Christ, was intended of God to be kept in the lively expectation of His speedy return in glory.

"2. That in the Divine councils a long period, of nearly two thousand years, was to intervene between the first and the second advent; and to be marked by a dispensation of grace to the Gentiles.

"3. That in order to strengthen the faith and hope of the church under the long delay, a large part of the whole interval was prophetically announced, but in such a manner that its true length might not be understood, until its close seemed to be drawing near.

"4. That in the symbolic prophecies of Daniel and St. John, other times were revealed along with this, and included under one common maxim of interpretation.

"5. That the periods thus figuratively revealed are exclusively those of Daniel and St. John, which relate to the general history of the church, between the time of the prophet and the second advent.

"6. That in these predictions each day represents a natural year, as in the vision of Ezekiel; that a month denotes thirty, and a time or year, three hundred and sixty years. The first of these maxims is plain from the statements of scripture, and the second from the actual history of the world. The third is, on a priori grounds, a natural and reasonable inference from the two former, and is the true basis of the year day theory viewed in its final cause. The three following present the theory itself under its true limits. Perhaps no simpler method could be suggested in which such a partial and half veiled revelation could be made, than that which the holy Spirit is thus supposed to adopt, resting as it does on a plain analogy of natural times."[173]

A summary of Professor Birks's argument will be found in "The Approaching End of the Age" (pp. 306-322). The argument is an exceeding able one, and affords a complete demonstration of the year-day theory.[174]

Starting Point of the 1,260 Years of Papal Dominion

In the Prophetic calendar appended to my work on "The Approaching End of the Age," and also in "Light for the Last Days," I have shown that the decree of the emperor Justinian, in 533, and that of the Emperor Phocas in 607, conferred on the Bishop of Rome headship over all the churches of Christendom. The latter decree is memorialized by the Pillar of Phocas in Rome, bearing inscription and date "Die prima Mensis August. Indict. Und. ac Pietatis ejus Anno quinto. Pro innumerabilibus Pietatis ejus Beneficiis." The usurper Phocas was the murderer of the lawful Emperor Mauritius, of four of his sons, of his brother Petrus, and of the Emperor's widow, Constantina, and her daughter. Such was the man who bestowed universal headship over

---

173 The analogy of the earth's diurnal and annual revolutions.

174 Professor Birks thus sums up his masterly argument: — " The year-day theory rests on a surprising combination of scriptural arguments, some of which it is true, are indirect, and some doubtful, but the great majority are full, clear, and unambiguous. First of all there are four or five distinct presumptions of a general kind, that the dates have some secret meaning. There are, then, three plain and certain, and one more disputable passage which supply an express rule of interpretation, and a key at once simple and comprehensive, the direct appointment of God Himself. When we further proceed to examine the passages in detail we find that every one, without exception, yields some peculiar argument, in support of this same view; and several of them furnish us with two or three distinct proofs. And besides all these distinct evidences for the system, it is found to have a basis in the heavenly revolutions themselves, and to be confirmed by its manifest harmony with the most exact elements of natural science."

the churches of Christendom on Boniface III.[175]

Justinian Starting Point of the 1,260 Years

"The commencement of the twelve hundred and sixty years," says Cunninghame, "is to be marked by the giving of the saints, and times and laws, into the hands of the little horn.

"That the little horn is the papacy, has been established with such force of evidence by Mede, Bishop Newton, Mr. Faber, and other writers on prophecy, that I do not consider it at all necessary to enter upon the proof of it. The papacy being a spiritual power within the limits of the Roman empire, Mr. Faber argues, I think rightly, when he says that the giving the saints into the hand of the papacy, must be by some formal act of the secular power of that empire constituting the Pope to be the head of the Church. It is not, in fact, easy to conceive in what other mode the saints could be delivered into the hand of a spiritual authority, which, in its infancy at least, must have been in a great measure dependent upon the secular power for its very existence, and much more for every degree of active power which it was permitted to assume or exercise.

"Accordingly we are informed, by the unerring testimony of history, that an act of the secular government of the Empire was issued in the reign of Justinian, whereby the Roman Pontiff was solemnly acknowledged to be the head of the Church. That emperor, whose reign was marked by the publication of the volume of the Civil Law which was afterwards adopted through the whole extent of the Roman empire, by the different nations who had divided among themselves its territories, was no less ambitious of distinction as a theologian than as a legislator. At an early period of his reign, he promulgated a severe Edict against heretics, which contained a confession of his own faith, and was intended to be the common and universal standard of belief to his

175 Calendar, "Approaching End of the Age," p. 618.

subjects. The severest penalties were enacted by it against all who refused implicit submission.

"A second Edict of the same nature was issued by Justinian in the month of March, 533; and on this occasion he formally wrote to the Pope, as the acknowledged head of all the churches, and all the holy priests of God, for his approbation of what he had done. The epistle which was addressed to the Pope, and another to the Patriarch of Constantinople, were inserted in the volume of the Civil Law; thus the sentiments contained in them obtained the sanction of the supreme legislative authority of the empire; and in both epistles the above titles were given to the Pope.

"The answer of the Pope to the imperial epistle was also published with the other documents; and it is equally important, inasmuch as it shows that he understood the reference that had been made to him, as being a formal recognition of the supremacy of the See of Rome.

"From the date of the imperial epistle of Justinian to Pope John, in March, 533, the saints, and times, and laws of the Church, may therefore be considered to have been formally delivered into the hand of the papacy, and this is consequently the true era of the twelve hundred and sixty years."

Phocas Starting Point of the 1,260 Years

It is manifest that the rise of the papacy was gradual. A second decree similar to that of Justinian was issued by the Emperor Phocas in 606 or 607, and a long list of prophetic interpreters from the sixteenth to the nineteenth centuries can be shown who adopted this latter decree as the proper starting point of the 1,260 years of papal domination.

From the decree of Justinian in A.D. 533 the 1,260 years' period reached its termination in A.D. 1793, the central year of the French Revolution — that of the reign of Terror, and the execution of Louis XVI and Marie Antoinette.

From the decree of Phocas in A.D. 606-7, the 1260 years, reckoned as calendar or prophetic years of 360 days each, ended in 1848-9; the year of the great European Revolution which witnessed the formal deposition of the Pope from his temporal authority, and the establishment of a Republic both in France and Italy.

Reckoned in full solar years, 1,260 years from the decree of Phocas terminated in 1866-7. The years 1866-1870 witnessed the overthrow of Papal Austria by Protestant Prussia; the Spanish Insurrection, and deposition of the Queen; the Ecumenical council at Rome, and declaration of papal infallibility; the overthrow of the Imperial power of Papal France in its conflict with Prussia; and the rise of the Kingdom of United Italy, and of the Protestant Empire of Germany.

Thirty-four years have now elapsed since the memorable year 1870, when the Pope of Rome was decreed infallible, and lost the Temporal Sovereignty which he had held for more than a thousand years. As there is not the slightest probability that United Italy will consent to give up its dearly won position, and restore the secular dominion of the Popes, we are warranted in considering the year 1870 as that which witnessed the End of Papal Temporal Power.

Chapter 6. Anticipations Of The Years 1848, And 1866-7, As Those Of The Final Fall Of Papal Dominion

THE APPLICATION and adjustment of the prophetic times to the order of historical events has, during the last nineteen centuries, advanced continually in the degree of its correctness. This was of course to be expected. The mysterious form in which the prophetic times in Daniel and the Apocalypse are stated, and the ignorance of the church as to the duration of her pilgrimage, and of the long apostasy which was to cast its shadow on her career, account for the errors of her earlier interpretations of these times; while the growing revelations of history explain the gradual advance in her comprehension of prophetic chronology so distinctly visible in later centuries, and especially during the last 700 years.

From Cyprian's time, near the middle of the third century, as Elliott reminds us, "even to the times of Joachim and the Waldenses in the twelfth century there was kept up by a succession of expositors in the church a recognition of the precise year-day principle of interpretation; and its application made, not without consideration and argument, to one and another of the chronological prophetic periods of days, including the shorter one of those that were involved in the prophecies respecting Antichrist; though not, so far, to that of the 1,260 predicted days of Antichrist's duration. An inconsistency this very obvious; and only to be accounted for, I think, by the supposition of some providential overruling of men's minds; whereby they were restrained from entertaining the view, and carrying out their own principles, so long as it would necessarily have involved the conclusion of Christ's' advent being an event very distant. Further it appears that so soon as ever it was possible to entertain the year-day principle, and yet to have an expectation of Christ's advent being near at hand, so soon the application was made of it to the 1,260 days predicted of Antichrist's duration in Daniel and the Apocalypse. At the close of the twelfth century Joachim Abbas, made a first and rude attempt at it; and, late in the fourteenth the Wicliffite Walter Brute followed."[176]

The commentary on the Apocalypse by Joachim Abbas, Abbot of the monastery of Curacio in Calabria, was written about the year 1183.[177] Having become famous for his gift of scriptural research he received permission from Pope Lucius III, in 1182, "to retire awhile from the abbacy and its active occupation in order to give himself more entirely to these studies." Nearly 1,260 years had elapsed from the nativity of Christ to the period in which Joachim wrote. Had Antichrist already come?"We may probably conclude," says Joachim, "that Antichrist is even now in the world," though the

---

176 Elliott, *Horae*, III, p. 283.
177 Fleury, Histoire Ecclesiastique, Liv. LXXIV.

hour of his clear manifestation has not yet come. The holy city trodden down during the prophesying of the witnesses he held to be the Latin Church and Empire, and the forty-two months in which the witnesses preach clothed in sackcloth signify" so many generations of the cleric and monastic witnessing orders"; i.e., according to his own explanation elsewhere of the five months of the scorpion locusts, a period of 1,260 years. It was impossible, of course for Joachim, the abbot of a Roman Catholic monastery, to apply the 1,260 years prophesying of the witnesses to definitely anti-Romish testimony. He saw that the harlot city of the Apocalypse meant Rome; that the Antichrist would be the counterfeit of Christ; and that false prophets would issue out of the bosom of the church; but to rightly value the Protestant testimony which had even then commenced among the Waldenses, and was to grow in later times to such gigantic proportions, was beyond his power. Not so, however, with Walter Brute, the Wicliflite, in 1391, whose testimony is given to us by the venerable Foxe from original documents. To him the 1,260 and 1,290 days of prophecy were so many years, to be reckoned from the Hadrian desolation of Jerusalem to his own day.[178] But what if the Hadrian date was too early a starting point? To reckon the 1,260 years from the rise of the papacy would throw its termination into the distant future. Who should be bold enough to do this? A hundred and seventy years roll away. The Reformation has come, and the Romish anti-Reformation movement is in full flood. The massacre of the Huguenots in France is imminent; the dreadful massacre of St. Bartholomew. It is the year 1571. David Chytraeus ventures to indicate the decree of Phocas as the possible commencing point of papal domination. He says that if reckoned from the beginning of the overthrow of the Western Roman Empire by the Gothic Alaric, in 412, the termination of the 1,260 years would be in 1672, or a hundred years later than the date at which he wrote, while if reckoned from the Pope exalting decree of Phocas in 606 its termination would fall in 1866, or 295 years later. According to this

---

178 Foxe, "Book of Martyrs," Vol. Ill, pp. 131-188.

there might remain about 300 years of the fatal dominion of Antichrist.

Bullinger in 1573 states strongly the view that the Pope exalting decree of Phocas is the initial date of papal dominion, and refers to the notable preceding action of Gregory the great.

"The Byshop of Constantinople blynded wyth ambition, required to have the supremacie given hym, whom Palagius and Gregory Byshops of Rome wythstode: And this latter so impugned the supremacie of the Patriarch of Constantinople, that he sticked not to call hym the vauntcurrour of Antichrist, which would usurp the tytle of generally byshop. There remaine not a fewe espistles written of this matter, in his register. Nevertheless, a fewe yeares after, when the Byshops of Rome were sore afrayde, least the dignitie should be geven to the Byshops of Constantinople, Boniface the 3, obteyned of the Emperour Phocas the murtherer, that he which was byshop of olde Rome, should be taken for the universal bishop, and Rome for the head of all churches: which constitution set up the Pope in authoritie, so as he was now taken of the most part of the west byshoppes for Apostolicall, and many matters were brought before hym to determine: whereby he got in favor of many princes, chiefly of Fraunce, by whose ayde he drove out of Italy both the Emperour of Greece, and the kings of Lumbardie, and brought Rome, and the best and most flourishing parts of Italy under his owne subjection."[179]

Such too had been the view of Bishop Bale, who in 1550 called Phocas "the first Pope maker," and of that of the Magdeburg Centuriators in their monumental history published in 1559-1574. Napier, the famous inventor of Logarithms, in his remarkable work on the Apocalypse dated A.D. 1593, powerfully advocates the year-day theory. "In Prophetic dates of daies, weeks, moneths and yeares, everie common propheticall day is taken for a yeare." He thought that the interval 1541 to 1756 would be marked by the downfall of Romish power.

---

[179] "Bullinger on Apocalypse," p. 177.

Pareus in his commentary on the Apocalypse A.D. 1643 boldly reckons the 1,260 years of papal dominion from the decree of Phocas in 606. His work represents the substance of lectures delivered in the year 1608 to the Academy of Heidelberg, over which he presided. Boniface III, he says was exalted by a decree of Phocas to "the chaire of universal pestilence" in 606. "From the yeare of Christ therefore 606, untill this time the holy citie hath been trodden under foot by the Romane Gentiles, which is the space of 1,037 yeeres, and is yet to be trodden down 223 yeefes more, to wit, untill the ye ere of Christ 1866 ." A bold prediction, based on the prophetic times! There is no hesitation about the language. From his chair at Heidelberg, in the seventeenth century, Pareus looked forward 223 years into the future, and guided by the sure word of prophecy pointed out the year 1866 as that which would witness the overthrow of papal dominion. And history in the events of 1866-70, justified his anticipation.

Seven years later, in 1650, Holland in his work on the Apocalypse says that according to prophecy "there remain 216 years more" for the papal power; which calculation also places the termination of the 1,260 years in 1866.

Forty years later Cressener in 1690 stated that the years of the period should in his view, be reckoned as prophetic years of 360 days each, which would shorten the 1,260 years to 1,242. Following in the same line Robert Fleming in his memorable work on the "Rise and Fall of Papal Rome," published in 1701, anticipated the year 1848 as a critical year in the downfall of the papacy. He added, "Yet we are not to imagine that these events will totally destroy the papacy, although they will exceedingly weaken it, for we find that it is still in being and alive when the next vial is poured out." He also indicated the year 1794 as one which would witness some notable papal overthrow. There was not a sign in the political heavens when Fleming wrote that such events were impending; he foresaw them only in the light of chronological prophecy. Both his anticipations proved correct: 1794, and still more 1793, the year of the Reign of Terror in France, and 1848, the year of the great

Revolution, witnessed the preliminary overthrow of the papacy. Events further showed that the 1,260 years of prophecy should be reckoned both as calendar years of 360 days each, and as solar years; and that reckoned in these two forms from the decree of Phocas in A.D. 606 the period terminates first in the revolutionary year 1848, and secondly in the year 1866, so long anticipated as that of the end of papal power.

In the year 1746, Dr. Gill in his well known voluminous commentary, similarly placed the ending of the 1,260 years in 1866. The beginning of the Pope's reign, he says, was in the year 606; "if to this we add 1,260 the expiration of his reign will fall in the year 1866, so that be may have upwards of a hundred and twenty years yet to continue. But of this," he adds, "we cannot be certain; however the conjecture is not improbable."

Reader in his Apocalyptic commentary (A.D. 1778) placed the 1,260 years in the interval A.D. 606-1866.

Twenty four years later Galloway at the commencement of the nineteenth century, in 1802, also points to 1866 as the termination of the 1,260 years of papal dominion. So did Faber, in 1805, Frere in 1816, Holmes in 1819, Bickersteth in 1823, Irving in 1828, and Elliott in 1844. Burder in 1849 says, "The year 606 appears to me to be the grand and momentous date from which it is most satisfactory to compute the 1,260 years of the Papal Antichrist. If this be agreed then the eventful termination of his reign will be in the year 1866, and we are now approaching a period most momentous to the Church and to the world."

Five editions of Elliott's great work on the Apocalypse were issued between 1844 and 1861. I have before me Elliott's diagram of the prophetic times in his last edition, (Vol. IV, p. 240), tracing their termination in the year 1866. That diagram of the convergent ending of the chief prophetic times stands as a last witness to the marvelous anticipation whose existence we have traced for three hundred years, in the writings of Chytraeus, Pareus, Holland, Fleming, Gill, Reader, Galloway, Faber, Frere, Holmes, Bickersteth,

Irving, Burder, and Elliott, or from the middle of the sixteenth century down to within five years of 1866; the anticipation that that year, as terminating 1,260 years from the decree of Phocas, would bring about the predicted fall of papal power. We have now to trace the fulfillment of this remarkable and long continued anticipation, in the events of the years 1848, and 1866-70.

Chapter 7. Fulfillment Of The Foregoing Anticipations Of Prophetic Interpreters In The Fall Of The Papal Power In The Years 1848 And 1866-1870

THE PONTIFICATE OF PIUS IX, the last Pope exercising temporal sovereignty, witnessed a double overthrow of papal power. The first of these took place in 1848. Marvelous were the events of the period! In a single fortnight in that year "a conflagration broke out which blazed from the shores of the Atlantic to those of the Vistula." France, Germany, Austria, and Italy were convulsed by the earthquake shocks of Revolution. Thrones fell like trees before a tornado. Lamartine and Louis Blanc, who were eye-witnesses and actors in the Revolution have each written its history. The literature of the subject is voluminous. Granier de Cassagnac, Reynault, Lord Normanby, Caussidiere, Emile Thomas, Proudhon, Grey, Lespez, Prevost Paradol, Guizot, Jules Simon, and other writers of various nationalities have told its tale. In his "Century of Continental History," Rose has given a synopsis and diagrammatical summary of the revolutionary events of 1848. In July, 1847, the profound tranquility of the western world was proclaimed from the thrones of England and France. On the 23rd of February, 1848, the Revolution broke out at Paris. Barricades were thrown up, the Tuileries ransacked, the prisons opened, and frightful disorders committed. Louis Philippe abdicated on February 24th. A Republic was proclaimed from the steps of the Hotel de Ville on February 26th. The perpetual banishment of

Louis Philippe and his family was decreed on the 26th of May. The election of Louis Napoleon to the national assembly followed on the 18th of June. On the 25th of June Paris was in a state of siege, in which 16,000 people were killed or wounded. On the 20th of December Louis Napoleon was proclaimed President of the French Republic. On March 15th, a little more than a fortnight after the fall of Louis Philippe a constitution was proclaimed at Rome. The Pope fled to Gaeta, on the 24th of November, where an asylum had been provided for him by the King of Naples. On the 8th of February, 1849, the Pope was formally deposed from his temporal authority, and a Republic proclaimed. The revolutionary contagion penetrated with amazing rapidity into every stronghold of European despotism. " Metternich fled before it, leaving the once powerful empire whose policy he had so long guided, a prey to terrible calamities. It descended the Rhine along its entire course from the mountains of the Black Forest, stirring its dukedoms and electorates into tumult and insurrection. It struck eastward into the very heart of Germany, still producing wherever it came the same commotions, popular assemblies, demands, threats, insurrections, skirmishings — all hostile to the royal prerogative. The great kingdom of Prussia felt its shock, and was well-nigh prostrated. The force of the movement was spent only when it had reached the Russian frontier. Providence had said to it 'Hitherto but no further'; and now accordingly its progress was arrested. It did not cross the Vistula, for Russia forms no part of the Roman earth, and Providence has reserved this powerful kingdom, it would appear, for other purposes. Such was the extent of the movement. On almost the same day the various nations inhabiting from the hills of Sicily to the shores of the Baltic met to discuss the same grievances, and urge the same demands. They did not act by concert; nothing had been arranged beforehand; none were more astonished at what was going on than the actors themselves in these scenes. One mighty influence had moved the minds of a hundred nations, as the mind of one man; and all obeyed a power which every one felt to be irresistible. Then suddenly were all the lights of the political heaven smitten, and as it seemed at the time, extinguished." a All

over Papal Europe royalty was smitten — suddenly, terribly
smitten. Laws were abolished; armies were forced to flee; dynasties
were sent into exile; the supreme Power was in the dust; and the
mob was the Monarch."[180] The flight of the Pope from Rome was
followed by anarchy, and the dissolution of civil society in Italy.
The Roman Republic which had been proclaimed proved short-
lived. In 1849 it was forcibly suppressed by the French Republic,
and the Pope restored to temporal dominion by French
soldiers."The sight of the soldiers of republican France in the
streets of Rome compelling the Romans to submit to a very much
worse government than that which the French themselves had
rejected at the cost of revolution, and doing so professedly for the
sake of French religion, was a singularly loathsome one, and
grievously revolting and demoralizing to the conscience of
Europe."[181]

Restored to his throne by French bayonets, against the will of
the Italians, the Pope was maintained in his unnatural position by a
French army of occupation for twenty-one years longer, till the
fatal year 1870, in which the French Empire of Louis Napoleon,
and the papacy suddenly fell together. Isolated during this period
as a temporal ruler, Pius IX turned his attention to becoming a
great Pope, and promulgated the new dogmas of the immaculate
conception of the Virgin, and the infallibility of the tiara crowned
priest. The latter was the climax of papal self-exaltation.

Events of 1866-70

The overthrow of Papal Austria by Protestant Prussia took place in
1866. Prussia declared war on the 18th of June, and was victorious
in a series of battles. The total defeat of the Austrians at Sadowa,
followed on the 3d of July. Italy declared war against Austria on the
18th of June. The Austrians retired from Mantua, Verona, and
Venice on October 9-17. The invitation of the Pope to all Catholic

---

180 Wylie, "The Seventh Vial," pp. 195-6, 202.
181 Trollope, "Life of Pius IX," Vol. I, p. 330.

bishops to celebrate the eighteenth centenary of the martyrdom of Peter and Paul was issued on the 8th of December. We pause before this fact. Such was the period reached in 1866-7, the eighteenth centenary of Paul's martyrdom at Rome. Such was the appointed time of papal downfall. Five hundred and ninety-nine bishops, and thousands of priests were present at the allocution delivered by the Pope on the 26th of June, 1867. Twenty-live martyrs were canonized by the Pope on June 29th. Then followed on September 13th the publication of the Pope's encyclical letter summoning the (Ecumenical council at Rome for the 8th of December, 1869. Immediately after, on September 1 8th a general insurrection broke out in Spain. Ministers resigned, the queen fled, and was deposed. The Jesuits were suppressed, and freedom of religious worship was decreed.

The twenty-first general council was opened at Rome on the 8th of December, 1869. At this great (Ecumenical council were present six archbishop princes, forty-nine cardinals, eleven patriarchs, six hundred and eighty archbishops and bishops, twenty-eight abbots, twenty-nine generals of orders; eight hundred and three in all. Four public sessions were held and between ninety and one hundred congregations. New canons were issued on the 24th of April, 1870. The Infallibility of the Pope, as head of the Church, affirmed by 547 placets against two non-placets, was decreed and promulgated the 18th of July, 1870.

The dogma was read by candle-light, amid the rolling thunders of a storm which burst over Rome. "The definitions of the Roman Pontiff are of themselves, and not from the consent of the Church Irreformable. But if anyone presume to contradict this our definition, let him be Anathema." "The reader ceased. The storm alone was speaking. For a moment no human tone disturbed the air. But memory was repeating two terrific words, and imagination kept saying that the winds were whispering, 'Irreformable! Anathema!'"[182]

---

182 William Arthur, "The Pope, the Kings, and the People," Vol. II, p. 401.

This great and memorable Vatican decree, the *ne plus ultra* of Popery, involved no less than "The legal extinction of Right, and the enthronement of Will in its place, throughout the churches of one half of Christendom." It subjected the Church to "more than Asian despotism." "The effect of it, described with literal rigor, was in the last resort to place the entire Christian religion in the breast of the Pope, and to suspend it on his will." "Whatsoever was formerly ascribed either to the Pope, or the Council, or to the entire governing body of the Church, or to the Church general and diffused, the final sense of the great Christian community, aided by authority, tested by discussion, mellowed and ripened by time — all — no more than all, and no less than all — of what God gave, for guidance, through the power of truth, by the Christian revelation, to the whole redeemed family, the baptized flock of the Saviour of the world; all this is now locked in the breast of one man, opened and distributed at his will, and liable to assume whatever form — whether under the name of identity, or other name, it matters not — he may think fit to give it."[183]

"Idle is it to tell us that the Pope is bound 'by the moral and divine law, by the Commandments of God, by the rules of the Gospel'; and if more verbiage and refutation could be piled up, as Ossa was set upon Olympus, and Pelion upon Ossa, to cover the poverty and irrelevancy of the idea, it would not mend the matter. For of these, one and all, the Pope himself, by himself, is the judge without appeal. If he consults, it is by his will; if he does not consult, no man can call him to account. No man, or assemblage of men, is one whit the less bound to hear and to obey. He is the judge of the moral and divine law, of the Gospel, and of the Commandments; the supreme and only final judge; and he is the judge, with no legislature to correct his errors, with no authoritative rules to guide his proceedings; with no power on earth to question the force, or intercept the effect of his decisions."[184]

---

183 Gladstone, "Vaticanism," pp. 92, 93, 101, 102.
184 Gladstone, "Vaticanism," pp. 92, 93, 101, 102.

Fall of the Papal Power, 1870

Speedily was the blasphemy of this infallibility decree rebuked by the Most High! The same day that it was published there was dispatched from Paris to Berlin the declaration of war which sealed the fate of the second French Empire, and with it that of the temporal power of the papacy. On July 18th, when the Pope read, amid the thunder and lightning of an awful storm the decree which marked the climax of papal pretension, the announcement of his own infallibility, Napoleon III dispatched his challenge to Germany. We know what followed; how Protestant Prussia humbled herself before God by a day of special prayer on the 27th, and besought His blessing on her quickly gathering armies; how the wicked, and withered, and blood-stained emperor of Catholic France, accompanied by his poor unfortunate boy, assumed the next day the command of the wretchedly organized French troops at Metz; how the Germans defeated the French, both at Wissemburg and at Geisburg on August 4th, and on the 6th at Woerth and Forbach; how they bombarded Strasburg and defeated Bazaine, and drove him back into Metz, gained another great victory at Gravelotte, and forced the emperor and the entire army into Sedan, where on September 2d, they had to surrender, and were all taken prisoners; how 300,000 men marched on Paris, and establishing their headquarters at Versailles, besieged it in September; how other German armies overran all France; how Bazaine had to surrender Metz and 173,000 men in October; and how before the end of the year France lay bleeding and prostrate at the feet of her Protestant foes, without an army in the field, or an ally in Europe. And we know how also, long before this crisis arrived in France — Rome having been evacuated by the French troops which were sorely needed at home — the Pontifical government fell, to rise no more. The king of Italy forewarned the Pope of his intention to occupy Rome on September 8th, and did so in the following month. Rome decided, by an overwhelming vote, for union with Italy, and was with its surrounding territories incorporated by Royal decree with the Italian kingdom in October,

1870.

This was the full and final fall of the temporal power of the papacy. It was on the day of the last meeting of the Council, which had deified a man by declaring him possessed of the Divine attribute of infallibility, that Victor Immanuel's announcement reached Rome; it was on the day that the German armies closed round Paris that the Italian general Cadorna invested Rome. The struggle lasted but a few hours; the Pope understood that further resistance would be mere wanton waste of life, for his Zouaves numbered but 8,000, and 50,000 Italians were arrayed against him. As soon as a breach had been made in the walls of Rome, the word to surrender was given.

"There, yea, there on the dome of proud St. Peter's, being raised and beginning to flutter, was the white flag, and there unwinding itself did it float out upon the September breeze, and waved in the forenoon sun, — waved over Pontiff and Cardinal, over the Circus of Nero and the Inquisition of the Popes. Was it real? Eyes would be wiped to see if they did not deceive. Eyes, ay, the eyes of soldiers, would be wiped from thick, hot tears. Could it be — could it ever be? Come at last! The hour for which ages had impatiently waited, for which myriads of Italians had died. Italy one! her arms outstretched from Etna and from Monte Rosa, clasping at last every one of her children, and even availing by their returning strength to lift up her poor old Rome from under the load of the priest and the stranger.

"He who two brief months before had, amid deep darkness at noonday, read out, by artificial light, the decree of his own unlimited power and irreformable law, lay down that night amid a rude and intrusive glare streaming from across the Tiber into the multitudinous windows of the Vatican. It came from the lights of Rome all ablaze with illuminations for the fall of the temporal power."[185]

---

185 William Arthur, "The Pope, the Kings, and the People," p. 430.
Events and dates of Franco-German War; fall of Papal Temporal Power, and
   unification of Italy. Decision to declare war against Prussia, July 15th.

Can anyone suppose that these things happen by accident? Consider what a combination is here! Far back, at the beginning of the dark ages, a wicked usurper and murderer, thinking perhaps to atone for his crimes, presumes to bestow a prerogative which pertains to Christ alone — the headship of all the Christian churches east and west — on the bishop of the ancient seat of the Empire, Rome; and the ambitious and worldly-minded bishop dares to accept the gift, and seat himself in the temple of God, as if he were God. Divine prophecy had foretold, more than a thousand years before, the uprising of this power at this period, and had foretold also that it should endure in the Roman world for 1,260 years. We pass on through the centuries, and note how this same

---

Declaration signed, July 17th. Delivered at Berlin, July 19th, on the day after that signalized by the decree of papal infallibility.

Day of general prayer observed in Prussia, July 27th. Napoleon assumes chief command of army at Metz, July 28-9; Saarbruck, July 30th. Crown Prince crosses the Lauter, the boundary of France, and defeats the French at Wissemburg and Geisburg, August 4th. Defeats McMahon at Woerth, August 6th. Forbach, August 6th. Bombardment of Strasburg, August 14th. Bazaine defeated before Metz, Gravelotte, August 18th. Battle round Sedan, September 1st. Capitulation of Sedan; the Emperor surrenders to the King, September 2d. Revolution at Paris, and proclamation of Republic, September 4th. Seven German Corps (about 300,000 men) approaching Paris, September 13th. Siege of Paris begun, September 15th. Completely invested, September 19th. Versailles surrenders, September 19th. Capitulation of Strasburg, September 27th. Orleans captured, October 11th. Foissons surrenders, October 16th. Marshal Bazaine surrenders Metz and his army, including three marshals, sixty-six generals, 6,000 officers, 173,000 men, including the Imperial Guard, October 27th. Phalsburg surrenders, December 12th. Tours submits, December 21st Sortie of Trochu repulsed, January 19th, 1871. Capitulation of Paris, January 28th. French loss about 350,000 in January. German loss: killed, 17,570; died of wounds eventually, 10,707; total killed and wounded, 127,867. German troops enter Paris, March 1-3, 1871. Treaty of Peace, May 10th. Ratified by French National Assembly, May 18.

Fall of Papal Temporal Power. Rome completely evacuated by French troops in consequence of the war, August 21st Letter from Victor Emmanuel to the Pope announcing his intention to occupy Rome, September 8th. Italian troops enter Papal territories, September 12th. Enter Rome, after a short resistance, September 20th. Plebiscite, overwhelming vote for union with Italy, October 2, 1870.

Rome and its provinces incorporated with the Italian Kingdom by Royal Decree, October 9, 1870. — Author's work, "Approaching End of the Age," Calendar, p. 666.

power grows greater and greater, till it wields an authority mightier than that of the Caesars at the pinnacle of their glory, for it rules over two hundred millions of mankind, and, according to its own account, rules not in earth only, but in heaven and in hell. We note how the saints are given into its hand, and perish by millions at its instigation. We note how all the monarchs of the Roman world give it their voluntary submission for centuries, and how at last they rebel against it, and seek to overthrow it; how they succeed in doing this time after time, though not fully or finally, till, when eleven centuries have been left behind us we see this power declining and failing. Twelve pass away; it is weaker still! Will it last out to a thirteenth? No; its duration is fixed at 1,260 years. We scan its condition more closely. Fall succeeds fall; yet it rises again, or rather is helped up again. The last four years are come; it still stands trembling. The fateful year is ushered in. Its first six months pass, and there is no sign of a crash; midsummer comes, and, lo! the storm breaks, and before winter appears all is over — as a reigning dynasty in Europe it has fallen to rise no more! Is not this the finger of God?[186]

Chapter 8. Further Confirmation Afforded, By The Visible Commencement Of The Restoration Of The Jews, At The Close Of The Prophetic Period Of 1,260 Years From The Conquest And Occupation Of Palestine By The Saracens A.D. 637.

Are we truly living at the close of the prophetic "Times of the Gentiles?" Have we reached the final stage in the predicted course of the church's pilgrimage? Is the fourth and last watch of the "night" of her appointed suffering history shortly to expire; and does the dawn of a new age, and a new world, already lighten with

---

186 Author's work, "Light for the Last Days," p. 174.

its early rays the eastern sky? We have seen and set forth clear and multiplied proofs that "the end of the age is near at hand"; that its last sands are swiftly running out; but are all the signs we might have expected of this fact fulfilled? Writing in 1861, correcting his fifth and last edition of the "Horae Apocalypticae," Elliott said, "some signs are still wanting, especially the non-gathering as yet of the Jews to Palestine, and predicted troubles consequent. Forty-three years have elapsed since Elliott thus wrote, and now we behold the commencement of the Jewish restoration so long foretold, and its commencement at the time indicated ages ago in the prophetic word. The sight is a wonderful one, and a glorious confirmation of our faith, and of the correctness of our interpretation of"the sure word of prophecy."

On every stage of Jewish history prophecy has shed its antecedent light. Their four hundred years' captivity in Egypt was foretold;[187] their forty years' wandering in the wilderness foretold; their seventy years' captivity in Babylon foretold; their a seventy weeks," or 490 years of restored national existence in Palestine ending with the advent of Messiah foretold; their dreadful overthrow by the Romans, involving the destruction of Jerusalem, and the Temple, foretold; their long subsequent dispersion, and unexampled sufferings, their falling by the sword, and being "led captive into all nations," and Jerusalem's being trodden down by the Gentiles until the "times of the Gentiles" are fulfilled, was foretold;[188] the "seven times" or 2,520 years, of their subjection to Gentile sovereignty, under the succession of the four Kingdoms of Babylon, Persia, Greece, and Rome, was foretold; the "three and a half times," or 1,260 years, of the last "scattering of the holy people" by the desolating power occupying "the Sanctuary," whose "sacrifice" had been "taken away," was foretold;[189] and the final reversal of all this oppression, dispersion, and misery was foretold; that He who had "scattered Israel" would "gather them";[190] that He

187 Daniel 12:7.
188 Luke 21:24.
189 Jeremiah 31:10.
190 Isaiah 11:13.

would assemble the outcasts of Israel, and gather together the dispersed of Judah from the four corners of the earth ";[191] that He would"gather them out of all the countries" where he had "driven them in His anger," and bring them again into the "place" from which they had been exiled, and would "rejoice over them to do them good," and "plant them in that land assuredly" with His "whole heart" and with His "whole soul"; 'that He would make them "one nation in the land upon the mountains of Israel," and that they should be "no more two nations, neither be divided into two kingdoms any more at all";[192] that "the children of Judah and the children of Israel should be gathered together, and appoint themselves one head";[193] that the Lord would make "her that was cast off a strong nation," and that He would "reign over them in Mount Zion from henceforth and forever";[194] that He would "make them a praise and a name whose shame had been in all the earth";[195] that He would "pour upon them the spirit of grace and supplication," and that they should "look" on Him "whom they pierced, and mourn for Him as one mourneth for an only son, and be in bitterness for Him, as one that is in bitterness for his firstborn"; that there should be "a great mourning in Jerusalem, as the mourning of Hadadrimmon in the valley of Megiddon."[196]

That the Lord would "cleanse them from all their filthiness and idols," and give them "a new heart, and a new spirit," and "take away the stony heart out of their flesh, and give them an heart of flesh"; and put His "spirit" within them, and "cause them to walk in His statutes, and to keep His judgments, and do them"; and that they should "dwell in the land that He gave their fathers," and be "His people," and that He would be "their God"; and that "the land which was desolate" should be "tilled, whereas it was a desolation in the sight of all that passed by"; and that they should say "this land that was desolate is become like the garden of Eden,

191 Jeremiah 32:37-41.
192 Ezekiel 37:1-28.
193 Hosea 1:10, 11.
194 Micah 4:6-8.
195 Zephaniah 3:14-20.
196 Zechariah 12:8-14.

and the waste, and desolate, and ruined cities are fenced and inhabited."[197] All this was foretold, and to confirm his declarations Jehovah had said "then shall the nations that are left round about you know that I the Lord have builded the ruined places, and planted that which was desolate: I Jehovah have spoken it, and I will do it."

But not all at once, or by a single act, was this great restoration of the Jewish people to be accomplished. In his memorable vision the prophet Ezekiel portrays several successive stages in this work. He sees, representing figuratively the children of Israel, a valley filled with dry bones, and hears the question, "Can these bones live?" Then comes the command, "Prophesy upon these bones, and say unto them, O ye dry bones hear the word of the Lord. Thus saith the Lord God unto these bones, behold I will cause breath to enter into you, and you shall live." Then the prophet beholds the bones coming together, "bone to his bone," "but there was no breath in them." Later on at the call "Come from the four winds, O breath, and breathe upon these slain that they may live," "the breath came into them, and they lived, and stood upon their feet, an exceeding great army."[198] In explanation of the vision the Lord said to the prophet, "Son of man, these bones are the whole house of Israel; behold they say, our bones are dried, and our hope is lost; we are cut off for our parts. Therefore prophesy, and say unto them, thus saith the Lord God, Behold O My people, I will open your graves, and cause you to come up out of your graves, and bring you into the land of Israel, and ye shall know that I am the Lord when I have opened your graves, O My people, and brought you up out of your graves, and shall put My spirit in you, and ye shall live; and I shall place you in your own land: then shall ye know that I the Lord have spoken it, and performed it, saith the Lord." "Behold I will take the children of Israel from among the heathen, whither they be gone, and will gather them on every side, and bring them into their own land; and I will make them one

197 Ezekiel 36:22, 38.
198 Ezekiel 37:10.

nation in the land upon the mountains of Israel, and one king shall be king to them all."[199] First the unification of the lifeless people of Israel should take place; then their national restoration to their own land; and lastly their spiritual quickening, with all its glorious results. Such was the foretold order. Not forever are the Jewish people to be a dispersed, despised, down-trodden race; not forever is their unbelief and rejection of Messiah to continue; for as Paul tells us "blindness in part is happened to Israel, until the fullness of the Gentiles be come in, and so all Israel shall be saved"; for this is God's "covenant" with them; "for the gifts and calling of God are without repentance,"[200] or irrevocable.

And now the thing foretold is taking place before our eyes. There is a stir in the Valley of Vision. The immobility and disjointed condition of the bleached bones, which had continued for ages, exists no more. Israel is still spiritually lifeless as a nation, but bone is coming to his bone. The Jews are unifying. They have proclaimed before the world the "solidarity" of Israel: and are beginning to return to their own land. And when did this movement commence? It began at the time of the French Revolution. Both events commenced at the close of the "seven times" of the four empires; at their first, or initial termination; the era of the seventh trumpet, with its seven vials of judgment on apostate Babylon. And the last 100 years which have witnessed the casting down of the Papal and Mohammedan powers, by the successive shocks of war and revolution, have seen the lifting up of the people of Israel from the depression of ages; their rapid emancipation, and national renaissance.

The first act in this marvelous modern movement was the enfranchisement of the Jews in England in 1753. In 1755 Moses Mendelssohn published the first of those writings which gave him a foremost place among the literary men of his time. In 1776 the United States of America embodied in their constitution the principle that Gentile and Jew were "equal" in right and privilege

---

199 Ezekiel 37:1-21.
200 Romans 11:25-39.

before the law. In the convulsion of the French Revolution "the chains fell from the limbs of Israel wherever the victorious armies of France appeared, and the Jews once more began to be accounted men." In 1805 Russia revoked the edict of Jewish banishment. In 1806 the Jews were made citizens in Italy and Westphalia, as they had been previously in Holland and Belgium. In 1809 Baden, and in 1813 Prussia and Denmark followed the example of other nations, and emancipated the Jews. Acts of Parliament were passed in England in their favor in 1830, 1833, and 1836; and in 1858 they were made eligible for election to Parliament. In 1866 Turkey had pledged herself to protect them from persecution; and in 1867 she gave them the right to hold real estate in the land of their fathers. In 1878 the Congress of Berlin made the full emancipation of the Jews in Roumania a condition of promised autonomy. And then in 1860 was formed the Universal Israelite Alliance, "an organization which has for its object the promotion and completion of the emancipation of the Jews in all lands, and their intellectual and moral elevation, as also the development of Jewish colonization in the Holy Land." This great Jewish society has some three thousand branches widely scattered throughout the world. Beneath the device on the title page of its report representing the tables of the law illuminated with the glory of the Shekinah, two hands are pictured, closely clasped in friendship and unity, with the motto '*Toutes les Israelites sont solidaires les uns des autres.*' All Israelites are one!"

The aim of the Society, next to the realization of Jewish unity, is the cooperation of Jews throughout the world in efforts on behalf of their suffering and oppressed brethren, efforts to secure "*l'emancipation de nos freres qui gemissent encore sous le poids d'une legislation exceptionelle.*" Various associations are connected with the Alliance as national branches, as the Anglo-Jewish Association, under the presidency of Baron de Worms, Sir Barrow Ellis, Sir Julian Goldsmith, Sir Benjamin Phillips, Sir Saul Samuel, and Sir Albert Sassoon. Its records tell of efforts on behalf of suffering Jews in Morocco, Roumania, Russia, and Persia; of schools for neglected Jewish children established in Bagdad, Bey rout, Bombay, Constantinople, Corfu, Damascus, Fez, Haifa, Jerusalem, Kezanlik, Philippopolis, Salonica, Samacoff, Sophia, Tunis, and elsewhere. Jewish journals have been created or aided for the instruction and elevation of the Jews in various countries, and "to knit more closely the bond of union amongst the different Jewish communities." But here the work of the Alliance stops. It has not sought to secure for the Jews a national position, or to bring about their restoration to Palestine.

The unity and emancipation of the Jews at which this Alliance aims, however desirable, fails to satisfy the heart of the Jewish people, which naturally turns to Palestine, the land of their fathers, with longings for restoration to their national position, and their original divinely-given inheritance and home. And hence the various attempts which have been latterly made to found Jewish colonies in Palestine; attempts to a considerable degree successful; and the large number of Jews who have returned to, and are settled in that land. But beyond these efforts a further movement was needed to bring about the reconstruction of the Jews as a nation in their own land. Was it possible that such a movement, vibrating far and wide throughout the scattered people, could arise? This is a prosaic and practical age. For long centuries the Jews have been domiciled in Gentile lands. Palestine has long lain desolate, and exists at the present day under the misgovernment of the Turks. Was it likely that the Jews, already to a considerable extent emancipated from Gentile oppression would undertake the gigantic work of restoring their people to the land from which they had been exiled so long? It is true that the scriptures of the prophets had said that this would come to pass. But how could this thing be? How could the Jews be brought, in any wide and general way, to entertain the thought of such a restored national existence in Palestine? And how could they be led to attempt its practical realization?

Difficulties vanish in the presence of infinite, eternal power. Had not God brought forth the Jewish nation from Egypt; had He not restored them from captivity in Babylon, and could He not bring them again to their own land from the ends of the earth?"Tremble thou earth at the presence of the Lord, at the presence of the God of Jacob." And now, lo! as the foretold period of 1,260 years from the Saracenic conquest of Palestine in A.D. 637, expires, as the year 1897 arrives, a new movement among the Jews springs into existence; Zionism arises, with its clearly defined aim "to procure for the Jewish people an openly recognized and legally assured home in Palestine."

The first "Zionist" Congress was held at Basle, in 1897. Each year since that date the annual Congress has increased in numbers and influence.

I have before me a description from the pen of an intelligent Christian eye-witness, Mr. Schonberger, of the fifth Zionist Congress, held at Basle. Three hundred Jewish delegates, and about a thousand Jewish hearers, crowded the large hall of the Stadt Casino. The delegates were highly-educated men, speaking a great variety of languages. "The three great speeches were those of Dr. Hertzl on the opening day, of Dr. Nordau on the second day, and of Mr. Israel Zangwill, of Ghetto fame, on the evening of the fourth day. Dr. Hertzl's address which was most eagerly looked forward to, and listened to with profound interest, had all the soberness, earnestness and statesmanlike character which mark the commanding personality of the respected and honored founder of the movement. There was no brilliancy of diction, nor any attempt at oratory in its delivery; but its principal points, as well as the whole setting testified of the man who had undertaken a great task, and felt the full weight of his responsibility. It gave in a most concise and telling way the whole story of Zionism, its achievements and prospects; and described the spirit and means by which it strives to attain its end. An altogether different thing was Dr. Nordau's great address on the 'Physical, economical, and intellectual amelioration of the Jews/ Dr. Nordau is a masterful orator and most gifted word-painter, who brings to his task all the abilities of a savant, a writer and a journalist combined. His personality and his gifts are alike striking. He is a veritable giant, and his strokes go home to friend and foe alike. His addresses are characterized by sweeping assertions, anatomical and pathological laying bare of Israel's diseases, woes, and miseries; searching analysis of the deplorable physical and economic condition of the great masses of Jews, and their causes; a fiery denunciation of the rich — especially the 'lost' Jewish millionaires. Israel Zangwill's task was to expose the Jewish Colonial Association, and the Trustees of the Baron Hirsch Fund, on account of their standing aloof from Zionism."

It is a significant fact, indicative of Jewish progress that the delegates at the Congress "total at more university degrees than the House of Commons, though the membership is not half that of the mother of Parliaments." These delegates "come from everywhere, from Dawson City and Stockholm, from Astrachan and Tetuan; from Morocco, from Anatolia and the Argentine. In less than five years the movement has run through the British Empire, Russia, Roumania, and Galicia, and is making headway in Austria, Germany, France, Italy, Holland, Belgium and Switzerland, and has its advocates for the return among the returned in Palestine."

"The movement is distinctly liberal. The central authority is the Vienna executive, but each country has independent power within the framework of the movement. The most marked liberality of thought exists on religious matters. At one end is the rabbi, in fur cap, gabardine and side curls; at the other the rank Freethinker. Every shade of political thought is represented, and differences ignored in favor of the main idea of the return, and blood kinship of Israel. Nearly half a million of Jews have become interested Zionists. Next to no one is paid j volunteers do nearly everything except the sheer routine work. Its zeal has given birth to Neo-Hebrew. The old tongue lives again. It has its newspapers, magazines, novels and poetry, and 'Daniel Deronda' or Byron's Hebrew Melodies may be picked up in the tongue of Isaiah and the Talmudic Rabbis. Even London has its Hebrew newspaper, and a new Hebrew encyclopedia is being issued. Zionism has made Hebrew the language of instruction in the Jewish colonies in Palestine. The Zionists have managed to arrest the attention of the German Emperor, to obtain an audience of the Sultan, and raise £ 300,000 from 126,000 shareholders." They are opposed by a certain set of rabbis under the influence of the more wealthy and worldly Jews, but as Dr. Hertzl said, "The poor and the wretched understand us; they have the imagination created by distress. They know from the experience of today and yesterday what the pangs of hunger will be tomorrow. In this condition there are many hundreds of thousands of our people. Judaism is an immense hostelry of misery, with branches throughout the world. Of the 'Protest-Rabbis' of the west who oppose the movement Dr. Max Nordau said, 'with them we have already settled, and I hope that soon the whole Jewish people will have settled with them.'"

This eloquent Jew, Dr. Max Nordau, addressing the delegates to the Congress said, "It seemed as if we were witnessing a miracle which affected ourselves, and all around us. We felt ourselves part and parcel of a fairy tale, in which we saw. our brethren, thousands of years buried, again become flesh and blood. We wanted in the joy of this reunion to rehearse the sad history of the hundreds of years in which we had been dead in our tomb, in a grave which lacked the peace of a grave." "We have honestly striven everywhere to merge ourselves in the social life of surrounding communities, and to preserve only the faith of our fathers. It has not been permitted to us. In vain arise loyal patriots, in some places our loyalty running to extremes; in vain do we make the same sacrifices of life and property as our fellow citizens; in vain do we strive to increase the fame of our native land in science and art, or her wealth by trade and commerce. In countries where we have lived for centuries we are still cried down as strangers; and often by those whose ancestors were not yet domiciled in the land where Jews had already made experience of suffering. We are one people — our enemies have made us one in our despite, as repeatedly happens in history. Distress binds us together, and thus united, we suddenly discover our strength. Yes, we are strong enough to form a State, and a Model State."

Zion the Capital of a Jewish Nation In his account of the International Zionist Congress at Basle in August last Richard Gottheil says, "A full seven years of service and work have passed by since a little band of one hundred and fifty enthusiasts met in the small hall of the Stadt Casino of that city in the year 1897. This year nearly six hundred delegates crowded to its utmost capacity the large meeting hall in that building; and these were little more than one-half of those that have been elected to represent Zionist constituencies. In 1897 delegates came from only a few European states — notably Austria, Russia, Germany, France, and England. In 1903 there was hardly a corner of the globe in which Jews reside which was not represented. In Europe, from northern Scandinavia to southern Italy, from Ireland to the confines of Asia; and from North and South America, from far off Australia and South Africa; even from the Russo-Chinese frontier, these delegates came to meet their brethren and to sit in the Jewish Congress. The telegrams of greeting which poured into Basle showed that the Zionist organization is as far reaching as is the present day dispersion of the children of Israel. Even China proper was heard from in a communication from the Shanghai Zionist Association. It was not out of idle curiosity that these representatives had come to Basle; it was not the excitement of a moment that prompted these messages. Both men and messages bespoke, not only an underlying sentiment in the heart of the Jewish people, but also definite work in this great Jewish movement. The meeting in 1897 was tentative. That of 1903 was evidence of a fixed institution. The growth in members is paralleled by the growth in internal organization, and in other work of a most varied character. So large has become the number of delegates that a change has been found necessary in the method of representation, the basis of that representation being now two hundred in place of one hundred for each delegate.

"Within the Congress itself various parties have been formed. There is the government party, led of course by Dr. Hertzl, and the central committee at Vienna. There is the strictly orthodox party, called the Mizrachi, led by a Russian Rabbi in the long caftan of his own country j there is the young Zionist party, made up largely of former and present Russian students at German and Swiss universities. Though not opposed to one another, and all working for one and the same end, they differ as to the means by which this end is to be reached; and these very differences show that the movement is pulsating with life — that it is not dead formalism, but the expression of the soul of Judaism.

"At the meeting in 1897 the question discussed was the eternal one — to be, or not to be. At the Congress of 1903 definite propositions were made which demanded in their treatment the wisdom of experience, and the restraint of calm judgment. The road traversed by the Zionists between 1897 and 1903 was not only strewn with many obstacles, but covered by almost impassible barriers. A way had to be cleared through the jungle, and the undergrowth which centuries of neglect had allowed to arise in the path of the Jews. Opposition, more especially Jewish opposition had to be overcome at every point; for attacks had been made upon the Zionists in the open, and from behind ambushes. 'The rich ones among us, those who have gained fame and wealth in the international market of the world, have held severely aloof. Those who believed they would be looked upon as better citizens by crying out loudly their allegiance to the country in which they lived, fought us with all the weapons of satire and detraction. But a movement which is of the people, and for the people, which has its roots firmly set in the conscience of that people, will not down even at the insistence of the mighty, or at the satire of the garrulous. The movement progressed, and indeed gained strength from the opposition which it provoked. A Jewish Congress had been hailed as an impossibility. It was shown to be a fact. A Jewish bank for strictly Jewish purposes had been decried as an anomaly. Yet the Jewish Colonial Trust was founded in London; a branch, the Anglo-Palestine bank, was founded in Palestine, and branches are now in the process of formation both in Russia and in America. A

Jewish national fund was laughed at as the dream of enthusiasts. Yet such a fund has been founded and bids fair to give the material resources to Zionism without which of course it cannot work. But more than this, the Zionist movement is responsible for a great awakening of the Jewish conscience; for a return of many of our best and most intelligent Jews to Judaism; for a tremendous advance of culture among the Jews along Jewish lines in philosophy, in literature, in art. If the Jews have still a message to the world it is through this reawakened conscience that this message is spoken."[201]

Our beloved brother David Baron of London who has as a converted Jew, deeply interested in the welfare of the Jewish people, attended the Zionist Congress, says in The Scattered Nation, "I am of the conviction that if Zionism does not as yet sufficiently represent the wealth and material resources of the Jewish nation, it does certainly represent a large proportion of its head and brain; and as I looked upon those hundreds of earnest, intelligent faces, gathered from all parts of the earth, and listened to the able, and often impassioned speeches made in different languages, I felt in my soul that Israel is God's great reserve force for the future blessing of the world; and my heart goes out in yearning for the time when 'the spirit shall be poured upon us from on high,' and when these remarkable gifts, and this zeal and ability, shall be consecrated to the service of making known their long rejected Messiah and King among the nations."

Chapter 9. Primary Ending Of The 1,260 Years Of Jewish Desolation In 1860, And 1897, As Reckoned From The Conquest Of Palestine By The Saracens, A.D. 637.

[1.] From the Saracenic conquest and occupation of Jerusalem and Palestine, in A.D. 637, to the formation of the Universal Israelite

---

201 Richard Gottheil, in the Cosmopolitan, December, 1903.

Alliance, in 1860, extend 1,260 lunar years.

[2.] From the same Saracenic starting point in Palestinian history, A.D. 637, to the First Zionist Congress in 1897, extend 1,260 solar years.

THE NARRATIVE of the Saracenic conquest of Jerusalem and Palestine by the Saracens is told by Gibbon in his work on "The Decline and Fall of the Roman Empire" (Ch. LI): "Jerusalem, in the year 637," says Gibbon, "was defended on every side by deep valleys and steep ascents; since the invasion of Syria the walls and towers had been anxiously restored; the bravest of the fugitives of Yermak had stopped in the nearest place of refuge; and in the defense of the sepulchre of Christ the natives and strangers might feel some sparks of enthusiasm which so fiercely glowed in the bosoms of the Saracens. The siege of Jerusalem lasted four months; not a day was lost without some action of sally or assault; the military engines incessantly played from the ramparts; and the inclemency of the winter was still more painful and destructive to the Arabs. The Christians yielded at length to the perseverance of the besiegers. The Patriarch Sophronius appeared on the walls, and by the voice of an interpreter demanded a conference. After a vain attempt to dissuade the lieutenant of the Caliph from his impious enterprise, he proposed, in the name of the people a fair capitulation, with this extraordinary clause, that the articles of security should be ratified by the authority and presence of Omar himself. The question was debated in the council of Medina; the sanctity of the place, and the advice of Ali, persuaded the Caliph to gratify the wishes of his soldiers and enemies; and the simplicity of his journey is more illustrious than the royal pageants of vanity and oppression. The conqueror of Persia and Syria was mounted on a red camel, which carried beside his person, a bag of corn, a bag of dates, a wooden dish, and a leathern bottle of water. Wherever he halted, the company, without distinction was invited to partake of his homely fare, and the repast was consecrated by the prayer and exhortation of the commander of the faithful. But in this expedition or pilgrimage, his power was exercised in the administration of justice; he reformed the licentious polygamy of the Arabs, relieved the tributaries from extortion and cruelty, and chastised the luxury of the Saracens, by despoiling them of their rich silks, and dragging them on their faces in the dirt. When he came within sight of Jerusalem, the Caliph cried with a loud voice, 'God is victorious. O Lord give us an easy conquest!' and pitching his tent of coarse hair, calmly seated himself on the ground. After signing the capitulation, he entered the city without fear or precaution; and courteously discoursed with the Patriarch concerning its religious antiquities. Sophronius bowed before his new master, and secretly muttered, in the words of Daniel, 'the abomination of desolation is in the holy place.' At the hour of prayer they stood together in the church of the Resurrection; but the Caliph refused to perform his devotions, and contented himself with praying on the steps of the church of Constantine. To the Patriarch he disclosed his prudent and honorable motive. 'Had I yielded,' said Omar, 'to your request, the moslems of a future age would have infringed the treaty under color of imitating my example.' By his command the ground of the temple of Solomon was prepared for the foundation of a Mosque; and during a residence of ten days he regulated the present and future state of his Syrian conquests."

The Mosque of Omar still stands in Jerusalem on the foundation of Solomon's Temple, as a witness of the Saracenic conquest whose initial date was the year A.D. 637.

In a series of works on the fulfillment of prophecy published during the last twenty-six years I have pointed out the importance of the year A.D. 637 in relation to the 1,260 years of Jewish and Palestinian desolation.

I. The Four Kingdoms

In the year 1878 I published my work on "The Approaching End of the Age," and in a subsequent edition issued the following year added a Calendar of the Four Gentile Monarchies of Babylon,

Persia, Greece, and Rome, commencing with the Era of Nabonassar, B.C. 747, the starting point of Ptolemy's Canon of the kings and times of these four empires.

In my calendar of the four kingdoms (p. 622) I stated that the capture of Jerusalem by the Saracens took place in the sixteenth lunar year of the Mohammedan Hejira, A.D. 637, and added the following chronological and historical facts.

"From the date of Nebuchadnezzar's burning of the Temple (B.C. 587, 5th month, 10th day), to the setting up of the Mohammedan desolation in Jerusalem (A.D. 637), there extend 1,260 lunar years. From Omar's capture of Jerusalem (A.D. 637), there extend 1,260 lunar years to A.D. 1860. Mohammedan massacre of 3,300 Christians at Damascus (July 9, 1860), followed by English and French intervention; 4,000 French troops landed at Beyroot, August 22nd; Lord Dufferin, British Commissioner in Syria, reaches Damascus, September 6, 1860. From the same initial date there extended 1,260 calendar years to A.D. 1879; total defeat of Ottoman armies by Russia in 1877, followed in 1878 by British occupation of Cyprus, and protectorate in Asia. Berlin Treaty depriving the Porte of its most important possessions in Europe, and binding it to introduce 'necessary reforms,' signed July 13, 1878, in the beginning of the 1,260th calendar year from the summer of A.D. 637. From A.D. 637, 1,260 solar years extend to A.D. 1897."

II. The Initial Stages of Jewish Restoration

Ten years before the arrival of the year 1897, in my work "Light for the Last Days" (published in 1887), I again pointed out, and with stronger emphasis the importance of the years 1860 and 1897, in connection with initial stages of Jewish restoration.

The following is the diagram of dates there given, and the paragraph which follows it:

A.D. 637 ——— 1,260 ——— lunar years ——— 1860.

A.D. 637 ——— 1,260 calendar years ——— 1877-8.

A.D. 637 ——— 1,260 solar years ——— 1897.

"The first of these years, 1860, was a most critical one in the history of the Porte, and in the history of the Jews. It was the first stage in the liberation of the Holy Land from direct Turkish rule, — an early stage in the cleansing of the sanctuary from the power of the desolator; (being the date of the Druze massacre, and of the placing of the Lebanon under a Christian governor), and it was also the year of the formation of the 'Universal Israelite Alliance ,' an initial step towards Jewish national reorganization. The action of England and France in Syria on this occasion might be considered a marked stage in the decline of the Ottoman power, as each such interference with its governmental action is an additional demonstration to the world of its loss of independence. The calendar termination from this Omar date (end of 1,260 years of 360 days each), is the year 1878, the year of the Berlin Conference, with its wholesale dismemberment of Turkey. The remaining solar termination is still ten years distant, 1897. What is it likely to witness? Some more final and fatal fall of Ottoman power? Or some more distinct stage of Jewish restoration? Time will declare."[202]

III. The Termini Of 1260 Lunar and Solar Years.

In my work "Creation Centered in Christ" published in 1896, I again indicated the importance of 1860 and 1897 as the termini of 1,260 lunar, and 1,260 solar years, reckoned from the Saracenic conquest of Palestine in 637.

---

202 "Light for the Last Days," pp. 176, 177.

The following is the paragraph in that work referring to these dates.

"The prophetic times belong chiefly to the fourth Gentile kingdom, and especially to its latter half, or 1,260 years Papal and Mohammedan period. The French Revolution of last century and the fall of the papal temporal power coincident with the decree of papal infallibility in 1870 marked the termination of 1,260 years as measured from the Justinian and Phocas starting points in papal history. Reckoned from the Saracenic capture of Jerusalem and subjugation of Palestine in A.D. 637, 1,260 lunar years expired in 1860, the date of the liberation of the Lebanon district from Turkish rule, consequent upon the massacre of Christians in Syria, and also of the formation of the Universal Israelite Alliance, which has now branches throughout the world. Reckoned in solar form $1^{\wedge}260$ years will terminate in and present events in Armenia confirm the view that we are on the eve of the break up of Mohammedan power in the East. It may be noted that the prophetic period of 2,300 years in lunar form extends from B.C. 336, the initial date of Alexander's conquest (prominent in the prophecy of the ram and he-goat, Dan. 8), to A.D. 1897, the date expiration of 1,260 solar years from the setting up of Sarcenic rule in Palestine. Among all the signs of the nearness of 'the end of the age' none perhaps are more important than those connected with the state of the Jewish people. The removal of Jewish disabilities, and coincident rise of Jewish wealth, learning, and social and political influence; the unification of the Jews by various alliances, especially the Universal Israelite Alliance, which has countless branches in the present day all over the world; the persecution of the Jews on the continent, and particularly in Russia, where they are so numerous, and the constant growth of a national desire on the part of the Jewish people to return to the land of their fathers, all point to the proximity of the close of the 'Times of the Gentiles,' which are throughout times of the depression and dispersion of the Jews."[203]

---

203 "Creation Centered in Christ," pp. 492, 493.

The Zionist Congress held in Basle in 1897 remarkably fulfilled the anticipations which I had expressed from time to time during the previous eighteen years, with reference to the importance of that date as marking an initial stage of Jewish restoration.

The confirmation is so striking and important as to justify a fresh and close examination of the system of times and seasons which I have set forth in a series of volumes during the last twenty -six years. We cannot give this here, but we point out some salient suggestive facts.

First as to Jewish dates.

The importance of the date B.C. 587, as marking the completion of Jewish captivity at the destruction of the city and Temple of Jerusalem, by Nebuchadnezzar should be realized.

Then the fact that from that date

[1.] One thousand two hundred and sixty lunar years extended to the Saracenic capture of Jerusalem in A.D. 637.

[2.] Two thousand five hundred and twenty lunar years (1,260x2) to the formation of the Universal Israelite Alliance in 1860: an important initial date in the Jewish restoration movement.

Then the further facts that from the Saracenic capture of Jerusalem in 637

[1.] One thousand two hundred and sixty lunar years extend to the above date A.D. 1860.

[2.] One thousand two hundred and sixty solar years to the first Zionist Congress in A.D. 1897.

This confirms the importance of reckoning the prophetic times both in lunar and solar form. In my "Calendar of the Four Kingdoms," published in 1879, 1 have so reckoned them; and have set forth the discovery which I made in the study of the times of history and prophecy, that the period extending from February 26, B.C. 747, the Babylonian Nabonassar era, to August 22, 476, the date of the deposition of Romulus Augustulus, and of the termination of the Western Roman Empire, is exactly 1,260 lunar years.[204]

The unquestionable fact that the duration of the four kingdoms of prophecy, of history, and of Ptolemy's Canon, Babylon, Persia, Greece, and Rome, from the Babylonian era of Nabonassar B.C. 747, to the end of the empire of western Rome, A.D. 476, should be limited by, and contained in, the prophetic period of 1,260 years, in lunar form, is suggestive of a system of times, measuring the full duration of the four kingdoms of prophecy, starting with the Babylonian Nabonassar era. That such a system exists long continued examination of the subject has amply convinced me. Thus while 1,260 lunar years measure the four kingdoms from the Nabonassar era to the end of the western empire of Rome, the full period of 2,520 solar years (twice 1,26p years) extends from the Nabonassar era to A.D. 1774, the date of the accession of Louis XVI; recognized in the histories of Carlyle and Alison, as the date of the commencement of the era of the French Revolution.

A striking fact which I discovered that the difference in measure between 2,520 lunar years, and the same number of solar years, is seventy-five solar years, the very period placed by the recording angel in Daniel 12, at the termination of the prophetic times, plainly indicates that these times should be reckoned both in lunar and solar form; and that their epact, or the difference between their lunar and solar measurement, is adjusted to the terminal periods of these times, as measuring closing eras. Thus the period from 1859-1860, to 1934 is seventy-five years; and is the epact, or difference between 2^20 lunar years, and the same number of solar years, reckoned from the completion of Jewish captivity at the destruction of the temple by Nebuchadnezzar B.C. 587.

---

[204]"Approaching End of the Age," p. 606.

B. C. 587 ——— 2,520 *lunar* years ——— A. D. 1859–1860
=2,445 solar years
B. C. 587 ——— 2,520 *solar* years ——— A. D. 1934
2,520 lunar years=2,445 solar years

$$\underline{75}$$

2,520 solar years

Now as B.C. 587 the nineteenth year of Nebuchadnezzar, witnessed the completion of the captivity of Judah, whose commencing dates were the first, fourth and eighth years of his reign, M seven times/' or 2,520 years in full solar measure from these captivity dates are likely to extend to corresponding dates in the course of Jewish restoration.

Dates of completion of Jewish Captivity in the first nineteen years of Nebuchadnezzar's reign; and corresponding dates at close of the prophetic period of "seven times."

B.C. 605 ——— 2,520 solar years ——— A.D. 1916

B.C. 602 ——— 2,520 solar years ——— A.D. 1919

B.C. 598 ——— 2,520 solar years ——— A.D. 1923

B.C. 587 ——— 2,520 solar years ——— A.D. 1934

Chapter 10. Coming Events In Jewish History

TO THESE the last chapter of the prophecy of Daniel is both a historical and chronological key. Its dates are reckoned from the cessation of the "daily sacrifice," in Jerusalem, and placing there of the "abomination that maketh desolate," the idolatrous ensign of the desolating power.

The first fulfillment of this event took place B.C. 168. Antiochus Epiphanes having captured Jerusalem with great slaughter, caused the daily sacrifice to cease, polluted the Temple, and dedicated it to

Jupiter Olympus, erecting his statue on the altar of burnt offerings, and putting every one to death who resisted his decrees.[205]

The second fulfillment, of which the first was typical, took place in A.D. 70, when during the siege of Jerusalem by the Romans, foretold by our Lord, the daily sacrifice ceased, the Temple was burned, and Jerusalem overthrown with great slaughter. Referring to this awful event, and to the previous erection of the idolatrous standards of the Roman army in the precincts of the" holy city," our Lord had said in reply to a question as to the approaching destruction of the Temple, "When ye therefore shall see the abomination of desolation spoken of by Daniel the prophet, stand in the holy place (whoso readeth let him understand) then let them which be in Judea flee to the mountains, ... for then shall be great tribulation such as was not since the beginning of the world to this time, no, nor ever shall be" (Matt. 24:15, 21).

More fully recorded in Luke, our Lord's prediction was as follows, — "When ye shall see Jerusalem compassed with armies, then know that the desolation thereof is nigh. Then let them which are in Judea flee to the mountains; and let them which are in the midst of it depart out; and let not them that are in the countries enter thereinto. For these be the days of vengeance, that all things which are written may be fulfilled. But woe unto them that are with child, and to them that give suck in those days! for there shall be great distress in the land, and wrath upon this people. And they shall fall by the edge of the sword, and shall be led away captive into all nations, and"Jerusalem shall be trodden down of the Gentiles, until the times of the Gentiles be fulfilled" (Luke 21:20-24).

Our Lord had previously foretold with tears this coming judgment, and again when on the way to crucifixion He speaks of it in His touching words, "Daughters of Jerusalem, weep not for Me, but weep for yourselves and for your children," "for if they do these things in a green tree what shall be done in the dry?"

---

205 Macc., Book II, Vol. 1, p. 54.

The third fulfillment of the placing and setting up of the desolating power in Jerusalem took place A.D. 637, when at the capture of the city by the Saracens, and the clearing of the temple area for the erection of the Mosque of Omar, the Mohammedan power became supreme; thenceforward to exercise dominion in the Holy City and Holy Land, "until the times of the Gentiles be fulfilled." To the entrance of the polluting presence of this power the Patriarch Sophronius strikingly referred in the sentence quoted by Gibbon, "The abomination of desolation is in the holy place."

Contemporaneously with this setting up of the Mohammedan desolating power in the East, took place the setting up of the idolatrous Papal power in the West; and a comparison of the seven passages in Daniel and the Apocalypse relating to the 1,260 years continuance of the desolating power, yields proof of the conclusion that they refer to the duration of Popery and Mohammedanism.

These twin antichristian powers in the West and in the East, rose together, dominated together, have declined together, and are coming to their end together. Hence various general predictions as to the expected Antichrist may well include both of these in their range of meaning; as the declaration in the first epistle of John that the Antichrist will "deny the Father and the Son." Popery virtually denies both in exalting the Pope to occupy the place of God, in the temple or church of God, and the place of Christ as the Head of that church; while Mohammedanism actually and openly denies both, in its implacable opposition to the truth revealed in scripture that Christ is the only begotten Son of the Father.

This breadth of range in the meaning of the prophetic word surely harmonizes with the vastness of the mind of its author. Analogous events are comprehended under the same expression, and room is given for the progressive unfolding of the divine meaning in the prolonged course of history.

Thus the "time of trouble" foretold in Daniel 12, seems to include both Jewish and Christian aspects. The "time of trouble" predicted by our Lord is certainly Jewish, and, judging by a,comparison of Matthew 24 and Luke 21, commenced with the Roman destruction of Jerusalem, and continues throughout the period in which Jerusalem is "trodden down by the Gentiles," and the Jews "led captive into all nations"; while the mention of "Michael" as "the great Prince which standeth for the children of thy people" (Dan 12:1) connects "the time of trouble" with the warfare of "Michael and his angels" with "the dragon and his angels"; the seven headed ten horned dragon representing the satanically inspired Roman empire, in its heathenish warfare with the early Christian Church; a warfare renewed under the revived Roman power of Revelation 13, in the "war with the saints," of later mediaeval and modern Reformation times. It is important to observe that both in the prophecies of Daniel and those of our Lord the "time of trouble" is immediately followed by the resurrection of the dead. "Many of them that sleep in the dust of the earth shall awake," says the revealing angel to Daniel, "some to everlasting life, and some to shame and everlasting contempt. And they that be wise shall shine as the brightness of the firmament, and they that turn many to righteousness as the stars for ever and ever."

"Immediately after the tribulation of those daysf says our Lord,"shall the sun be darkened, and the moon shall not give her light, and the stars shall fall from heaven, and the powers of the heaven shall be shaken. And then shall appear the sign of the Son of man in heaven: and then shall all the tribes of the earth mourn, and they shall see the Son of man coming in the clouds of heaven with power and great glory. And He shall send His angels with a great sound of a trumpet; and they shall gather together His elect from the four winds, from one end of heaven to the other " (Matt. 24:29-31).

The same order of events is predicted in Zech. 14, where the gathering of "all nations against Jerusalem to battle" is foretold; the capture of "the city," and "captivity" of the people, followed by the advent of the Lord to deliver, when "His feet shall stand upon the Mount of Olives," and "the Lord my God shall come, and all the saints with Thee"; an advent to be succeeded by the manifestation of the universal kingdom of God; "the Lord shall be king over all the earth; in that day there shall be one Lord, and His name one" (Zech. 14:1-9). Nor is this order different from that which is revealed in the prophecies of Paul, and in the Apocalypse.

If the ending epoch of Jerusalem's treading down by the Gentiles be the epoch also of Christ's second and glorious advent, to what great events are we now near at hand! The "fig tree" which on the Jewish rejection of Christ had withered away, begins to shoot forth leaves after its long period of barrenness, whereby we may know "that summer is nigh" (Matt. 24:32, 33). The Jews after the dispersion of ages are again being gathered to their own land. Trouble awaits them there. Joseph's brethren must be brought to self-judgment in a closing crisis of anguish and distress before Joseph reveals himself to them, as the brother whom they had sold into Egypt, and treated as dead. Then shall their tears of repentance be mingled with his tears of forgiving love. Then shall there be "a great mourning in Jerusalem," for God will "pour upon the house of David, and the inhabitants of Jerusalem, the spirit of grace and of supplications, and they shall look upon Me whom they have pierced, and they shall mourn for Him, as one mourneth for his only son, and shall be in bitterness for Him, as one that is in bitterness for his first-born" (Zech. 12:10-14). Then shall be the national affliction and humiliation of the "Day of Atonement" for Israel; following the "blowing of trumpets" which opens the "first day of the seventh month" (Lev. 23), the future Sabbatic portion of their history. There shall sound on the day of atonement for all their sins the jubilee trumpet of restoration to the land, and liberty to the people (Lev. 25); followed in its turn by the still more glorious "Feast of Tabernacles," whose celebrations are bright with the joys of future ages.

An intelligent consideration of the present position of the Jewish people, of their long continued preservation, and of their deeply rooted national hopes, can only confirm the anticipation of their coming restoration to their own land; while the clear and multiplied promises of the word of God as to their conversion to Christ leave no room for doubt as to the accomplishment of that blessed event. "The remnant shall return, even the remnant of Jacob unto the mighty God: for though thy people Israel be as the sand of the sea a remnant of them shall return" (Isa. 10:21, 22). Most of the Jews are now in Russia, where expulsive forces are at work which shall yet drive them out of the country in large numbers. The anti-semitic feeling in Germany is extremely strong, and growing in intensity; it exists in the Balkan states, in France, Algiers and other countries. Forces are thus in existence, ready to expel the Jews in considerable numbers from Gentile lands. The increasing wealth of the Jews, and modern means of travel, facilitate migratory movements on a national scale. But both experience and scripture indicate that the restoration of the Jews will be gradual, and that the early settlers in the land will be chiefly drawn from the poorer classes. Steam communication from South Russia, and the eastern states of Europe, makes the journey to Palestine an easy one. Railways are in operation, and others being built in Palestine in several directions. The Turkish government which has possessed and ruled the land for more than four hundred years, is in a dying condition. The eastern question remains unsolved. Everything points to its solution by the return of the Jews to the land of their fathers. On the other hand the mutually antagonistic powers which surround Palestine, especially the Russian and Turkish, forecast by their presence coming struggles for the possession of the land which are likely to involve the restored Jews in great suffering, and even to expose them to threatened destruction. The Turks are accustomed to perpetrate massacres, and the Russians when roused are still barbarous in their modes of warfare. That Russia covets Palestine is a well known fact. Ten thousand Russian pilgrims annually visit Jerusalem, and the Crimean war which originated in a dispute as to the holy places in that city is a witness to Russian interest in the land of the nativity and the crucifixion.

Beyond the immediate prospects in relation to the Jews and Palestine rises the glowing and glorious picture of the future of that people and land, as portrayed in scripture, and illuminated by a study of the physical conditions, and ethnographical surroundings involved. Placed at the junction of three continents, and at the gateway of commerce between the West and the East; possessed of tropical valleys, and snow-clad mountains, the land of the palm and the cedar, of the olive and the vine, holds forth its hands of promise to the wandering exiled Jews. Carmel and Sharon covered in spring with their roses, the fields of Bethlehem, and hills of Nazareth with their anemones, the plain of Esdraelon with its corn-fields, the Jordan valley with its luxuriant foliage, the wilds of Bashan with their pastures, all wait for the Jewish hands and homes which are yet to cultivate and occupy them. The long neglected Gulf of Akaba with its noble headlands projecting into the Red Sea shall yet become a highway of commerce to southern Palestine. Ezion-geber at the head of that gulf will be connected by railway with the Dead Sea, the Jordan valley, and the Lake of Gennesareth. The waters of Merom, and sources of the Jordan shall be linked with the crowded streets of Damascus, and the snow-clad steeps of Hermon. The slopes of Lebanon will be populated, the city of Antioch revived. Beyrout already connected with the ports of the Mediterranean and with Damascus, shall be the gate of a highroad through the Euphrates valley to the Persian Gulf, India, and the East. Africa traversed with railways shall lie at the feet of Palestine, and Europe with its wealth of civilization shall flourish at its side. The Jews restored from all countries, and speaking all languages, shall be fitted for the work of evangelizing the world. Their marvelous commercial, political, and literary gifts shall come into fullest play. No more shall they be a despised and outcast people. The natural brethren, the blood relations of the King of Glory shall take a foremost place among the nations. The sigh of sorrow, the wail of grief shall be turned to the song of gladness, and the shout of praise. The voice of redeeming love and mercy shall swell from innumerable multitudes; Jerusalem shall vibrate with its music, Carmel prolong its cadence, and Lebanon echo back its strains. The song of angels shall awake again above the fields of Bethlehem; and heaven and earth unite their voices as never before in the anthem which shall celebrate the triumph of redeeming grace and mercy.

Chapter 11. Confirmation Of The Year Day Theory Afforded By The Astronomical Character Of The Prophetic Times

THIS SUBJECT has been more or less elucidated in the works I have written during the last twenty-six years, including, "The Approaching End of the Age," published in 1878; "Light for the Last Days," in 1887 "The Divine Program of the World's History," in 1888; and "Creation Centered in Christ," in 1896. The Astronomical Appendix to the last named work fills a volume of 627 pages, and contains tables of 101,217 so solar and lunar dates, for a period of 3,555 years, from B.C. 1622, to A.D. 1934, stated in days, hours, and minutes, calculated from the prophetic times contained in the book of Daniel. The complete and unanswerable demonstration afforded by these extensive tables — tables which have been accepted, and are in use, by astronomers throughout the world, — of the yearday theory, according to which the 1,260 and 2,300 "days" of the prophecies of Daniel, and the Apocalypse, are interpreted to mean 1,260 and 2,300 years, settles the question of the historical fulfillment of these periods. Astronomy proves that these periods are vast in their dimensions, twelve to twenty-three centuries in length; and that therefore they cannot be measures of the brief course of events in any single lifetime, as according to the Futurist theory they are;, but measures of great and long continued historical movements, as the rise and fall of the Papal and Mohammedan powers, or the down treading of the Jewish sanctuary, from the invasion of the west by Persia, to the decline of the Turkish power in the present day.

I will now briefly relate the facts connected with the origin of my interest in the prophetic times, and the progress I subsequently made in their elucidation.

It was in the early part of the year 1870, that I crossed the Pyrenees on my way from France to Spain. The snow lay thickly on the hills, and glittered on the Sierras, whose sharply pointed peaks stood outlined against the clear southern sky. The trains were crowded with travelers, largely of the agricultural class. There was a perfect babel of patois, in which through familiarity with French, and the study I had bestowed on Spanish, I could distinguish here and there intelligible sentences. On reaching Madrid I went with Mr. William Green, the friend and biographer of Matamoros, to see the newly opened Quemadero. Some workmen employed in cutting a road across the summit of a low hill close to the city had inadvertently dug into a broad bank of ashes, which had been buried for one or two centuries. Mingled with the ashes they had found a large quantity of charred human bones, together with fragments of rusted iron, and melted lead. The spot was speedily verified as the famous Quemadero, or place of burning, one of twelve places where so called "heretics" were annually burned in Spain, during the reign of the Inquisition. I found the road had been cut through the center of this bank of blackened bones and ashes. The strange stratum displayed seemed about six feet in depth, and covered quite a large area. There, then, exposed to the light of day were the ashes of Spanish martyrs. I stood in silence and looked at the ghastly monument. I had seen before not a little of Romanism on the continent, and in other countries, and had read of the multitude of martyrs who had suffered cruel deaths in past centuries at the hands of Spanish priests and inquisitors, on account of their faith in the pure gospel of the grace of God, and their opposition to Popish superstitions and idolatries. Now, for the first time, I found myself face to face with a terrible demonstration of the truth of these histories. There, lying before me were the bones and ashes of Spanish confessors and martyrs who had suffered death at the stake. I could examine them, and satisfy myself of their character. I could handle them, and did. Reverently I removed some burnt bones from the general mass, and wrapped them, together with a quantity of ashes, in a Spanish newspaper which I still possess, bearing the date of the day. Sadly turning from the spot I carried the parcel to my hotel where that evening under the influence of strong emotion, I wrote the following lines, —

> Ye layers of ashes black, and half-burnt bones,
> Ye monuments of martyrs' stifled moans,
> Of human agony and dying groans,
> Cry out till every ear has heard your tones!
> Cry till the murderess trembles, though her brain
> Is drunken with the blood of millions slain;
> She did not mean to show you; 'twas the spade
> Of simple workmen which your horrors laid
> Unearthed and bare before the light of day;
> They only dug to open a new way.
> As they advanced, the ground beneath them grew
> In patches softer, changed its wonted hue,
> And with the smell of death defiled the air.
> They dug, and they discovered layer on layer,
> Black bones, and rusted chains, and human hair.
> And iron nails, and bits of melted lead.
> And the burnt fuel of unnumbered dead.
> They cut the heap across — it crowns a hill;
> Its length is shown — its breadth lies buried still.
> Doubtest thou, reader? I was there today;
> I saw them at their work; I brought away
> Some pitiful remains which, while I write
> These very words, are lying in my sight
> A piece of paper on this table holds
> Some of this martyr-dust within its folds.
> I pause and gently touch it with my hand; —
> It is not common earth; it is not sand:
> I look at it; the tears have filled my eyes;

My God, what is it that before me lies?
The ground beneath was gravel and was red,
But this is dark and formed a separate bed.
How soft it is and light! it feels like soil
That has been saturated once with oil:
'Tis full of small black cinders; most is gray
And ashen; here is something burnt away
Black as the blackest coal; this was the meat
Of some relentless and devouring heat.
A little box beside the paper stands;
Its relics I collected with these hands:
I take a something from it like a stone,
Tis gray and light, ah 'tis a piece of bone;
This was the side on which the muscles grew,
The other side its chambers are burnt blue.
These four are lumps of iron; they are red,
Like fetters that have rusted off the dead.
This was an iron bolt, 'tis long and curved,
To hold a chain or cord it doubtless served;
This is a hollow bone burnt through and through, It leaves
upon my hand a dusky blue;
This was a bar of iron, now mere rust;
And this is indistinguishable dust
O Rome! thou Mother of a cherished race.
Blush not to show the world thy kindly face!
Thy bosom — hide its demons, hush — thy breast,
'Tis there alone that suffering men find rest
How mild the chastisements thy love has used
Whene'er thy children have thy laws refused!
Gentle coercion! pity's tender tones!
Tell me, thou murderess black, what mean these bones?
These bones before me, those upon that hill,
Who, what were these thus slaughtered by thy will?
What did these helpless women? these poor men?
Why didst thou shut them up in thy dark den?
Why didst thou rack their limbs, and starve their frames.

And cast them bound into devouring flames?
True, they reproached thee for thy crimes and lies,
And prayed for thee with sin-forgiving sighs;
Thy multiplied idolatries abhorred,
No mediator honored but their Lord;
Condemned thy priestcraft, and thy love of gold;
Clung to God's word, and for its truths were bold;
Adorned by blamelessness the name they bore;
Loved not their lives to death: what did they more?
Were they adulterers — these prisoned saints?
Or murderers — these who died without complaints?
Hush! for they sleep in Jesus — soft their bed;
His suffering saints their Lord hath comforted!
Hush! for the sevenfold wrath of God grows hot!
Hush! for her deep damnation slumbereth not

That very year, 1870, within a few months from the date when I wrote these lines the papal temporal power fell, and fell forever.

Such was the origin of my interest in the fulfillment of prophecy in papal history. It was that day when standing breast deep in the ashes of Spanish martyrs, that my attention was specially and strongly directed to it; and it was the promulgation the same year of the blasphemous decree of papal infallibility, and the coincident fall of the papal temporal power, which led me to study and write on the subject. The lines which I wrote in Madrid on the opening of the Quemadero subsequently grew to a volume entitled "The City of the Seven Hills." As the fruit of eight years of study, from 1870 to 1878, I published "The Approaching End of the Age," a work which has since gone through many editions. Other works on the same theme followed. In 1896 my Astronomical Tables, based on the prophetic times regarded as astronomical cycles, were published. The discovery of the astronomical character of the prophetic times was made in the following way.

In July, 1870, while the Vatican council was being held in Rome, and at the date when the decision was arrived at in France to declare war against Prussia, I left Paris, terminating a gospel mission, which had extended over nearly two years, in which with the help of twenty-five Protestant pastors, including Bersier, Pressense, Armand de Lille, Lepoids, Cook, Jaulmes, Hollard, and others, I had organized and held eight hundred gospel meetings, in seventeen parts of the city, attended by many thousands drawn from all ranks and persuasions, Protestants, Romanists, and Infidels.

The decision of Napoleon III to declare war against Prussia was made Friday, July 15th. The declaration of war was signed on Sunday, July 17th. The infallibility of the Pope was decreed by the Vatican council on Monday, July 1 8th. The declaration of war was delivered at Berlin on Tuesday, July 19th. In the war which followed Imperial France, and the Papal power fell together.

The startling coincidence of the papal self-exalting act, with the overthrow of the papal temporal power, profoundly impressed me. The spectacle of the Paris in which we had just held so many gospel services, suddenly invested by German armies, surrounded by a gigantic ring of artillery fire from which there was no escape; of the tragic fall of Napoleon, the rise of united Germany, the unification of Italy, all pointed to the passing away of the old order of things on the continent, and the advent of a new era. And then the question arose, what had the Word of God to say about these events? What did it indicate as to the rise, course and fall of the papal power? The search for an answer to that question led to a careful and extensive study of the subject. In the course of that study I met with the very able work of Professor Birks, of Cambridge University, on "The Elements of Sacred Prophecy." The four last chapters of that book contain an admirable elucidation and defense of the year-day theory. The argument in these chapters appeared to me absolutely unanswerable, and in fact has never been answered or confuted. One section of these chapters proved of special interest, that on the Cyclical character of the

Prophetic Times. A prolonged subsequent sojourn in England gave me the opportunity to examine this subject minutely, and to make the calculations necessary to prove that the prophetic times are astronomical cycles of long range, and surprising accuracy. In the course of this mathematical investigation I made further discoveries confirming and extending the evidence of the astronomical character of the prophetic periods, and of their fulfillment in the history of the four kingdoms of Babylon, Persia, Greece and Rome; and in the duration of the Papal and Mohammedan powers.

The work of Professor Birks on "The Elements of Sacred Prophecy" has been long out of print, and is difficult to procure. I therefore quote the brief section whose study led me to the investigation of the prophetic times.

> "The cyclical character of the prophetic times," says Professor Birks, "seems to have been first unfolded by M. de Cheseaux, a French writer, [A Swiss astronomer, known as the discoverer of De Cheseaux's comet.] purely as a curiosity of science; but it is Mr. Cunninghame who has revived attention to this interesting topic. Though unable to concur in the whole superstructure which he has reared on this basis, the first principles, I believe, are both true in fact, and form a remarkable and collateral confirmation of the figurative view of these prophetic times. Two or three remarks will perhaps make the subject plain to general readers, so far as it bears on the present argument.

> "I. On the fourth day of creation it was announced as the divine purpose in the appointment of the heavenly luminaries — 'Let them be for signs, and for seasons, and for days, and for years.' The division of time was one main purpose of their institution as lights in the firmament. The word rendered 'seasons' is the same which here denotes the times, and there is consequently a tacit reference to that original ordinance of God.

"The revolutions of the sun and moon have thus, in every nation, formed the basis of the calendar. The day, the month, and the year, are the first elements on which it depends. If the natural month and year had been each a complete number of days, or a simple fractional part, the calendar would have been quite simple. But this is not the case, and hence the various intercalations used to bring them into agreement.

"Where the calendar is adapted to the sun only, its construction is very simple. The Julian year is a close approximation, and the Gregorian is practically correct for some thousands of years.

"But in the sacred calendar of the Jews, and those of Greece and the eastern nations, the motions both of the sun and of the moon enter into the reckoning. And hence arise mixed calendars, more natural, since they are fitted to the motions of both the natural lights of heaven, but more complex in their adjustment.

"The most natural mode of adjustment is by taking the nearest integer of the lowest period contained in the higher, and making this the unit for the next higher denomination, intercalating where necessary.

"Thus the natural month is nearer thirty than twenty-nine days. Therefore thirty days will be the calendar month, and the unit of every reckoning where months occur.

"Again, the year is nearer twelve than thirteen calendar months. Therefore twelve calendar months will form* the calendar year, and five days are intercalated to complete the whole number.

"2. Now just as the day and the month were taken for the basis of these shorter periods, so may the month and year be taken as the basis of higher intervals. These give us cycles, or periods of complete years which are almost exactly a complete number of natural months.

"The intervals of years which most fully possess this character, adopting the most exact scientific measures of the lunar month and solar year, are 8, 11, 19, 30, 49. .. 315, 334, 353, 687, 1,040 years. After this limit the increasing accuracy of the series is limited by the moon's acceleration, and the uncertainty of our measures of time.

"Now from this series there result several interesting conclusions which bear on the present question.

"The period of nineteen years, though not directly recognized in the Jewish calendar, formed the basis of that used by the Greeks, and was no less an integral element of it than the month or the year. Now the very next period to this, in the above series, is thirty years; which, on the year-day theory, is the prophetic month, and has thus a real existence as a cycle, no less than the natural month of thirty days, to which it bears a close analogy.

"The next period is that of forty-nine years; which, according to the dates in Josephus of sabbatic years, and the more probable view of the sacred text, is the interval from jubilee to jubilee; and therefore is fundamental in the Hebrew calendar. This will be a second scriptural instance, like the prophetic month, of a luni-solar cycle adopted for a higher unit, composed of a complete number of years.

"Let us now pursue the analogy a step further. As twelve common months of thirty days, form a year of three hundred and sixty days, which, with five days intercalated, make the solar year; so twelve prophetic months of thirty years will form a 'time' of three hundred and sixty years, exceeding by seven only the very exact luni-solar cycle of three hundred and fifty-three years; which forms a kind of natural unit in the series.

"Again, a 'time, times, and a half' will compose a period of one thousand two hundred and sixty years. And this is exactly four times the accurate cycle three hundred and fifteen years, and, therefore, partakes itself of the same cyclical character.

"The most perfect cycle, perhaps, which can be certainly ascertained, in consequence of the moon's acceleration affecting the higher periods, is one thousand and forty years. Now, on the year-day theory, this is exactly the difference between the two grand numeral periods of one thousand two hundred and sixty, and two thousand three hundred years.

"Finally, the highest prophetic period, two thousand three hundred years, is itself a cycle — 4x315+1,040, — and is perhaps, the only secular cycle composed of centuries only, that is known to exist.

"From these remarks it appears that the prophetic month of thirty years, and the 'time,' composed of twelve such months, as such have a scientific character, though less distinct, yet of the very same nature with those of the common month and year. It appears also that the two main periods of one thousand two hundred and sixty, and two thousand three hundred years are cycles; and that their difference, one thousand and forty years, is the most perfect cycle certainly ascertained. The interval of one thousand, two hundred and ninety years is also a cycle, and that of one thousand three hundred and thirty-five is defective only by one single year.

"These remarks seem to prove that the year-day interpretation, besides its direct scriptural evidence, has a further and collateral support in the analogies of science. The same principles of the intersection of the solar and lunar periods, by which the units of the ordinary calendar is determined, when carried further up the ascending series of time, produce, even from the abstract relations of the celestial periods, the larger but corresponding units of thirty, and three hundred and sixty years, or the prophetic month and time.

"And surely, in the view which is thus unfolded, there is a simple grandeur which harmonizes with all the other features of the inspired predictions. A fresh light is thrown upon the words of the Psalmist, where the same word is employed as in these mysterious dates — 'He appointed the moons for seasons.' We are raised out of the contracted range of human reckonings to a lofty elevation of thought, and catch some glimpses of that mysterious wisdom by which the Almighty blends all the works of Nature and of Providence into subservience to the deep councils of His redeeming love. A divine ladder of time is set before us, and, as we rise successively from step to step, days are replaced by years, and years by millennia; and these, perhaps, hereafter, in their turn by some higher unit, from which the soul of man may measure out cycles still more vast, and obtain a wider view of the immeasurable grandeur of eternity. When we reflect, also, that the celestial periods by which these cycles are determined are themselves fixed by that law of attraction which gives the minutest atom an influence on the planetary motions, what a combination appears in these sacred times of the most contrasted elements of omniscient wisdom ı Human science sinks exhausted at the very threshold of this temple of divine truth. It has strained its utmost efforts in calculating the actual motions of the moon and the earth; but the determining causes which fixed at first the proportion of their monthly and yearly revolutions have altogether eluded its research. Yet these elements of the natural universe are linked in, by these sacred times and celestial cycles, with the deepest wonders of Providence, and the whole range of Divine prophecy. How glorious, then, must be the inner shrine, lit up with the Shechinah of the Divine presence, when the approaches themselves reveal such a secret and hidden wisdom!

"Every one of the passages in Daniel yields distinct evidence in favor of the year-day system. And when these various indications are compared together, and combined with the truth which has just been unfolded, of the connection of these numbers with the natural cycles of science, the proof seems the highest almost of which such a subject is capable, and forms little short of the convincing power of a mathematical demonstration."

For more than twenty years I pursued the study of the astronomical character of the prophetic times. The further I investigated the question the more evident it became that not only these, but the whole system of Revealed Redemption Chronology, Levitical, Historic, and Prophetic, is adapted to the time order of Nature. The revealed periods vary from a few days to thousands of years, yet their character in this respect is the same. Calendars of human invention, both sacred and civil, invariably fall out of agreement with solar and lunar revolutions in the lapse of time. The number of such calendars is very great. .They are of Egyptian, Assyrian, Babylonian, Greek, Roman, Jewish, Christian, Mohammedan, Indian, Chinese and other origin. All alike fail to keep time with Nature. But not so is it with the divinely revealed time system in Scripture. The Levitical times are adjusted to both solar and lunar revolutions, and adjusted in such a way that their slowly accumulating errors are corrected in the prophetic times; while the adjustment of the latter to solar and lunar revolutions is far reaching and complete; so complete that it is possible to calculate from the prophetic times regarded as astronomical cycles tables of the whole course of vernal and autumnal equinoxes, of summer and winter solstices, of mean and true new moons, of the new moons of solar eclipses, and the full moons of lunar eclipses; in short all the solar and lunar elements required in a calendar of times extending over thousands of years, embracing the whole course of human history.

In my work entitled "Creation Centered in Christ" I have published such tables; and have given the following account of the incommensurateness of the natural time units, days, months and years; and of the cycles to which these incommensurate periods give rise, in which their harmonization is accomplished ("Creation Centered in Christ," Vol. I, pp. 324-330).

Cyclical Character Of The Prophetic Times — Discoveries Of M. De Cheseaux

The perplexities and difficulties which encumber the attempt to adapt brief periods of time to both solar and lunar movements, as in the Civil Calendar, disappear directly it is a question of longer intervals.

Short periods have to be artificially harmonized, larger ones harmonize themselves. There exist various periods which are naturally measurable both by solar years and lunar months, without remainder, or with remainders so small as to be unimportant.

Such periods are therefore soli-lunar cycles, and we shall henceforth speak of them as such. They harmonize with more or less exactness solar and lunar revolutions, and they may be regarded as divinely appointed units for the measurement of long periods of time, units of precisely the same character as the day, month and year (that is, created not by artificial means, but by solar and lunar revolutions), but of larger dimensions. They are, therefore, periods distinctly marked off as such, as much as the fundamental revolutions on which our calendar is based; that is, they are natural measures of time furnished by the Creator Himself for human use.

The lunar cycle of nineteen years employed by the Greeks is one of these periods, and the ancient cycle of Calippus is another. Their discovery has always been an object with astronomers, as their practical utility is considerable. But it was exceedingly difficult to find cycles of any tolerable accuracy, especially cycles combining and harmonizing the day and the month with the year.

About the middle of last century a remarkable fact was discovered by a Swiss astronomer, M. de Cheseaux, a fact which is full of the deepest interest to both Jews and Christians, and which has never received, either at the hands of Bible students or scientists the attention which it merits.

The prophetic periods of 1,260 and 2,300 years, assigned in the Book of Daniel and in the Apocalypse as the duration of certain predicted events, are soli-lunar cycles, cycles of remarkable perfection and accuracy, but whose existence was entirely unknown to astronomers until, guided by the sacred scriptures, M. de Cheseaux discovered and demonstrated them to be such. And further, the difference between these two periods, which is 1,040 years, is the largest accurate soli-lunar cycle known.

The importance of this discovery, and the fact that it is exceedingly little known, will explain our entering into a somewhat full account of the matter here. It is, besides, vital to our own immediate subject, and was, indeed, the means of leading me to the present investigation.

M. de Cheseaux was the astronomer who observed and described the six-tailed comet of the year 1744. His book on the cyclical character of the prophetic times is out of print, difficult to procure, and even to consult. A copy of it exists in the library of the

University of Lausanne, and another in the British Museum. It is entitled, "*Memoires posthumes de M. de Cheseaux*," and was edited and published by his sons in 1754. It contains "*Remarques historiques, chronologiques, et astronomiques sur quelques endroits du livre de Daniel.*" The calculations of the astronomical part were submitted to Messrs. Mairan and Cassini, celebrated astronomers of the Royal Academy of Sciences at Paris, neither of whom called in question the accuracy of M. de Cheseaux's principles, or the correctness of his results. M. Mairan, after having carefully read his essay, said "that it was impossible to doubt the facts and discoveries it contained, but that he could not conceive how or why they had come to be embodied so distinctly in the Holy Scriptures." M. Cassini wrote, after having read the treatise and worked the problems, that the methods of calculating the solar and lunar positions and movements which M. de Cheseaux had deduced from the cycles of the book of Daniel were most clear, and "perfectly consistent with the most exact astronomy"; he wished the essay to be read before the academy.

From the year 1754 to 1811 M. de Cheseaux's discoveries seem to have almost completely dropped out of sight. The stirring events of the French Revolution, which took place in the interval, may have caused his remarkable treatise to be forgotten. In the year 1811 Mr. William Cunningham, of Lainshaw, in Scotland, the author of several valuable works on prophecy, noticed a reference to de Cheseaux's discoveries in the writings of M. Court de Gibelin. Mr. Cunningham published the fact in an article which appeared in the Christian Observer for that year. In 1833 Mr. Cunningham published a letter in the Investigator, a monthly journal of prophecy, describing his finding a copy of M de Cheseaux's work. "During the twenty-two years," says Mr. Cunningham, "which have elapsed since my communication to the Christian Observer I have sought for the work of M. de Cheseaux without success till the present year. A young relation of mine having last year gone to Heidelberg to complete his studies, I requested him to endeavor to procure the book for me. His inquiries among the booksellers, were quite unavailing. At length, having become acquainted with a student from Lausanne, where the work was originally published, by his assistance search was made in the library of the university of that city. The first attempt was unsuccessful; but on a second and more careful search, the book was discovered, and a manuscript copy of that part which relates to the book of Daniel was taken for me, and is now in my possession." The cyclical character of the prophetic periods of 1,260 and 2,300 years, and the 1,040 year's period which measure their difference, was subsequently called in question by Mr. Frere, a well-known writer on prophecy. In a letter to the Investigator, dated January, 1835, Mr. Cunningham says, "With regard to Mr. Frere's vain endeavor to shake the cyclical periods of de Cheseaux... if a scientific friend, who last summer favored me with some remarks entirely confirmatory of the importance of the conclusions of M. de Cheseaux, and also showed me the principle of calculating the cycles by continued fractions, shall not take up Mr. Frere's paper, I will myself do it." The scientific friend here alluded to was believed by the editor of the Investigator to be Professor Birks, of Cambridge, who subsequently published in the pages of that journal a letter on the method of calculating these soli-lunar cycles by continued fractions, and also embodied in his valuable work on the elements of prophecy, published in 1843, a brief account of the astronomic character of the prophetic times. It was when reading this work of Professor Birks just after the fall of the Papal Temporal power in 1870, that my attention was arrested by that portion of it referring to these remarkable cycles, and I was consequently led to investigate their character with considerable care, and in doing so made a number of chronological discoveries, some of which I have since published in my writings on the fulfillment of prophecy. The astronomic portion of my work on "The Approaching End of the Age" was submitted, prior to its publication, to the criticisms of Professor Adams, of Cambridge. For this purpose I became Professor Adams, guest at the Observatory in Cambridge, and he verified de Cheseaux's calculations with reference to the prophetic times. I still possess the papers in his handwriting in which the calculations are worked out.

The following is a translation of M. de Cheseaux's account of his discovery of the astronomic character of the 1,260 and 2,300 years' prophetic periods:

"We all know what a cycle is — that is to say, a period of time which harmonizes different celestial revolutions, comprehending, each of them, a certain number of times precisely, without fractional remainder. Such is, for example, the period of Julian years, or 1,461 days, which, according to the ideas of the ancients, should contain exactly 'solar years and 1,461 days; so that, supposing the sun on the 12th of April, 1749, at noon in Paris to be in 22° 40' of Aries, it should in 1,461 days, and at the same hour of midday, be found again precisely in the same position. The error is, as we know, 44' of an hour. This cycle belongs to the first order — those which are employed to harmonize solar years and days.

"Cycles of the second kind are designed to bring lunar years or months into agreement with solar years. Such is Meton's cycle of 19 years. This ancient astronomer supposed that if the sun and moon were found, for example, on the first day of the year in conjunction at a certain point of the ecliptic, they ought to return again at the end of 19 solar years, or of 235 complete lunar months, to the same position without fractional remainder. The error of the cycle is about 2h., 3m; by which the solar year finishes earlier than the lunar.

"Cycles of the third kind are those which harmonize solar days with lunar months, as, for example, the cycle of 1,447 complete days, which comprehends at the same time 49 lunar months with 1½ nearly.

"Lastly, we may make a fourth kind of cycle of those which unite the previous classes, and harmonize at the same time the solar year, the lunar months and the day. Such ought to be the cycle of Meton, and still more the period of Calippus. The discovery of these cycles has been an object of the researches of almost all astronomers and chronologists, and it has seemed to them so difficult that they have almost laid it down as a fact that it was impossible to find those of the fourth class. It has been thus far a kind of philosopher's stone in astronomy, like perpetual movement in mechanics. There have been times when, seeking to assure myself effectually that it was not possible to succeed in the matter, I commenced my research by the second kind of cycle. Supposing a lunar month of 29 d., 12 h., 44 m., 3 s., the error is 7''' by defect: in a solar year of 395 d., 5 h., 49 m., the error is not more than; 5 s. by excess. I observed that by adding on the one side and on the other two periods of time proportional to these two revolutions, that is to say, 57'' to the first and 11' to the second, their agreement became very approximately as 29 d., 12¾ h. to 365¼ d., or as 2,835 quarters of an hour to 35,064 quarters of an hour; or in dividing these two numbers by 9, which is their common measure, as 315 to 3,896. This agreement was at the same time so simple and exact that, giving the lunar month its true length of 29 d., 12 h., 44 m., 3 s. 7''', the resulting measure of the solar year is 365 d., 5 h., 48 m., 16 s., that is to say, 39 s. only too short. From that I concluded that at the end of 315 solar years or 3,896 lunar months the sun and the moon should meet very nearly at the same point in the ecliptic. We find, in fact, that at the end of 315 Julian years, 2 d., 4 h., 27 m., or at the end of 115,051 days, 4 h., 27 m., the sun and the moon return, to the 7th or 8th minute of a degree nearly to the same point of the heaven from which they started. This 7' or 8' of a degree makes an error of 3 h., 24 m. as to the solar year, which ends 3 h., 24 m. after the lunar; that is to say, which recommences for the 316th time at the end of 115,051 d., 7 h., 51 m. This difference of 3 h., 24 m. between the duration of 315 lunar years and that of 315 solar years, or the error of 315 years' cycle, is that of the cycle of Meton as

$$\frac{3 \text{ h., } 24 \text{ m.}}{315} \quad \frac{2 \text{ h., } 3 \text{ m.}}{19} \text{ or } \frac{8 \text{ h., } 12 \text{ m.}}{76} :: 3{,}838 : 38{,}745$$

or as 1 to 10; that is to say that it is only the 10th part.

"The cycle 315 years thus found, I forthwith observed that it was the quarter of the 1,260 years' period, or the 3 ½ 'times' of Daniel 8:12, and 12:7, compared with Apoc. 12:6, 14; and consequently that this prophetic period was itself a lunar cycle of such a character that at the end of 1,260 Julian years — 10 d. + 6 h., 14 m., or of 460,205 d., 6 h., 14 m., the sun and the moon return within ½° nearly to the same point in the ecliptic, and that at the end of 1,260 Julian years — 10 h. + 7h., 23 m., or of 460,205 d., 7 h., 23 m., the sun returns to the same point of the ecliptic exactly.

"This period has not only the advantage of comprehending a round number of years, a number sufficiently remarkable on account of the number of its aliquot parts [for 1,260 is divisible by 1, 2, 3, 4, 5, 6, 7, 9, 10, 12, 14, 15, 18, 20, 21, 28, 30, 35, 36, 42, 45, 60, 63, 70, 84, 90, 105, 126, 140, 180, 210, 252, 315, 420, 630; that is to say, by 35 divisors, which is, I believe, the largest number of divisors a number of this kind can have], but also that of containing a number of days whose length occupies about the mean between those of the lunar and solar years comprised in this number.[206]

"The agreement of this period, destined by the Holy Spirit to designate civil periods, with the length of the most remarkable periods of celestial movements, led me to conjecture that it might also be such with the period of 2300 years. I examined then this last period by astronomic tables, and I found that at the end of 2,300 Gregorian years less 6 h., 14 m., or of 840,057 d. less 6 h., 14 m., the sun and the moon return within half a degree nearly, to the place from which they started; and at the end of 840,057 d., 7 h., 23 m. the sun returns exactly to the same point of the ecliptic; from which it follows that the prophetic period of 2,300 years (remarkable also by the number of its aliquot parts, and because it contains a complete number of cycles) was also a cyclical period, and this cyclical period was also so perfect that although 30 times longer than the Calippic period, its error is, however, much less

---

206 The length of the solar year which I employ here is that which results from a perfect cycle of the fourth kind, of which we will speak presently, and which occupies the mean between the different determinations of the most able modern astronomers.

than double, since it only extends to 13 h. - 37 m., and being proportionately subdivided in the period of 70 years, it is reduced to 29 m., that is to say, to the 17th part of the error of the Calippic period, which I said just now was 8 h., 12 m.

"The equality of the errors of this cycle of 2,300 years with those of the preceding led me to conclude that their difference, that is, 1,040 years, ought to be entirely exempt from error, and should give a perfect cycle, and one all the more remarkable because it unites at the same time the three kinds of cycles, and forms consequently this famous cycle of the fourth kind vainly sought so long, and ultimately believed to be chimeric or impossible. Having then examined this period of 1,040 years by the tables of the most celebrated modern astronomers, I found that it held about the mean between them, as one may see in this little table:

According to Messrs. ——	The sun makes in 379,852 entire days 1,040 complete revolutions with reference to the first point of Aries.	The moon makes in 379,852 entire days 12,863 complete revolutions with reference to the sun.
Cassini	+2′ 1″	+ 1′ 59″
Flamsteed	—1′ 39″	+ 7′ 40″
De La Hire	+3′ 33″	+ 3′ 30″
Bouillaud	—5′ 18″	—11′ 30″
Tycho	+7′ 23″	+ 4′ 20″
Certain others	—1′ 30″	— 8′ 37″
Mean	+0′ 45″	— 0′ 26″

"These differences are absolutely insensible for so large a period, and it would be impossible that the best astronomic tables should be exempt from them, on account of the imperfections of ancient observations upon which they are founded, from which it seems that we should conclude, according to all appearance, that this period of 1,040 years, or solar revolutions, indicated in a certain way by the Holy Spirit, is a cycle at once solar, lunar, and diurnal, perfectly exact... May I be permitted meanwhile to give to this cycle the name of THE DANIEL CYCLE?"

Convinced by the studies which I have conducted that the prophetic times are so closely adjusted to the revolutions of the sun and moon that I could derive the one from the other, and believing that it would clearly demonstrate the astronomical character of the prophetic times in Daniel to do this, i. e., to derive the course of solar years and lunar months, in days, hours, and minutes, for thousands of years, either past or future, from these prophetic times, I have had the solar and lunar Tables calculated, contained in the second volume of my work on "Creation Centered in Christ." These astronomical Tables contain more than 100,000 solar and lunar positions, verified by 12,000 eclipses; and the whole of these 100,000 positions have been calculated by means of the prophetic periods regarded as Astronomical cycles. The tables have been submitted to the highest astronomical authorities, and approved as correct and trustworthy. The demonstration they afford of the truth of the year-day theory, according to which the "days 99 of the prophetic times in Daniel and the Apocalypse are interpreted as signifying years, is complete. These mysterious prophetic times are not brief periods adapted to the measurement of events in any individual life, but vast periods, stretching over thousands of years, adjusted to the chronology of the history of Israel, of the Christian Church, and of the Gentile kingdoms, outlined in the word of God.

Chapter 12. Practical Use Of The Apocalypse

> "Ye are of God, little children, and have overcome them,
> because greater is He that is in you than he that is in the
> world." — 1 John 4:4.

I. The Primary Practical Purpose

THE PRIMARY PRACTICAL OBJECT of the Apocalypse is to make the Church victorious over the world, the flesh, and the devil. The Bible opens with defeat; it ends with victory. At its outset, man fallen, Satan triumphant; at its close Satan conquered, all his world powers overthrown, and the redeemed with the Redeemer, crowned as victors, and glorified.

At the close of His earthly life, looking back over its temptations and conflicts, Jesus said, "I have overcome the world." In the beginning of His risen life, exalted and endowed with "all power in heaven and in earth," He went forth leading His Church, "conquering and to conquer." In His heaven sent messages to the Churches which He left as His witnesses on earth, all the inestimable rewards of His kingdom are promised "To him that overcometh." In the prophetic visions which succeed these messages, tracing the gradual subjugation of all things to Christ, the conflicts, sufferings, and victories and final glories of Christ's saintly followers are described. This is the theme of the prophecy, and its object is practical. It was a gift to the Church militant from Christ triumphant. The Son of God had overcome the world. The sons of God were now to overcome it. Faith was to make them victorious. They were to conquer their visible foes by faith in things invisible. All the powers of the world were to be arrayed against them. They were to be hated, persecuted, hunted into dens and deserts, cast into dungeons and flames. Yet were they to conquer. "Greater is He that is in you than he that is in the world." Who spoke that triumphant word? A lonely exile; a persecuted and banished saint and apostle. And when? In the days of proud Domitian, master of the world; in the time of Pagan Rome's supremacy. How calmly he writes it in his letter of love to his "little children." There is no flourish of trumpets; simply the clear note of victory. 4i Out of the mouths of babes and sucklings Thou hast ordained strength, that Thou mightest still the enemy and the avenger." And so Christ led His Church to the battle-field. Calmly and unflinchingly He conducts them with open eyes into the deadly arena of their warfare. They are to fight with wild beasts in the Colosseum; to be driven into the darkness of the Catacombs; to die under the worst tortures pitiless Rome can inflict. They are later on to contend with worse enemies than heathen Rome. They are to fight with the

powers of hell in the apostate Church which should succeed to the
throne of the Caesars. The harlot Babylon was to be drunken with
their blood; yet were they to overcome, and the victors were "to
stand on the sea of glass mingled with fire, having the harps of
God." No music so lofty as theirs; no song more glad and glorious;
followers of the Lamb, of Him who died on Calvary's Cross, the
Conqueror and Saviour of the world. To nerve such warriors, to
arm them for the battle, to conduct them to victory, the
Apocalypse was written. He who has not grasped this salient fact,
has missed the meaning of the prophecy. Not to satisfy curiosity as
to the future was this wondrous prophecy indited; nor merely to
close the sacred volume, to bind its several portions into unity as
with a golden clasp, nor was it written to complete the book by
shedding the glories of sunset, or rather of sunrise, over its con
eluding pages, to fill its last skies with splendor, with the light of
the rising of a morning without clouds, the advent of a world
where sin and sorrow and death can never come; not for these ends
though doubtless they were contemplated, but for nobler
purposes; to form the characters, guide the steps, maintain the
faith, and inspire the courage of those who were to pass through
flood and flame to that final world of glory and immortality; to
make the saints and martyrs who were to share its triumphs and
wear its crowns. And hence the glorious rewards promised in the
seven letters to the Christian Churches with which it opens, letters
purely practical in their object, are largely the theme of the
succeeding prophecy. For in it the selfsame rewards are seen, and set
forth in their most glowing colours, and in their true and proper
relations, their place, and time, and circumstance, for the
contemplation of the servants of Christ; that they may behold in
advance the things promised, and the future world become as real
to them as the present, as seen with the open eye of vision; so that
the confessors might witness in the presence of Rome's Caesars,
standing the while in spirit before the throne of God; or tread their
way amid the awful shadows of the Catacombs, as beholding the
golden streets of the New Jerusalem. Yea to open heaven itself to
the gaze and contemplation of God's pilgrim people was this

prophecy given; that their conversation, or "citizenship" might be there, even while they wandered as strangers amid earth's transient and troubled scenes; and that while journeying or warring on earth, they might be seated in heaven, where Christ is seated "at the right hand of God."

And turning now to those practical letters which preface the Apocalypse, we ask what are the promised rewards which they hold forth "to him that overcometh?"

First, to the victors of the Church of Ephesus it is promised that they shall eat of "the tree of life which is in the midst of the paradise of God." Behold then the promised tree of life in the visions of the prophecy, bearing twelve manner of fruits, whose leaves are for the healing of the nations. See it there in its true location growing by the river of the water of life, clear as crystal, "proceeding out of the throne of God and of the Lamb."

Secondly, to the victors of the martyr Church of Smyrna the crown of life is promised; and the revealing spirit adds "he that overcometh shall not be hurt of the second death." But what that second death, and for whom destined? The prophecy replies, "the fearful, and unbelieving, and the abominable, and murderers, and whoremongers, and sorcerers, and idolaters, and all liars shall have their part in the lake which burneth with fire and brimstone, which is the second death." "Death and Hades" it tells us are to be finally "cast into the lake of fire, which is the second death."

To the Church of Thyatira the promise runs "to him that overcometh, and keepeth My works unto the end, to him will I give power over the nations; and he shall rule them with a rod of iron; as the vessels of a potter shall they be broken to shivers: even as I received of My Father. And I will give him the morning star." In the prophecy the shivering of the nations as the vessels of a potter with a rod of iron is portrayed. A woman clothed with the sun, and crowned with twelve stars brings forth "a man child who was to rule all nations with a rod of iron." The man child is caught up to God and to His throne, and the woman flees to the wilderness from the presence of the persecuting dragon. Later on the all conquering "Word of God," the "King of Kings and Lord of Lords, comes with the white robed armies of heaven," "to judge and make war," to "smite the nations with the sword of His mouth," and "rule them with a rod of iron"; even He whose voice declares "I am the root and offspring of David, and the bright and morning star."

To the Church of Sardis which had a name to live and was dead, the command "be watchful, and strengthen the things that remain, that are ready to die," is followed by the warning "if therefore thou shalt not watch, I will come on thee as a thief, and thou shalt not know what hour I will come upon thee," and the promise "he that overcometh the same shall be clothed in white raiment and I will not blot out his name from the book of life." In the prophecy the thing promised is beheld; the bride of the Lamb is seen in her purity and perfection "arrayed in fine linen, clean and white, for the fine linen is the righteousness of saints." And at the final judgment "the book of life is opened"; while those who enter the New Jerusalem are only "they which are written in the Lamb's book of life."

To the Church of Philadelphia the encouraging promise is given, "him that overcometh will I make a pillar in the temple of my God, and he shall go no more out; and I will write upon him the name of my God, and the name of the city of my God, which is New Jerusalem, which cometh down out of heaven from my God: and I will write upon him my new name." In the visions of the prophecy the New Jerusalem is seen "descending out of heaven from God, having the glory of God." Her walls, her gates, her streets, and her foundations are all described. Her beauty and her glory fill the bright closing vision. And of Him who is called "Faithful and True," it is declared, "He had a name written that no man knew, but He Himself"; analogous with that secret name which He will yet write upon the victor's brow.

To the degenerate Church of Laodicea, boasting herself "rich, and increased in goods, and needing nothing," not knowing that she was "wretched, and miserable, and poor, and blind, and naked," after the gracious offer of tried gold, and white raiment, and healing eye salve Jesus declares His long-suffering love, and says, "Behold I stand at the door and knock," promising to the individual soul that opens to Him the supper of His own personal and private fellowship: and promising further "To him that overcometh will I grant to sit with Me in My throne even as I also overcame and am set down with My Father in His throne." And in the succeeding prophecy the glorious reward thus promised is beheld, for there are seen the victor saints enthroned with the Lord, first in His millennial kingdom, and then in His eternal reign.

These relations of the prophetic visions of the Apocalypse to the hortatory letters addressed in its opening pages to Christian Churches, reveal the practical character of the prophecy; and the important practical uses which the Church, under the Spirit's guidance, has made of the prophecy during the last nineteen centuries is a confirmation of its intended adaptation to practical ends. For first, the Martyr Church of the second and third centuries armed herself for her conflict with heathen Rome with weapons drawn from the arsenal of the Apocalypse. To her heathen Rome, seated on her seven hills was the Apocalyptic Babylon, drunken with the blood of saints and martyrs. Every feature of Rome's character and history she saw delineated in the prophecy, in bold outlines, and vivid colors, her place, her power, her wealth, her wickedness, her doom. And the martyrs of those days beheld the exact picture of their experience in the slain beneath the altar portrayed in the prophecy, whose blood called for vengeance; a vengeance delayed but to come at last when in Babylon, the smoke of whose judgment should go up forever, "the blood of prophets, and of saints, and of all that were slain upon earth" should be found.

Secondly, on occasion of the fall of persecuting heathen Rome the early Church of the fourth century recognized the prediction of that great event in the vision of the Apocalypse, and celebrated it in the triumphant language of the prophecy, and commemorated it in symbols drawn from that sacred source. To the newly liberated exultant Church the fall of heathen Rome was none other than that represented by the casting down of the great red dragon, who had sought to devour the man child destined to rule all nations with a rod of iron. As predicted the victory had been that of Christ and His martyr followers. "They overcame Him by the blood of the Lamb, and by the word of their testimony; and they loved not their lives unto the death." The triumphant song of the Church ascended in the Apocalyptic words "now is come salvation, and strength, and the kingdom of our God, and the power of His Christ, for the accuser of our brethren is cast down which accused them before our God day and night."

The coins of Constantine the Great bear witness to the use of the symbol of the dragon prostrate beneath the cross to commemorate the overthrow of the dominion of ancient heathen Rome.

Thirdly, the overthrow of the Roman Empire by Gothic invaders which followed, and especially the burning of the city of Rome by Alaric, in the year 410, led Augustine to write his noble book on "The city of God"; a book whose central conception is drawn from the Apocalypse, in which the two societies of the world, and of the people of God, are represented by the harlot city Babylon, and the Bride, the New Jerusalem. Augustine recognized Rome as Babylon, and devotes a large part of his work to the delineation of its character and history. On the other hand he dwells with loving appreciation on the past, present and future of the society of saints, "the city of God," that city which has, unlike Rome, enduring foundations. The work of Augustine defended the Church, whose views it illustrates, from the accusation that it was the cause of the woes which had befallen the empire; and gave popularity and permanence to a conception of the relation of the society of the world to the society of saints, in striking harmony with the teachings of the Apocalypse.

II. Preservation of True Christianity from Extinction.

The second great practical use of the Apocalypse lay in the aid which it rendered to the preservation of true Christianity from the extinction by which it was threatened in the Middle Ages. The Gothic overthrow of the Roman empire was succeeded by the gradual rise in the sixth and following centuries of Papal Rome. The wars and jurisprudence of Justinian in the sixth century laid the foundation of a new imperial power. The bestowment on the Bishop of Rome, by Justinian and Phocas, of universal oversight in the Christian Church, exalted the Pope to the position of the Spiritual Head of the restored empire, while the work of Charlemagne completed the movement by the creation of "the Holy Roman Empire" of mediaeval and modern history.

The empire thus restored became the support of apostate papal Christianity, and the oppressor and persecutor of the true saints of God, whom it drove into obscurity, and reduced in the course of centuries to almost complete extermination.

Foreseen and foretold in Apocalyptic prophecy the persecuting papal power, and idolatrous Romish Church became objects of dread and abhorrence to the faithful saints of the Middle Ages, who in their separate communities and mountain solitudes kept the "commandments of God," and continued the testimony of Jesus Christ. The records of the Albigenses, and Waldenses, of Wyckliffe and the Lollards, of Huss, Jerome of Prague and their followers, amply attest the preserving influence of Apocalyptic teachings during this perilous period. By means of this prophecy the lamp of divine truth was kept burning which later on was to illuminate the world. The historian Gibbon justly connects the Paulicians, Albigenses, Waldenses, and other pre-reformation separatists from the apostate Church in the East and West, with the reformers of the sixteenth century. The faith of the Reformation and pre-reformation reformers was one; their testimony was one, their attitude to the Bible was the same, and their martyrs suffered in a common cause. The reformation movement did not commence with Luther, nor was he the first to translate the Bible into the vernacular. The exalted Head of the Church had maintained an unbroken line of faithful witnesses to His Truth during all the Christian centuries, and had fulfilled His promise that against the Church which He had founded upon a rock, the "gates of hell" should never prevail.

III. Justification and Support of the Reformation.

The third great practical use of the Apocalypse lay in its justification and support of the Reformation movement, by its delineation of the Church of Rome, and its command to the people of God to separate from that apostate Church, to republish the Scriptures, and to rebuild the Spiritual Temple, as the Jewish reformers Ezra and Nehemiah had restored the temple at Jerusalem after the Babylonish captivity. Ample materials exist for the verification of these statements in the voluminous works of the Reformers of the sixteenth century. The reformation was built by them on doctrinal, practical, and prophetic grounds: there is no possibility of separating these elements in its foundation. To the Reformers the Pope of Rome was the "Man of Sin," and Antichrist, and the Church of Rome the Babylon of the Apocalypse; a doctrine not only embodied in the confessions of faith of the reformed churches, but sealed by the blood of their countless martyrs. Who can estimate the value and importance of the aid thus rendered to the Reformation by the delineations and warnings of prophecy? Let the learned Bishop Wordsworth have a hearing on this subject, for no other has written upon it with clearer understanding, and in nobler and more eloquent language, — "The Holy Spirit, foreseeing, no doubt, that the Church of Rome would adulterate the truth by many gross and grievous abominations, that she would anathematize all who would not communicate with her, and denounce them as cut off from the body of Christ and the hope of everlasting salvation; foreseeing also that Rome would exercise a wide and dominant sway for many generations, by boldly iterated assertions of unity, antiquity, sanctity, and universality; foreseeing also that these pretensions would be supported by the civil sword of many secular governments, among which the Roman Empire would be divided at its dissolution, and that Rome would thus be enabled to display herself to the world in an august attitude of imperial power, and with the dazzling splendor of temporal felicity; foreseeing also that the Church of Rome would captivate the imaginations of men by the fascinations of art allied with religion, and would ravish their senses and rivet their admiration by gaudy colors and stately pomp and prodigal magnificence; foreseeing also that she would beguile their credulity by miracles and mysteries, apparitions and dreams, trances and ecstasies, and would appeal to such evidences in support of her strange doctrines; foreseeing likewise that she would enslave men and (much more) women by practicing on their affections and by accommodating herself with dangerous pliancy to their weakness, relieving them from the burden of thought and from the perplexity of doubt by proffering them the aid of infallibility, soothing the sorrows of the mourner by dispensing pardon and promising peace to the departed, removing the load of guilt from the oppressed conscience by the ministries of the confessional and by nicely poised compensations for sin, and that she would flourish for many centuries in proud and prosperous impunity before her sins would reach to heaven and come in remembrance before God; foreseeing also that many generations of men would thus be tempted to fall from the faith and to become victims of deadly error, and that they who clung to the truth would be exposed to cozening flatteries and fierce assaults and savage tortures from her, — the Holy Spirit, we say, foreseeing all these things in His divine knowledge, and being the everlasting Teacher, Guide, and Comforter of the Church, was graciously pleased to provide a heavenly antidote, for all these dangerous, widespread, and long-enduring evils, by dictating the Apocalypse. In this divine book the Spirit of God has portrayed the Church of Rome such as none but He could have foreseen that she would become, and such as, wonderful and lamentable to say, she has become. He has thus broken her magic spells; He has taken the wand of enchantment from her hand; He has lifted the mask from her face; and with His divine hand He has written her true character in large letters, and has planted her title on her forehead, to be seen and read of all: 'Mystery, Babylon the Great, the Mother of Harlots and Abominations of the Earth."

IV. Confirming Faith In God's Plan Amidst Skepticism.

The practical use of the Apocalypse in the present day, as casting light upon the whole course of Christian history, revealing the plan of Providence, and confirming faith amid the assaults of modern skepticism.

"The Church of Christ in these last days," says Professor Birks of Cambridge, "is exposed to strong temptation, from the spread of a secret and disguised infidelity. Many causes have conspired in promoting it, — the long years which have passed since the first preaching of the gospel, the superstition of the middle ages, the religious feuds of later times, the progress of physical science, with the consequent occupation of men's thoughts, more than ever, about sensible and outward things, and the widening intercourse with all the various creeds of the whole earth. Hence the faith of real Christians has often been severely sifted, and that of many others entirely undermined. A vague loose form of skepticism has crept in, and become fashionable, which does not care openly to discard Christianity, but is content to reduce it to the rank of uncertain opinion, a harmless and even beautiful form of the religious sentiment; while it denies the binding authority of its message, and treats the word of God with a hollow politeness, or perhaps with scornful indifference.

"At such a time we need to use every help which God has given us to expose this fearful evil. One of the chief of these is the word of prophecy. For here the Almighty Himself withdraws the veil, that we may see His hand clearly at work amidst all the changes of time, and discover the seal of His own prescience, whereby His word is stamped with a divine authority. Once let its truths enter our minds and infidelity can have no place within us. The history of our world becomes bright with the very sunshine of heaven. Where all before seemed to be disorder and darkness we can now discover light, love, order, and beauty. The gulf which appeared to separate us from the times of the gospel, and the personal history of our Lord, is bridged over; and the meanest events that are now passing around us are seen to be links in one mighty chain of Providence, which reaches from a past eternity, and loses itself in an eternity yet to come. The Church of Christ does well in taking heed to this word of prophecy, until Christ Himself, the true Daystar shall return to scatter the darkness. Amidst all the dimness of earthly hopes and human fancies, it is this holy light which alone can reveal the mysteries of divine Providence, while it leads our thoughts onward to the glory which shall be revealed."

We occupy today a more advanced position than has ever been previously reached in the course of the five kingdoms of history and prophecy — a position from which we can trace with clearer light and fuller knowledge than that possessed by those who have gone before us, the plan of Providence directing the development and decline of human governments, and the rise and establishment of the kingdom of God. Standing as we do at the close of the fourth, or Roman kingdom of the visions of Daniel and the Apocalypse, we behold the fulfillment of their predictions as to the four kingdoms, and especially as to the last, in its pagan and papal stages, the long course of its antichristian and persecuting action, and the outpouring of the vials of God's wrath by which its destruction is being accomplished. We trace the fall of the western and eastern divisions of the Roman empire, under Gothic, Saracenic and Turkish invasions; the rise of the Papal and

Mohammedan apostasies, their dominion and decline; the fall of the Papal temporal power at the date so long foretold, and the parallel wasting away of Turkey, and subjection throughout the world of Mohammedan countries to Christian rule, — together with the marvelous rise of the Jewish race to wealth and power, and the commencement at the predicted period, of their national reconstitution, and restoration to the land of their fathers.

In all these mighty movements, with their world-wide effects, we can clearly see the fulfillment of the sure word of prophecy, the actual realization in the history of the past, and in present events, of the course of things predicted thousands of years ago in the writings of holy apostles and prophets contained in the scriptures. Our faith in the inspiration of the Bible is thus confirmed; the ceaseless assaults of skepticism are resisted and repelled as the foaming waves of the sea by the lofty rocks against which they hurl themselves in vain; and the very oppositions of unbelief, of skepticism, naturalism and materialism, as foretold in prophecy among the salient characteristics of the closing days of the present dispensation, confirm our faith in the Word of God, which has forewarned and forearmed us against these attacks.

In the "divinely pictured visions of the Apocalypse," as Elliott has admirably shown, the philosophy of the history of Christendom is set before us, "the chief eras and vicissitudes of the Roman Pagan Empire," and "the sketch of the Christian body such as it would present itself to the all-seeing eye of God's spirit," the sealing of an elect number out of the professing church, or mystic Israel, and the subsequent "fortunes and histories of Christendom and the church distinctly in two different lines of succession: — the one the visible professing and more and more antichristian church: — the other no visible corporate Christian body (the once visible faithful Catholic church being now hid from men as in a wilderness), but Christ's own real church, the outgathering and election of grace, individually chosen, enlightened, quickened, and sealed by Him with the holy spirit of adoption; a body notable as"God's servants" for holy obedience; and though few in number as compared with the apostate professors of Christianity, yet in God's eye numerically perfect and complete. Thenceforward the prophecy traced them in their two distinct lines of succession, through their respective fortunes and histories... down even to the consummation. On the one hand there was depicted the body of false professors, multiplied so as to form the main and dominant constituency of apostate Christendom, as developing more and more a religion not Christian but antichristian, it being based on human traditions, not on God's word: and, after falling away to the worship of departed saints and martyrs as mediators, in place of Christ, as alike in its western and eastern division judicially visited and desolated by the divine avenging judgments of emblematic tempests, scorpion-locusts, and horsemen from the Euphrates: in other words, of the Goths, Saracens, and Turks: — then as in its western division, rising up again from the primary desolating judgment of Gothic invasion, in the new form of an ecclesiastical empire, enthroned on the seven hills of ancient Rome: its secret contriver being the very Dragon or Satanic spirit, that had ruled openly before in the Pagan empire; its ruling head proud, persecuting, blasphemous, and self-exalting against God, even beyond his pagan precursors; its constituency and priesthood characterized by "un repented idolatries, and fornications, thefts, murders, and sorceries": in fine as continuing unchanged, unchangeable in its apostasy, notwithstanding the repeated checks of woes and judgments from heaven, even until the end; and therefore then at length in its impenitency to be utterly abandoned to judgment, and, like another Sodom, made an example of the vengeance of everlasting fire: — this being in fact the grand essential preliminary to the world i s intended and blessed regeneration.

On the other hand, with regard to Christ's true Church, the election of grace, consisting of such as should hold to Christ as their head, and keep the word of God, and testimony of Jesus, the Apocalyptic prophecy represented them as almost at once entering on a great and long tribulation; yet though in number few and fewer, and reduced soon to a state spiritually destitute and desolate, like that of the wilderness, so as to constitute them a church invisible rather than visible, as still secretly preserved by their Lord; ... and then as witnesses for Christ's cause and truth made war on by Rome's revived empire, as by a beast from the abyss of hell; and so being at length conquered and apparently exterminated: yet suddenly revived and exalted in the presence of their enemies; a revelation from heaven of Christ as the Sun of righteousness introducing and accompanying this glorious revival of God's slaughtered witnesses; and "a political revolution attending, or following, under which the tenth part of the ten-kingdomed ecclesiastical empire would fall. All this the prophecy figured as the result of God's second great intervention for His Church;" and "fulfilled in the great Reformation of the sixteenth century: the discovery introducing it of the doctrine of justification simply by faith in Christ Jesus; and the downfall following it of the tenth part of the Popedom in Papal England. Thus was the Protestant Reformation distinctly figured in the Apocalypse as a glorious, divine act."

"As to the subsequent 'indifferentism in religion/ which followed in the seventeenth and eighteenth centuries, it was not unforeshown in the further developments of the Apocalypse. Yet it seemed also pre-intimated how, as if from some gracious revival of religion in God's still favored Protantism, there would afterwards speed forth in the latter times three missionary angels, flying through midheaven, with voices of faithful gospel-preaching throughout the length and breadth of the world, of warning against Papal Rome, and denunciation of its quickly coming judgment: a contemporary energetic revival and going forth of the spirit of Popery, conjunctively with other kindred and allied spirits of Pagan-like infidelity, and pseudo-Christian priestcraft, being but the last putting forth of its bravery, to hasten the final crisis, and constitute the precursive and justification of its fall: acts these that would be nearly the last public ones promoted, or mingled in, by the little body of Christ's faithful ones on earth. For it was foreshown how that Christ's advent would speedily follow; and contemporarily therewith, and with the mystic Babylon's destruction by fire, His witnessing saints and all that fear Him, small and great, have the reward given them of an entrance into the everlasting kingdom of their Lord; and that so, and then (not before, or otherwise), the promised regeneration of all things, the Christian's great object of hope, should have its accomplishment, in Christ's own reign with His saints; and therewith, at length, the true and only complete evangelization of the world.

"Such is the Apocalyptic moral philosophy of the history of Christendom, its rule of faith not tradition, but the Bible; its Church of the promises that alone of true believers in Jesus; and God's glory in Christ the grand and final object ever set forth in it."[207]

In the foregoing view there is a consistency with the Apocalyptic figuration, and the actual history of the Christian Church which cannot fail to deeply impress those whose minds have not been blinded by prejudice, or warped by erroneous conceptions as to the subject of Apocalyptic prophecy, and the philosophy of Christian history. For the Apocalypse is manifestly "the story of Christ's kingdom its faithful and suffering saints are none other than those who M keep the commandments of God, and have the testimony of Jesus Christ" (chap, 12:17), who overcome in their warfare with the satanically ruled world power "by the blood of the Lamb, and by the word of their testimony, and loved not their lives unto the death" (v. 11), those who "keep the commandments of God and the faith of Jesus" (chap, 14:12), those who are "the martyrs of Jesus" (chap, 17:6), those who are "called, and chosen, and faithful" (chap, 17:14), those whom God calls "My people" (chap, 18:4), those who "have the testimony of Jesus" (chap, 19:10), those who were "beheaded for the witness of Jesus, and for the word of God" (chap. 20.). They form "a great multitude, which no man could number, of all nations, and kindreds, and people, and tongues," they ascribe their "salvation to

---

207Elliott, *Horae*, IV., pp. 250-255.

our God which sitteth upon the throne, and unto the Lamb"; they have come "out of great tribulation, and have washed their robes, and made them white in the blood of the Lamb"; they are the "palm bearing" multitude before the throne (chap, 7:9), the victors who "sing the song of Moses the servant of God, and the song of the Lamb" (chap, 15:3), the hundred and forty-four thousand who stand with the Lamb on Mount Zion, "having His Father's name written in their foreheads," who "follow the Lamb whithersoever He goeth," who were "redeemed from among men, being the first fruits unto God and to the Lamb" (chap, 14:1—4). They are the "blessed" who "are called to the marriage supper of the Lamb" (chap, 19:9), the "blessed and holy" persons who "have part in the first resurrection," on whom "the second death hath no power," "priests of God and of Christ" who "reign with Him a thousand years" (chap, 20), and later on "reign forever and ever" (chap, 22:5). They are the citizens of "the holy Jerusalem," who constitute "the bride the Lamb's wife," a city which is yet to "descend out of heaven from God," "having the glory of God" (chap, 21); in which city the saints of the Seven Churches addressed in the opening Epistles of the prophecy have their part, and receive their reward, for on them Christ promises to "write the name of the city of My God, which is New Jerusalem, which cometh down out of heaven from My God" (chap, 3:12), the saints to whom He promises that they shall "sit with Him on His throne," when He comes in the glory of His kingdom (chap, 3:21).

The Apocalypse describes the double conflict or warfare of these saints and martyrs of Jesus, first their conflict with Pagan Rome (chap, 12), and then with Papal Rome (chaps, 11, 13, 17), first the warfare in which they overcome, and secondly the warfare in which they are overcome, and utterly silenced, but from which slain condition they rise, and are exalted to power, in manifest analogy to the experience of their Lord, the Lamb, who had been slain, and raised and never bowed the knee to Baal, how confirmatory to faith becomes the marvelous Apocalyptic anticipation of the course of Christian history! How clearly we behold the evidence of divine inspiration in the prophecy, for by no mere human wisdom could the strange and checkered history of the Church, its apostasies, its contrasts, its conflicts, its victories, have been foreseen; yet here is all the story told in advance, the events described long before they came to pass, sketched with masterly power, drawn in striking colors, ineffaceable by time, portrayed not only with fidelity, but with an insight into their deepest meaning most manifestly divine. And every century by its fresh fulfillments has only added to the evidence of that inspiration, while the events of the present, as they unfold before our eyes, still further confirm it. Upon "the impregnable rock of holy Scripture" then we take our stand, nor fear the assaults of modern skepticism; our faith in the Bible as the Word of God, confirmed and deepened, assured that while "heaven and earth shall pass away," the word of the Lord as contained in that sacred volume shall abide as living and life-giving truth forever.

V. Keeping Before The Church The Ever Brightening Hope

The use of the Apocalypse in setting and keeping before the Church from age to age the ever brightening hope of the Coming and Kingdom of Christ.

The foregoing marvelous fulfillments of prophecy having taken place, confirming our faith, and indicating our advanced position in the revealed course of the present dispensation, we have but to follow the further delineations of the prophecy in order to perceive the character of the events which lie before us, in the ever advancing development of the Kingdom of God set, and the books opened "; but a comparison of this earlier and briefer prophecy with the more detailed predictions in the Apocalypse reveals the fact that the fourth empire, that of Rome, with its persecuting papal head, is overthrown under the judgments of the seven vials; and that the advent of Christ in judgment, accompanied by His saints, has more than one stage, for a period of a thousand years is to separate between His revelation"to tread the wine-press of the wrath of God" as described in Rev. 19, and His coming on His great white throne to judge "the dead small and great," out of the things" written in the books," described in Rev. 20. The recurrence of the remarkable expression" the books were opened" in Dan. 7:10, and Rev. 20:12, links together these two descriptions of the final judgment, as relating to the same event; but while the judgment of Rev. 20:12 is certainly postmillennial, the destruction of" the beast," or persecuting Roman power is, according to Rev. 19:20 a premillennial event; indicating the conclusion that the judgment described in Dan. 7 includes both the pre and post-millennial stages of the judgment of "the Beast," and of "the dead small and great," more fully portrayed in the Apocalyptic prophecy.

The existence of these stages in the divine judgment will cause no surprise when we reflect on the character of the present and millennial dispensations taken as a whole; for as Jonathan Edwards has shown in his "History of Redemption," the whole period from the ascension and enthronement of Christ to His final coming to judge "the dead small and great," is characterized by the taking down and removing of antagonistic world powers, one after the other, until every foe is placed in subjection beneath His one are apt to ignore or deny the other. Hence while some are pessimists others are optimists, in the interpretation they attach to contemporaneous events. But time corrects such partial views, and with added years, and widened observation, we come to occupy a position midway between these opposite extremes. "Are you a pessimist?" said one to the late Dr. A. J. Gordon of Boston. "No," said he, "I am not." "Are you then an optimist?" asked the interrogator. "No," he answered, "I am not." "What then are you?" he was asked. "I am a truthist ," he replied.

If I may be permitted to refer to my own experience as a student of prophecy for more than forty years, I can distinctly trace two stages in the development of my views, in which the downward and upward movements of the age, successively occupied my attention. Briefly to narrate the facts I may say that when evangelizing in

France before the outbreak of the Franco-German war of 1870, I saw everywhere around me the prevalence of Romanism and infidelity. Visits to Spain and Italy only extended the view of this sad state of things, while growing acquaintance with Germany showed the reign of Rationalism in a country which had taken a leading part in the reformation of the sixteenth century. In all these lands there still existed a small body of evangelical Christians, but they were inconspicuous compared to the mass of the population under the sway of Romish or Rationalistic errors. By the Vatican Council of 1870 which decreed the Pope of Rome to be "The Infallible Teacher of Faith and Morals," the errors and superstitions of the Church of Rome were practically declared to be "irreformable." Nothing then awaited that apostate church but the destruction foretold in new world rising up, like some vast continent emerging from the depths of the ocean. Extending my study of the movement it became evident that this new world had been rising up for the last three or four hundred years, but especially since the Puritan colonization of America in the seventeenth century. The growth of civil and religious liberty, the marvelous progress of science, the extension of the British empire, the rise of the United States, of United Germany, of United Italy, the political regeneration of India, the exploration and uplifting of Africa, the opening and evangelization of China, the amazing progress of Japan, the ever increasing approximation of all peoples by steam and electric communication, the rapid spread of education, the multiplication and extension of Christian missions, all were evident features of a world movement, analogous to, though far surpassing that in the history of Greece and Rome which preceded the advent of the Christian religion, and prepared its way; or like the terrestrial changes which prepared the world for the appearance of man; the dawn of light, the retreat of the submerging waters, the clearing of the sky, the rise of islands and continents, and the clothing of the waste and desolate places with the wonders of vegetable and animal life.

On considering these two contrasted world movements several broad facts as to their nature, causes and tendencies became apparent.

First, considering their history in the past, and the forces from which they spring, the inveterate tendency in fallen man to depart from the living God, and the law of progress, both natural and spiritual, under which we are placed, it became evident that both these movements, the downward and the upward, will continue to operate in the fu- [original page 441 was missing from the source book -ed] ...the second. We know "neither the day, nor the hour" when our Lord cometh.

What is the teaching of the New Testament on the subject of the second Advent of Christ? What place does it assign to it? How far does it give it prominence? To what practical uses does it put the prospect of the Lord's coming? And what position does that coming hold in the last great prophecy in the Bible, the sacred prophecy with which it ends? Let us turn to the New Testament, and patiently scanning its pages seek to collect in one view the substance of its testimony on this great subject. Surely such a doctrine deserves this effort to understand its meaning and its place in the word of God! Our examination must of necessity be brief and superficial, little more than a grouping of scripture passages, but the glance which we bestow on these may lead to further and deeper study of "the whole counsel of God" in the matter. Let us then turn to "the sure word" of scripture prophecy, given by "inspiration of God"; inwardly praying for the illumination of the Holy Spirit that we may be led into all truth.

We begin with the Gospels. There, on the mount of beatitudes, we behold Jesus teaching the multitudes, preaching the righteousness of the kingdom of heaven, whose establishment was then at hand, and as we listen awed and borne away by the divine wisdom and authority of His discourse, we hear Him speak of that day of Judgment in which His word shall decide the eternal issues of our destiny, how He will say to false professors of His name, "I never knew you, depart from Me ye that work iniquity." We tremble at the message and take heed; while He Himself, rises before us in the vision of that coming judgment as our great and final Judge. [original page 443 was missing from the source book -ed] ...one end of heaven to the other." And for that coming the world and the Church should be unprepared, for it should overtake an ungodly world as did the flood in the days of Noah, and find an unfaithful Church slumbering — slumbering till wakened by the midnight cry, "Behold the bridegroom cometh, go ye out to meet Him." The wise virgins having oil for their lamps trim them, and go in to the marriage; the foolish virgins having no oil, their lamps gone out, are excluded. In a later parable our Lord tells us that His coming would not take place speedily; "after a long time," the master of the household should return to reward his faithful servants. And every act, even the most trivial ministration of kindness to suffering men whom He calls His "brethren" would be remembered and rewarded as done to Himself, when He should come "in His glory, and all the holy angels with Him," and seated "on the throne of His glory" should separate His true disciples from false professors of the Christian name, as a shepherd divides the sheep from the goats. Then should the wicked go into everlasting punishment, but the righteous into life eternal.

Following Christ to the upper chamber in Jerusalem, we witness the paschal supper the night before His crucifixion. He is comforting His disciples, sorrowing in the prospect of His departure. "Let not your hearts be troubled," He says. "I go to prepare a place for you. And if I go and prepare a place for you I will come again and receive you unto Myself that where I am there ye may be also." Earth is not all. "In My Father's house are many mansions." Words of tender love, and lofty meaning, how have ye comforted the sorrowful from age to age, and kept the lamp of hope burning through the long night of Christ's absence; the vision of those many mansions shining above the gloom; and world was committed to her; a work to this day but half accomplished, if even that. Great fields unreaped though white to harvest, still remain. And still the great commission presses upon the Church "Go," "preach the gospel to every creature," and the twofold promise is hers; that of the Spirit's baptism; and that of the perpetual presence of her Lord.

While the words of the great commission were still sounding in the ears of Christ's disciples, "while they beheld, He was taken up; and a cloud received Him out of their sight."

Gazing after Him they remained rooted to the spot. Then two angels, "in white apparel" stood in their midst, and in a brief memorable sentence, turned their thoughts from the Lord's departure to His return. "This same Jesus, which is taken up from you into heaven, shall so come in like manner as ye have seen Him go into heaven."

A few days later Peter and John, having received with the other disciples the baptism of power, of cloven fiery tongues, for gospel testimony, are standing in the temple witnessing for Christ. "Repent" they cry to the crowds around them, "be converted that your sins maybe blotted out, when the times of refreshing shall come from the presence of the Lord, and He shall send Jesus Christ, which before was preached unto you, whom the heavens must receive until the times of the restitution of all things, which God hath spoken by the mouth of all His holy prophets since the world began."

Later on Paul is standing on Mars Hill, preaching to the Athenians the gospel of the resurrection. "God," he says, "commandeth all men everywhere to repent, because He [original page 447 was missing from the source book -ed] ...orders had appeared among them. He comes to the subject of the Lord's supper, and reminds them of Christ's own institution of the ordinance, and of its meaning."As often as ye eat this bread and drink this cup ye do show the Lord's death till He come." To remember Him; to show forth His death; to anticipate His return; to link the first advent yrit h the second; to bind them together with an unbroken chain of sacramental acts and seasons; such the object, the effect of the sacred ordinance. And so in lowly tabernacles, in lofty temples, in upper chambers, in prisons, in caves, in deserts, has the Church kept without intermission this sacred ordinance of communion and commemoration, during the long centuries which have elapsed since her Lord's departure, waiting for His return.

With a marvelous and matchless chapter on the resurrection of the dead Paul closes the Epistle. "Every man," he tells us, shall be raised "in his own order. Christ the first-fruits, afterwards they that are Christ's at His coming then later on the end, when death should be destroyed. But should all die?"we shall not all sleep, but we shall all be changed in a moment, in the twinkling of an eye at the last trump." Then shall death be "swallowed up in victory."

In his second Epistle to the Corinthians he resumes the subject, and reminds them that "we must all appear before the judgment seat of Christ, that every one may receive the things done in his body, according to that which he hath done, whether it be good or bad." A salutory view of a solemn subject, never to be forgotten or ignored. To the Ephesians he writes his epistle of unity, speaking of "unity of faith and knowledge; of one body, one spirit, one hope, [original page 449 was missing from the source book -ed] ...that are fallen asleep. For the Lord Himself shall descend from heaven with a shout, with the voice of the archangel, and with the trump of God; and the dead in Christ shall rise first: then we that are alive, that are left, shall together with them be caught up in the clouds, to meet the Lord in the air, and so shall we ever be with the Lord." He reminds them that "the day of the Lord so cometh as a thief in the night, when they are saying peace and safety, then sudden destruction cometh upon them, as travail upon a woman with child, and they shall in no wise escape." But that day should not overtake God's faithful people "as a thief." And he prays for them that their "spirit and soul and body be preserved entire, without blame at the coming of our Lord Jesus Christ."

In his second Epistle to the Thessalonians he tells them that God will "recompense affliction to those who afflict them," "at the revelation of the Lord Jesus from heaven with the angels of His power in flaming fire, rendering vengeance to them that know not God, and to them that obey not the gospel of our Lord Jesus."

"Touching the coming of our Lord Jesus Christ and our gathering together unto Him," he tells them that that day should not come "except the falling away come first, and the man of sin be revealed"; "and now ye know that which restraineth, to the end that he may be revealed in his own season. For the mystery of lawlessness doth already work, only there is one that restraineth now until he be taken out of the way. And then shall be revealed the lawless one, whom the Lord Jesus shall slay with the breath of His mouth, and bring to nought by the manifestation of His coming." "But the Lord is faithful who shall stablish you, and guard you from the evil one. And the Lord direct your hearts into the love of God, and into the patience of Christ."

To the Hebrews he writes that Christ who had appeared "once at the end of the ages to put away sin by the sacrifice of Himself," and was now appearing "before the face of God for us," would "appear a second time, apart from sin, to them that wait for Him, unto Salvation." "For yet a very little while He that cometh shall come, and shall not tarry."

To Titus he writes of "looking for the blessed hope and appearing of the glory of our great God and Saviour Jesus Christ." To Timothy of keeping the commandment without spot "until the appearing of our Lord Jesus Christ: which in its own times He shall shew who is the blessed and only Potentate, the King of Kings and Lord of Lords." "I charge thee," he adds, "in the sight of God and of Jesus Christ, who shall judge the quick and the dead, and by His appearing and His kingdom, preach the word: be instant in season, out of season; reprove, rebuke, exhort, with all long-suffering and teaching, for the time will come when they will not endure the sound doctrine, but having itching ears will heap to themselves teachers after their own lusts, and will turn away their ears from the truth, and turn aside unto fables." For "in later times some shall fall away from the truth giving heed to seducing spirits and doctrines of devils": and "in the last days grievous times shall come." But "I have fought the good fight," says Paul, in this his last Epistle; "I have finished the course, I have kept the faith: henceforth there is laid up for me the crown of righteousness, which the Lord the righteous Judge shall give to me at that day; and not only to me, but also to all them that have loved His appearing."

In his brief practical Epistle James writing to "the twelve tribes which are of the - Dispersion" exhorts them to "be patient until the coming of the Lord... stablish your hearts for the coming of the Lord is at hand."

Peter in his Epistles of hope encourages "the elect who are sojourners of the Dispersion" to expect that their faith "though proved by fire" would be found unto praise and glory and honor at the revelation of Jesus Christ." Partakers as they were of His sufferings, "at the revelation of His glory" they would "rejoice with exceeding joy." As "a witness of the sufferings of Christ, and a partaker of the glory that shall be revealed," he exhorts the elders "Tend the flock of God which is among you... and when the chief Shepherd shall be manifested ye shall receive the crown of glory that fadeth not away." In his last epistle he foretells that "in the last days mockers shall come with mockery walking after their own lusts, and saying, Where is the promise of His coming? for, from the day that the fathers fell asleep, all things continue as they were from the beginning of the creation." But such "willfully forget" the flood, and its solemn lessons. "Forget not this one thing," he says, "that one day is with the Lord as a thousand years, and a thousand years as one day. The Lord is not slack concerning His promise, as some count slackness, but is long-suffering to you-ward, not wishing that any should perish, but that all should come to repentance. But the day of the Lord will come as a thief in the which the heavens shall pass away with a great noise, and the elements shall be dissolved with fervent heat, and the earth and the works that are therein shall be burned up... but according to His promise we look for new heavens and a new earth wherein dwelleth righteousness."

In his first Epistle John writes, "Little children, it is the last hour: and as ye heard that antichrist com£th, even now have there arisen many antichrists, whereby we know that it is the last hour." Therefore "abide in the Son, and in the Father." "And now my little children, abide in Him, that if He shall be manifested we may have boldness, and not be ashamed before Him at His coming."

Jude in his brief Epistle adds his final warning, — "remember ye the words which have been spoken before by the apostles of our Lord Jesus Christ; how that they said to you, In the last time there shall be mockers, walking after their own ungodly lusts. These are they who make separations, sensual, not having the spirit. But ye beloved, building up yourselves on your most holy faith, praying in the Holy Spirit, keep yourselves in the love of God, looking for the mercy of our Lord Jesus Christ unto eternal life."

Lastly, in the Apocalypse, the key-note of the final revelation is sounded. "Behold He cometh with the clouds, and every eye shall see Him, and they which pierced Him; and all the tribes of the earth shall mourn over Him." To that coming all the preliminary letters to the Churches, and all the subsequent actions of the prophecy are directed; the opening of its seals; the sounding of its trumpets, the pouring forth of its vials. Under the sixth vial the startling utterance is heard "Behold I come as a thief; blessed is he that watcheth, and keepeth his garments, lest he walk naked, and they see his shame."

After the fall of Babylon heaven is opened and "the King of kings and Lord of lords," whose name is "Faithful and True," the "Word of God," comes forth, followed by the army of His white robed saints. He treads "the wine-press of the fierceness and wrath of Almighty God."

[original page 454 was missing from the source book -ed] ...we cannot but be impressed by the fact of the close connection which exists between the coming and the kingdom of our Lord Jesus Christ, and that these constitute the goal of redemption history.

"Human history," says Dr. Henry Smith, "has no other center of convergence and divergence than the Cross of calvary." He adds, "history has no other prophetic end than the Kingdom of Immanuel."

Nowhere in Scripture is this latter fact more clearly set forth than in the prophecies of Daniel and the Apocalypse, for in these the kingdom of God is revealed as the last of five universal kingdoms, diverse in source, in character, and in duration from the four great kingdoms which it follows, and replaces; the goal to which they advance, the end to which their entire movement is subject. The Apocalypse, as we have seen is the story of the fourth and fifth of these kingdoms, of the last great earthly empire, and the eternal kingdom of the God of heaven.

The glory of the kingdom of God irradiates this closing prophecy, and the history of the people who are to inherit that glory fills its pages. As "the sufferings of Christ and the glories which should follow," are the chief theme of Old Testament prophecy, so the sufferings of His saintly people, and the glories which constitute their reward occupy this closing New Testament prophecy, the gift to his suffering and witnessing church of the ascended Saviour.

The greatest of all the events to which the Apocalypse directs the attention is the second Advent of Christ, in glory and majesty, to raise the dead, to judge the world, and to reign with His saints forever.

From the opening sentence "Behold He cometh with clouds, and every eye shall see Him," to the last utterance. "Surely I come quickly ," the second coming of Christ occupies in the prophecy a prominence accorded to no other event; and on the subject of Christ's coming and kingdom its revelations are far in advance of those presented in preceding prophecies.

The Apocalypse is thus the crown of all the progressive revelations in the word of God concerning these final events. For whereas in the second of Daniel we see the Kingdom of God as a great mountain filling the earth, and in the seventh of Daniel with increasing clearness as the kingdom of the Son of man, and of the saints of the Most High; and in the gospels of the New Testament, as the kingdom of the Father, and of the children of the resurrection, introduced by the advent of Christ with His angelic hosts, at the close of the times of Jewish trouble and desolation; and in the Epistles as the coming of Christ to raise the sleeping and translate the living saints to meet Him in the air at His advent; and then to manifest them in the glory of their risen life when He Himself is manifested with the angels of His mighty power, to destroy "the Man of Sin," and to remove from His kingdom all that offend and do iniquity, and effect "the restitution of all things," promised through all the prophets from the foundation of the world; in the Apocalypse the precursory events which are to introduce that advent are represented in a long series of marvelous visions, its effects and consequences described in scene after scene of matchless glory and sublimity, and an entirely new revelation granted of a kingdom in which Christ and His risen saints shall reign for a thousand years after the destruction of all antagonistic world powers, and before the final day of the resurrection and judgment of "the rest of the dead," and the establishment of the new heaven and earth of the eternal state.

And this sublime and glorious prophecy completes and closes the volume of Divine revelation. Borrowing its symbols from the earlier writings of the law and the prophets, gathering together in one the doctrinal and practical teachings of previous Scriptures, as converging rays meeting in a luminous center, unveiling the vistas of eternal glory and felicity to which all the previous dispensations and ages of redemption history lead, and in which they issue, the Apocalypse forms the golden clasp of the entire volume of Revelation. And as the gift of the ascended Saviour, His own and His final utterance to the church; as His own opening of the mysteries of providence and of the future previously hidden from both men and angels, an unveiling granted to Him as the Lamb of God, as a reward of His sufferings, and crown of His victory, this closing prophecy possesses an altogether celestial position, and an incomparable glory. It speaks to us, not from earth as other prophecies, but from heaven. It is the voice of Him that liveth and was dead, and is alive forevermore, who holds the keys of death and hades; Him to whom every knee shall bow and every tongue confess; Him whom all angels worship and serve; and from whom shall flow the light and life of that eternal kingdom, in which sin and sorrow and death shall be no more.

Conclusion

NO NEWLY INVENTED SYSTEM of Apocalyptic interpretation have we set forth in this volume, but the old interpretation which has been "from the beginning," ripened and mellowed by the influence of time.

"None Other Things"

If the Apocalypse could speak today concerning itself it might employ the language of Paul, "I continue unto this day, witnessing both to small and great, saying none other things than those which the prophets and Moses did say should come;"for while opening to us new mysteries of Providence, it gives us no outline of futurity but that which was set forth from the dawn of revelation. It is but the expansion of preceding prophecies. The promise that the seed of the woman should bruise the serpent's head contains it all. The king seated on Zion in the second Psalm, breaking in pieces his enemies with a rod of iron is the same as the King of kings and Lord of lords, wielding the rod of iron to subdue His foes in the visions of the Apocalypse; and the king of the one hundred and tenth Psalm, seated at God's right hand, who is a priest forever after the order of Melchizedek is none other than the exalted Redeemer of the Apocalypse, who offers before the throne "the prayers of the saints," sanctified and sweetened with the "much incense" which mingles with them in the golden censer of His high priestly service. Ezekiel saw in his prophetic visions the "living creatures" of the Apocalypse, and Isaiah its "new heavens and earth." Daniel beheld in vision its wild beasts, saw its ten horned Roman empire, its persecuting Antichrist, its suffering saints, its mysterious "times and seasons," its coming in the clouds of heaven of "the Son of Man," its resurrection of the dead, its final judgment scene, and its everlasting kingdom of the God of heaven. Zechariah beheld its meek majestic King whose dominion was to be "from the river to the ends of the earth," saw Him coming "with all His saints" in that day "known to the Lord," to be "king over all the earth," when there should be "one Lord, and His name one." John the Baptist beheld its "Lamb of God who taketh away the sin of the world." And above all our Lord Jesus Christ Himself revealed that clear and comprehensive outline of the future which contains within its framework all the series of events set forth in the visions of the Apocalypse; the progress of the kingdom of God, the wars, the famines, the pestilences, the persecutions, the false prophets, the apostasies, the tribulations, the universal preaching of the Gospel; the shaking of the heavens, the darkening of the luminaries, the falling of the stars, the calling of men on the rocks to hide them from the wrath of the Lamb, the coming of the Son of Man in the clouds of heaven, with His angels, to gather His saints from the uttermost parts of the earth, the judgment and reward of saints, the marriage of the Lamb, the final judgment of the world deciding the eternal issues of life and death, and the Palingenesia, or regeneration of all things, in which the "children of the resurrection" are to be made "equal to the angels"; all these great and wondrous events were foretold by our Lord during the course of His earthly ministry. And the apostasy predicted by St. Paul, and the other apostles, with its "Man of Sin," its "Son of perdition," its Antichrist, its profaned temple, its deluded multitudes, and the saints protected from its peril and doom, is that apostasy with its blasphemous persecuting head, its idolatrous worship, and its suffering witnesses occupying so large and central a place in the visions of St. John. The New Jerusalem, the city of the living God, on its Mount Zion, with its "innumerable hosts of angels," its "general assembly and church of the first-born enrolled in heaven," and its "spirits of just men made perfect," so gloriously described by Paul in the epistle to the Hebrews, that "Jerusalem which is above which is the mother of us all" of which he speaks in the Epistle to the Galatians, is none other than the New Jerusalem of the visions of the Apocalypse, the city of saints, bearing in its foundations the names of "the twelve apostles of the Lamb," and on its gates the names of the tribes of Israel. God's long-suffering patience, deferring the Advent of "the day of the Lord" in mercy to a sinful race, yet bringing it at last, when unexpected, "as a thief in the night," when the heavens shall be wrapped together as a scroll, and the earth dissolved with fire, to make way for the new heavens and earth, all these which John beheld in Patmos, were seen by Peter years before, and made the subject of his last warning words. For the testimony of prophecy is one: and the Apocalypse but the last and most complete "unveiling" of that course of things partially and progressively revealed in previous prophetic teachings. Thus the last book in the sacred volume of Revelation teaches us "none other things" than those which the voices of the prophets declared from the earliest times; as the light of the noon is none other than the brighter radiance of the light which had shone from the dawning of the day.

O holy harmony of inspiration, O sacred continuity of testimony, thou art worthy of the God of Truth, to whom all things have been known from the foundation of the world.

Time as an Interpreter

We have shown in the preceding pages that history has all along revealed the meaning of prophecy; that it did so in Old Testament times; that it did so at the advent of Christ, the accomplishment of His sufferings, and glories, expounding by their fulfillment the prophecies of these events; and that it has done so ever since, opening from century to century, the meaning of the mysterious predictions relating to the course of Christian history. We have thus shown that

1. The events of history explained the meaning of the Six first Seals of the Apocalypse.

The early victories of the gospel of Christ, the rapid spread of Christian teachings, and extension of the Christian church throughout the Roman Empire, in the face of tremendous opposition from Jew and Gentile, explained the meaning of the first seal, the going forth of the rider upon the white horse, "conquering and to conquer." No doubt whatever rested on the minds of the primitive Christians, as to the significance of this opening Apocalyptic seal; and the view they took has held a leading position ever since. It can be traced in every century, from the first Apocalyptic commentary extant, that of Victorinus, down to Alford's commentary on the Greek New Testament published in our own days. The application of this vision to the conquests of Christ is confirmed by the analogous vision in the nineteenth chapter of the going forth of the rider on the white horse of victory, and the name the rider bears, "The Word of God," "the King of Kings, and Lord of Lords."

The calamities which fell upon the Roman Empire in the second and third centuries, explained the second, thirds and fourth seals. The dreadful civil wars by which the empire was long distracted, the oppressive fiscal policy resulting in widespread famines, and above all the desolating plague which in the third century swept off one half the population, explained the meaning of the going forth of the riders on the red, black, and livid horses, whose mission it was "to take peace from the earth," that "men should kill one another"; to tax the necessaries of life; and to "kill with sword, with hunger, with death, and with the beasts of the earth." The commentary ©f Victorinus recognizes the application; and the view became current in the early church that the calamities which were weakening the Roman Empire and preparing the way for its destruction, were not only fulfillments of Apocalyptic prophecy, but also of our Lord's last great prophetic discourse on the Mount of Olives in which He forewarned His disciples of wars, famines, and pestilences as precursors of His coming, and of "the end of the age."

The cruel persecutions of the Church by pagan Rome, especially in the time of Diocletian, giving rise to the era of the martyrs, explained only too clearly the meaning of the fifth seal, the seal of martyrs.

The overthrow of the pagan Roman Empire which followed in the fourth century, shaking as with an earthquake, and darkening as with an eclipse of the heavenly luminaries the state and religion of ancient Rome, interpreted the sixth seal; especially as that appalling event was viewed as an adumbration of the final judgment of the world, in the great day of "the wrath of the Lamb."

2. The triumph of Christianity over Paganism in the fourth century

The triumph of Christianity over Paganism in the fourth century explained to the Church of that period the meaning of the vision in Revelation 12, of the casting down of the persecuting dragon from his throne. Representations of the prostrate dragon were inscribed by Constantine upon his coins, and above it the symbol of the victorious Cross; and the joy and triumph of the early Church found expression in the glowing words in the Apocalypse, "Now is come salvation, and strength, and the kingdom of our God," and the power of His Christ; for the accuser of our brethren is cast down which accused them before God day and night; and they overcame him by the blood of the Lamb, and by the word of their testimony; and they loved not their lives unto the death (Rev. 12:10, 11). This notable victory of Christianity over Paganism led the early Church to adopt an erroneous interpretation of the vision of the millennial reign of Christ and His saints and martyrs. The binding of Satan for a thousand years, that he should "deceive the nations no more till the thousand years should be fulfilled," was regarded by the Church of the fifth and following centuries as an accomplished fact. The Church of the Middle Ages erroneously believed herself to be living in the millennium! Not till the seventeenth century did the church escape from this false interpretation of prophecy, compelled to abandon it by the stern teachings of historical events.

3. The Gothic invasions of the fourth and fifth centuries

The Gothic invasions of the fourth and fifth centuries, by which the Western Roman Empire was overthrown, and broken into fragments, amid terrible bloodshed and desolation, explained the meaning of the four first trumpets; while the Saracenic and Turkish overthrow of the Eastern Roman Empire which followed revealed the significance of the fifth and sixth trumpets. In the light of their fulfillment in history the trumpets of the Apocalypse are seen to possess the same character, and general purpose. Without exception they are "woe" trumpets; trumpets of war and desolation, heralding and sounding forth the overthrow of the Roman Empire Western and Eastern. The meaning of the seventh trumpet, with its seven vials of judgment on "Babylon" and the "Beast" remained a mystery till the outbreak of the French Revolution. The fifth and sixth trumpets had long before been clearly understood to refer to the Saracenic and Turkish conquests in the East. As the first four trumpets precede the fifth and sixth their application to the Gothic invasions which overthrew the Empire of Western Rome became a natural, and almost inevitable inference.

4. The Holy Roman Empire

The rise of the Papacy and revival of the Roman Empire under Charlemagne, the "Holy Roman Empire" which from its foundation in A.D. 800, continued for a thousand years till its overthrow by Napoleon, cast unexpected light on the marvelous prophecy in Revelation 13, of the restoration of the Roman Empire in its second, or Gothic form, under its revived eighth head; the "deadly wound" of the seventh head having been "healed." The identity of this eighth head with the "little horn" of Daniel 7, arising together with the ten horns of the divided Empire, is so plain and evident as to need no comment. Both occupy the same place, both have the same "mouth speaking great things and blasphemies," both are cruel persecutors of the saints, and both last for the same period. Long has the Church recognized in these symbolical predictions the representation of the Roman Papacy. In a multitude of particulars history has here fulfilled prophecy, and illuminated its meaning as with the light of day.

5. The Glorious Reformation

The glorious Reformation of the sixteenth century explained the vision in Revelation 10, of the sudden descent and action of the rainbow crowned Covenant Angel, whose voice was as the roar of a lion, and who held in his right hand "a little book open."[208] That Reformation gave back the Bible to the nations, and inaugurated the age of the book. It fulfilled the command of the angel of the vision to republish the gospel to "peoples, and nations, and tongues, and kings." It fulfilled the command to "measure," or reform and restore, the Church, represented by the temple, altar, and worshiping people; while rejecting or "casting out" the portion of the professing Church answering to "the court which is without," which was "given to the Gentiles" to be trodden under foot for 1,260 years (Rev. 11:2). Clearly comprehended by the Reformers, of the sixteenth century this great prophecy was acted on by them to the letter, as the divine plan, and authorization of their work.

At this point the revealing angel of the vision, standing "upon the sea and upon the earth," as claiming both for the sphere of his command, lifts up his hand to heaven and swears "by Him that

---

208 Elliott, *Horae*, II, p. 126.

liveth forever and ever, who created heaven and the things that therein are, and the earth and the things that therein are, and the sea and the things which are therein, that there should be time no longer (or that time shall no further be prolonged), but in the days of the voice of the seventh angel, when he shall begin to sound, the mystery of God should be finished, as He hath declared to His servants the prophets" (Rev. 10:5-7). The sense gathered is that time should no longer be extended "to the so far permitted reign of evil, the seventh trumpet's era being its fixed determined limit"

A comparison of this oath of the revealing angel with that in Daniel 12, relating to the three and a half "times" of the "scattering of the power of the holy people," sheds additional light on its meaning, and confirms its solemnity and importance, — God's oath, sworn in Reformation days, as to the proximate termination of the prophetic times, their ending with the seventh trumpet, whose sounding was even then at hand.

6. The Papal Reaction

The tremendous papal reaction of the sixteenth and seventeenth centuries by whose anti-Protestant wars, persecutions and massacres Europe was deluged with blood, and far more martyrs put to death than in all the persecutions of the early Church by Pagan Rome, explained the "war" against Christ's sackcloth clothed witnesses of the wild beast power in Revelation 11; and the cruel suppression of the Huguenots and Waldenses at the time of the Revocation of the Edict of Nantes: and the immediately succeeding English Revolution, with its restoration of the persecuted Protestant church to civil and religious freedom, and political ascendency, occurring at the predicted close of the sixth trumpet woe, and shortly before the sounding of the seventh trumpet of the French Revolution, cast a flood of light upon the meaning of the death, resurrection, and ascension of the witnesses — Christian witnesses whose position, action, testimony, sufferings and success, were typified of old by those of the Jewish prophets and

Reformers, in the dark days of Baalitical and Babylonish apostasies.

7. The French Revolution

The French Revolution in which as by the explosion of the long pent-up forces of a volcano the papal church and state were suddenly torn from their foundations, and overwhelmed in common ruin; and its repeated after waves of war and desolation affecting every throne and country of Europe, explained the outpouring of the introductory Vials of judgment under the seventh trumpet; vials expressly stated to be poured forth on the persecuting wild beast power, his followers, worshippers, and throne; those who had "shed the blood of saints and prophets," and to whom in righteous vengeance blood was given "to drink." The wasting away of the Turkish power which has followed in the East has explained the "drying up" of the Euphratean flood of the sixth trumpet, or Turkish woe; a drying up represented under the sixth vial. The seventh vial poured out on "Babylon the great," remains to be fulfilled. There may be a doubt as to its commencing point, but the accomplishment of its main predictions is certainly future, though near at hand.

8. The Church of Rome

The character and history of the Church of Rome, her proud position as seated on "the seven hills" of the Imperial city, and "reigning over the kings" and peoples of the earth, her gorgeous self-adornment, her fabulous wealth and luxury, her adulterous association with kings and princes of the Roman Empire, her multiplied idolatries, and cruel persecutions of the saints, and her judgment as finally hated and cast off, stripped and torn by the ten horned wild beast power which had previously carried her, and done her bidding; all this has been recognized as marvelously portrayed in the Apocalyptic vision of the harlot "Babylon the Great," drunken with "the blood of the saints, and of the martyrs of Jesus."

Like the apostle John who "wondered" as he gazed on this vision "with a great wonder,"[209] so do we contemplate it with admiration and astonishment; so marvelous has been the historic reality, and so marvelous its prediction. Its representation forms the most complete and striking portrait in the Apocalypse; a portrait whose terrible outlines and vivid colors have arrested the attention of the Church for ages; a portrait set as a warning to God's people in danger of being deceived and ensnared by the pretensions and wiles of the great church of the apostasy, and called to separate themselves from her sins, that they may escape her doom.

9. Duration of Papal Power

The duration of the papal power for the long period of 1,260 years from its commencement under the Pope exalting decrees of the Emperors Justinian and Phocas to its fall in the French Revolution of 1793, the revolution of 1848, and the final overthrow of the Temporal Power in 1870, has established the meaning of the "1,260 days" of the Apocalyptic prefiguration; has demonstrated the truth of the year-day theory; a demonstration sealed by the discoveries of astronomy as to the secular and cyclical character of the prophetic times in the book of Daniel and in the Apocalypse; confirming and settling with exactness their duration; and exhibiting their position, as integral parts of a great system of times, natural and revealed.

Slowly thus, century by century, time has interpreted the meaning of the mysterious visions of prophecy relating to the long and complex course of Christian history, clearing away their obscurities, as it has translated their anticipations into accomplished facts. Under its operation the apocalypse of prophecy has to a large extent given place to the apocalypse of history; the shadowy outline of the one to the substance of the other. Providence has proved the key to prophecy; and has confirmed on the whole that historic interpretation to which the

---

209 R. V.

Church of Christ has most commonly given her adhesion. The Praterist interpretation which would confine the reference of Apocalyptic prophecy to events in the time of Nero, and the fall of Pagan Rome, — disproved by the post-Neronic date of the Apocalypse as revealed in the time of Domitian — has been cast into oblivion by the discoveries of time; and on the other hand the reveries of Futurism have been shown to be speculations concerning future fulfillments of predictions which for the most part have been already accomplished. As time has been the great interpreter of prophecy in. the past, so doubtless will it continue to be in the future. To wait and watch for its discoveries is clearly the wisest course; curbing the premature flight of speculation; standing on the firm ground of ever evolving fact; leaving God to be His own interpreter in the Providential acts destined to fulfill and illuminate His spoken words.

Nineteen centuries of the fulfillment of New Testament prophecies concerning the course of events during the Christian dispensation lie behind us. The fall of Jerusalem, the triumphs of the Gospel, the vicissitudes of the Roman Empire, the sufferings of the Church under Pagan Rome, the victory of the martyrs, the abolition of Paganism and establishment of Christianity, the gradual development of the great apostasies in the West and in the East, the overthrow of the Western Empire by Gothic invasions, and of the Eastern Empire by the Saracens and Turks, the depressed and hidden condition of the true Church during the middle ages, the great Reformation of the sixteenth century, the slaughter and resurrection of the Christian witnesses, the retributive judgments of the French Revolution, the universal proclamation of the Gospel in modern times, the fall of the Papal temporal power at the moment of the highest act of papal self-exaltation, and at the date anticipated for centuries by students of the prophetic word, the wasting away of Turkish power, the issuing forth of spirits of delusion, Romish, Ritualistic and Infidel in our own days, and the visible commencement of the rise of the Jewish people from the depression of ages, of their unification, and of their restoration to the land of their fathers, all these events by their striking fulfillments of the anticipations of prophecy have confirmed our faith in the divine inspiration of the Scriptures. In vain do the restless waves of skepticism dash against the base of that impregnable rock. And now astronomy is adding its testimony to that of history in confirmation of the prophetic word. The stars in their courses are fighting for Israel. The sacred "times and seasons" of the law, equally with those of the prophets are found to possess a hidden astronomic character, binding them together as a systematic whole, linking them indissolubly with the System of Nature, proclaiming their true measures, settling their historic place, and demonstrating the divineness of their origin.

The folly of those who misled by the rash speculations which have arisen in modern times under the name of science, have denied to Scripture all insight into the system of nature, is becoming apparent. There is no science, say they, in the Bible! There is a deeper science there than they have investigated, a science yet to be developed in the future with convincing clearness, and taught in class-books among the elementary facts of Bible knowledge. The law of Moses, say they, was the compilation of unscrupulous priests in later times. But astronomy is rising up to rebuke them with its evidence of the profound connection of Mosaic and Prophetic Times and Seasons, as a harmonious system adjusted to the chronology of redemption history.

The Bible, say they, contains the grossest errors. But the fresh examination of its teachings which Bible criticism has provoked, reveals the fact that no absolute disproof exists of a single historic or doctrinal statement in Scripture. The creation of the world in the stages described in Genesis has never been disproved, but is even confirmed as to its general outline by the findings of geology. Astronomy proclaims light to be the eldest occupant of the universe, just as does the sublime opening of the Bible account of creation. The creation of man in the image of God has never been disproved, and his merely animal origin is but the theory of a skeptical naturalist who confessed that he had lost the sense he once possessed of the presence of God in nature, and his action in the government of the world. The fall of man has never been disproved, but is confirmed by the witness of history, and the voice of experience. The occurrence of the flood has never been disproved but is confirmed by universal tradition. What if we have to modify our ideas as to its absolute universality, if it was universal as to the race of man, and the then known habitable world? The account of the Bible as to the postdiluvian population has never been disproved, its Japhetic, Semitic, and Hamitic elements, and their dispersion from the valley region of the Tigris and Euphrates. The discoveries of archaeology are exalting our ideas of the antiquity of civilization in the region of Assyria, and evidences are accumulating of the migration of races from that ancient world center. The noble narrative of the call of Abraham from Ur of the Chaldees which opens the Jewish and Christian pages of redemption story has never been disproved, and the history of the patriarch remains today like the inscriptions engraved on the granite monuments of Egypt, indestructible by the ravages of Time. The very name of Abraham, father of many nations, is a prophecy which every age has fulfilled, and whose marvelous anticipation of the future is but enlarged and exalted by the widening course of events in Jewish, Mohammedan, and Christian history. The Sinaitic revelation has never been disproved, and the Jews remain today a witness to its reality by their adherence to its legislation.

The conquest of Canaan and its division among the tribes has never been disproved, and the history of the Jewish occupation of the land confirms its truth, while the labors of Palestine exploration in our day have served to verify the names and positions of countless places mentioned in the book of Joshua. The inscriptions of Moab, of Shishak king of Egypt, in the days of the son of Solomon, the records of the Assyrians, the Babylonians, and the Persians, but confirm the truth of later Jewish history, which from the time of the captivities moves in the full light of amply verified events. The same may be said of the whole of New Testament history. As to the doctrines of the Bible none of these have been disproved, or ever will be. We repeat it, no one important historic event, or doctrine in the Bible has ever been absolutely disproved, while on the other hand the proofs of the truth of Bible history and doctrine are accumulating year by year, and this largely as a result of the attacks to which they have been subjected. And the inward witness of the human soul to the truth of Bible teachings remains unaltered and unanswerable. No sooner has skepticism completed in the writings of Spencer its alleged destruction of religion than the breath of a divine revival makes the reality and power of religion more apparent than before.

The skeptic boldly proclaims the retreat of the tide of Christian faith, but scarce have the words fallen from his lips than the incoming waves of the advancing tide of spiritual religion roll over the spot he occupied, and falsify his presumptuous declaration.

And thus the last great prophecy in the Bible, the Apocalypse, which has suffered from the baseless speculations of its friends, and the unscrupulous attacks of its foes, lifts up its voice in these our days, clear as a trumpet, to teach the true philosophy of Christian history, and to confirm the faith of God's people by its exhibition of a knowledge of the future possessed in apostolic times, immeasurably transcending that of mortal man. In the course of events which it reveals we behold the mirror of the decline and fall of the Roman empire so eloquently narrated in Gibbon's monumental work, and of the complex and troubled story of the Christian church, the story of its trials and triumphs, of its apostasies and reformations, and of its actual condition in the days in which we live. And as we study the one and the other, the story of the decline of human governments, and the rise of the divine, we are impressed with its profound connection with the remoter history of the past, and with the progress and prospects of the world. The kingdom of God is seen to be the true goal of history, and the revolutions of the past take their place as acts in a general movement whose course has been foretold from the earliest ages, a movement as much beyond the power of man to arrest as the sweep of worlds in the amplitudes of space. And who can measure the power which the apocalyptic prophecy has exerted on the faith and practice of the Christian church from age to age? Who can measure its influence on Christian hope and Christian courage? Has it not been the strength of the martyrs, the inspiration of the reformers, the support of the confessors and witnesses of all the Christian centuries? Has it not been a lamp in the darkness of the darkest ages of the past? Is it not as the bright and morning star of the times in which we live, the herald of a new and better day? And are not its visions of the future the lofty and luminous vistas through which the church militant gazes into an eternity to come, the magic mirror in which she beholds the glories of the church triumphant? Does she not sit in the auditorium of its sublime revelations, and listen as through a telephonic instrument adjusted to the sounds of the celestial region, to the songs of innumerable harpers harping with their harps, and the thunders of redemption praises? Is she not brought by its wondrous revelations, while still journeying in the world which is, under the power of the greater and more glorious world which is to come? Is not the future, in its sublimest features thus made present to her, and the unseen made visible, and as enduring, more real even than the fleeting things around her? Are not those celestial visions the inspiration of her sweetest songs, and do they not shine before her gaze in the supreme moment when she reaches the boundary of mortal life, and the things of time and sense fade from her view forever?

O glorious and sacred prophecy, thou sublimest chapter in the sublime volume of revelation, thou wonder of our childhood's imagination, thou mystery of our manhood's thought, thou star of our pilgrim wanderings, thou sunburst of our maturist conceptions, by thee we behold death's conqueror planting his triumphant feet upon our deadliest foe. By thee we behold the morn in which He will wipe all tears from off all faces, when sorrow and sighing shall flee away. Thy trumpets of woe are but the preludes of thy trumpets of victory, and the darkness of thy night of sorrow of the brightness of thy morning without clouds. Thine are the martyrs, thine the conquerors. They stood amid thy flames, they stand on thy sea of glass mingled with fire. Thine is the wilderness of desolation, thine the paradise of God. Babylon and Jerusalem are thine, the proud city on its seven hills of sin and shame, and the city of holiness on its abiding Zion. The lonely isle of banishment is thine, and the society of blissful multitudes in the habitations of saints and angels. Thine is the widowhood of the church, and thine the marriage of the Lamb. The sackcloth clothed witnesses are thine and thine the saints in their shining robes of light. Yea thine is the Victor, who died, and rose, and lives forevermore. From him radiate all thy beams of glory, for thou art "the revelation of Jesus Christ," and "the testimony of Jesus is the spirit of prophecy." And thou art the final chorus in the anthem of revelation, the climax of its triumphant praise. In thy fields of glory, in thy city of felicity, the last utterances of revelation sound upon our ears. In thine endlessness is its finis, for thine end has no end, and is but the beginning of eternity. Fit termination of the volume of the book of the eternal, in thee ends the deathless story of redeeming love. In thy multitude that no man can number, of all nations, kindreds, tribes, and tongues, who have come out of great tribulation, and washed their robes and made them white in the blood of the Lamb, the palm-bearing multitude before the throne of God, we behold the fruit of the Redeemer's travail, the reward of the anguish of the divine sufferer on Calvary's cross. In that innumerable host of blood-washed victors we behold the fulfillment of the prevision of His troubled yet triumphant soul, "I, if I be lifted up, will draw all men unto Me." "A multitude that no man can number," a joy that none can measure, a life that shall never end. Sin thou art pardoned; sorrow thou art no more, death thou art swallowed up of life, Thanatos thou art replaced by Athanasia. In thee, thou Palingenesia the goal is reached; in thee thou victory of goodness the love of God is perfected. Shine deathless day, sound ceaseless hallelujahs, and let all nature, all worlds, all angels, join the chorus of joy. For behold a New Creation rises never more to be dimmed with shades of sin and grief, and sheds its transcendent light on a measureless universe.

"Behold   I   come   quickly,   and   My
reward   is   with   me,   to   render   unto
each man according as his work is."

"Occupy till I come."

Appendix A. Explanation Of The Astronomical Tables In The Author's Work, On "creation Centered In Christ," Volume II.

For the sake of those who desire a brief and simple explanation of the nature and use of the Astronomic appendix to this work, we put the required information in the form of answers to the following elementary questions:

Q. You state that the Prophetic Times in the book of Daniel are Astronomical cycles. What is the most conclusive proof that they are so?

A. The calculation of the Astronomical Tables contained in the Appendix of this work (Vol. II) from those Prophetic Times.

Q. What is the nature of the Tables?

A. They are tables giving the dates of all the Vernal Equinoxes and mean and true new moons for 3,555 years; from the probable date of the Exodus, B.C. 1622 to A.D. 1934.

Q. What number of new moons do the tables contain?

A. 87,938 new moons (43,969 mean, and 43*969 true new moons). They also contain 4,862 mean foil moons, and 4,862 true foil moons connected with lunar eclipses.

Q. What is the number of Solar and Lunar dates in the Tables taken together?

A. 101,217 Solar and Lunar dates.

Q. What is their degree of accuracy?

A. They are calculated to days, hours, and minutes.

Q. How is their correctness proved?

A. By their correspondence with historically recorded dates, and especially with more than 1 2,000 Solar and Lunar eclipses, ancient and modern, including all the calculated eclipses, in Oppolzer's Canon der Fins ter nisse, up to A.D. 1934.

Q. Are the dates of the Tables stated in Greenwich Time?

A. No. For the convenience of students of Sacred Chronology they are stated throughout in Jerusalem Civil Time, which is two hours twenty-one minutes in advance of Greenwich Civil Time.

Q. How do the Propheric Times in Daniel yield these dates?

A. The Prophetic Times in Daniel are astronomic cycles harmonizing lunar months with solar years. From these very accurate cycles the measures of the synodic month and equinoxial year can be derived. The measure of the anomalistic month and the anomalistic year can be similarly derived from the Prophetic Times. On the basis of the measures thus obtained the Tables have been computed.

Q. What are Synodic and anomalistic months, and equinoxial and anomalistic years?

A. The Synodic month is that measured by the return of the moon to conjunction with the sun; the anomalistic month is measured by the return of the moon to the Perigee or Apogee point in its orbit; the anomalistic year by the return of the sun to the Solar Perigee, or Apogee; while the equinoxial year is the year of the four seasons, and is measured by the return of the sun to the equinox of Spring.

Q. Why is it needful to take into account anomalistic months
and years in constructing such tables?

A. Because the sun and moon do not go round and round with
the regularity of the two hands of a watch, but are

alternately accelerated and retarded in their movements, owing
to the elliptical form of the orbits in which they travel. The
anomaly of a celestial body is its angular distance from a point in its
elliptic orbit intersected by the longer diameter of the ellipse. As
the speed of the revolving planet or satellite differs according to its
anomaly, to know its anomaly at a given moment is to know how
far it is in advance of its mean place or behind it. A comparison of
the mean and true moons in the tables will show the movement
here referred to.

Q. You stated on page 167 that the speed of a planet is exactly
adjusted to its distance and magnitude. Is this strictly true?

A. It is only strictly true when the maxima and minima of the
planet's motion are taken into account, or the limits of its varying
speed in its elliptic orbit.

Q. Would you explain in the simplest way possible the method
of the derivation of these astronomical measures from the
Prophetic Times?

A. The simplest and most interesting way to explain the matter
is the historical. The leading facts in the narrative are as follows: —
A Swiss astronomer when searching for a cycle which would
harmonize lunar months with solar years lit by calculation upon
the very accurate cycle of 315 years. It then occurred to him that this
cycle is the quarter of the 1,260 years' period prominent in the book
of Daniel, and in the Apocalypse, and that the period of 1,260 years
must therefore be a luni-solar cycle. On examining it he found it
was so. The thought then struck him that as the 1,260 years' period
in Daniel was a luni-solar cycle it was likely that the 2,300 years'
period in Daniel was also a luni-solar cycle. Since the Creator of

Nature and Revealer of Scripture had made one of these two connected periods a cycle harmonizing months and

yean, it seemed probable that He had also made the other such a cycle. On examining the 2,300 yean* period, this astronomer found that it was a luni-solar cycle, and that it was remarkably exact, and the only secular cycle (or cycle measured by complete centuries) possible, within limits applicable to the course of human history. Considering further the mutual relation of these two interesting cycles, he noticed that each had a slight error of a few houn, and that these errors were in opposite directions. From this he concluded that 1,040 yean, which is the difference of 1,260 and 2,300 years, must be a still closer cycle harmonizing months, yean, and days very exactly. On carefully testing it by the best tables in existence at the time, and by ancient and modern observations, he found it was such a cycle. Impressed with its singular accuracy, he named it the Daniel cycle. Thus were these cycles discovered. Had the Prophetic Times not been in the Bible, the cycles in question would have remained unknown to the present day.

How was it discovered that the 2,300 years' Prophetic period is a cycle of Solar and Lunar anomaly?

That discovery was a much later one, and was not made till more than a hundred years after the death of the Swiss astronomer to whom I referred. It was in the year 1870, when the decree of Papal Infallibility was immediately followed by the Franco-German war, the overthrow of the French Empire, and the fall of the Papal Temporal power, that my attention was directed to the fulfillment of historical and chronological prophecy taking place. Noticing in a book by Professor Birks, of Cambridge, a reference to the astronomic character of the Prophetic Times discovered a century previously by a Swiss astronomer, I investigated the matter, and soon made further discoveries. I found that the seventy-five years added by Daniel to the period of "seven times," or 2,520 years, is the epact of the period, or the difference between 2,520 lunar and the same number of solar years. I also found that the historic interval from the Era of Nabonassar, Ptolemy's starting point for the Babylonian Kingdom, to the fall of the Western Roman Empire was just 1,260 lunar years. These and other discoveries stimulated enquiry, and I conceived the plan of deducing tables of mean Synodic months and Equinoxial years from the Prophetic Times, for practical uses. But I required more than this. I wanted the true new moons as well as the mean, and there was no way of readily getting them on an extensive scale but by employing in the computation some cycle of lunar anomaly. A convenient and accurate cycle for the purpose is Houzeau's cycle of 7,412 days (twenty years and 107 days), in which time the synodic and anomalistic months closely agree. Mr. Walter Maunder, the present Secretary of the Royal Astronomical Society, kindly undertook to calculate for me a table of true new moons for twenty-five centuries, employing Houzeau's cycle as a basis. While calculating this table he found to his surprise that the 2,300 years' prophetic period is a cycle of a similar kind, only much superior to Houzeau's cycle. In Houzeau's cycle of 7,412 days, the 251 synodic months closely agree with 269 anomalistic months, but the period is not one of complete years, whereas in the prophetic period 28,447 synodic months equal 30,487 anomalistic months, and both closely agree with 2,300 Equinoxial years. Mr. Maunder's discovery led me to examine the relation of the 2,300 years' period to the anomalistic year, and I found that in the course of 2,300 years the Solar Perigee advances forty days with reference to the Equinoxes, which gave 21,000 years for its complete revolution. From these discoveries I saw that it was possible to derive the true new

A. They are of practical value in the study of civil and sacred history and chronology. Without a knowledge of the exact times of new moons and vernal equinoxes it is impossible to fix or verify the dates of a great variety and multiplicity of events in Jewish and Christian history, and in Egyptian, Assyrian, Grecian, Roman, Mohammedan, Indian and Chinese chronology. The chief value of the Tables is the demonstration they afford of the Astronomic character of the Prophetic Times, and the complete mutual adjustment of natural and revealed chronology. The adjustment is such as to imply and involve the revelation of Levitical and Prophetic Times, and hence the inspiration of Moses and the Prophets.

Appendix B. Testimonial to my Tables from Dr. Downing, F.R.A.S.

Superintendent of the Nautical Almanac. Nautical Almanac Office, 3 Verulam Buildings, Gray's Inn, W.C. March 23rd, 1895.

DEAR SIR: I have examined your volume of Astronomical Tables containing Dominical letters, Vernal Equinoxes and New and Full Moons for some thirty centuries. I think you have shown that De Cheseaux's cycles of 2,300 and 1,040 years (by means of which your times are deduced) are not only curiosities of astronomy, but are sufficiently accurate to be turned to practical use for the computation of the positions of the Sun and Moon at distant epochs. The comparison of your results with those of Oppolzer's *Canon der Finsternisse* and other authorities to which you refer in the introduction would of itself be sufficient to justify you in claiming a remarkable degree of accuracy for your Tables. But in addition to this I have examined a great number of your results, and find that a discordance of about three hours between your times and those computed from various Tables that were accessible to me, is the greatest discordance to be apprehended. For any purposes therefore, for which an error of this magnitude in distant dates is immaterial, your Tables may be used with the greatest confidence. You have made your Tables considerably more interesting and useful by giving, in addition to the times of Mean, New and Full Moon, those of true New and Full Moon, deduced

381

from the former by the application of the two principal inequalities.

Yours faithfully,

A. M. W. DOWNING.

Testimonial from Dr. Dreyer, F. R. A. S., Director of the Armagh Observatory, Formerly Editor of the Astronomical Journal "Copernicus."

These Tables give the date, hour, and minute of every new moon from the year B.C. 1622 to A.D. 1934, as well as the Dominical letters and the time of Vernal Equinox for every year of this period. Hitherto chronologists who required the time of any new moon have had to calculate it from Largeteau's Tables published in the *Connaissance des Temps pour l'an 1846*; or, if very great accuracy was required, by Oppolzer's *Syzygien-Tafeln fur den mond* (Leipzig, 1881); but Dr. Guinness's Tables give the time of new moon by mere inspection without any calculation whatever. In his introduction the author illustrates the accuracy of his Tables by a comparison with the time of the first solar eclipse of each century, taken from Oppolzer's *Canon der Finstemisse*, and shows that his Tables never differ from these more than two hours, while the differences frequently amount to only a few minutes. I have myself tested the Tables by means of a number of eclipses rigorously computed by Stockwell (eclipses observed in India B.C. 1386, 1301, 1250), by Schjellerup (B.C. 707, 599, and 547, observed in China) and by Newcomb (Arabian eclipses from the middle ages), and with the same result. These Tables art therefore somewhat more accurate than those of Largeteau, and of of Largeteau, and ofcourse vastly more convenient, as they do notentail any calculation. These Tables have been calculated by means of the luni-solar cycles discovered by the Swiss Astronomer De Cheseaux, about themiddle of last century, but hitherto very little noticed by scientific men. Thecyclical new moons thus found are given in the Tables side by side with the truenew moons obtained from them by equating for solar and lunar anomaly.Astronomers will be much interested in the remarkable accuracy obtained in thisway by Dr. Guinness.The Tables will be of great practical value to chronologists and historians,who can find from them the day of the week and the age of the mooncorresponding to any date. Particularly to students of Oriental history they will beinvaluable, as the moon is the clock hand of Eastern nations.But they will also in many cases be of great use to astronomers as aready means of finding, by a mere glance, the whereabouts of the moon in thesky at any time during the last three thousand years.

I. L. E. DREYER.

Armagh   Observatory,
April 8,1895

How Can You Find Peace With God?

The most important thing to grasp is that no one is made right with God by the good things he or she might do. Justification is by faith only, and that faith resting on what Jesus Christ did. It is by believing and trusting in His one-time *substitutionary* death for your sins.

Read your Bible steadily. God works His power in human beings through His Word. Where the Word is, God the Holy Spirit is always present.

Suggested Reading: *New Testament Conversions* by Pastor George Gerberding

Benediction

Now unto him that is able to keep you from falling, and to present you faultless before the presence of his glory with exceeding joy, To the only wise God our Savior, be glory and majesty, dominion and power, both now and ever. Amen. (Jude 1:24-25)

Encouraging Christian Books for You to Download and Enjoy

Devotional

- *The Sermons of Theophilus Stork: A Devotional Treasure*
- Simon Peter Long. *The Way Made Plain*

Theology

- Matthias Loy. *The Doctrine of Justification*
- Henry Eyster Jacobs. *Summary of the Christian Faith*
- Theodore Schmauk. *The Confessional Principle*

Novels

- Edward Roe. *Without a Home*
- Joseph Hocking. *The Passion for Life*

Essential Lutheran Library

- The Augsburg Confession with Saxon Visitation Articles
- Luther's Small Catechism
- Luther's Large Catechism
- Melanchthon's Apology
- The Formula of Concord

The full catalog is available at LutheranLibrary.org. Paperback Editions of some titles at Amazon.

Made in the USA
Monee, IL
27 January 2024

52485853R00249